W9-CUZ-963

THE WHEELS OF JUSTICE

One of the cops walked back to the bus ramp with Icky Peace. Brandley stood up. The cop paused and stared at the two of them, the black man in his white T-shirt and shabby jeans, the little white man with the thick glasses and the ballooning belly.

"One of you two is gonna hang for this," said the cop. Then he turned to Brandley. "Since you're the nigger, you're elected."

———————

WHITE LIES

RAPE, MURDER, & JUSTICE TEXAS STYLE

NICK DAVIES

AVON BOOKS ◆ NEW YORK

Grateful acknowledgment is made to Edward B. Marks Music Company for permission to reprint an excerpt from the song lyrics "Strange Fruit" by Lewis Allan. Copyright 1939 by Edward B. Marks Company. Copyright renewed. Used by permission. All rights reserved.

AVON BOOKS
A division of
The Hearst Corporation
1350 Avenue of the Americas
New York, New York 10019

Copyright © 1991 by Nick Davies
Published by arrangement with Pantheon Books, a division of Random House, Inc.
Library of Congress Catalog Card Number: 90-53407
ISBN: 0-380-71845-6

The Pantheon Books edition contains the following Library of Congress Cataloging in Publication Data:
Davies, Nick
    White lies : rape, murder, and justice, Texas style. Nick Davies.
    p.   cm.
    1. Brandley, Clarence—Trials, litigation, etc.   2.Trials
(Murder)—Texas—Conroe.   3.Racism—Texas—Conroe.
4.Corruption (in politics)—Texas—Conroe.   I.Title.
KF224.B73D38   1991
345.73'02523'09764153—dc20   90-53407

First Avon Books Printing: January 1993

AVON TRADEMARK REG. U.S. PAT. OFF. AND IN OTHER COUNTRIES, MARCA REGISTRADA, HECHO EN U.S.A.

Printed in the U.S.A.

RA   10   9   8   7   6   5   4   3   2   1

For Sheridan

Prologue

This is a true story. When I started work on it in the fall of 1987, I intended to write a short feature for a magazine in London, and I assumed I would be finished within a week. Instead, the story took over my life for the next two and a half years. One of the reasons that happened was that by the time I arrived on the scene, many of the details of the story had already been exposed in extraordinary detail by the efforts of attorneys and private investigators who had invested hundreds, thousands of man-hours in attempting to discover the truth. While I had imagined that I was working on a simple story about one man's fight for justice, their work showed that this was really the story of a whole community and of the survival of a way of life that I, at least, had been happy to assume was dead. The more I looked, the more I found, and so I became embroiled.

The hard work that had been invested by the attorneys and the investigators had a more fundamental importance. Even though some of the central characters were still trying to smother the truth in lies and confusion, the facts the investigators had uncovered now had such force that even the courts of Texas, which had resisted them in the past, were compelled to accept them. This, in turn, gave me the chance to reconstruct the whole story with unusual accuracy and confidence. The times, dates, places, and events are all now matters of record. Where I wanted to reproduce dialogue, I was often able to work from sound or video recordings made by the attorneys and their investigators or from the transcripts of court hearings. Many of the people in the story were inspiringly generous with their time (the first time I sat down to talk with Don Brown, eleven hours passed before we got up), and these interviews gave me the raw material for the thoughts of characters and occasionally for their dialogue. With all this support, I was able to set out to produce a narrative that would be accurate in all its details. If I have succeeded, it is largely due to the hard work of these people.

Clarence Brandley, who has through his unusual experiences become an unusually philosophical man, urged me to see that the people of Montgomery County are not all bad. He is, of course, right, and when working in the county I was treated with great courtesy and kindness even, oddly, by those who have at other times been willing to behave with terrible cruelty. Brandley wanted me also to thank the people in the county who have fought so courageously for him against such awesome opposition, and I, too, in my less significant role, would like to add my gratitude to all those who were brave enough to tell the truth.

STRANGE
FRUIT

Southern trees bear a strange fruit,
Blood on the leaves and blood at the root,
Black bodies swinging in the southern breeze,
Strange fruit hanging from the poplar trees.

—FIRST SUNG BY BILLIE HOLIDAY IN 1939

Chapter One

Conroe is the kind of town that strangers never notice. From a distance it is no different from the last town they passed, just the usual muddle of power lines and road signs, a glimpse of rooftops and railroad tracks. Conroe squats on the edge of the Sam Houston National Forest about forty miles north of the city of Houston just after Interstate 45 crosses the San Jacinto River on its way up to Dallas, but to a stranger's eye it could be any town on the edge of any freeway. Even those who, for some reason, leave I-45 where it bends to the west and take the northward fork up Frazier Street and into the center of Conroe find little to distinguish it: gas stations, shopping malls, billboards lining the road like beggars in a bazaar: KRISPY CHICKEN—EIGHT PIECES FOR $3.89; A BIGGER DEAL AT THE NEW BURGER KING; FEED AND FARM SUPPLIES; BEER AND BAR BQ AND BAIT . . .

Halfway through the town Frazier Street is crossed by Route 105, which runs from east to west so that the two roads together form a crucifix, dividing Conroe into four quarters. The crucifix is shadowed by railroads, the Missouri Pacific running north and the old Santa Fe Railroad cutting across it. At the center of the crucifix is the courthouse square, the town's heart, where the scene is just as familiar. There is Scott's pharmacy with the chipped and fading sign outside; the Casey Jones Bar BQ with its rows of empty seats; Nita's beauty shop (WALK-INS WELCOME); the Capitol drugstore with a handwritten sign offering VALENTINE CANDY, 60% OFF; a restaurant where the grubby window bristles with credit card signs—Visa, American Express, Texas Restaurant Association, Carte Blanche—and a notice that says it

3

is closed for good. There are usually a few pickup trucks with men in baseball caps sprawling spread-legged in the back and a couple of old Fords with rusting dents sitting soaking up the heat outside the Montgomery County Courthouse.

The courthouse—a squat square five-story block of brickwork with flags flying on its roof and janitors spiking scraps of trash from its grass—is the only building that might catch a stranger's eye. Its featureless walls shine as bright as a whited sepulcher. What marks the courthouse out from its humbler neighbors is not only the self-evident pride of the building but also the air of business that surrounds it. The rest of the courthouse square—the old Crighton Theater as well as the restaurants and stores—have been more or less deserted in favor of brash new shopping malls with names like U Save and Crossroads that were built out by I-45 in the 1970s, but the courthouse is still a thriving place. White men in shirtsleeves talk earnestly on the steps; deputy sheriffs with holsters jiggling on their hips keep pushing through the double doors. Up on the top floor the holding cells are usually packed with prisoners from all over Montgomery County. On the lower floors five district judges dispense justice. Yet this, too, is really nothing special, just another courthouse in a small town.

There was a brief period in the 1930s when Conroe was raised from normality after a geologist named George Strake struck oil just outside the town and Montgomery County was suddenly the biggest oil-producing area in Texas. People called Conroe the Miracle City. It had more millionaires per head than any other town in the United States. Families who had been land-poor, who had been scratching twenty-five or fifty cents out of an acre and bartering bushels of peas for a pair of shoes, suddenly found that their barren land was floating on liquid money. Thousands of itinerant workers, pushed south by the Depression, descended on the town to share the spoils. Oil-rich families tried to polish up the town to match their new status. That was when the townspeople built the gleaming white courthouse so they no longer needed to hold prisoners on a chain strung between two trees and when they put up the theater, which they decked out like a Venetian garden with an Italian ceramic tile floor and Grecian garden scenes on the ceiling. They started a country club, too, with a golf course. But the boom faded, pigeons infested the new theater, wild hogs got through the fence onto the golf course, and Conroe subsided into peaceful indifference again.

There, as far as a stranger can tell, the town still rests. Its couple of thousand old-time residents keep cattle and horses and sell timber and creosote. They have been slowly outnumbered over the years by newcomers from Houston and the North, who have built high-priced new satellite communities with names like Village Hill and Willow Ridge out on the edge of town. There is a bottling plant for Pepsi and a factory that makes reinforced elevators to move nuclear warheads about in submarines. There are new roads and a little airport, two new fire stations, and a new sewage plant. It is, to all appearances, a peaceful, plump little town, just like a thousand others, entirely devoted to its own obscurity.

The events that finally betrayed the truth about Conroe began one hot, sticky Saturday in the summer of 1980, when the lives of two people who had never even heard of each other crossed and became ruined.

One of them was Clarence Lee Brandley, who was then aged twenty-eight, a stocky, round-faced black man with a cheerful, easygoing disposition. He liked to wear his hair a little too long, and when he shaved, he carefully preserved a thin black mustache running down both sides of his chin. In August 1980 Brandley was living in a small apartment in a housing project in the southeast quadrant of Conroe and working as a janitor in the high school on the other side of town. He had been married, but he had separated from his wife and left her and his five children in Houston. He lived alone unless his girlfriend Beverley was visiting.

This particular morning Brandley was not feeling too good. He was tired, his head hurt, and he needed a smoke. The last thing he wanted was to go up to the high school and spend the day working, moving chairs, and picking up other people's trash, especially on a Saturday. All he really wanted to do was to fall back into bed with Beverley. She was lying there now, all warm and soft and telling him not to go to work today and telling him he should just stay in bed with her. Still, he had to go.

School was starting in ten days. There was a lot of work to be done, and he was determined to do it. This job meant a lot to him. Not that it was the best job in the world. He had had better down in Houston, working for the light company and driving the Metro buses. But it was a steady job and a steady life, and he had made up his mind that if he was ever going to settle down, he had to keep this damned job. That was why he had left Houston: to get out of the fast lane and get away from the fast life he had been living there. The money here was OK, better since he had been promoted a few weeks back to be supervisor of the other janitors at the school. It was the best he was going to get in a town like Conroe.

He stripped and headed for the shower, calling back: "Beverley, you gonna have to give me a ride."

Under the spray of water he rubbed the tiredness out of his eyes. It had been a rough night. He knew he should have stayed in with Beverley. But he had gone out to one of the juke joints and started shooting dice, and before he had known it, the whole night was gone, and most of his week's money, too. He was not going to do that again. He had had enough of spinning his wheels, living for just one day at a time and burning up his money. And there was something else: his eldest son, Clarence, Jr.

He had talked to his wife, and she had agreed that if he could settle down and earn enough money, Clarence, Jr., could come live with him. He wanted that badly. So apart from working up at the high school, he was working part-time at a gas station and also down the road at Oscar Johnson's funeral parlor, looking after the mourners, who seemed to like him. People had always said he had a friendly way with him.

He reckoned he had been doing OK since he came back to Conroe. He had been going to work every day. He hadn't had any trouble with anyone. He had already put aside some money. And he had been looking for a school for the boy. It was plain dumb to go blow a whole week's money on dice like that. This was a new life he was making here. In this town. In his part of this town.

Ten minutes later Brandley was in his worn blue jeans and his white T-shirt, sitting next to Beverley while she pointed her old Mercury out of the shade of the housing project and bounced over the potholes into the sun on South Seventh Street.

None of the roads in this part of town had a regular name. It was different on the other side of Conroe, where there was Shady Oaks Drive and Cochran Street and all kinds of names that referred to people who had lived there or places they wanted to remember. Not here. The townspeople did not even call this place Conroe. They called it Dugan. On the maps it was part of Conroe. For the mailman it was part of Conroe. But for everybody who lived in Conroe, it was Dugan. Nobody even remembered where the name came from, but everybody knew what it meant if a person came from Dugan.

Brandley looked out the window and wished he had a smoke. He watched the wooden houses with the peeling paint, the windows patched with plastic sheets, the roofs of rusting corrugated iron, the old people sitting silently in the shade, the dogs and children playing in the dirt. Beverley turned right along Avenue E, past the shack where he and most of his brothers and sisters had been born in the front room and where his mother, Minnie Ola, still lived, past the rotting brown shed where his aunt lived in a single room with the clothes drying on a line over the bed and the rain always finding its way through the roof. At the head of the bed, where a crucifix might have hung, she kept pinned to the bare wooden wall a magazine page with the face of Martin Luther King, Jr., gazing down from it.

Then the shacks thinned out until there were only a few hiding behind the trees, as if they were not quite sure if they should show themselves at the main road. The last one was a battered yellow cabin with a rain-stained roof and a sign tacked on the front that said JEANNE'S BEAUTY SALON. They had come to the railroad track.

Beverley slowed down and the old Mercury tripped over the tracks. The sign said STATE LAW—OBSERVE WARNING SIGNS. Beverley turned left and drove down Route 105 toward the center of town. She drove carefully. She didn't want any trouble. It was seven-fifteen in the morning on August 23, 1980.

The stranger whose life was to cross that of Clarence Brandley was a sixteen-year-old schoolgirl with blond hair and blue eyes named Cheryl Fergeson. She was tall and slim, and people always said she was pretty.

She lived with her father. Her mother had died a year earlier of cancer. Her brothers had grown up and had their own homes, in Houston. Apart from her Siamese cat, Crook, with the bent tail, she lived alone with her father and looked after him on the ranch at Kenney, ten miles outside Bellville.

She was always busy with one thing or another. She liked drawing and painting, and she had just finished designing a big mural at Bellville High, all about sports, with pictures of different team mascots and a slogan that said in big letters GET WITH THE SPIRIT. She worked on the school paper, taking photographs, and she had been to a seminar about journalism and photography at the University of Texas. But more than anything she liked roller-skating; she spent every spare minute down at the Rolling Oaks rink in Bellville. She even had a part-time job there, so she could earn some pocket money and skate with her girlfriends and with Frank, too. She was going to marry Frank when they were through with school.

Cheryl liked to wear western-style clothes, like her daddy, who used to ride the rodeos. She often wore boots of cowhide or suede, blue jeans slung low at the waist, and a heavy leather belt with an ornate iron buckle. Across the back her name was stamped into the leather in big letters: CHERYL. Around her neck she always wore a delicate gold chain with a crucifix.

Right now Cheryl Fergeson was in a hurry. She had got up early, eaten breakfast on the run, and left home without having a chance to say good-bye to her daddy, so she could be at the high school on the edge of Bellville by seven-fifteen, in time to catch the bus for the volleyball tournament. She had been manager of the volleyball team for only a couple of weeks, and she was eager to do well, so she was right on time.

She parked the big blue-and-white Chevy Blazer at the back of the school, grabbed her purse, pillow, scorebook, and red bag full of volleyballs, and ran across to where half a dozen other girls were standing around in their gray sweat suits, waiting for Susan Norris, the volleyball coach, to show up with the big yellow school bus. But Mrs. Norris was late. Then, when she finally turned up, apologizing and explaining that she had had trouble getting the engine started, they realized there was still one girl missing from the team— Dierdra. She had overslept, and by the time she arrived, they were even later. It was ten to eight when Mrs. Norris finally started the bus and set off with a plume of black smoke in her wake for the tournament, sixty miles to the northeast at a high school where they had not played before, in a town called Conroe.

Beverley pushed the old Mercury along Route 105, past the railroad intersection where the freight trains crooned, past the pawnshop (WE PAY CASH FOR ALMOST ANYTHING), alongside the white slab outline of the county courthouse in the center of town, across Frazier Street, driving slowly near the pickup trucks with the bumper stickers that said I'M OK. YOU'RE THE SHITHEAD. and DON'T MESS WITH TEXAS, through the shopping malls, and then out to the western edge of town, where the high school, Conroe's most precious jewel, lay.

With the long, low red brick high school on her right, Beverley slowed and turned onto the side road at the far end of the main building. She stopped between the end of the school and the new Vocational Building, in the area where the students waited for their buses every afternoon. The other four janitors had already arrived.

Brandley could see Icky Peace, perched behind the wheel of his battered green Chevrolet, like a pudding on a plate. Icky was very short, maybe four feet ten inches, and very fat, probably 170 pounds, and he had a voice like a little girl, pure and high-pitched. He wore thick glasses, he could neither read nor write, he had false teeth, which he pulled out when he ate, and he claimed to have diabetes. He was in his late thirties and unmarried, and so far as Brandley knew, he had never even had a girlfriend. He had lived with his mother until she died, and now he lived with his sister in Cleveland, thirty miles east of Conroe. It was his sister who had nicknamed him Icky, after the noise he made when he was a baby. His real name was Henry Martin Peace, Jr., but that never did suit him. So he was Icky. Brandley had never met anyone quite so strange as Icky Peace, but he liked him.

When he had first become supervisor a few weeks earlier, Brandley had had a little trouble with some of the other janitors, who were not too happy to work for him. But Peace had never given him any problems. He just did as he was told, and when he did well, he was proud of himself, like a child. But Brandley had discovered that in spite of some strange habits, Peace was not nearly as dumb or as innocent as he made himself out to be.

As Beverley drove off, Brandley waved at the little fat janitor. "All right, Icky?"

Peace bounced out of the Chevrolet, rubbing his hands and ready for work. "Mornin', Clarence," he piped.

Brandley nodded toward the other three, who were sitting together in the shade of the bus shelter. They didn't bother to reply, just got up and flipped their cigarette butts into the road and started strolling slowly over to the school doors.

Gary Acreman was the last to move, his hands jammed into his pockets as he walked, sneering as usual. Just turned twenty-one, he was tall and thin, like a slice of a normal man, with reddish brown hair and a face like a fox—long thin snout and small dark eyes. Acreman had been at the high school only a couple of months, but Brandley had already learned to beware of him. Brandley had tried to treat him right, had even bought him food when he turned up without money one day, but there was something sly about the guy that he didn't trust. He was always wisecracking and mouthing off about something. Brandley knew his type.

Brandley stood with his back to the Vocational Building, fished the fat bunch of keys out of his back pocket, and unlocked the door at the end of the main school building.

"OK," he said. "Let's get to work."

"Man, this had better be worth it." It was Acreman. "I ain't coming in on no Saturday just for some one hour's pay."

"Y'all can leave it to me," said Brandley. "We'll take it easy. There ain't so much to do. We'll work till around noon, and I'll put y'all down for a full day. Just take it nice and easy."

As he opened the door, Brandley could smell the booze on John Sessum beside him. Sessum had been drinking for years, and he carried a thick scar across his right temple as a reminder of some long-forgotten barroom where a fight had gotten out of hand. He was always dirty and disheveled and usually quiet, sunk in some private misery or just plain drunk. He was from Mississippi originally, but he had been in East Texas for years now, drinking and dragging himself from one dumb job to another. Brandley did not know him too well. He did not normally work at the high school. He had just been called in for this Saturday job because the other regular high school janitors were not interested in working overtime. He lived out to the east of town, in a little bunch of shacks and trailers called Cut and Shoot. Brandley had never been out there. He knew he would not be welcome.

Icky Peace and Gary Acreman were behind them along with Sam Martinez, a young Chicano with bushy black muttonchop sideburns and a frizz of curly dark hair. Martinez, too, had been called in from another school to help out. He seemed like a straight guy to Brandley. He was married to a woman who lived in Dugan. He was pretty quiet. He came to work; he did his job; he took his pay and went on home.

The five men set off down the main hallway, which ran like a spine through the school, with different rooms on each side like ribs. First on the right was the teachers' lounge. That was going to have to be cleaned up. Opposite it, on the left, was the little janitor's office. That was where Brandley was headed the first chance he got; he was going to buy himself some smokes and take some time out in there, try to wake himself up.

Some twenty feet farther on, Brandley stopped at the edge of the main lobby, which opened up to his right and led to the big parking lot on Route 105. The lobby was dominated by a large glass case containing a stuffed tiger, the high school mascot. Right now the lobby was also cluttered with folded tables and orange plastic chairs, all stacked in piles.

The hallway stretched on in front of him, down through the school, with the cafeteria running down on the left and the big auditorium running down opposite it on the right. In the distance, at the end of the auditorium, he could see the characters from "Sesame Street" painted on the wall near the rest rooms, and past that the sports area, where the gymnasiums and dressing rooms were.

There was work to be done with all these tables and chairs lying around in the lobby. Brandley reached for his bundle of keys, turned down a short flight of steps to his left, and let the others into the end of the cafeteria. He told them how he wanted the tables and chairs laid out in there in rows. Coming up on Monday was a big meeting of all the teachers in the Conroe School District, getting together to prepare for the new term. Everything had to be set up and ready for them. Brandley started moving some chairs himself, so they would understand what he was talking about. He went off and found a two-wheel dolly to help them.

Acreman shook his head and leaned against the back wall of the cafeteria with his arms folded, while drunken John Sessum and Sam Martinez started to walk laboriously to the lobby to get some chairs for themselves. Brandley told Peace to come with him, and he and the little pear-shaped janitor returned through the lobby toward the teachers' lounge, but they were still within earshot when one of the others spoke.

"Goddamn nigger. He can kiss my ass."

*   *   *

The yellow school bus plowed along the back roads, through Hempstead and Magnolia and onto Interstate 45. Mrs. Norris did not want to be late. She pushed northward as fast as she dared.

A few seats behind her Cheryl Fergeson, curled up on the pillow she had brought with her, sat quietly reading. Bright sun beat on the windows. Endless days of heat had laid the land to waste. Fruit withered on the vine; lawns lay like brown blankets; woodland was burned black; fields were scorched from fires kindled by sparks from passing trains. Everything was brittle and dead.

Cheryl Fergeson read her book. The bus pressed on into Conroe, past new stores and supermarkets, past Tudor-style houses with central air-conditioning and private swimming pools, past the Safeway, where the Republican Women's Club was holding its white elephant sale, past the auditions for the Conroe Chorale, and past the Conroe Ballroom, where the Southbound Country and Western Band was rehearsing for the evening's entertainment, on past the Lincoln Continentals and the Buick station wagons with their bumper stickers: JESUS IS MY SPECIAL FRIEND and CHRISTIANS FOR RONALD REAGAN.

The yellow bus swung off I-45 and mounted the slope of Route 105, west toward the high school. Susan Norris saw other buses lined up in the big parking lot in front of the school, and she joined them. As soon as she stopped, she checked her watch. She had wanted to be there by nine.

"We're late," she told the girls. "Nearly ten minutes. Still, I guess it could have been worse. Let's hurry on now."

The seven volleyball players climbed out of the bus and into the sticky heat. Cheryl came last, carrying the big red bag full of balls, the scorebook, and her purse. She made sure the bus door was shut.

They headed off to their right and found a gym door open. Inside, the room was filled with the sound of shouts and sneakers squeaking on the polished floor. The tournament had started. They hurried to find a dressing room.

Brandley started to roll slowly through his routine: trash cans, toilet paper, locks and keys. He felt dog-tired, he was more or less sleepwalking, but he was going to do this damned job the way it should be done.

He took Icky Peace back down to the beginning of the hallway to the teachers' lounge and showed him how he wanted the floor cleaned up: how to stack all the furniture by the walls and mop the wooden floor with soap and water, then how to mix wax with water and spray that on, and, finally, how to use the big electric buffer to polish it all so it shone. He helped Peace to haul the buffer up out of the closet and into the lounge. He told him, "I know you going to make a real good job of this, Icky."

The little janitor rolled up his sleeves and got down to work. Brandley set off to get his cigarettes. It must have been about eight-thirty. There was not too much to do, and there was plenty of time to get around to it. It was just another day. It was no big deal.

Brandley walked down between the cafeteria on the left, where he could see Acreman and Sessum and Martinez slowly laying out the chairs, and the auditorium on the right, which was all locked up, and then past the "Sesame Street" mural where the rest rooms were, up on a landing. He went up and checked in the boys' rest room and made a mental note to bring some toilet paper later on. He would have to find someone to check the girls' room for him.

He walked on toward the gymnasiums and was surprised to find some white woman trying to prop open the big swing doors at the end of the hallway with a trash can. That was the first time he found out there was supposed to be a volleyball tournament in the school that day. The woman, who turned out to be one of the volleyball coaches from Conroe High, told him that eight teams were going to be playing there today and that she had to get these doors to stay open. He took out his allen wrench and showed her how to fasten it onto the crash bar so that the door no longer automatically locked itself. This end of the school turned out to be full of people. A girl in a sweat suit came by, and he asked her to go down and look in the girls' rest room there by "Sesame Street" to see if it needed toilet paper. He never liked to go in the girls' rooms himself. By the time he had finished putting his wrench on the door, she was back to tell him he didn't have to worry about the paper down there.

It was eight forty-five. He was desperate for a smoke. But if there was going to be a tournament, he had to get busy.

He would have to unlock all the doors to the gymnasiums—
they were using the boys' gym as well as the girls'—and
make sure the right rest rooms were open, as well as do all
his regular duties. The cigarettes were going to have to wait
some more.

He shuffled quietly from one job to the next, wondering
how Beverley was, worrying about Clarence, Jr., fixing trash
cans and toilet rolls. He unlocked the rest rooms in the dressing room, where he guessed these volleyball teams would be
getting into their gear. He went and locked the rest rooms up
by the bleachers in the gym. The white lady had opened them
with her own key, but he didn't want them all messed up.
There were already some girls going inside when he got up
there. He grinned at them. "You better be out quick, or I'll
lock you in."

It was ten past nine before he finally finished and walked
out the end of the building toward the town and down to the
Shamrock gas station on Route 105 to buy a pack of Kools.

Cheryl Fergeson hurried through the gym, following the
seven team players in their gray sweat suits with the bright
red letters that said BELLVILLE GIRLS ATHLETICS. As manager
she did not have to wear a sweat suit. She could wear a shirt
and her regular western-style blue jeans and her cowboy belt,
though she was wearing sneakers instead of her normal boots.
They were late. All the space in the dressing room was taken.
They had to leave their things in the corner of a little warm-up
gym. There was no rest room in there.

Mrs. Norris told the girls to loosen up, start doing some
stretching exercises and throw a ball around. It was going to
be at least thirty minutes before they played their first game.
Mrs. Norris went off to find the Conroe High coach, to check
on the playing schedule.

Cheryl dropped her red bag full of volleyballs and her
scorebook and her purse on the floor of the warm-up gym.
There was just time to go find a rest room before she got
busy, setting up the game with Mrs. Norris and then keeping score.

She walked out into the hallway. At first she turned toward
the dressing room, where the other teams had changed; but the
door was closed, and there was no sign to tell her that there was
a rest room in there. If Cheryl Fergeson and her team had not
arrived late, she would have been inside that dressing room,

and she would have seen that there was a rest room there; but as it was, she turned and walked away, away from the gyms and away from her friends, down the long, empty hallway.

A minute later Mrs. Norris was back in the warm-up gym. She needed her team manager.

"Where's Cheryl?" she said. "Anyone seen Cheryl?"

Nobody had.

It was nine-fifteen in the morning on August 23, 1980.

Clarence Brandley wandered slowly down to the Shamrock station, feeling the heat of the day building on his shoulders. He never felt good in this part of town. Ever since he could remember, it had been like that. When he was a little boy, his grandma used to bring him across the railroad tracks to go shopping downtown near the courthouse. She always told him he had to be on his best behavior, so as not to antagonize any of the white people who lived there.

So he had learned how to address white people—respectfully, standing a yard or two back so they didn't think he was trying to touch them, with his head bowed and his hand raised, waiting for permission to speak.

It was nothing he had ever felt mad about. It was just a fact of life. When he used to go downtown to see movies at the Crighton Theater, he always went straight upstairs to the black seats, and he never hung around downstairs where the white kids were. Or when the black kids used to go to the old McGee Hotel to get hamburgers, they had to go in the side door, right next to the kitchen, while the white kids went in the front and sat down.

It was just a fact of life, though sometimes it hurt. His brother O. T. had gotten into trouble one time when he had gone to a white lady's house where their mama, Minnie Ola, was working as a maid. O. T. hadn't known any better, so he went right up and knocked on the front door. That white lady looked at him with her eyes so hard, and their mama had told them they must never go to the front door again or she could lose her job.

Another time Minnie Ola was working in one of the restaurants downtown, near the courthouse. It was the time of integration, and when some black people came to eat in the restaurant, Minnie Ola felt proud, and then it hurt her heart when the owners broke the plates the black people had eaten from so white people would never have to use them.

It was a fact of life for anyone who lived in Dugan. It had always been that way. Long as anyone there could remember. The blacks all knew the stories, the bad things that happened to people who got out of line. And often enough they happened to people even if they weren't out of line. Like the black man who had lived up at Montgomery, the old county seat fifteen miles northwest of Conroe. He was well known in the town, and everyone called him by his nickname, Putt.

Putt worked on the Santa Fe Railroad, fixing the track; but he was also a gardener and a handyman, and by simple hard work he managed to save enough money to buy forty acres of land. That was no easy thing around Conroe in the 1940s. Very few black people owned land; those who tried were often laughed at or threatened, and no white bank would lend them money. Often they could do it only if some sympathetic white person agreed to front for them. But Putt did it, and he planted his land with cotton and corn and sugarcane, and in his own small way he began to prosper.

One Saturday morning Putt rode into Montgomery on his horse, and he was just walking down the main street in the middle of town when a white man walked up to him and shot him. Then, in front of all the people who came running out of the stores to see what all the noise was about, the white man walked over to Putt where he lay moaning on the ground and put two more bullets in his black body.

Everyone knew who the white man was. He was the town bully. He had a job at the First State Bank, but he spent most of his time frightening people. No one really knew why he had done it—if he had had some argument with Putt or if he just did not like the sight of a prosperous nigger. But Putt was dead, and the white man was never even arrested.

Brandley often heard that story at home because Putt's real name was Dennis Brandley and he was Clarence's grandfather.

These were just facts of life. It made no difference what laws came and what laws went. Brandley never felt good in this part of town. He bought his pack of Kools and trudged back to the high school. It was nearly nine twenty-five now.

On the way back down the hallway he saw the white lady from Conroe High again and took the trash can out of her office and asked her if she was sure there was enough toilet paper in the girls' room in the dressing room. It was hot. He was worried about the volleyball teams, so he went into the gym and opened the windows and switched on the big electric fans.

Then he stopped by one of the janitor's closets near the gyms and picked up some rolls of toilet paper. He would just drop them off in the boys' rest room by "Sesame Street" and then finally get into that nice quiet little office at the end of the hallway opposite the teacher's lounge and have himself a peaceful smoke.

He was halfway to "Sesame Street" before he realized that all the other janitors were standing around there. Gary Acreman was hanging about at the top of the staircase that led up to the rest rooms. John Sessum and Sam Martinez were lurking around by the water fountain at the bottom of the stairs.

Acreman looked at the toilet paper in Brandley's arms and said: "Don't go in the girls' rest room, Clarence. There's a girl in there."

Brandley reckoned this was Acreman's idea of a wisecrack, just trying to stop him from doing his job. Since he didn't want to go in there anyway, he paid it no mind. "I ain't going in there," he said. "Y'all finished in the cafeteria?"

They nodded.

"What you want us to do now?" asked Martinez.

"Well, we gotta fix some stuff in the Vocational Building. You go back across the street and wait for me. I'll be on over soon enough, let y'all in."

It must have been nine-thirty by now. Brandley was beginning to think he was never going to get that smoke. But what the hell? They could wait for him. It would do them no harm, and it would help to kill some time so they could claim a full day's money.

He put the toilet paper in the boys' room and headed down the hallway to his office, where finally he managed to sit down, switch on his little black radio, put his feet on the desk, and light up his cigarette. He would go across and see to them soon enough and check in on Icky, too, to see how he was getting on with buffing the teacher's lounge.

He began to feel a little better. The smoke was really good. Brandley sat quietly in the warm air, resting his eyes. He might even have dropped off for a moment. He thought he might take Beverley out partying that night. If he could get away around noon and catch up on some sleep in the afternoon, he would be all right for the night.

Eventually, he heaved himself up from his chair. He had better let those guys into the Vocational Building. He had no idea how long he had left them waiting. He had no watch on. But it must be after ten o'clock now, and there was something like eighty-five chairs they had to lay out in there for Monday morning. There was going to be a meeting of all the janitors in the Conroe School District. While the teachers were over in the main building, talking about the new term, the janitors would be in the Vocational Building with their boss, Mallie Davis, talking about their work.

As Brandley came out of his office, he saw that the outside door at the end of the hallway had been propped open with a trash can. That was not right. It was his job to make sure all external doors were closed and locked. He slid the trash can out of the way, stepped out into the bright sun, and almost collided with Icky Peace.

"Clarence," chirped the baby-faced janitor, "when you gonna let us in?"

"You finished in the teachers' lounge already?"

"Sure I am. I done a real good job. You wanna see?"

"I'll check it later, Icky. Here, take the key."

Brandley lobbed him the key to the Vocational Building. Across the road Brandley could see Gary Acreman, sitting sullenly on the steps of the Vocational Building, with a cigarette in his mouth, and John Sessum lying flat out on the top step, apparently fast asleep. By the side of the building Sam Martinez seemed to be checking out the pay phone. Brandley explained to Peace about the chairs that had to be laid out and left it to him to get the other janitors up and working. He watched him waddle back across the road.

Back in his office Brandley lit up another Kool. That Icky Peace truly was a strange person. He might look like a big baby, but he had some grown-up thoughts in his head. Several times now, when they had been working together on their own, Peace had got on at him about women, complaining that he couldn't get one because he was short and ugly and asking Brandley to get a woman for him. Brandley just used to smile at him and shake his head.

Peace might seem dumb, but in his own way he was pretty smart. He had been kicked around all his life, and he had learned to spot trouble coming and talk his way out of it. Brandley had seen him tell tales—just like that, off the top of his head, and you would never know he was making it up.

Icky Peace knew how to look after himself. He had a gun, too. He had been showing it off one day in school. And there was talk about how he did some kind of work for the police. He even had his own identity card with his picture on it and everything that was something to do with the police. He was a strange one.

Brandley sighed and smoked and listened to the radio and let the time roll by, and it was after eleven by the time he pulled himself together and wandered back out of his office and over to the Vocational Building. He checked the work there and decided to call it a day. They had done four hours since seven-thirty.

"Y'all can go on home now," he told them.

"What about our money?" It was Acreman's familiar whine. "You said we'd get a full day."

"I'll put y'all down for a full day. Eight hours."

As the four white janitors turned to leave the Vocational Building, Brandley caught Peace's eye. "Hey, Icky, can you give me a ride? I just gotta lock up and we can go."

"OK, Clarence."

With the egg-shaped janitor at his side, Brandley had started to cross the road to the main building when something caught his eye. It was a police car, a Conroe Police Department car, sitting by the bus ramp with a cop at the wheel.

Brandley was curious. "What's the problem?" he asked.

"They're looking for a girl," said the cop, who was young and white. "She's been reported missing."

The cop didn't seem too worried. Brandley led Peace inside, praised him to the skies for his work on the floor of the teachers' lounge, checked in the cafeteria, and found the other three had not finished the job. He and Peace were just laying out the last remaining chairs when they heard voices. It was girls shouting.

"Cheryl! Cheryl!"

Brandley and Peace went out to the hallway to take a look. There were three girls there in sweat suits. "Is that you hollerin'?" asked Brandley.

The girls seemed worried. They had lost their friend. She had been missing for two hours now. She was blond, and wearing blue jeans and a shirt. They weren't too sure what color shirt. But she was missing. She had even left her purse behind. Nobody had been too worried to start with; but now they had stopped the tournament, and one of the coaches had called the police. They were all looking.

"I guess we better look, too," said Brandley. "C'mon, Icky."

While Brandley locked the cafeteria, Icky Peace drifted over to the main lobby by the stuffed tiger. His voice sang out. "Hey, Clarence, this door's open."

He was right. One of the double doors that led from the lobby into the parking lot on Route 105 was unlocked. That was not right. Brandley was just about to lock it when he noticed that one of the doors that led from the lobby into the auditorium was also open. "We better go take a look, Icky. Could be somebody in there vandalizing things."

They pushed through the door. Inside the auditorium it was dark. Icky shot a nervous glance toward Brandley and hesitated, but Brandley was determined to go in. He had cleaned this whole place up during the week, ready for the new term. Then he had locked it and left it so it would stay clean. If there was anyone skulking around in there in the dark, he wanted him out before he messed the whole place up again.

"Anyone there?" he shouted, and started walking along the dark aisle between the seats. "Anyone there?"

Twisting his fingers into a knot, Peace shuffled into the dark behind him, his head sunk down between his shoulders, round eyes switching from side to side, feeling his way to his left, to the side wall that ran alongside the main hallway. Finally, he found the light switch and flicked it on.

Now they could see the whole auditorium, the rows of seats running down to the stage, a door to the left in front of the stage that went out to the rest rooms at "Sesame Street," a door on the other side of the stage that went out to the parking lot and Route 105. Brandley was already down at this door. "Icky," he shouted. "Look here. This one's open, too."

Brandley was now very suspicious. Someone had been playing around with these doors. He had heard about all this from some of the old janitors: kids hiding in the auditorium and missing class or boys and girls going in there to make out. "We better check this out, Icky. Take a look up on the stage there. I'll check around these seats."

Brandley walked back up the aisle, away from the stage, looking down each row of seats to see if anyone was crouching down and hiding. He climbed up to the little spotlight booths at the far end of the auditorium. There were couches in the booths. Some of the janitors had found incense sticks and cigarette butts up there. But Brandley found no one now.

He headed back to the stage, where Peace was still shuffling around, avoiding dark corners and gawking at the shadows as if he expected to see a ghost. "Icky, I'm gonna check behind the stage here. You go up them stairs there. See what's up there."

Peace started to walk very slowly up a winding metal staircase. "Go on, Icky. There's nothing to be scared of. I'm right here, man."

Brandley could see the little janitor was getting nowhere. "OK, man. I'll come with you."

Their feet rang dull chimes on the metal steps. The stairs wound upward past ropes and pulleys to a small loft. The loft was dimly lit and cluttered. There was a sled and a big yellow mat and a bunch of wooden flats with different scenes painted on them. It was some kind of props loft. The only light came from a row of colored bulbs along one side of the loft. It was hot and dusty. They started feeling their way about. Peace turned over one of the wooden flats, and the body of a blond girl with blue eyes rolled away from the wall and lay back on the floor, her eyes staring upward, her mouth frozen open, the tip of her tongue lying on her bottom teeth. Her hands were wide open, the palms pressing upward. She was naked except for her socks. Peace screamed.

"Oh, my God," said Brandley. "I'll go get help. Stay here."

"Clarence, couldn't I go get help? I don't wanna stay here."

"Just stay there, Icky." Brandley was already clambering down the metal steps. "Don't do nothing. Just stay there."

Peace pulled his work knife out of his back pocket and clasped it to his breast. His mouth was trembling.

Brandley raced along the aisle, burst out of the open door at the end of the auditorium, around the corner and out into the open air by the bus ramp, where he and Peace had seen the cop in the car. He was gone. There was another cop driving by. Brandley waved him over.

"Come with me. We found something. Come with me."

Events started to race. Brandley became a spectator.

The cop looked at the body and called another cop on his radio. Then they called more cops, who called the detectives and the justice of the peace and the funeral home and the school officials and the press. Soon there were white men in big boots swarming all over the props loft and the auditorium and up and down the hallway, opening doors and asking questions, herding schoolgirls into different rooms and asking questions, while Brandley and Peace sat in the front seats of the auditorium trying to figure out what was happening.

Peace was almost in tears. Brandley tried to comfort him. He had been in the army for a couple of years after school, and he had seen dead people before; but the truth was it had shaken him up, too. He could still see it in his mind's eye. She had seemed so young, but she was surely dead: her lips had been blue, and all around the front of her neck there had been an ugly red, raw stripe. Brandley had been there when one of the cops checked underneath her body. He had seen the mark in the middle of her back, right between her shoulder blades, where the weight of her killer, pressing her down against the floor, had printed the shape of her crucifix in the flesh.

After an hour or two the cops seemed to run out of things to do. A couple of them came up to Brandley and Peace and asked them if they would come downtown to make a statement. They said OK. The cops drove them away. On the side of the car a sign said CONROE POLICE DEPARTMENT. WE CARE.

Brandley felt strange sitting in that car. He had never had much to do with cops. There was no big reason. It was just another one of those facts of life you learned when you grew up in Dugan. No one there had forgotten what happened to Greg Steele a few years back.

Greg Steele was only a kid, eighteen years old, just out of school and about to join the army. He was a big, soft kind of guy, like Yogi Bear, with a permanent grin across his face. He spent his time playing football and basketball in Dugan, listening to loud music, and hanging out with his girlfriend. And that was where the trouble started, because the girl was white.

At first it was nothing too heavy. People in Dugan warned Greg there had been some white man driving around looking for him, making threats about the girl. Greg just shrugged and said there wasn't much he could do about that. Then one Saturday night, just before Christmas 1973, Greg got into some kind of trouble in a juke joint in Dugan called the Blue Jacket. It seemed he had been in there drinking beer and shooting pool and some drinks got spilled and the people who had lost their drinks turned ugly. The owner called the police, who came and arrested several of them, including Greg. The next thing that anyone in Dugan heard was four or five hours later, when Greg's mother and stepfather went up to the police station to bail him out and they were told their boy was dead.

The police said Greg had pulled a knife on an officer who had had to shoot him in self-defense. No one in Dugan believed it. The others who had been arrested with Greg said they had all been searched and Greg never had any knife. They said they had heard Greg being beaten. The police could not explain why if Greg was attacking the officer, all three bullets that had hit him had gone into his back. Nor could they explain why the knife he was supposed to have been holding was never splashed with any of his blood. People in Dugan knew that Greg's white girlfriend had an uncle who was a policeman. They had no doubt about what had happened, but all the same the officer who killed him was cleared of committing any crime and allowed to stay on the police force.

Brandley stared out the window of the cop car and tried to relax. Downtown he and Peace were led to a portable cabin behind the old city jail. Peace was taken to one room, Brandley to another. Two white men asked him what happened. He told them. They wrote some of it down. He signed it. The two white men took his work knife from his pocket. They took his fingerprints. Then they asked if he would mind coming down to Medical Center Hospital to give them some samples of blood and hair. He said OK.

They put Icky Peace in the back of a police car with him. Brandley could see he was frightened. His eyes were as round as an owl's at night, and he was gaping about him as if he had just woken up on another planet.

"You OK, Icky?"

Peace nodded.

At the hospital a police officer took Brandley to a room. He sat and waited. A nurse and a doctor came in. They took samples of his spit and his blood. Then the nurse used a pair of tweezers to pull a couple of hairs out of his head and then a couple more from his pubic area. The white doctor looked at him hard.

"You know what you're doing?" he asked.

Brandley shrugged. He didn't know what he meant. "I guess," he said.

A couple of cops drove Brandley and Peace back to the high school. Peace had had samples taken from him, too. He was worried. He started saying that he needed his sister and that he couldn't read or write and that he didn't know what all was going on here. Brandley told him it would be OK.

At the school the cops told Brandley to sit down by the bus ramp and then took Peace across to his '72 Chevrolet Impala, which was still parked where the little janitor had left it that morning. The officers started searching it. Brandley watched. He saw an officer pull out a little knife from the front of the car and then a bigger knife and then some kind of billy club and then the handgun that Peace had been showing off in school that time. Peace looked uncomfortable. The cops told him it was an offense to carry weapons in a car. Peace was wide-eyed.

Then one of the cops walked back to the bus ramp with Peace. Brandley stood up. The cop paused and stared at the two of them, the black man in his white T-shirt and shabby jeans, the little white man with the thick glasses and the ballooning belly.

"One of you two is gonna hang for this," said the cop. Then he turned to Brandley. "Since you're the nigger, you're elected."

James Harold Keeshan, Jr., was nobody's fool. He had sailed through law school at the University of Texas in Austin, built himself a career in the air force as a judge advocate, and then arrived in Conroe and become district attorney of the Ninth Judicial District of the state of Texas when he was still only thirty-five. Everyone in the courthouse always said how smart he was and how he could dance his way past any defense attorney who tried to take him on. And how charming, too. That was Jim Keeshan—with the dapper suits and the way with words and the sharp blue eyes. If he couldn't win a case with the evidence, he could win it with his smile.

For a district attorney in Montgomery County, winning was not always easy. Some of the people he had to work with were not so highly trained and sharp as he was. Just two months earlier, in June, there had been a bad fire at the county library in Conroe. Two days later the fire department announced that it had investigated the incident and ruled out the possibility of arson. Three days later it announced that it had investigated it again and it was arson after all. The county sheriff's department was no better. Last month an officer in a patrol car had seen a motorcyclist speeding down I-45 and set off in pursuit, calling for backup as he went. A couple of miles down the road the officer had lost the motorcyclist and stopped, at which point a backup patrol car, which had responded to his call for help, had run straight into the back of him, totaling both cars. In the jailhouse, Keeshan had just had to deal with a whole lot of fuss about a man who had been charged with killing a twelve-year-old girl. In court the man claimed that he had been abused and threatened by jailers who tried to make him eat maggots from the dead girl's corpse. That was bad enough, but then the jail supervisor got up in court and confirmed the man's story. Keeshan had sorted things out, and the jail supervisor had left for another job; but it all made winning more difficult.

Still, Jim Keeshan's record spoke for itself. In five years as district attorney, he had never lost a single jury trial. There were people outside the courthouse who said that Jim Keeshan was too damn smart for his own good and that he cared more about his career than he did about justice. There were even some defense attorneys who went so far as to say that he did not play fair. But they all agreed that he was nobody's fool.

That Saturday evening, when Jim Keeshan switched on the television in his comfortable house on the edge of Conroe and saw the news of the murder at the high school, he watched very carefully. The news bulletin caught all the commotion at the high school—the shocked students and the detectives pointing to the spot where the body was found—and it closed in on Monty Koerner, the potbellied captain of detectives.

When he was cornered by the reporters, Captain Koerner seemed lost for a moment. Then he started stammering, as he often did, and finally told them: "We've got an investigation going. There's nothing staring at us in the face, but we're running down several possible leads."

Keeshan watched carefully and did nothing. He would just wait awhile and see what old Monty Koerner came up with. The murder of Cheryl Fergeson would come his way soon enough.

It was hot again that Sunday, the kind of heavy, humid day when young kids and old men like to take their fishing lines out to the nearest water and swat the flies and talk a bit. That is what John Henry Faulk was doing that day, just a little to the north of Conroe.

Faulk was a household name in Texas, famous as a folklorist and a stand-up comic who took his one-man show from town to town, playing out the parts of dozens of different Texans he had met over the years, satirizing them and teasing them about their weaknesses, especially their racism. Many of the characters he played onstage were modeled on people he had met in Montgomery County.

This particular Sunday afternoon Faulk was down by the river with an old friend, who had lived all his life in that part of Texas and who now provided the raw material for one of Faulk's most popular characters. Faulk looked on him as a living symbol of a certain kind of white Texan. Soon enough the conversation turned to this dreadful killing at the high school. It had been all over the front page of the *Conroe Courier* that morning: GIRL FOUND SLAIN AT CONROE HIGH. POLICE SAY TEENAGER STRANGLED. Faulk's fishing partner explained that there was one thing for sure. "When they catch him," he said in his slow drawl, "when they catch the man who did that thing, it'll be a nigger."

Faulk looked at him and sighed.

"Sure as you're born," continued his friend. "That's a typical damn nigger crime."

John Henry Faulk nodded slowly, not because he agreed with one word of it, but because he knew that was the kind of thing that his friend was bound to say. Faulk had been listening to it all his life. Onstage he often launched into a monologue that was entirely built out of the words of his friends in Montgomery County. It was all about "good niggers" and "bad niggers."

"You gotta unnershtan'," he would start with his voice creaking out of the side of his mouth in a parody of an East Texas accent. "There's good niggers, and there's bad niggers. You gotta know how to treat 'em right. Take, for example, if you got a good nigger and you gotta whup him, don't go haulin' him out in front a his wife and children and humiliatin' him 'cause that's how you turn a nigger bad, see? You can run a nigger off doin' a thing like that. No. You gotta treat a good nigger with respect—take him down ta the woods and give him a whuppin' there where no one can see!"

Then he would laugh, and even in a place like Montgomery County, he would get his audience laughing with him, teasing them with the truth about themselves, and he would speak a few more of their hidden thoughts. "Y'see, if a nigger keeps his place, he'll get no trouble. No trouble at all. He can sit there in his little ol' shack and eat his corn and play with his old nigger woman and no one's gonna pay him any mind. But you know, once a nigger's gone bad, there's no helpin' him, and he'll cause nothing but trouble till you get shot of him. And nothing makes a nigger go bad quicker than thinkin' 'bout white pussy."

If they were still laughing with him at this point, Faulk could go deeper, right into the heart of their prejudice. He would talk about his aunt, Ol' Miss Waters, who reckoned little black boys tried to spy on her in the toilet "because they develop their sexual urges young, the little stinkpots" and who would never let her children go swimming down by Grogan's Mill because of the black men who worked there. "They got the biggest ol' organs you ever seen and they just love to catch a little white girl and the first thing they'd do is just rape you, just get you and there'd be an orgy of violence right there." Then he would talk about one of his earliest confidants, old Mr. Brodie, who explained the other side of the story in his parched voice: "You know one of the greatest wonders in the world? Is why God put all the best pussy on the nigger woman. You ever think of that? 'Cause it's the truth. You tried any yet?"

If his audience was really good, Faulk could spell out how as a boy he had discovered that as a white man he was allowed to take any black woman he saw. Just like the old slavemasters who had had their way with the slave women and who offered a little black girl to any white man who came to stay as a houseguest. It was not so different today, he would say. No white man was ever going to get into trouble for raping a black woman. No white woman could sue for adultery if her husband was playing around with a black woman. But a black man had better not even look at a white woman—not even look—or he would touch a nerve so bare, so vital that every white man in the area would only be doing his manly duty if he helped hunt that black-assed nigger boy down and taught him a lesson once and for all.

As he watched his fishing line trail through the water that Sunday afternoon, John Henry Faulk's heart was heavy.

By Monday morning no one in Conroe felt safe, on either side of the railroad tracks.

The *Conroe Courier* said that the dead girl had been raped as well as strangled. The justice of the peace who had been called to the scene of the crime, J. P. Bailey, warned parents and teachers not to let any child go off anywhere alone. "They should go in numbers," he said. "Never go alone, and this goes for boys as well as girls. It isn't safe. If it can happen in Conroe, it can happen anywhere."

And it had happened in the high school—of all places! That building was Conroe's pride, a shining symbol of the town's stability, a cornerstone of its future. It was supposed to be safe. Everybody had always trusted the school. But now the head of security at the school, Calvin Blake, was taking calls from thirty different parents a day, trying to reassure them that they could trust his security arrangements. At the school board the superintendent, Chuck York, was beginning to feel the heat. Parents were threatening to keep their children away from the start of term next week unless the killer was caught. Some of them were even buying Mace gas for their children to carry in their lunchboxes.

Then there was talk that the dead girl's family or school might sue Chuck York and the school board for failing to protect the volleyball tournament. York pleaded that he had done all he could. "We can't put a person in every hallway every hour of the day," he said.

He promised he would try to be more vigilant, but there was not much time. The new term was due to start next week. Monday was Labor Day, and then Tuesday the school doors opened. At least Chuck York hoped that they would. He kept calling the police and begging them to get a break in the case. He went off to see the security director for all the schools in the Conroe area, Lonnie Williams, and told him they were going to have a problem if they could not calm this panic among the parents. But what could they do? They fixed it so that someone stood guard while the Golden Girls practiced their cheerleading routine in the high school auditorium. They told the school night watchman that he should look out for people as well as property. But what else could they do? They just hoped for a break.

Chuck York was not the only person calling the police. Half the townspeople seemed to be on the phone to the police department, demanding action, demanding that their school be made safe again. But the police did not have much to say. Captain Koerner tried to be reassuring. "It's priority number one," he said. "We hope to have this thing wrapped up before school starts."

In Dugan the grapevine was twitching with talk about the murder: a strange man had been seen up at the school dressed as a woman; the dead girl had been killed because she had stumbled on a drug ring using the school labs to make speed; the killer was a Mexican who had followed her from Bellville; another girl had been raped, but the authorities were trying to keep it quiet. The gossip was a veil for fear—for the old fear that anyone who had ever lived in Dugan had felt at some time.

Minnie Ola Brandley felt it badly now. She had gone to her son when she heard about the murder, and she had told him: "Clarence, don't you go back there. Don't you go back to that school."

He had smiled and shrugged the way he often did. "Mama, I ain't done nothing."

"I know. All the same, why don't you leave off working up there?"

"It's my job, Mama. I ain't done nothing."

So Brandley went to the school again on Monday morning, determined that he would not be afraid, and did some of his regular duties, checking the rest rooms and throwing trash out into the Dumpsters before going over to the Vocational Building to sit with all the other janitors from all the schools in Conroe and listen to Mallie Davis talk about trash cans and toilet paper.

Afterward they all hung around talking. Icky Peace told Brandley something that made no sense at all. According to the little janitor, while they had all been sitting outside the Vocational Building on Saturday morning waiting for Brandley to unlock the door, Gary Acreman had gone back into the main building. When he came back, he had told Peace he had seen some girl's clothes scattered around in there. Brandley didn't know whether this was just Peace making up stories again or whether this was somehow important. Since he was the supervisor, he decided he should try to find out. He found Acreman in the crowd and asked him about it.

Acreman twisted his mouth and shook his head. "Oh, man, I was just bullshitting Icky," he said. "I never saw no clothes."

Brandley guessed Acreman had just been mouthing off as

usual. It made no sense to him. Just then Mallie Davis came over. He had heard from the Conroe police. They wanted to see Brandley and all four white janitors who had been at the school on Saturday. They were all to go downtown right now to the police department.

Brandley wished he could just get on with his work. He had helped the police all he could. He told them everything he knew and even given them his hair and blood. Still, he had better go.

When they got down to the old city jail, Acreman and Sessum and Martinez were taken away to give statements about what they had seen on the day of the crime. Then some cop came up to Brandley and Peace and asked them if they would mind going down to Houston to take a lie detector test.

Brandley couldn't see what they wanted with a lie detector test. He had already told them the truth. But he guessed he might as well do it. He had nothing to hide. The way he figured it, as long as he cooperated, he couldn't go wrong.

But Peace was worried. "I need to talk to my sister," he pleaded. "I don't know about lie detector tests. I can't read nor write. I need my sister." The police persuaded a minister to go down to Houston with them to hold Peace's hand.

The lie detector test was simple enough. Brandley sat in a chair. The cop ran a bunch of wires all around his arm and chest and asked him a lot of questions about himself. Then he looked at the machine and asked him some more questions about the crime. Had he killed the girl? Had he raped the girl? Had he ever raped anyone?

Brandley just answered the questions and told his story, the same as he had on Saturday. Then the cop looked at his machine again. "OK," he said. "You passed. You don't got nothing to worry about."

Brandley felt relieved, and that was strange. Until that moment he had not admitted to himself that he had ever been worried.

The murder of Cheryl Fergeson was finally brought to the district attorney's office on Tuesday morning, when Captain Monty Koerner stomped over to the courthouse to brief Jim Keeshan on the investigation so far. The captain of detectives tried to be upbeat about it.

He told Keeshan that he was doing everything he could.

The police had collected a whole bunch of stuff at the scene. There were these hairs that one of his men had seen on the dead girl's thigh, and he had saved them—put them straight into his cigarette pack so they wouldn't get lost. They had found a bit of her bra up there in the loft. It looked as if it had been cut off her. There was a paper towel lying nearby, and her crucifix, though the chain was missing somehow.

Then Sunday they had shipped the body down to Houston, and the medical examiner there, Dr. Joseph Jachimczyk, had done an autopsy. They were still waiting on the report, but the medical examiner had given him some more stuff: grit and dust from her body and the pair of white socks that was all she was wearing when she was found. Monday they had been out to the school again, and they had found the rest of the dead girl's clothes in a trash bag in one of the big Dumpsters behind the main building. Everything they had found was on its way up to the Department of Public Safety in Austin, so the lab there could have a look at it all.

Although he tried to be upbeat about it, the captain of detectives could not conceal the fact that his investigation was moving slowly, not least because he had allowed his men to take off on Sunday so the trail had been left to go cold from Saturday afternoon right through to Monday morning. By the time his men went back to the high school, the cleaning women had already been around the place with their mops and swept up anything that might have been useful to them.

His men could not even be sure how the dead girl's clothes came to be in the Dumpster: they might have been put there by the murderer on the day of the crime, or they might have been thrown out by the cleaners, who had collected trash bags from all over the school on Monday morning.

His best suspect had been the black janitor. He had had a knife on him, too. But he had passed the lie detector test. And he had also found the body. The killer had gone to a whole lot of trouble to get that girl's body up into the props loft and hide it behind the wooden flats. It was as if he'd wanted to get well away and out of town before anything was discovered. It wouldn't make too much sense to go straight back up there the first chance he got and find it again.

Jim Keeshan listened carefully to Captain Koerner's briefing, told him to get things moving, and let him go back to work.

He would give him a little longer to get a break in the case, but he was toying with an idea of how he might get things moving himself.

It was on Tuesday that Brandley first sensed it, just the way you sense a storm coming, from the way the ground darkens, without ever needing to look up in the sky. Something strange was happening up at the school.

It was the way people looked at him and then the way they looked away when he caught their eye. People were acting weird with him. Students who usually smiled and said hi pretended they had not seen him. Teachers who usually talked had nothing to say. He saw strange cops walking around the school, looking at him as if they knew him, as if they were saying, "Oh, yeah, that's the black janitor we all heard about."

It got worse. It got to the point where he felt he was being watched. And he knew he was not crazy. People couldn't think it was him. They must know he had nothing to do with it. They wouldn't be watching him about that. It must be something else. Unless he was imagining it. But he knew he wasn't. By Wednesday it was really starting to get to him. And it was not just the funny looks. As far as he could tell, the police were paying extra attention to him.

The three white janitors had not had to go to the hospital and give samples from their body like him and Icky Peace. They had not had to go down to Houston for a lie detector test. He found out he was the only one who had had to give his fingerprints. So what was that all about?

Then he heard on his little black radio the captain of detectives, Monty Koerner, going on again about how they were definitely hoping to catch the killer before school started next week.

Brandley was not saying he was frightened. Damn it, he didn't see why he should be. He had hardly ever been in trouble. And he had told them the truth and helped them every way he could. But his mother kept going on at him, telling him to stay away from the school, going on about Conroe and the way the townspeople did things. Finally, he gave in and agreed with her that they had better do something about it. There wasn't much they could do except go see an attorney. So Thursday evening after work they went down to Houston to see an attorney there called Ray Reeves who had helped one of his brothers one time. Reeves spent only a couple of minutes with them. He said so far as he could see, they had nothing to worry about, and anyway, there was nothing much he could do to help them unless Brandley was arrested. If he was arrested, Reeves said, he should be sure to call him.

Cheryl Bradford had been worrying all week. She knew the dead girl only to say hello to, but she had seen her there at Conroe High School that Saturday. She played volleyball for her school, Waller High, and she was sure she had seen Cheryl Fergeson in the hallway, maybe even walking down toward the rest rooms by "Sesame Street." But that was not what was worrying her.

The strange thing that stuck in her mind was the two men. They were both white and both young, maybe early twenties. One had shaggy dark hair, and the other had sandy hair. She had noticed them only because they had been in the gym, and they obviously did not belong there. They had not seemed to have anything to do with the school at all. They had come into the gym from the hallway, from somewhere near the auditorium, and walked across the room and out the other side toward Route 105.

At the time she had not thought much about it. But later, at home, Cheryl Bradford wondered about the two white men and what they were doing there and where they were coming from. Could they have been coming from the auditorium, where the body was found?

It started to worry her so much that she told her volleyball coach, who seemed to think it was important. So they called the Conroe Police Department to tell them what they knew.

John Wesley Styles is a Texas Ranger. On the Thursday after the murder he was on vacation at his aging parents' home in Baylor County, up near Wichita Falls in North Texas, when the call came through from ranger headquarters in Houston. He was to get down to Conroe and report to District Attorney Jim Keeshan and try to help him get a break in the rape and murder of a white schoolgirl there.

To Wes Styles it was just another job. Styles had been a lawman all his life. He had been sheriff in Baylor County, near the Oklahoma border, for eighteen years before he decided to join the Texas Rangers. That was in 1969, and he had never regretted it.

He had signed up with Company A, whose job it was to range across East Texas helping local sheriffs and police chiefs with their work, and it was his particular duty to concentrate on three counties: Trinity, Walker, and Montgomery. He had become a familiar sight in many a courtroom with his big, heavy body and his baggy green eyes and his paunch sagging over the top of his pants.

He had been in and out of every kind of crime: rape, robbery, murder, including the big siege at the Huntsville Jail in 1974, when four men died. There were those who said he cut corners and put the fear of God into his witnesses to get them to say what he wanted to hear and that he was too rough and too tough and a solid-gold son of a bitch. That didn't worry him. He got results, and to a Texas Ranger, that was what mattered.

Friday morning, wearing his tall leather boots and his white Stetson hat, Ranger Styles reported for work in Conroe.

Friday afternoon in the high school, about four o'clock, an announcement came over the public-address system calling Clarence Brandley to the principal's office.

He stopped what he was doing and walked down the long hallway toward the main lobby and the tiger in the glass case. He knocked gently on the door of the principal's office and walked in and saw a big man with tall leather boots and a white Stetson, another guy with a neat suit and sharp blue eyes, a potbellied cop who he knew was the captain of detectives, and a whole bunch of other cops, and they all just looked at him with angry faces, and then the big guy with the Stetson stepped forward with this deep voice and said, "I have a warrant for your arrest on a charge of capital murder," and then the cops took his arms and cuffed his hands behind his back and marched him out the door.

Chapter Two

There were several good reasons why Ray Reeves wasted no time when he heard that Clarence Brandley had been arrested, though not all of them were obvious.

The truth about Ray Reeves was that a lot of people did not have a very high opinion of him. That included Ray Reeves. It gave him no pleasure, but he admitted that he was not the greatest attorney in the world and that he had never been considered sharp or worth a damn and that he had probably pulled more dumb stunts than any other damned lawyer in the whole state of Texas. He admitted it.

He did not even look like an attorney. He looked more like a European peasant: stubby, fat body with a ruddy, round face on top. His language was coarse, foul even. He always looked as if he had just walked in from a high wind. God never intended Ray Reeves to sit on the Supreme Court.

Something else he admitted was that he was a racist. Not the kind of racist who would do anything very much about it—he was not about to join the Ku Klux Klan or pick a fight with black people who wanted to move into his street—but the way he saw it, he was bound to be a racist. Back in the little town where he was born in Gray County up in the Texas Panhandle, the townspeople would not even let a black person stay overnight. If blacks broke down in a car, they would push the car down the road to the next town. That was the way it was and always had been, especially since there had been a big murder there—a white family had been killed and chopped up and hidden down crevices in the earth and everyone said it was blacks who'd done that. He simply never had felt for black people the way he did everyone else; he never had socialized with them or wanted to, and he admitted he just considered niggers on a different basis from regular people.

Despite all that, there were several good reasons why Ray Reeves hurried up I-45 from Houston to Conroe as soon as he could that Saturday morning to see if he could help Clarence Brandley.

One reason was that Ray Reeves did not screw his clients. He figured he was never going to get rich out of being an attorney, and he was never going to win any prizes, so he might as well try to help a few people. There was always this feeling in the back of his mind that he owed it.

As a young man, during World War II, he had been shot out of the sky over France on a bombing mission in a B-24. Everyone else in the plane had been killed, and for a while he had thought he was dead, too. He knew he would never have survived on the ground if a family of poor peasants had not taken him in and hidden him and healed him and then passed him on to the French underground, which took advantage of his coarse features to disguise him as a farm worker and smuggle him into Spain. That was probably what had made him feel so restless when he got back to Texas after the war and started working as a sheriff's deputy. He just felt it was chickenshit work with chickenshit people, and he owed it to someone, if only to a poor French family in a village whose name he could not pronounce, to get out and help people. So he became a defense attorney, and whatever his limitations, he made up his mind never to screw the people he worked for.

There was a second reason that kept pricking his mind as he headed north from his home in Houston. He knew the kind of town that Conroe was.

He drove fast up Interstate 45.

On a Saturday morning the road was clear, and it was less than an hour before Reeves swung his car off the freeway, up Frazier Street and into the courthouse square. The sun was warm, and the streets were quiet. Reeves had no fancy strategy worked out. He knew next to nothing of what was happening here. Anyway, that was not his style. He just wanted to tell Brandley that he was going to do what he could for him and that in the meantime he should keep his mouth shut. The police had had him in custody for less than a day, so they should not have done too much harm. Not yet.

Reeves paced across the courthouse square and over to the old city jail. But when he asked to see Brandley, the officer on the front desk shook his head and sent him over to the county jail, which was up on the top two floors of the courthouse.

Reeves paced back across the square and made his way up to the county jail and found a deputy sheriff. He explained who he was and that he needed to see his client. The deputy shrugged and turned his mouth down.

"We don't got him here," he said.

"What you mean? Y'all arrested him, didn't you? Y'all got him in custody, don't you? And I need to see him. I'm his damned attorney."

"Well, we don't got him here."

It was happening again. Conroe. Reeves never had liked the place. He might be a racist and a whole lot of other things, but this town was too damn much. Once these people got it into their heads that someone was guilty, they did not give a damn. Especially with a black man. Reeves looked at the deputy. "Where's that Keeshan?" The deputy pointed at the floor—downstairs in the DA's offices.

"Is that where I'm going to find my client?"

"I reckon," said the deputy.

That meant one thing and one thing only: the prosecution had already started questioning Brandley. Reeves shook his head and made for the stairs. Keeshan certainly hadn't taken the black man down there to make him comfortable. Never mind his civil rights. Never mind that he was supposed to have his attorney with him. Keeshan was a slick operator. Reeves knew it. He'd always said that Keeshan could crawl bare-ass through a barrel of thistles and never get a scratch. And he was smart as a whip.

The last time Reeves had been in Conroe, he had been defending a man on a murder charge and Keeshan had thrown so much damned evidence at him that Reeves didn't even try to beat the charge, just did his best with the jury to get his man a life sentence instead of the death penalty. Now Keeshan was going to try to do the same thing, try to tie up Brandley with a confession before he had had a chance to talk to his attorney.

By the time he got down to the district attorney's offices, Reeves was ready with a lungful of law for James Keeshan, but Keeshan was nowhere to be seen, so Reeves had to make do with one of the DA's assistants, and when the assistant claimed that the DA's office didn't have Brandley either, it was a lungful of righteous anger that came out: "Son of a bitch Keeshan . . . my damned client . . . goddamned civil rights . . . goddamned, son-of-a-bitch town . . . son of a bitch Keeshan . . ."

The assistant said he would see what he could do.

Clarence Brandley felt as if he had been pitched into a circus ring. He had never heard of anybody being arrested this way before. The cops had led him out of the school and driven him down to the courthouse square, and instead of taking him around to the back of the old city jail the way they were supposed to, they had walked him right across the street into the front of the courthouse. There were people everywhere, and reporters and photographers. They must have told the press to be there. It was as if they were putting him on a stage and showing him off, with his hands cuffed behind his back.

Inside, they had made him take his clothes off and then gone all over his body, looking for scratches. They had shot pictures of him from every angle and then taken his belt away. Then they had stuck him in some little room and started asking him questions about the dead girl. The big Texas Ranger with the Stetson had tried it first, and Brandley had just told him he had nothing to say and he wanted to call an attorney. Then one of the young cops had come in and tried it, and he had told him the same thing. So then they had sent in a black cop, as if that were going to change anything. He knew the way their minds worked.

Finally, they had let him call Ray Reeves, who had told him to stay calm and say nothing. Reeves had told him he would be up there first thing in the morning and he would talk to the cops and make sure they didn't try to question him any more before then.

Brandley had spent his first night in jail, haunted by half-remembered stories from his childhood. Greg Steele had died here, in this building, at the hands of these white men. Brandley had known him and played basketball with him. But Greg was not the only one. There had been others. Brandley had never met them, but he knew the stories. There was one story in particular that the old people told, about a man called Joe Winters.

He had lived in Dugan years ago, in the 1920s, and worked out at one of the mills near Leonidas on Route 105. He was married to a woman named Anna, but all the same he had a white girl he was going with. A lot of black people knew they were seeing each other, but no white people did until one day, one Friday afternoon, when they were in the woods together close by the river and a white man saw Joe Winters with his white girl. When she got home, they asked the girl: "What you doing in the woods with a nigger?" And in her fear she said the black man had raped her.

All the old people in Dugan knew what happened next. They still recalled the day when as children they had seen the white men with guns and sticks coming down through the streets and into their homes. "They came to get him. There was white men searching in all the houses. It went on all night. . . . Sheriff Hicks came through our house. My mama was crying. Everybody was crying. I didn't know why. But I started crying, too. . . . They had dogs, bloodhounds, searching everywhere. There was white men on horses in the streets. Everybody just stayed inside, hoped there wouldn't be no trouble. . . . Just before they came the first time, I saw him walk by my house. Joe Winters. He didn't know he was in trouble. He just walked by, and they never saw him. . . . They were coming through all the doors, saying they were looking for the man who raped the white girl. There was a lot of men looking for him, white men with torches. . . . Everybody was frightened."

The search through Dugan was only part of the manhunt, which soon became such a big affair that it made the front page of the newspapers. Within hours of the first report on that Friday afternoon, May 19, 1922, news and rumors were sweeping Montgomery County that a black man had raped a white woman—a girl of only fourteen years, according to some. Sheriff Hicks called in the bloodhounds from the Huntsville Jail, and by nightfall several hundred men were helping comb Conroe and the surrounding fields and woods.

At first the woman did not tell them the name of the man they were hunting, and during that Friday evening the hunters caught a black man named Rudolph Manning who they believed was guilty of the crime. Some deputies took him down to Houston to keep him safe, but Sheriff Hicks went off after him and brought him back at three in the morning and showed him to his supposed victim, who said he was the wrong man.

The hunt went on all night. By Saturday morning white men had poured into Conroe from all over Montgomery County. Several thousand of them were now hunting the black rapist, and for the first time they knew the name of the man they were chasing. They went to Joe Winters's house on Avenue J. There were rumors he was hiding underneath it, but he was not there.

They took his clothes to give the scent to bloodhounds, which chased a trail more than a mile out to the west of Conroe, but then they lost it. There was a rumor that the fugitive had taken a mule from a black boy out there. The dogs had given up when word came from the other side of town, from Waukegan, that Joe Winters had been seen there.

White men converged on Waukegan in trucks, on horses, with their dogs and their guns. Soon the woods were alive with the sound of the hunt, the dogs yelping, the men shouting, all crashing through the undergrowth. This time they were on the right track, and early on Saturday afternoon, May 20, 1922, word came through to Conroe that they had caught Joe Winters in the woods two miles from Waukegan and were bringing him back.

Just before four o'clock in the afternoon the white men dragged Joe Winters into the courthouse square. The whole place was boiling with people, all the men who had come to join the hunt, their wives, children too, hundreds of white faces filling the square and the surrounding streets. Out on the city limits the sheriff's men blocked the roads and turned away black people.

Joe Winters was in chains when they hauled him through the crowd, which jostled and shoved to get a look, to jeer and shout "nigger" and kick him and spit. First they tried to fix him in front of Wahrenberger's store, but Mr. Wahrenberger wouldn't let them in case his place got damaged, so they chained him to an iron post at the end of the fence that ran around the old courthouse.

Most of the crowd watched and waited while a few of the men organized everything, fetching old boxes from Wahrenberger's, piling them up around the black man's body till they reached up over his head, bringing oil and kerosene, and splashing them all over all the boxes till they were good and soaked. Then one of them struck a match, and all the white men, women, and children stood and watched while Joe Winters was burned alive.

In Dugan the old people still recalled how they heard about the end of the hunt in broken scraps of rumor: " . . . I was only a kid, maybe five or six, and I was riding on a wagon with my mother, coming to Conroe from about nine miles out. When we got to the edge of town, a deputy turned us back. He told my mama: 'You can't come through. They gonna burn a nigger.' . . . I remember a man came down our street and he said they had burned him and he said they were trying to burn the heart, which you can't do. . . . I heard they tried to take pictures of him, but he wouldn't straighten up. . . . There was one man who rode up to him on his horse and hit him so hard he fell out of his stirrup. . . . He was trying to make them kill him before they burned him. He was hoping they would shoot him. But they didn't want to do that. . . . You could smell it all around. Smell the kerosene and the meat. Burning meat. . . . He didn't die straight away, not till the flames went down his throat."

Later the fire died down, and with it, the crowd. Families went home to eat and sleep. The *Courier* reported: JOE WINTERS BURNED HERE. NEGRO PAYS PENALTY FOR ASSAULT UPON 14-YEAR-OLD GIRL. The *Courier* described the manhunt and its conclusion and said: "Winters was regarded by both white and negro population as a bad character. He is said to have had three women, one at Waukegan, one at Conroe and one at Leonidas, and his favorite occupation was smoking a cigar as he loafed the streets and refused hard work when offered him."

Then Conroe got on with its life, and all that was left of Joe Winters was memories. In his cell above the courthouse square Clarence Brandley lay alone with his fear.

Saturday morning the questioning started again. Brandley protested that the authorities had told Ray Reeves they would stop. It made no difference. By this time Brandley was feeling pretty weak. He had hardly slept, and he had not eaten a thing since they took him in. He was hungry all right, but he was not going to eat anything they gave him. He had heard about some of the things that had been going on behind these bars. Earlier that year, in January, some prisoners had tried to pick a lock, and the jailer had caught them and taken a dozen prisoners into the freezing night air, made them strip, and then hosed them with icy water and left them there to freeze for the night. The way Brandley saw it, if they were mean enough and crazy enough to arrest him for something they must know he hadn't done, then it would be no surprise if they tried to finish him off with something in the food. He would wait till his family brought him a meal.

The Texas Ranger kept asking him a lot of questions. Brandley kept refusing to answer. He had given up thinking he was going to do himself any good by helping these guys. And down beneath his fear and weakness, he was mad at them—not so mad that he dared argue with them, but mad enough to stare back, dull and sullen, and be sure he would not play their game. Anyway, he had no idea who had killed that girl. He knew he hadn't. He guessed it wasn't any of the white janitors. They had all been working. They had never had time to do a thing like that. He guessed the girl must have wandered outside, or some vagrant or someone must have got into the auditorium through one of those open doors. The truth was, he did not know.

Finally, word came through that Ray Reeves was kicking up a stink outside, and the ranger got up and stood over Brandley and told him: "If I had my way, I'd take you out now and blow your goddamn brains out."

By the time Reeves made it in to see him, the attorney was cussing and swearing about Keeshan and about the ranger. Reeves told him he knew both of them from this other case he had worked on up in Conroe, and in that case, he said, there had been witnesses who had had the shit beaten out of them and all kinds of other crap. So his advice was to say nothing and keep his head down. Brandley needed more than that. When was he going to get out of here? What did these guys have on him? How could they do this? The two men talked about trying to raise some money to pay for the defense, and Reeves said he would go see Brandley's family and talk to them about it. They talked about bail, though Reeves could not see how he was going to have much luck on a charge as bad as this. Brandley was getting angry. He kept telling Reeves that he had done everything the police had asked him. He had even taken a lie detector test. And he had passed it. So why had they gone ahead and arrested him?

Reeves had a pretty shrewd idea about why Brandley had caught their eye, but he kept that to himself. Reeves tried to get him to tell him what happened on the day of the crime, but Brandley could hardly remember. It had just been another day. He couldn't even remember what time it was when he turned up at school. All he knew was that he and Icky Peace had found the body and that was the first time in his life he had ever seen this girl.

Reeves leaned forward and looked straight into Brandley's face. "Clarence, it don't make a whole lot of difference to me whether you done this thing or not. I need to defend you. You gotta tell me the truth, see? Now, did you have a damned thing to do with this?"

Brandley looked straight back and said: "No, Mr. Reeves. I did not."

Reeves could not exactly explain why, but for some reason, he believed him.

It had been a long time since anyone had built a new scaffold in Conroe. In the old days the city council had often met and set aside $22.50 to pay the carpenter to go to work in the courthouse square. There was one time, back in 1905, when the council paid the money and the scaffold was built and the prisoner, who was from Dugan, cheated them by hanging himself in his cell the night before he was due to die. But there had been no public hangings since 1924, when the state ordered that executions should be carried out by the Texas Department of Corrections in Huntsville.

Now Brandley sat alone in his cell and watched the town get ready to stage an execution. The foundation of the scaffold was already being laid.

The *Conroe Courier* carried Brandley's picture on its front page, as he was led in handcuffs into the courthouse, his face morose and dull and black. People who did not even know him discussed his guilt in the paper. Everyone in Conroe— everyone who might eventually have to sit on his jury—could read all about this monster called Brandley. A Conroe detective said the police had "an airtight case" against Brandley. The district attorney said Brandley would not be entitled to be released on bond. The captain of detectives said he was reluctant to have anybody like Brandley loose in society. The school superintendent said he was relieved that Brandley had been caught so now they could start school. The father of the dead girl said he was proud the police had caught their man so quickly and he hoped Brandley would be convicted. Some reporter wrote, "Conroe can sleep safe at night once again."

But there was something worse than that, something that had started off so simply, the way bad things often do. It must have been a couple of years ago that his mother, Minnie Ola Brandley, had been out walking behind the shack on Avenue E, where he had been born and where she still lived. Out along the railroad track behind the shack she had spied something in the weeds, and out of curiosity she had taken a closer look. It had turned out to be an old shotgun, all riddled with rust and useless, but she had had the idea that she would take it home and clean it up and maybe it would come in useful one day for shooting a jackrabbit or scaring off a prowler.

As it turned out, she never had cleaned it up, and it had just lain under the big bed in the front bedroom of the shack—the same bed where he had been born—gathering dust and making a home for a whole bunch of spiders. He had still been living down in Houston at that time, driving a Metrobus, and he hadn't known a thing about it.

One weekend, back in the spring of '79, he had come up to stay in the shack on Avenue E. His mother had gone down to Houston to see her doctor, so he was alone up there. This had been at a time when he was still living in the fast lane, drinking in the juke joints and spending all his money on a good time, and he had gone out that night to a place in Dugan called the Doll House.

He had been sitting in the Doll House drinking with some people when a guy came in and started shouting at a prostitute who was sitting in there, a white girl called Mary Zavaba, and had started dragging her out by the hair. Brandley and some of the others had got up and helped the girl and told the guy to get lost. After that he and another guy had started drinking with Mary Zavaba and a friend of hers, another prostitute, a black girl called Jo Ellen Parrish. One thing had led to another, and many hours and many drinks later Brandley had ended up taking this black prostitute back to the shack on Avenue E. Not that he was going to pay for her. It was just a friendly thing. She had been kind of worried because she had some boyfriend—Brandley guessed he was her pimp—who was going to go crazy if he found out she was with Brandley. In the end, all that had happened was that they had cooked themselves a meal in the shack and Brandley had been so drunk that he had just passed out on the bed. He had awakened in the morning and found that Jo Ellen Parrish had vanished and taken his long coat with him. He had thought nothing about it. He had been too hung over to be interested. But the next thing he had known, some cop was outside saying Jo Ellen Parrish was accusing him of raping her.

It had turned out that while he was asleep, she had got all worked up about what her boyfriend was going to say. So she had gone off and told her boyfriend that Brandley had made her go back to his place and had raped her or tried to rape her or some such thing. The boyfriend had bought the story and made her go to the cops.

The cop had had no search warrant, but he had proceeded to search the shack all the same, and there, under the bed in the front room, covered in rust and dust, he had found Minnie Ola Brandley's old shotgun. So Brandley had ended up being charged with some kind of sexual assault on Jo Ellen Parrish and with unlawful possession of a shotgun. Parrish had soon backed off and withdrawn her charges, and the cops had quickly dropped all the talk about the rape; but he had been left with the shotgun charge. Brandley had wanted to plead not guilty. That gun had had nothing to do with him. But if he said that, the cops were only going to come around and accuse his mother of unlawful possession. So he had talked to an attorney and had been advised to make a deal. He had ended up pleading guilty and getting three years on probation. That had been more than a year back.

The attorney had said it was nothing to worry about. He was not likely to get arrested for anything else, so the probation would never mean anything. Just two weeks ago the attorney had filed papers with the courthouse to have the probation discharged. That was the rule: If you did more than one-third of the time without trouble, then you could get the whole sentence lifted. All it had needed was for the judge to stamp a piece of paper, and it would have been out of the way. But now he still had it hanging over him.

Still, so far as he was concerned, he had never been in trouble before. Well, nothing bad. But that was not the way it looked in the paper. All across the top of the front page of the *Courier*, in big letters, the paper talked about Brandley being on probation for a felony offense. That damned piece of old rust. It made it sound as if he were an armed killer. "Brandley was serving a three-year probated sentence for possession of a prohibited weapon—a sawed-off shot gun." All across the front page. It was as if he could see this whole town building the scaffold.

*   *   *

Only a few blocks away from the city jail, where Brandley sat watching his fate unfold, a group of men and women were gathered in the office of a Conroe taxi company called City Cab. Like almost everyone else in Conroe, they were talking about the black janitor who had been arrested for the high school murder.

There was the dispatcher sitting behind her desk taking calls and scribbling notes, a couple of drivers sitting around waiting for work, a teenage boy who had stopped in to wait for his grandmother, and Connie Miller, a large white woman with light brown hair who had until recently been the manager there. She had just stopped by to see her old colleagues. It had been only a few weeks since she had left, but already there were new faces, like the lean, scruffy young man who had just walked in.

Connie Miller did not like the look of him. Everything about him looked dirty. He seemed drunk or stoned, and it looked to her as though he had wet the front of his pants. She watched in distaste as he walked over to the other drivers and told them he had been signed on as a new part-time driver.

"Name's Gary," she heard him say, "Gary Acreman."

He went into the back room while they continued to discuss the murder and to agree that they could hardly believe that such a thing had happened in their high school. Connie Miller was just telling the others her theory: that she did not necessarily believe the police had arrested the right man.

"Anybody could have come in off the street and done it," she was saying. "It would be easy to get into that school. If you were going to watch the volleyball. Or if you just wandered in."

That was when Acreman first spoke up, when he came back and settled down on the couch and rested his cup of coffee on an empty chair and told them that he worked up there as a janitor himself and he knew this Clarence Brandley, who had been arrested.

"Well," said Miller, "my honest opinion is that I feel with school fixing to start they had to find someone. They had to pin it on someone real quick to clear it up before they started school to, like, calm the community down."

She looked across at Acreman on the couch by her side. "I mean, I honestly don't think that that Clarence Brandley did it."

Suddenly, Acreman was out of the couch. And he was shouting at her. "Clarence did not kill that girl. I know who did. Clarence didn't do it. But I will never tell."

She would never forget his eyes like a cat and his yellow teeth and his foul breath. Right in her face he was shouting. She would never forget it.

Then, just as suddenly, he was back on the couch again, lying back with his eyes shut and a dim smile on his face and the wet patch on the front of his pants. Connie Miller felt shocked and shaken, and the others all went quiet. They changed the subject.

A few minutes later Connie Miller got up and left the office of City Cab and drove home. The dispatcher took some more calls. The drivers went to work, and the teenage boy went home with his grandmother. Nobody walked a few blocks across town to tell the black man in the prison cell that somebody out there knew something, that somebody out there said he was innocent.

The Reverend John Daviss watched and worried. For forty years now Daviss had lived in Conroe and ministered at the First Missionary Baptist Church in Dugan, and he had come to know the town well. With his graying hair and his moon-round face, he had a calm, owlish kind of air about him, and on both sides of the railroad tracks he had built a reputation as a solid, wise old black man. He had become an unofficial spokesman for the people of Dugan. Reverend Daviss knew Clarence Brandley and his family, and he wanted to help; but it was hard to know how he could. When he was just a boy, his granddaddy had often told him that no matter what you did, there would always be white folks who hated Negroes.

It went back to the days of slavery, which were not so long ago. In those days Montgomery County had been one of the biggest slave-holding counties in the state of Texas. Boatloads of slaves had been shipped up the Trinity River to a town called Cincinnati, which yellow fever had since wiped out, and had been sold in markets all across the county. The last witnesses of the old days had died in the sixties: Phillis Bates, who remembered her father's being whipped at the post for drinking and trying to run away from his master; the last of the Easley family, who had belonged to a rich farmer named Raleigh Rogers until he gave them all away as a wedding gift to his daughter, Mrs. Pleasant Yell.

Conroe had not even existed until the 1880s—twenty years after the slaves were freed—when a Union army captain from New Jersey named Isaac Conroe set up a sawmill in the Big Thicket from which the new town grew. But John Daviss had come to believe that the old hatreds and inequalities of the county's slave days had become part of Conroe's way of life. Daviss came to Conroe during the oil boom, when there was terrible racism and no black people gained any benefit from the oil. In 1980 he looked around him and saw a town that was still built to keep blacks on one side of the tracks in shanties and whites up on the hill in big houses. He knew how Conroe sheriff's deputies used to harass black people who traveled through the town. Life for blacks in Conroe seemed to have got better for a while, but now with this killing at the school, it was as bad as ever.

Reverend Daviss had always tried to hold a hand out to white people. He did not believe in hate. In the 1960s he had worked on the human relations committee that was set up by black community leaders trying to get black people into jobs that were denied them. He had persuaded one of the Conroe bank presidents, the most liberal one, to hire a black. He kept working at it, trying to persuade young black people who graduated from Conroe College not to leave town but to stay and build the black community. He went to the white churches, the more liberal ones, and persuaded them to let him come and preach to their congregations. He met with the police to work together to keep the young blacks out of trouble. But in truth he could not say that he had been able to change very much. The county seemed to have drifted back to what it had once come out of.

Sometimes he had to wonder whether his granddaddy wasn't right after all. Only the other Sunday he had been to the Episcopal church to preach to a white congregation, and afterwards a white man had walked up to him and shook him by the hand and said how much he had enjoyed the sermon. All the while they were talking, the white man's wife stood there, and she didn't shake the minister's hand. She crossed her arms over her chest and scowled at the ground, and then, nodding at her husband, she said to the Reverend John Daviss: "He may want to shake your hand, but that don't mean I gotta."

* * *

Ray Reeves knew he was in trouble. The town was awash with rumors: that Brandley had raped a whole lot of other women, that he had raped one of his own sisters or maybe his mother, and that there was no doubt that he had killed the girl at the school because they had taken swabs from her vagina and it was "nigger semen." Reeves was afraid the prejudice was becoming overwhelming. He tried to do something about it. A Houston TV station wanted to interview Brandley; but when Reeves tried to set it up, Keeshan blocked it and the police wouldn't let the TV people into the jail.

That was only the beginning of his trouble. Reeves had no money. He had a client who had no idea what had hit him. He had no clue to who had really killed the girl. He had no witnesses, no scientific evidence. And he could not get one word of sense out of the damned district attorney, who would not even hand over a copy of the statement Brandley had given on the day of the crime, so he had no way of knowing why they had arrested Brandley or how in hell they hoped to convict him.

The nearest thing he had to a lead was some crazy psychic who called him up and insisted that they had got the wrong man, that the real killer was a white man with black hair. Reeves had nowhere to go and no way of getting there. Then Jim Keeshan offered him a hand.

Reeves knew he could not trust Keeshan. He told Brandley, he told Brandley's family, he told his wife at home that Keeshan would trick you and twist you, that he was so damned charming but he would as soon cheat you as look at you, and that no matter how much of a gentleman he might make himself out to be, Keeshan never could be trusted. Still, when Keeshan offered him a hand, Reeves took it.

Keeshan's offer was a simple one: if Brandley would agree to testify to the grand jury, Keeshan would not press for a high bail bond. That way, said Keeshan, Brandley would get a chance to put his side of the story to the grand jury, and he would also be released from jail to help prepare his defense, so it was all fair play.

Reeves could see the danger: the greenest law student, wet behind the ears, could tell you that you never feed your client to the grand jury. Reeves had said it often enough himself: "The grand jury are just a tool for the DA. The grand jury will do any damn thing that the DA tells them to do. If they don't, everyone calls them a runaway grand jury, and they get criticized in the press and looked upon as freaks. The DA just has to come in and say, 'We can make a case against this ol' boy,' and so they do. It's a farce."

There were not even regular rules of evidence at a grand jury hearing. Keeshan would be able to throw any kind of rumor and speculation at Brandley, and he would be on his own. Even if Reeves was in the room with him, he would have no right to make objections. Keeshan could slice Brandley up and feed him to the wild hogs. At the end of it all Brandley would have just about no chance of blocking Keeshan from getting an indictment from the grand jury, and he would have given the other side a preview of his evidence. Yet Reeves was tempted. He went to see Brandley and explained the deal that Keeshan was offering.

"I tell you, Clarence, I don't know what that son of a bitch is up to, and I can see where this is a dangerous move. It's extremely dangerous. It could finish up being a foolish move, not wise at all."

But Reeves explained that he was tempted because as long as Clarence was in jail, the defense was tethered. He wanted Brandley out so he could talk to him whenever he needed to, take him up to the school and get him to remember every minute of the day of the crime, let him loose in Conroe and see if he could find someone who knew something to help him. More than that, Reeves wanted to buy some time. He had never felt such a concerted effort to convict a man. It was all moving too fast.

"My God, Clarence. I don't know what to advise you. I can't advise you not to, because I can see where it could possibly help you. But if you're vulnerable, don't go, because that son of a bitch Keeshan will get you. You know, he's a pretty sharp ol' boy."

"Mr. Reeves, I didn't do it."

Reeves had that feeling again. "Clarence, if you really had nothing to do with it, and there's really no shit he can throw at you, then I can't see how it can hurt you too much to go before the grand jury. Maybe they'll ask some questions that will shed some light on the son of a bitch who did this. And we'll get you out of here on bail."

Reeves went back to Keeshan and sealed the deal. For what it was worth, he gave Keeshan his personal opinion that he was trying to indict an innocent man here. Keeshan said that was a big, broad statement to make, and for the first time he showed one of his cards: Keeshan told Reeves he had a witness who would say Brandley was missing for forty-five minutes around the time the girl was killed.

Reeves did not think that sounded like the most powerful evidence he had ever come across, but he could see where it might help a circumstantial case. Keeshan started prodding him, saying that if Brandley was really innocent, he should surely come and tell that to the grand jury. Reeves agreed, and in exchange Keeshan agreed that Reeves could have a transcript of the hearing, that he could sit next to Brandley to advise him—although not to intervene—and, most important, that the DA's office would not try to fix a high bond for his release from jail.

Reeves told himself it was what Clarence wanted, and it would be OK because, after all, Clarence was an intelligent guy, and it would give them a chance to find out what evidence Keeshan was sitting on; but he still could not help feeling that there was something wrong, that somehow Keeshan was playing him for a fool.

On Wednesday, September 3, only five days after his arrest, only eleven days after the death of Cheryl Fergeson, Clarence Brandley was led into the grand jury room on the second floor of the Montgomery County Courthouse. The room was stark and bare except for a long wooden table at which Brandley took his seat.

In front of him sat the twelve jurors. Brandley lifted his eyes and flicked them across their faces: all white. He looked back at the table. Ray Reeves sat on one side of him with a notepad. On the other side was the DA, Jim Keeshan, and his assistant, Jerry Winfree. Both white.

Keeshan spoke. "Brandley, I'd like you to stand and raise your right hand, please."

He stood up and swore that he would keep the proceedings secret. Now Ray Reeves spoke. Pointing to Brandley, he apologized to the jurors: "Sometimes he's a little, you know, a little bit difficult to understand."

Brandley knew what he meant. He talked the way he had been brought up to talk. These white folks would just have to understand him. He was going to tell the simple truth. Reeves had told him that was all he had to do. That was all he was going to do.

In jail he had been feeling angry, feeling the injustice of it all. Some cop in there had been riding him, telling him that if he ever got out of jail on bail, the cop would be out to get Brandley and he'd never be seen again. Now he felt a little nervous. He had never done this kind of thing before.

Keeshan started off slowly, explaining that the grand jury would decide whether he should be indicted and tried for murdering Cheryl Fergeson and that he had the right to remain silent, and then he asked him some simple questions about his childhood and his work record. Brandley kept saying, "Yes, sir," and "No, sir." Keeshan asked him if he had a criminal record.

"No, sir."

"Have you ever been arrested for rape before?"

"No, sir," said Brandley. The end of the answer. Then he thought for a moment and decided to tell the grand jury that Jo Ellen Parrish had once accused him of raping her but that there was nothing in it.

Ray Reeves winced. It was all very well being honest, but the odds were already stacked against them without Brandley's volunteering smears about himself. He glanced across at Keeshan, who looked as if he could hardly believe his luck. Then Keeshan slashed at Brandley.

"What about a woman by the name of Smith that accused you of rape one time?"

"No, sir."

"Do you know a woman by the name of Pokey that grew up here in Conroe?"

"I know Pokey."

Reeves did not know who the hell Pokey Smith was. What was Keeshan driving at?

"Is it true that about eight or nine months ago down in Dugan, you raped her?"

"No, sir."

If they had been in court, Reeves could have killed this. It was a rumor without any evidence. Brandley obviously did not know what Keeshan was talking about. It was pure prejudice. But Keeshan was up and running and dragging Brandley through the dirt.

"Did she report you to the police?"

"No, sir."

"You don't think she reported you to the police?"

"No, sir."

Keeshan paused. Reeves knew that the DA had scored his point. Without producing this Pokey Smith or any other evidence, Keeshan had planted the idea that Brandley had a history of rape, that he was some kind of bad nigger. Brandley had even helped him do it. And all the time Keeshan was so charming and persuasive with the jurors. Reeves had to hand it to him.

Now, for the first time, Keeshan started to ask questions about events at the high school. Brandley told him all about his job at the school and how his girlfriend, Beverley, had driven him up there that Saturday morning, about how he had been going about doing his work and opening all the doors for the volleyball tournament, and all about trash cans and toilet paper. He remembered how Gary Acreman had told him there was a girl in one of the rest rooms and how he had said he did not want to go in there, how he had sent the other janitors across to the Vocational Building while he had a smoke in his office, and, finally, how he and Icky Peace had joined the search for the missing girl and found her body in the little props loft over the stage.

That was when Keeshan started slashing at him again.

"You had never been up there before?"

"No, sir."

"Then I take it you had never had any reason to be up there with a girl before?"

"No, sir."

"And you had never had any reason to be up there by yourself before?"

"No, sir."

"Never had any reason to masturbate up there or have sex with anybody up there before?"

"No, sir."

"Is that right?"

It was the same trick. Keeshan had planted the idea. Reeves had known it all along. The grand jury was just a tool for the DA. Keeshan could tell the jurors any damned thing he wanted. And Reeves just had to sit there and let him do it. His only hope was that Keeshan would start throwing some real evidence at Brandley. That was when they might learn something about what the state was really up to.

Keeshan started asking if Brandley had been wearing a belt on the day of the crime or carrying a towel. Brandley said sure, he had been wearing a brown belt, and the police had taken it when he was arrested; but he never had a towel. Reeves guessed this had something to do with the state's case, but he was damned if he could see what it was. Then Keeshan started slashing again.

"When you worked for Oscar Johnson, did you ever go into the preparation room where the bodies are?"

"Yes, sir."

"What do you do in there?"

"I mostly assist."

"What about when you're there at night by yourself, do you have access to the preparation room?"

If this was in court, Reeves would have hit the son of a bitch with so many objections he'd have thought he'd died and gone to hell. What was this? It had nothing to do with Cheryl Fergeson. The son of a bitch was just trying to insinuate some idea about Brandley getting off on dead bodies. That damned Keeshan.

"When you stay there at night by yourself, do you have a key?"

"I never stay there at night by myself."

"Not even when they're having a wake and you're just sitting there waiting for it to be over?"

"No, sir."

"You've never been there by yourself?"

"No, sir."

"Why did you go into that kind of work? You had a job at the high school. Why did you go to work around dead bodies?"

The point was made. Keeshan was on a roll. "You're divorced? . . . Isn't it true that you're fairly rough on women? . . . Have you ever grabbed a woman by the throat and told her to have intercourse with you? . . . Have you ever hit a woman in the head with a gun? . . . How many women have you been having intercourse with in the past two months?"

Reeves could not see how any of it was relevant. Or even true. Keeshan was not pretending it was true. It was nothing but prejudice, but he could see that all of it was encircling Brandley tighter and tighter. Then Keeshan moved in and choked him.

"Do you feel sorry for this little white girl that was strangled and raped like that?"

"I feel sorry for anything like that that happens."

"Are you going to tell the grand jury that you didn't molest that little white girl?"

"Yes, sir."

That was a cheap shot. That was what had worried Reeves from the moment he heard Brandley had been arrested. OK, the girl may have been white, but waving that around in front of a Conroe jury like that was as good as booking Brandley his own private suite on death row. Now Keeshan was snapping at Brandley's heels like a dog at a rabbit.

"Isn't it true that you grabbed the little girl by the throat and took her in through the stage door?"

"No, I didn't."

"Didn't you have a strap or something and didn't you put it around her neck?"

"No, sir."

"You didn't? The poor little girl is dead and you had nothing to do with it?"

"I'm telling you, yes, I had nothing to do with it."

"The poor little girl was a sixteen-year-old virgin and wasn't ready for anything like that, was she?"

"I don't know. I didn't know or have anything to do with it."

"You didn't have anything to do with it?"

"No, sir."

"You swear to God, of course, and all that sort of thing?"

"Yes."

"You believe in God?"

"I sure do."

Finally, Reeves could see it. There was no evidence here. No eyewitness. No scientific breakthrough. No confession. The state did not even know whether the murder weapon was a towel or a belt or a strap or some other damned thing, never mind whether or not Brandley had ever been in possession of it, whatever it was. There was only prejudice.

Keeshan had needed Brandley to come and sit in front of the grand jury so he could throw all this trash at him. And if he threw enough, some of it would stick. In Conroe most of it would stick. Because Clarence Brandley was not the same as everyone else in that jury room, and just in case anyone had missed that fundamental point, Keeshan came right back to it.

"You ever had intercourse with a white woman before?"

"No, sir."

"Have you ever dated a white woman?"

"No, sir."

"Did you see any other Negro male that day inside the building?"

"No, sir."

It did not matter how many times Brandley said his "yes, sir" and his "no, sir." Reeves could see that all Keeshan needed was for that black man to sit there and talk in his black voice and point his black face at the table. That was all. There was no stopping Keeshan now. And Brandley was still sitting there telling him the truth.

"Do you think any of the custodians beside yourself might have been able to do this thing?"

"No, sir."

"You don't believe any of the other custodians did it?"

"Not after the experience I've had working around them. They don't seem to be the type of person that would do it."

Reeves could see that can't-believe-my-luck look on Keeshan's face again as Brandley swept suspicion away from the best alternative suspects. Brandley added that he was not sure about Gary Acreman because he made sly remarks and he guessed he might tell lies on him. Keeshan kept slashing.

He asked him about his time in Korea with the army. Had he ever killed anyone in Korea? Had he had intercourse with any young Korean girls? Brandley said he had never killed anyone, but he had slept with some Korean women. Pause. What about the Monday after Cheryl Fergeson's death? Hadn't Brandley taken some bags of trash out to the Dumpster, the same Dumpster where the dead girl's clothes were later found? Brandley said yes, he had taken out some trash. What about him and Icky Peace looking for the missing girl? Why had he done that? Was that part of his job? What about Jo Ellen Parrish? Had he raped her? What about Pokey Smith?

"You raped anyone else?"

"I never raped anybody."

"You haven't raped anybody?"

"No, sir."

"Isn't it true that you have some kind of psychiatric problem, that you have some problem about sex and meeting girls?"

"No."

"You don't have any kind of problem like that?"

"No, sir."

"You don't need any psychiatric help?"

"No, sir."

"You don't have any mental problems at all?"

"No, sir."

"You don't want a psychiatrist to look at you?"

"No, sir."

"You don't want to know what's wrong with you?"

"There's nothing wrong."

"You haven't got anything wrong with you?"

"No, sir."

"Have you ever been told you had any mental problems?"

"No, sir."

"Did your mother ever try to get you to go to a psychiatrist?"

"No, sir."

"Not one time? Never even suggested it?"

"No, sir."

"Never?"

"No, sir."

"What about the time you tied up your sister and beat her, why did you do that?"

"I never tied up my sister and beat her."

"You never did that?"

"No, sir."

"I believe that's all. Thank you for testifying."

Two feelings that had been wrestling their way through Ray Reeves's mind for the last four days had now become certainties. First, Brandley was innocent, and there was no damned evidence to show anything different from that. Second, Brandley was going to be indicted and very likely convicted and sentenced to death.

Ray Reeves was still in Conroe that afternoon when he heard that the grand jury had decided to indict Brandley and send him to trial. He was not surprised, not after the way Keeshan had treated Brandley. But he felt bad. He had fallen straight into Keeshan's trap. He had known it all along. He should never have fed Brandley to the grand jury. He knew the state would always cheat if it got the chance. That was any DA's rule: Screw the opposition. So he had been a dumb son of a bitch and let the state do it. He had only been trying to help. He guessed he had screwed up again.

The one gain he had made was that now he could get Brandley out on bail with a bond that was low enough for the Brandley family to afford. Keeshan had promised him that. All Reeves needed was for the district attorney to play fair.

Back in his cell Brandley was, visited by his mother. He could see she was trying to be brave, but she could not hide the way she felt. It was as if she were carrying a physical weight. Her old head sagged; her shoulders sloped; her arms were limp as string.

He told her not to cry, because he had done nothing, but she cried all the same because she felt it inside her. Just as before she had felt that he should never go back to that school, now she knew in her soul that the authorities were going to try to kill him.

His brother, O. T., a Baptist minister, came to see him. Brandley told him about Jo Ellen Parrish, about how it had been in the paper that he had a shotgun, and then how the DA had just tried to tell the grand jury he had raped Parrish. He told his brother about Pokey Smith. They all knew Pokey. He used to play in the dirt with her when they were kids. She was just a dumb little woman from Dugan. She spent a lot of time hanging around in the juke joints. He told his brother he had once had a fight with her, when he was drunk, and he had slapped her and she had called the police. He had paid fifty dollars right there, and that was the end of it. He was not proud of it. It was the kind of thing that made him get out of the fast life and try and settle down. But now this DA was trying to make out he had raped her, too. It seemed he had raped a whole lot of people if the DA was to be believed.

O. T. had bad news. He knew a black girl whose uncle was a cop, and he had told her to tell O. T. that they were going around looking for dirt on Clarence. So far as O. T. could make out, they had gone through their records looking for anything they could get on him, and they must have found that business with Jo Ellen Parrish's making out he had raped her, and he guessed they had found something about his slapping Pokey Smith that time. But that was not all.

According to what O. T. heard, the person who was digging up the dirt on Clarence, who had most likely been around to see Parrish and Smith, was Ted Morgan.

Ted Morgan was a legend in the Montgomery County sheriff's department. For them he was the deputy for "Dugan Nigger Town," the one man who knew every black face in every black juke joint, who knew all about how blacks lie and blacks cheat because he was black himself. Old Sheriff Gene Reaves used to get on his radio and sing out: "Where's ma nigger? Where's ma nigger?" And all the other deputies would wait till they heard the gravelly voice come back: "Ah'm here, boss." Then they'd laugh at that.

Ted Morgan had iron gray hair cropped down close to his scalp and dull, blank eyes, like a dead fish. He was one tough old man. They all knew the stories about how he used to get his confessions, how he would drive the suspects out into the Big Thicket with a shovel, and then he'd walk them into the trees and hand them the shovel and tell them to start digging a grave so he could kill them and bury them. Most of them never even started digging, just started talking. The white deputies all laughed at the stories, especially when Ted Morgan told them himself. One time he told them how he had caught some black-assed nigger boy who'd been stealing appliances out of empty new houses and had taken him into the Big Thicket down on the lowland by the river, cuffed his arms around a tree trunk, stripped the shirt off his back, and left him there for the skeeters to eat him while he went and sat in his patrol car. It wasn't five minutes, he said, before that damned ol' nigger boy started yelling and hollering and begging to confess—and he'd never laid a hand on him.

It was always a big deal when Ted Morgan brought in a suspect. He would lead him up to the desk, and he wouldn't fill in any forms or register any charge. He'd just croon in that low voice of his: "The nigger done it. Here's the nigger. The nigger done it." They'd all laugh at that because they knew the reason he never filled in any forms was that he could not read or write.

If Ted Morgan was down in Dugan trying to dig some dirt, Brandley knew that meant trouble. There was no telling what Jo Ellen Parrish and Pokey Smith would come out with.

Ray Reeves visited Brandley, too, full of anger at Keeshan for the trash he had been throwing around at the grand jury.

Brandley had a confession to make. He had fouled up in there on a question. He hoped it was not going to be important. He had told Keeshan that he had been wearing his brown belt on the day of the crime. Well, that was not right. He had been wearing it with his white pants when he was arrested. On the day of the crime he had been wearing his old blue jeans, which had a kind of built-in belt around the top. They didn't need any belt. He hoped it was not going to be important.

Reeves told him there was no damned way of knowing if it was going to be important because the damned DA himself couldn't make up his mind what the murder weapon was supposed to be.

Reeves asked Brandley about the forty-five minutes he was supposed to have been missing while the girl was raped and killed. It took Brandley a moment to realize that they were talking about the time that day when he had managed to get a moment for himself, when he had sat in his office and smoked his Kool and listened to the radio. Was he supposed to have had the girl in there with him? This was crazy. But how could he prove it? He had been alone. He had no alibi. If he were going to rape and kill a white girl, he would surely have planned something better than this. They could not be serious. And what about the lie detector test? Didn't that prove it? He had passed that damned test, and that cop had told him he had nothing to worry about.

Ray Reeves told him straight: "They changed their minds, Clarence. They're saying you failed the lie detector test."

Brandley felt the sweat prickle his face.

Ray Reeves was not sure, but as far as he could make out, it was the Texas Ranger, Wes Styles, who had done it. Back on Friday morning, a few hours before they had come to arrest him, Styles had called up the Houston Police Department and persuaded some supervisor there to go take another look at the polygraph test. The supervisor had looked at the graph and decided there was one answer where there could have been a deception. It was not the big question—whether he raped and killed Cheryl Fergeson. Not even the supervisor said that he had failed that. It was one of the general questions about whether he had ever had sex with anyone against her will. The supervisor was saying that his answer there might have been a deception, and he was saying the man who ran the test might have been a tad inexperienced. As far as Ray Reeves could see, that didn't matter a damn to this inquiry.

"It's just like a shrink in a divorce case," he said. "You pay him, and he'll say whatever you want him to. They gave you that test and you passed the son of a bitch. So they got another expert to say you failed it. It's so absurd."

But it seemed it was good enough for Ranger Styles. Now everybody in the DA's office and the Conroe Police Department was running around saying that Brandley had failed the polygraph test.

Ray Reeves still had no money to fight this case. He had talked to the Brandleys, and so far as he could see, he could have taken the whole bunch of them and turned them upside down and shaken them till their eyeballs rattled and he wouldn't have gotten more than four hundred dollars out of the lot of them. He told them: "From a business point of view, I'm sucking hind tit here."

But Brandley had put in his savings—the money he had been putting aside for Clarence, Jr.—and some of his aunts and uncles had put in the bit of cash they had. It was not enough to fight a big case like this, not much more than five hundred dollars, but it was enough to do one thing that Reeves badly needed.

The day of the grand jury hearing Ray Reeves hired himself a private investigator.

Lorna Hubbell was not exactly Ray Reeves's idea of a private investigator. She must have been six feet tall, and she was no more than twenty-five years old. She had lots of bouncy blond hair and a wide-eyed chatterbox kind of way about her. She was not an ex-cop, like most private investigators, and she had never taken any of the courses that they usually had. Instead, she had a degree in behavioral science. She was not even a Texan. She came from California, somewhere near Los Angeles, and she said things like "Houston is what happens when architecture catches venereal disease."

But Lorna Hubbell came highly recommended. She was working for a Houston agency, Burkett and Burkett, which was run by a husband-and-wife team, both of them ex-cops. They swore by her. She had plenty of guts, she could talk her way out of a tornado, she didn't mind what she did, and she would work from can to can't without stopping to draw a breath.

The day after the grand jury hearing, Thursday, September 4, 1980, Lorna Hubbell drove up from Houston to see Clarence Brandley. She was kind of disappointed. She thought this was a big, hot case. It had been in the papers in Houston and on TV just because it was such a horrible crime. And here she was interviewing the man in the middle of it all. But he didn't seem to know the first thing about it. And he was shy with her. Or something. Maybe he just wasn't used to white women. But he just said "No, ma'am" and "Yes, ma'am" in a soft voice.

He tried to explain to her what he had done on the day of the crime and how he had found all these doors open before they discovered the body. He seemed credible, but he seemed to have no idea of time the whole day of the crime. He ended up giving her the names of the four white janitors and of anyone else he could think of who worked up at the school.

She went to see Ray Reeves, who told her he knew no more than Brandley because the DA would not tell him anything, and they agreed that they were going to have to investigate this whole crime themselves. They had to clear Brandley, but before they could do that, they had to try to find out who had really committed this crime and—just as important—what evidence that district attorney was working on that made him think he could hang this black janitor.

The next day Lorna Hubbell went to Conroe High School in search of witnesses. The school authorities were not pleased to see her.

She spoke to the assistant principal, a tall, thin man with glasses who told her he was not allowed to discuss the case. She spoke to Brandley's boss, Mallie Davis, but he said he was not allowed to discuss the case. He said Brandley was a good and trustworthy worker, but he refused to put that on paper or come and say it to a jury. The volleyball coach told her she remembered Brandley's wandering around the gyms that day and asking her if there was enough toilet paper in one of the girls' rest rooms. She said that Brandley must be guilty and that he was the only person who could have committed the crime because he was the only one who had keys to the auditorium where the girl's body was found.

Finally, Hubbell found one friendly face, a woman named Marsha Porter who ran all the sports classes for girls in the school. She showed Lorna around the school, and they tried to retrace the black janitor's steps down the long hallway with the cafeteria on the left and the auditorium on the right and the rest rooms on the landing just past the auditorium, where the "Sesame Street" characters were. They knew from the newspaper reports that the girl had last been seen looking for a rest room. But they had no idea which one. She might have gone into the dressing room by the gyms and used the rest room there, in which case she must have been abducted and taken outside the building and into the auditorium. Or she might have walked down to "Sesame Street" and met her attacker there and been dragged off that landing and into the auditorium. For all her friendliness, Marsha Porter did not disguise her feeling that Brandley might be guilty. She thought it must be a janitor who had done it: he would have to have the keys to the auditorium, he would need to know that the props loft was up there, and he would need to be inconspicuous. An outsider, she thought, would surely have been noticed by someone.

Lorna Hubbell left the school feeling almost completely in the dark. Brandley's keys were obviously going to be used against him, so they would have to try to prove that these auditorium doors could have been opened by someone else. Beyond that, all she had discovered was that someone seemed to have talked to these people at the school and told them not to talk to the defense, that someone seemed to want to keep Clarence Brandley in the dark.

As Lorna Hubbell toured the school, Brandley was making his first court appearance. He had been taken from his cell and had walked a gauntlet of whispers to get to court. Ray Reeves, who had driven up from Houston, was huffing and puffing that Keeshan had better keep his end of the damned deal. Minnie Ola Brandley had put on her church clothes and set out across the tracks from Dugan. Half her family seemed to be crowding around her as she limped up the hard white steps and through the heavy double doors into the Montgomery County Courthouse.

The second-floor courtroom was clean and white, with a bright blue carpet. At one end, seated on a raised dais, was the judge, Lee Alworth, a small black-gowned white man whose hair was being eaten up by his forehead on both sides of his scalp. He had a tense, impatient air about him and a way of clenching his teeth so that his jaw muscles bulged in his cheeks. Brandley knew his face. This was the same judge who had given him three years' probation for that rusty shotgun.

The hearing was short. Ray Reeves asked the judge to set bail. Minnie Ola Brandley's brother Frank had come up from Houston to try to help. He got up in the witness box and answered some questions. He said the family had talked about raising some money for a bail bond. "We talked it over. But it's pretty scarce. We couldn't come up with too much. Some of 'em is working and some of 'em is not and I am on disability. I imagine we could come up with ten or twenty thousand dollars for a bond."

Reeves asked if that would be in cash.

"Cash? Well, that would be about a couple of thousand."

Could they really not raise any more than that?

"Well, I don't know. Money is pretty scarce the way we are living."

Judge Alworth said he would set bail at thirty thousand dollars and called for the next case.

To Minnie Ola Brandley and her family, the judge might as well have asked for the Empire State Building. They did not have it. But Ray Reeves tried to persuade himself that he was happy with it. He knew Keeshan could have pushed the judge for a much higher bond, and he reckoned the Brandleys could find the money if they put their minds to it, although it might take them a couple of weeks. It looked as if Keeshan were delivering his end of the deal. It was just that it seemed a little too easy, and he kept asking himself if there was not something he had missed.

Reeves did not have to wait long for the answer. That same day the office of the district attorney filed its first motion in the case of Clarence Brandley.

It was a motion to revoke Brandley's probation. Reeves had never claimed to be a legal scholar, but he knew what that meant. Brandley could not get bail. Not at any price. Not at thirty thousand dollars. Not at thirty million dollars. No bail. The whole deal with Keeshan was out the window. The motion said that Brandley had breached the terms of his probation by raping and murdering Cheryl Fergeson, and so he had to serve his three-year sentence. That motion had to go before the court to be ruled on, but in the meantime, the law said that the defendant automatically lost his right to bail.

Reeves was so angry he ran out of curses. It was not just the sheer two-faced deceit of it. What really made him sick was that he examined the papers and found that they had been drafted three days earlier—on Tuesday—before Brandley had been to the grand jury. Christ Almighty, that was the same day that Keeshan had made the deal with him.

* * *

Nobody in the Brandley family had ever expected an easy life. They had lived in this same shack on Avenue E ever since Minnie Ola had married Buck Brandley, which was back in 1931, when she was only sixteen. She was not from Conroe originally. She had been born forty miles north, in Huntsville, where she had lived with seven brothers and sisters who had a tough time after their mother died when she was small. When she was thirteen, her daddy had sent her to live in Conroe, to help his brother Frank, whose wife was sick. Her uncle Frank worked all night in the sawmill, and Minnie Ola looked after his wife and kids for him. Then she had met Buck Brandley, and before she knew it, she was married and having children of her own.

Buck Brandley was born in the town of Montgomery and raised in Conroe. Most of his life he repaired track for the Santa Fe Railroad, like his father, Putt, before him. He and Minnie Ola often had to move to follow the work, even when they had all eleven of their children—six boys and five girls—with them. Silsbee. Somerville. Brenham. Clay. Navasota. They had lived all down the line, but they always came back to Conroe, to the shack on Avenue E.

It was a pretty good place, they always said. Apart from the little kitchen and bathroom at the back, it had two bedrooms and a little dining room and a front room, too. They usually slept side by side, three or four to a room. In the back there was a little land, maybe as much as five acres, and Buck Brandley had worked hard on that land. He had a mule to plow it with, and a man called Mr. Prince, whom they always called the agriculture man, came from the government to teach him how to get the most out of it, how to rotate his crops. He planted everything on that land: peas, sweet potatoes, corn, potatoes, squash, beets, cucumbers, tomatoes, watermelon, even a bit of cotton. He had some cows and some chickens he kept there. They used to work on the land every evening, Brandley with the mule and plow, the children pulling up the weeds, putting in the seed and the fertilizer by hand. They sold a lot of what they grew, but there was always food. If they had a chicken to eat, they would eat all of it, the feet, the neck, even the gizzard; they kept the best parts for special days and did not throw anything away.

Buck Brandley was always trying to earn some extra cash on the side. He used to sell peanuts. Everybody in Conroe

knew Buck Brandley with his two-foot metal tray full of nuts.
He more or less had the peanut franchise for the town. He used
to buy a hundred-pound sack, and then the children cooked
them and put them into ten-cent bags that he sold at baseball
games or at the schools. Some of the schools did not let him
through their gates, so he sold the peanuts on the sidewalks
outside instead. Brandley used to get barrels and sell them to
politicians for them to use to give lemonade to the crowds
at their meetings. He would sell the calves that his cows
produced. If a mule or a horse died, he took it down the street
to Miss Griffith's house, and she made soap out of the corpse.
Clarence and his brothers and sisters had often wondered how
she did that, but they never were allowed to see.

Buck Brandley was always working. He might have been a
rich man if he had been white. As it was, they scraped along.
Minnie Ola Brandley used sacks to make dresses for the girls.
Neighbors gave them hand-me-downs. They never had a car,
though they had a pickup once. They never had a radio. One
time, after Buck Brandley had been selling peanuts, he said
he had some money and they could buy a TV, but Clarence's
eldest sister, Ola May, started fussing because she was courting
and she wanted to get something fancy to show her boyfriend,
so they got a dining-room table instead. Years later they did
get a secondhand TV for fifteen dollars, and the children were
all happy.

Sunday was always the biggest day. They had their Sunday
clothes and shoes. During the week they might look pretty
rough, but not on Sunday. They all went off together to the
Church of God in Christ in the white wooden shack a block
away on Avenue F and sat there from nine o'clock until eleven.
The children were supposed to pay attention all that time—no
talking, no reading, no gum—but they let the small ones go to
sleep on the bench if they got tired.

Elder Duncan was the preacher then, and everybody had a
lot of respect for him, a lot of reverence. If people were sick,
he came and put oil on them. What he said really mattered.
Each family in the congregation took turns giving him Sunday
dinner. When he came to the Brandley house, all the children
were very excited, and they all felt blessed and let him have
the best piece of chicken.

Clarence Brandley was still young when his parents broke
up. There had been trouble between them for a long time:
some drinking, some fighting. Some bad fighting. It got so bad

that Buck Brandley moved out around 1962, when Clarence was eleven, and eventually they got a divorce. Most of the children were grown up by then. But Clarence and his twin sister Florence were the youngest, and they were left in the shack with their mother and with the two other youngest boys, Tim and Ozell, who was always known as O. T.

Buck Brandley gave his ex-wife eighty dollars a month, but she couldn't make it on that, not with four children and bills to pay. She went to Mrs. Etheridge, whom she'd worked for part-time for thirty-five years, cooking and ironing and minding her children, and asked for a raise. Mrs. Etheridge turned her down, so she had to go on welfare.

Clarence Brandley went to Booker T. Washington School, the black school in Dugan, where he was an average student. He played a lot of basketball, broke his leg one time playing football. Then, when he was in the ninth grade, his mother became very ill. She had some mental trouble, couldn't even remember what day of the week it was. It turned out she had a blood clot on the brain. Doctors said it was the size of a golf ball, and it could have been something to do with one of her old fights with her husband. She was in a bad way. She could not even make it to O. T.'s graduation day. Surgeons operated on her, but she could not work anymore the way she used to, so she moved to Houston with Clarence and Florence and Tim to stay with her sister in the Fifth Ward.

For a long time Houston seemed like home to Brandley. He finished high school, fathered a baby daughter, and then was drafted to go to Vietnam. At the last moment the army switched him to Korea, and he spent seventeen months in uniform, mostly in communications. When his tour was over, he came back to Houston, married, had two more kids, including Clarence, Jr., separated, and had two more children with another woman. Finally, he got sick of it all and headed back up to Conroe, where his mother was back living on Avenue E. All he had been looking for was a steady job and a steady life.

That night, after Keeshan had broken his deal over Brandley's bail, Ray Reeves and Lorna Hubbell drove around to Avenue E to see Minnie Ola Brandley. Some of her other children were there, as well as Brandley's girlfriend, Beverley. They were very bitter. They all agreed that Brandley was being railroaded. And they all agreed why: the police had to arrest someone to stop the panic before school started, and Brandley was the black man nearest to the scene.

Tim Brandley said he had spoken about it to a white policeman who had said: "How come they're still holding your brother? Don't you know they found a white man's hair on the girl's body?"

They had all seen a story in the *Conroe Courier* about a fifteen-year-old schoolgirl in Cleveland, thirty miles away, who had been abducted and raped and strangled and left for dead, though she had survived. Wasn't that where that weird janitor lived? Icky Peace? How come they didn't arrest him? And why was the captain of detectives telling the paper, "Nothing is going to make me change my mind"?

And how could they take away Brandley's bail like that? And how could they just magically turn that lie detector test around? And what was all this about Jo Ellen Parrish and Pokey Smith? In Dugan there was talk that they had been paid fifty dollars each to say bad things about Brandley. Both had told Ted Morgan that Clarence Brandley had raped them. Pokey Smith was supposed to have said he had raped her four times. What was all this about?

Ray Reeves said he was doing his best to get on top of the case. But it wasn't easy with a son of a bitch like Keeshan. So far as he could tell, Keeshan was working on a circumstantial case. He was going to say Brandley was missing for forty-five minutes, that during that time he had come across the girl in one of the rest rooms or somewhere, that he had taken his belt or a towel to strangle her, and then that he had used his keys to get into the auditorium and hide the body there. Keeshan was going to have to say that Brandley had changed his mind about hiding her and decided to take Icky Peace and find her again. Reeves did not know. It did not make a hell of a lot of sense to him. He couldn't help fearing that Keeshan was hiding some stick of dynamite—a fingerprint or something—that was going to blow them clean out of the water.

But at the moment it looked to him like a straightforward circumstantial case. And a damned flimsy one at that. He told the Brandleys to stay cool, raise money, and hope there was justice in this town.

Chapter Three

The people of Dugan could offer Clarence Brandley little more than their sympathy. That was the way it had always been, though the Reverend Jerry P. Jones found it hard to believe.

Reverend Jones had just moved to Dugan from his birthplace, Birmingham, Alabama, to minister at the Pilgrim Rest Baptist Church on Third Street. Young and tall and strong, with a voice that boomed all the way to the back of the church, he was a commanding sight in his new pulpit. He was shocked by Conroe, which looked to him as if it had been completely forgotten by the civil rights movement. It seemed to him that the law might have changed, but the town hadn't.

He looked at the houses in Dugan that were nothing but shinny shacks, and he said, "You don't see shinny shacks anymore in Birmingham, Alabama, because we tore them down, and what we didn't tear down, we burned down." He saw the big brick churches on the white side of town, and it stirred a deep rage in him when white ministers called him up to give him the names of black people who had turned up in a white church so he could contact them and steer them back to one of the little wooden churches in Dugan. He saw people in Dugan who were submissive, who did not try to fight for their rights, and he protested: "Anything they put on you, you just accept." Most of all, he saw black people who had no power because nothing in the town belonged to them. "Everything you want— jobs, loans, credit at the store—whatever you want, you have to get from white hands. You don't own any businesses. You don't have any investment in anything. You don't have any decent clubs, no decent community centers, no facilities at all.

The only kind of black business you have here is a juke joint, a hole in the wall where you dance and drink some beer and raise hell and curse."

The more he looked into Conroe, the worse it got. There were no blacks on the school board, and there never had been any. There were none on the county commission, which ran Montgomery County, and there never had been. The mayor was white. So was the city administrator. So were all the judges, the district attorney, the county attorney, the sheriff, the chief of police, the captain of detectives, the fire chief, the president of the Chamber of Commerce, the county librarian, the four county constables, the tax assessor, the editor of the *Courier*, and all the reporters who wrote for the *Courier*. And they always had been. In the whole town, so far as he could tell, there had never been a black doctor or an architect or an accountant or any other middle-class professional who was born and bred in Dugan. No matter what Congress or the Supreme Court or the *New York Times* might say, the Reverend Jerry P. Jones could see that Conroe was still a white man's town. The only exception was Oscar Johnson, Jr.

Reverend Jones liked Oscar Johnson, and one of the reasons was that Johnson had no illusions about why he had become the first and only black man ever elected to public office in the history of Montgomery County. Johnson readily admitted that he had become a city councilman because he was no threat to the white man's town.

Oscar Johnson had grown up in Willis, just north of Conroe, at a time when he was told his place and what he could do, and he did not argue. He never expected anything else. That was how black people were then. When he went to the football game, he didn't try to sit in a white seat. When he went to the picture show, he went up to the top seats because that was where black people were supposed to be. When he moved to Conroe with his daddy in 1962 and started running the funeral parlor in Dugan, he knew the kind of town this was. His business often took him up to the courthouse. There were the different drinking fountains: WHITES ONLY and COLORED. Different rest rooms. Restaurants where you couldn't walk in the front door. He never expected anything else. He worked hard. He read *How to Win Friends and Influence People* and kept a copy near him in his office. He soon had a reputation as a moderate man, and so, in 1974, after Greg Steele was killed by the police and black people finally started to say they wanted someone from their end of town who could be on the council, they looked to Oscar Johnson. They knew no black person could be elected without white votes. The council had made sure that Conroe was never split up into voting districts, so the minority of black votes was always swamped by the white majority. Oscar Johnson, the blacks hoped, might be acceptable to the whites.

At his second try, in 1976, Johnson's moderate approach won him a seat on the council, but despite his easygoing, unthreatening politics, he had trouble. White people telephoned him and made threats. There were rumors that someone had hired the organized crime group the Texas Syndicate to kill him. One time someone came by his house in Dugan and emptied a .22 rifle through his front door. Oscar Johnson knew Conroe was still a racist town. You might not see the signs up anymore. It might not be on such a big scale as once upon a time. But he saw it every day in his work. In the old days of segregation there had been two cemeteries set aside for black people—Rosewood and Golden Gate—and in all the years since segregation ended, Oscar Johnson had still never buried a black body in the white cemetery, and even though his prices were the lowest in town, no white family had ever asked him to bury their dead.

There were times when the Reverend Jerry P. Jones despaired of Conroe. Around the corner from his church, he noticed one building in among the crumbling wooden shacks was built of brick, with a neatly clipped lawn. He soon discovered that this was the home of the man they called the "Head Nigger," who owned most of the shinny shacks, who had become rich off the rents he collected from those living there, and who now lived in great comfort. It had been no different in the days of slavery. The white masters would let one or two blacks get the upper hand over the others and pay them to whip the others into line. The "Head Nigger" was like some kind of Mafia Godfather who handed out favors in Dugan. There was nothing Reverend Jones could do about it; the man was also a church deacon.

Reverend Jones often heard that things had changed in Conroe. It was the steady refrain of white people in the courthouse and at the city council.

There had been a time in Conroe when white people made no attempt to hide their feelings about the people in Dugan. The *Courier* used to run a column called "A Little Fun—Jokes to Make You Laugh" in which black people were regular stars: the "colored" maid who was about to get married and asked her mistress to keep her savings for her because "ah hates to keep all dat money in de house wid a strange niggah man"; the black "mammy" who always signed her name with an *X*, then started signing with a *Y* because "Ise done got married yistidy an' changed mah name"; the church committee that met to discuss "de financial en pecuniary affairs ob dis chu'ch" and was told that "de treasurer done obscunded wid all de money"; the old "colored" lady who refused to go on a carousel because she had seen her friend Rastus on it and asked, "Rastus, yo' spent yo' money but whar yo' bin?"

The Ku Klux Klan had met openly in the town. In February 1923 the *Courier* reported on its front page: "The Conroe Ku Klux Klan enjoyed a most bountiful oyster supper at the Klan Hall in the Foster building last Thursday night in which several scores of Klansmen participated in devouring oysters, cakes and coffee, and several hundred valiant oysters lost their lives that the Kluxers might eat and be merry."

The history of Dugan was full of victims: an unarmed man shot dead by Deputy Floyd Cox in July 1932 because "he put his hands on the front of his shirt and I thought he was going to shoot me"; young Tommie Goffney, who in January 1951 wrote a letter to a white girl asking her for a date and was fined a hundred dollars by a Conroe judge who told him he wished the law allowed him to punish him more severely; Dedward Galveston, who had his head split open by a white man with a pair of ice tongs outside the Dude Ranch Café in July 1951; the unnamed man who was found dead by a roadside in August 1930 with his legs and arms broken and a hole in the back of his head and who was judged to have died accidentally; Happy Denman, who was given a lift by two deputies, who then locked him in a cell, fired tear-gas cylinders at him, beat him over the head with a pistol, and asked that he be declared a lunatic; Marshall Waters and Zeke Rollin, who in June 1922 were shot at a roadblock by police who heard rumors that black people were getting drunk on whiskey and planning an uprising. Even during the Second World War, when Montgomery County called on all men and women between the ages of fifteen and one hundred one to register for civilian defense, bitterly attacking Germany and Japan for their record of "enslaved people and the destruction of human freedom," the council stated clearly that only white citizens should apply.

All through Dugan's history the victims showed the same willing compliance in their oppression that frustrated the newly arrived Reverend Jones. It was expressed most clearly on a graduation day in the spring of 1923 at Conroe College, the only college to which black students were admitted. The new graduates—the cream of Dugan's rising new generation—were sitting quietly in their best clothes under the eyes of their proud parents. They were listening to the founder of the college, the Reverend J. Johnson, then the most respected figure in the black community, as he outlined for them the brave new future for which they had worked and which was now within their grasp. It was a future weighed down by the past. The new graduates were told to find work as domestic servants. "All sensible negroes know that the South only knows the negro as a servant, laborer and menial in the industries of the country, and we must prove ourselves worthy and indispensable in these vocations before we aspire for the higher industrial regions." There was no question of these bright young black people trying to influence the nation's future. "I do not wish to make you a power in the political world, but I am working to make you good in character and useful in life," their mentor told them. "You young people must be taught to know what duty means and that all service is honorable, and to know that politeness is cultural gentleness and not cowardice." In their quest to give satisfaction to the white man, the college founder advised them, they could do no better than to model themselves on the obedience of their ancestors who were slaves. "Their faithfulness to their mistresses and masters during the war between the states won for them the love and confidence of every southerner. Love, virtue, labor and economy will bring to you a greatness which no race can ignore or despise and this is the education my people need."

Reverend Jones was sure things had changed in Conroe, but he was not so sure it made a difference. White people still ran the town. Black people still let them. "You can cut the rattles off a rattlesnake," he liked to say, "but you can't stop him biting like a rattler all the same."

In the old days Conroe politicians never lifted a finger to help black people unless it suited them. There was a famous time in 1968, when the city's committee on civic affairs suddenly called on the council to clean up Dugan. The committee had visited Dugan and found piles of garbage alive with maggots, open sewers spilling waste into yards where barefoot black children played, pigs and dogs running wild, and row after row of dilapidated and unhealthy homes. The committee chairman, a wealthy white businessman named Rigby Owen, Jr., explained that the reason he wanted to clean up Dugan was that the town's schools were now being integrated. "And I don't like the idea of those kids bringing diseases from their filthy homes to school and exposing our children to them." In 1980 the politicians still did nothing for black people unless they had to. Even when federal law compelled them to integrate the schools, they held a referendum and voted 2,337 to 218 to ban the busing of children between racially segregated areas. Earlier that year, in May 1980, the Justice Department in Washington, D.C., had ordered the school board in Houston to stop discriminating against black schoolchildren, and Conroe's school superintendent, Chuck York, had stood up and attacked the Justice Department for interfering.

As far as Reverend Jones could see, most of the changes seemed to have driven the racism a little way underground, but not to have stopped it. White people in Conroe might not print jokes about niggers in the paper anymore, but he didn't doubt they told them in private just the same—and what was more, they still liked to believe that black people were just as stupid and dishonest as the niggers in the jokes. Black people in Conroe still became domestic servants and gardeners and cashiers in stores even though the white schools pretended to be grooming them for professional careers. They were still victims. Right now there was a white woman called Florence Sassie on trial who was charged with paying someone to kill her daughter because she was going out with a black man. The Klan was still active in Texas. It had little of the political power it once had, but it had been running "white youth self-defense and survival camps," and it was planning a protest against Vietnamese immigrants that its grand dragon, Louis Beam, described in the papers as "an old time political rally with a fish fry, flag-waving, some speechmaking, maybe some apple pie and a cross-lighting."

There were very few people in Dugan who would even think of fighting. Charles Henry might have fought if he had thought anyone would join him. He had been in school with Brandley, and unlike many of his classmates, he had not only left Conroe but had traveled around the world a bit, particularly in the Middle East, where he worked as an oil hand, and had learned that life did not have to be the way it was in Conroe. Charles Henry had tried to get Dugan moving by launching the Montgomery County Black Awareness Committee. People said they supported it, but joining was another matter. So far as Henry could see, people were too frightened of trouble. As long as they had bread on the table, they said, "What the heck." Charles Henry and his wife sponsored an annual Black History Week during which a black beauty queen was elected. That was a victory of a sort, to give black women pride in themselves; but it was a defeat, too, to admit that they had no chance of winning in the rest of Conroe. Henry had no doubt that Conroe was still essentially the same in 1980 as it had been when he was a child in the 1950s and used to go down to the river and lie real quiet in the bushes to watch the white men burn their crosses there. Things had changed enough that his white boss felt OK about inviting him to his wedding recently. But they had not changed too much: as soon as he sat down in the church, some white man came up and started asking who he was and what he was doing there. To his mind, they might not call him "nigger" to his face anymore, but white folks still didn't think his children were good enough to marry their children, and so long as white men ran this town, he guessed they never would.

He and the Reverend Jerry Jones were isolated. Reverend Jones liked to think he was not just a preacher but a fighter, too. There was no point in being afraid. "If you don't have something worth dying for," he used to say, "you don't have anything worth living for." It made him want to cry that a black man could still be railroaded in this day and age just because he was black. It reminded him of the crucifixion, when the crowd freed Barabbas and called out for Jesus to be killed. It was as if Conroe were calling out, "Give us the nigger. That will satisfy our thirst." Yet there seemed to be no one in Dugan who would stand up and fight for Clarence Brandley.

The young minister could only stand in his pulpit and warn them in his big booming voice: "They talk about Justice being blindfolded. That's the biggest lie. That woman can see. She knows the color of your skin."

If Clarence Brandley hadn't killed that girl, then who had? So far as Ray Reeves could see, it had to be either the white janitors or an outsider of some kind—someone who had got into the school that morning and tried to assault her or someone who knew her and maybe even met her there by arrangement, perhaps a boyfriend who wanted to have sex with her when she didn't. It could have been anyone.

To narrow down the suspects, Reeves needed to know about the scene of the crime. Had the attacker left anything there? Any item of clothing? Something that might have fallen out of his pocket? A footprint? Were there bloodstains or signs of a struggle to show whether she had been raped there or raped in some other place and then dragged up there when she was dead? But the district attorney would not let him look at the photographs the police had taken of the scene.

He needed to know about the dead girl's body. Had she scratched her attacker and got his skin or blood under her nails? Did she have semen on her body or in her vagina? Were there bite marks on her? Or even fingerprints, which could sometimes be lifted from a corpse? Were there bruises around her wrists to suggest she had been tied or handcuffed? Were there cuts or scuff marks on her legs to show whether she had been dragged or carried? What was this mark around her neck like? Had she definitely been strangled and, if so, with what? But the district attorney would not let him look at the autopsy report.

He needed to know the results of scientific tests. If semen or blood had been found, then what blood group was it? If there were prints, then whom did they belong to? Was it true that there was a white man's hair on the body? What other hairs or types of hairs were there? But the district attorney would not let him look at any of the scientific reports.

He needed to get hold of the dead girl's clothes, samples of her hair, and any other little clues that had been found anywhere in the school that day, so that he could send them off to be tested by his own scientists. But the district attorney would not release the girl's clothes or anything else he had found.

And most important, Reeves needed to get blood and hair samples from the white janitors, from the dead girl's boyfriend, Frank, and from anyone else who might have been near her. But the district attorney would not give him anything, and even worse, did not seem to be interested in getting them for himself.

That was what really got to Ray Reeves. Clarence Brandley had not killed that girl. Someone else had. But the district attorney and the Texas Ranger did not seem to want to find out. It was as if they were so focused on the black man that they were blind to everything else.

Lorna Hubbell was still looking for clues, but it was as if someone had been there before her and swept every one away. People were so clammed up they would not even tell her why they were clammed up; the other janitors, high school students, teachers, Brandley's bosses were all the same. Someone had always been there before her and gagged these people.

As the weeks passed, she began to feel more strongly that Brandley was innocent. It was not just that his story was credible. It was this sensation she felt of working against a whole town that was determined to see this man convicted, even if it meant sweeping away the truth. She could taste the prejudice.

She began to develop her own theory about the crime. She could see why people believed the murderer must be one of the janitors. They were in the building, they were inconspicuous, they would know about the props loft, and they could easily have gotten hold of keys. But in her mind Brandley was probably the least suspect of any of the janitors. It was not as if he had ever had a problem with women, and she had met Beverley and seen how crazy she was about him.

Lorna Hubbell's suspicion turned to Icky Peace. Brandley had told her that Peace was always complaining that women did not like him and that he had tried to get the other janitors to find a woman for him. So Peace had the simplest possible motive for trying to rape someone. Brandley also said the little janitor had been off on his own in the teachers' lounge for more than an hour that morning, so he had the opportunity.

But he was so small. How could he have abducted a healthy teenage girl and forced himself upon her? That was what most excited Lorna Hubbell's suspicion. If Brandley was telling the truth, Peace had been carrying a small armory in his car that day and had previously brought his handgun into the school. If Peace had had his gun with him, it would have been simple for him to confront the girl, take her at gunpoint up into the props loft, tie her up, rape her, and then strangle her. The big problem with her theory was that Brandley rejected it. He liked Icky Peace, and he would not believe that he was

capable of committing such a terrible crime. Lorna Hubbell
wanted to see for herself.

Within days of the murder Peace had been transferred away
from Conroe High School, and word at the school was that
he had been moved to stop him from talking. Lorna Hubbell
traced him to a junior high school in the town, drove there
before he was due to start work, spotted him waddling away
from his old green Chevrolet, and bounced up to him like a
long-lost friend. Peace said he would be happy to talk. "I got
nothing to hide," he piped, peering up at the girl, who was a
full foot taller than he. But before she could start asking him
any questions, he said something that sounded like an echo
from every interview she had ever started on this case.

"I can't say anything," he said. "I better call my attorney."

Lorna Hubbell watched him, fascinated. He was like a little
child playing at being a grown-up. He strode off into one of
the school offices, all businesslike, pulled out an address book,
and, frowning with concentration, dialed his attorney. As soon
as the attorney came on the line, Peace passed the phone to
Lorna. The lawyer said he had spoken to Jim Keeshan about
the case, and he did not want Icky Peace to talk. "He's a little
slow, you know."

Lorna was not so sure. Peace was watching her the way a
dog watches a bird. He was not missing a thing. And he was
beginning to look nervous, moving in a jerky kind of way,
even trembling a little, she thought. She said good-bye to the
attorney and gently started chatting with Peace. She did not
want to push him about the crime. She let him talk instead
about the police and how they had treated him. For the first
time she began to understand why people were refusing to
speak to her.

"They treated me real bad," he said, his eyes staring up at
her through his spectacles. They had called him names. They
had mistreated him. He had been scared. They had made him
sign a statement, and he never even knew what was in it. He
did not know how to read. He had just had to sign it. Then
there was the Texas Ranger. He had come by a week later
and scared him out of his wits. Peace fingered a silver chain
around his neck. It had a tag on the end that said he was
diabetic. He said the ranger had threatened him and grabbed
this chain and choked him with it. Now he couldn't sleep, and
he had nightmares about what had happened. It had all gone
blank in his mind. He could not remember what had happened.

Except when he tried to sleep, and then he could see the girl lying there.

"She was pretty," he confided. "Very pretty."

Lorna Hubbell watched him talk. She could not see why Brandley was so sure he was innocent. If she had been a cop, she would have been much more interested in this little guy than in the black man. And that was another thing: if Peace had been carrying all those clubs and guns around in his car, why hadn't the police charged him with unlawful possession of weapons? If Peace had that hanging over him, he would surely do anything these cops told him to. They could bust him and get him fired in hours if they wanted to.

She started to press him on the crime and was shocked to find that he did not share Brandley's feelings of friendship. Instead, the little janitor was damning. He was sure Brandley had done it. Brandley had a problem with women, he said, and he worked in a mortuary on the weekends, and that was mighty strange. Brandley must have done it because he had kept sending him, Peace, up into that props loft and getting mad at him until he found the girl's body. He must have known it was there.

That was news to Lorna Hubbell, and bad news, too. If that was what Peace was telling the police, it would look very damaging to a jury.

Peace said he had to get on with his work. Lorna Hubbell let him go and drove off to look for more clues. She could not quite make up her mind about him. He was obviously going to be a hostile witness. Maybe that was because he was guilty himself and wanted to cover it up. Maybe he was just too scared of the cops and the Texas Ranger to dare to quarrel with their version of events. She could not be sure.

It was the same way with these stories that the district attorney was spreading around that Brandley had a history of raping women in Dugan. She had been trying to find Jo Ellen Parrish, the black prostitute. The defense needed to know whether Brandley really had taken her out of the Doll House and raped her in his mother's shack or whether she had just said that to keep her boyfriend quiet. Lorna Hubbell suspected she was lying: if the rape had really happened and she had had the strength to get through the difficult part of reporting it and getting the police to believe her, she would surely not have dropped the complaint without explanation a few days later.

It sounded as if she had made up the story for her boyfriend and never meant it to get to the police.

Now she drove across town to find an elderly black lady named Rosie Holmes. She was Jo Ellen Parrish's grandmother, and somebody had called Ray Reeves's office to say that she knew the truth about the rape story. Lorna Hubbell stopped outside a small wood-frame house on the edge of Conroe. After a lot of knocking, a round old black woman with gray hair and wearing a cotton housedress opened the door. She stood back in the shadows of the house, talking through the screen door and saying she was not feeling good because she was just out of the hospital, where she had been for ten days. Lorna Hubbell explained why she had come.

"Oh, yeah!" said the old lady. "Now my grandaghter said all that stuff about being raped and all, and she told me that she never was raped, that there was never time for him to rape her."

Hubbell pressed her for more details. The old lady did not have many. All she knew was that Parrish had told her that this man was cooking her some food because she was hungry and that nothing had happened. That was all she knew. Except she was sure Parrish had just said the other day that she had lied to the cops about it. But she didn't know why and she didn't know if her granddaughter would speak to Hubbell about it.

It took several more days, but Lorna Hubbell finally found Jo Ellen Parrish and got her talking. She was sitting in a broken-down old red and white Cadillac outside a shack in Dugan. Someone was working on the engine, jerking the throttle cable and making it roar. The car radio was playing loud, and there was a crying baby on Parrish's lap. Parrish talked through the waves of noise.

She had told lies to the police. She admitted it straight away. She agreed now to tell the truth. She told her tale. Then she changed it. Then she wanted to change it again. It was as if every time a different song came blasting out of the car radio, a different version of the facts came out of her mouth. The one thing she was always sure of was that Clarence Brandley had never raped her. Sometimes she said Ted Morgan, the old black deputy, had made her say that. Sometimes she said that Ted Morgan had taken her up to the courthouse and it was Jim Keeshan who had threatened to drag her name through the dirt if she did not cooperate. Sometimes she said she never had told anyone that Clarence Brandley had raped her.

Lorna Hubbell took her statement denying that she had been raped. It was reassuring to know that Brandley had not raped her, but she could see that if Jo Ellen Parrish ever got anywhere near a witness stand, there was no telling what she would say, and if it was the police who put her there, it was not going to do Clarence Brandley any good.

And there was still Pokey Smith to worry about. The Brandleys had heard that Ted Morgan had got hold of Smith and that instead of complaining that Clarence Brandley had slapped her, she was now supposed to be saying that he had hauled her off and raped her four times in one night. Again, in Lorna Hubbell's eyes, the story made no sense. If she had really been raped four times, surely she would have mentioned it to the police at the time and they would not just have fined Brandley fifty dollars for slapping her.

She found Pokey Smith in the Holiday Inn south of Conroe on I-45, where she worked as a maid. She was short and skinny with small eyes and a dull look to her. Her hair was tied up in little cornrows, and she was chain-smoking. She did not want to talk. After some nudging, she started to say that it was true, that Clarence Brandley had raped her. Lorna Hubbell did not believe her. Her guess was that Pokey Smith was scared of Ted Morgan, and if she had just sworn a statement that Brandley had raped her four times, she was not going to risk a load of trouble from Ted Morgan by going back on it the first time anyone asked her about it.

A few days later one of Brandley's sisters contacted Lorna Hubbell to say she had spoken to Pokey Smith, who was now willing to tell the truth. Hubbell went back to Conroe and met her once more. This time she was ready to talk and even signed a statement. Pokey Smith said she had never been raped by Clarence Brandley. What had happened, she said, was that she had been in a bar in Dugan with a bunch of people and had gone to the rest room. When she had come back, she had found twenty dollars missing from her purse. She had been very upset and blamed Brandley because he had been sitting next to her and could easily have got inside her purse and taken it. So she had gone to the police and told them he had raped her. She was sorry now, and she did not think he had taken her money at all.

Her story made almost no sense. If she had told the police way back then that Brandley had raped her, why had they let Brandley off with a fifty-dollar fine? Pokey Smith said maybe she had not told them he raped her, just that he kind of assaulted her. But why hadn't she told them that he had stolen her money if that was what she believed?

The truth, it seemed, was that Brandley had slapped her, and she had told that to the police at the time, so they had fined him fifty dollars. Simple as that. But now both sides wanted to tell lies about it. Ted Morgan or someone had persuaded her to produce a grand story about rape so that Conroe could have its "bad nigger." And Brandley's family or friends had got her to tell this tale about stolen money because it explained why she had gone to the police, but it made Clarence out to be completely innocent. The simple truth—one slap in the face— was too dangerous for him in this climate of prejudice. It was a story born of fear and bred by years of life in Dugan.

Lorna Hubbell took Pokey Smith's statement. It said: "Ted Morgan came to my house and asked me to come downtown and state that Clarence Brandley had raped me. I guess he wanted me to lie. I don't think that Clarence messes with white women. I have never seen him force himself on a woman. I do not believe that Clarence is guilty of murder. I do not believe he is a rapist."

Hubbell drove away to report her findings to Ray Reeves. The bottom line was that Clarence Brandley had not raped Pokey Smith any more than he had raped Jo Ellen Parrish. But this whole cross fire of lies only served to remind her that the people in the courthouse wanted very badly to put that black man on death row and were not too worried about how they went about it.

In jail Brandley felt as if he had become a bystander at his own lynching. It was all happening so damned slowly. And he was trapped—physically trapped by bricks and mortar and iron bars and, beyond that, trapped by this whole tangle of prejudice. Nothing anyone did seemed to make any difference. It was as if people had built this scaffold for him and had bound him tightly and now were dropping the noose around his neck, getting ready to squeeze the breath out of him.

The other day Ray Reeves had come in to see him and said that his mother had found an alibi for him. She was saying that she remembered that he had come home on the day of the crime around ten in the morning. She remembered the time because the mailman had just been by. Clarence had been driving an orange pickup truck. She was sure of it. She had checked with one of her daughters, who had been there, and she agreed. Clarence Brandley had been at home on Avenue E when the girl was killed.

Brandley shook his head. "I'm sorry, Mr. Reeves. She's just trying to help. But it ain't true."

Reeves had thought as much. In a way he was kind of glad. An alibi would have been good for the defense. But if he had heard Brandley try to pick up a phony alibi like that, he would have been worried. Brandley was not so happy. He needed some help—not phony alibis, but real help. And he needed it fast. He was beginning to think Ray Reeves was not up to fighting this town.

On September 25 Ray Reeves went back to court.

The dumpy attorney had given up trying to persuade Keeshan to play fair in this case, so he had gone off to see the district clerk, a woman by the name of Peggy Stevens whom he found very charming. She smoked long, thin cigarettes in a holder, she carried her eyeglasses on a dainty gold chain around her neck, and her fingernails were beautifully painted strawberry red. He had filed two heavyweight legal motions with her. One said that District Attorney Jim Keeshan should stop interfering with witnesses and allow them to talk to the defense. Keeshan was guilty of "unethical and unprofessional conduct," Reeves complained. The second motion listed eighteen different types of evidence that he said the district attorney had to hand over if Clarence Brandley was going to have a fair trial.

Peggy Stevens had filed the motions with the court, and now Reeves was back in the courtroom, trying to persuade Judge Lee Alworth to order the district attorney to comply with these motions. The judge did not seem very interested. Ray Reeves began to wonder whether maybe this judge had been fed some of this horseshit about Brandley's raping half the women in Dugan. He stood up and tried to explain to the judge that all the witnesses they were approaching were scared to talk to them and that it was his belief that the district attorney was the cause of the problem. Keeshan stood up and said this was all untrue.

Ray Reeves put Lorna Hubbell on the witness stand and asked her to tell the judge what had been happening. She started to explain, but Judge Alworth cut her off and stopped Reeves's questions.

"There is no evidence that the state has interfered," he said. His voice seemed testy and impatient. It was up to the witnesses to decide whom they spoke to. The court was not going to help.

Reeves switched to his second motion and pleaded to be given access to the eighteen types of evidence he had asked for. Judge Alworth looked at the list and declared that the wording was too broad and that Reeves was asking the DA to do his work for him. Finally, he agreed to let the defense have a handful of items. Reeves was not impressed. He was to be allowed a transcript of Brandley's evidence to the grand jury. Since Keeshan had already promised him that as part of his deal to encourage Brandley to appear before the grand jury, Reeves saw that as no gain at all. He was to be given a copy of the statement that Brandley had made on the day of the crime, but he could have no access to anything that had been said by anyone else. So he and Lorna Hubbell were not only unable to speak to these witnesses but also unable to read what they had already said. The judge gave Reeves two things he needed badly: access to the dead girl's clothes and some of the photographs of the scene of the crime. They, at least, gave him something to start work on.

But there was still a lot missing. The judge refused to give the defense a copy of the autopsy report. Reeves had never come across a ruling like that in any case he had ever worked on. So far as he knew, it was just plain illegal. Nor would the judge give them the photographs of the dead girl's body, from which they might have been able to glean some clues, or any photographs of the rest of the school on the day of the crime, or anything on the criminal records of any of the witnesses in the case—such as the white janitors, for example.

And Reeves still had none of the scientific evidence—no blood or hair or semen swabs; none of the contents of the rape kit, the physical evidence routinely collected from the body of a rape victim. Jim Keeshan had preempted the judge by announcing in open court that he would give the defense all the scientific evidence he had. But Reeves had yet to see anything, and time was moving on. Pretty soon now they were going to start talking about fixing a trial date.

In the county jail that day Brandley marked his birthday. He was twenty-nine.

* * *

It was Brandley's oldest brother, Lawrence, who first worried out loud that Ray Reeves might not be doing the best possible job here and said maybe they needed a Conroe attorney who knew the town and its way of working. Lawrence Brandley knew nothing about attorneys himself, so he went to a well-respected white man, Mr. Gentry, who ran a menswear store on the courthouse square.

Mr. Gentry suggested that the Brandleys take their case to a couple of attorneys who worked upstairs from him. They were called Morris and Brown.

George Morris and Don Brown belonged together like a horse and carriage.

They sat up in their dark, cramped little offices over Mr. Gentry's store in an old building just across the street from the courthouse. In their waiting room the same brown carpet that covered the floor also climbed up the wall, the radio played country music, the ashtrays overflowed with old butt ends, and the words under the painting of a cowboy at a watering hole read: "Surely the Lord is in this place. Genesis 28:16." There they prepared for battle.

Then they emerged—two silver-haired men with bundles of legal papers under their arms, Morris well over six feet tall and stately like a Dickensian schoolmaster, Brown a bulky, shambling figure like a bear in a brown suit. In court they were a natural double act. Morris liked to play to the gallery. He would tease a friendly witness, slash a hostile one to ribbons, and try to play with a jury's affections. Brown was more of a scholar, who could pick apart the fine print of a scientific report and who knew the Texas Code of Criminal Practice in such intimate detail that people used to say he must be sleeping with it. Both of them habitually fought to the last drop of sweat.

Unlike many law partners, they were friends. They spent evenings drinking and smoking together in the Iron Horse on the courthouse square, swapping scuttlebutt about the courthouse, chewing over their cases, wheezing into their cigarettes, and occasionally stunning the room to silence with the volume of Don Brown's deep, dark, rumbling voice. But there was something deeper that held them together, a lesson they both had learned years earlier growing up in small-town Texas.

Morris learned it through his father, an old-fashioned family doctor with a battered bag and a never-ending list of patients in the old sawmill town of Magnolia, fifteen miles southwest of Conroe. As a child Morris used to go out with his father on house visits and helped him deliver babies. He got so good at it that by the time he was a teenager, he went out on his own to see women through their labor.

Some doctors picked their patients carefully, staying in the nice part of town, on the right side of the tracks. But George Morris followed his father through white ranches, black shacks, clean-as-a-whistle town houses, and lonesome backwoods trailers, and in all of them he saw life with the special intimacy that is granted to doctors. So he learned at first hand about the facts of life in Texas, about the rich and the poor and the black and the white, and when he went back to the comfort of life on his side of the tracks and he heard people talk in their ignorance, he learned in particular—and in a profound and passionate way—to loathe and despise his neighbors who were racists.

Don Brown came to the same point by a different route. He grew up picking cotton with his nine brothers and sisters on a small farm his parents owned in a tiny community called Cotton Gin, about 150 miles north of Conroe. He started his education in a one-room schoolhouse where most of the other children were his cousins and nephews. From the age of thirteen he worked in the oil fields earning money to stay in school. He was always set apart from the others: first he was just the brightest kid in the class, then he was the one who was going to go all the way to college and become a chemist, and finally, by the time he had got his chemistry degree, he was the owner of an intellect like a bulldozer, with emotions to match.

Brown would take an issue, simply tear it apart to get at the truth, and then doggedly defend his position against all comers. He was that way with his chemistry and with his politics (he fastened on to the liberal wing of the Democratic party when he was still a child and never let it go), and he was that way, too, about racism. It was a political target, a social disease, a moral evil, a human absurdity. No matter how Don Brown looked at racism, his intellect destroyed it.

Morris was the first to bring the fight to Conroe. When he came out of the navy at the end of World War II, he set out on a career whose course was always dictated by his passion for fairness. For a while, he worked in Houston with Percy Foreman, who was then one of the most famous defense attorneys in America, cheating the executioner of hundreds of intended victims, but Morris rapidly moved on to set up his own practice in Conroe in 1952. The little office soon became a garrison in a permanent war with the courthouse people across the street. Morris fought not only as an attorney but also as a member of the city council, to which he was elected in the 1970s with a combination of black and white votes.

Don Brown had tried at first to become a professional chemist and worked for Monsanto Chemical. He raised hell when he found the lunchroom was segregated. Then he ran into a storm when he refused to join the staff social club until blacks were allowed to use the sleek white clubhouse instead of the dingy little place that had been set aside for them.

He quit to study law and to run for the state legislature in 1962. He was elected from Galveston County and then scandalized the redneck wing of his own party by insisting on hiring a black woman as one of his aides. His party bosses ordered him to fire her and said she would not be paid. There was no black employee in the State Capitol in Austin at that time above the rank of janitor. But Brown told them to go screw themselves and led his new aide onto the floor of the House and won his point by sheer dogged defiance.

Then he drafted a bill to repeal every statute in the state of Texas that mentioned race, particularly the one that outlawed marriage between the races. He knew the bill had no chance. Two years later he narrowly lost his bid for reelection and set out to be an attorney instead.

For more than a decade he worked in Lamarque, south of Houston on the road to Galveston. Then, in May 1978, he decided to join forces with an attorney whose reputation attracted him, and he moved north and settled into the offices over the menswear store on the courthouse square. So the double act was born.

When Lawrence Brandley first went to see them about his brother, Morris and Brown were not too sure they wanted to get involved. They had too much work already, and they could see there was little prospect of the Brandleys' ever paying them. They knew, too, that Jim Keeshan was going to use every trick in his private book to get a conviction because the case was such a big deal in town. Yet something struck them about it. It gave them an uneasy feeling. Don Brown had had it ever since he had looked out of his window one afternoon at the end of August and happened to see a bunch of police

officers leading the black school janitor into the courthouse
with his hands cuffed tightly behind his back. It had struck
him then that it was too simple and easy—the white girl killed,
the black man arrested. It was all too familiar.

Morris and Brown agreed to help Ray Reeves, just to sit by
his shoulder and see if they could advise him at all. George
Morris went into court on September 25 and watched Reeves
get almost nowhere with his two big motions. He and Brown
took Reeves across to the Iron Horse and heard all about the
dumb deal he had made with Keeshan over the grand jury
and how Keeshan had given him a royal screwing. Morris and
Brown began to wonder how Reeves had gotten through law
school.

When Reeves started talking in his usual way, about "nigger" this and "nigger" that, at the top of his voice in front
of the young black kids who worked in the Iron Horse, they
wondered how he had ever come to take the case at all. It was
not long before they realized that if Clarence Brandley was
ever going to have a chance of beating this town, they were
going to have to do Ray Reeves's job for him.

Morris and Brown decided to mount an offensive. From
their base camp overlooking the courthouse square, they
unleashed a volley of writs and motions at the DA's office.
They found themselves fighting tooth and nail to obtain what
they believed was theirs by right.

They needed the autopsy report on the dead girl. As far as
Morris and Brown were concerned, they had an absolute right
to it. Don Brown went straight to the paragraph in the Code
of Criminal Practice that declared: "The detailed findings of
an autopsy shall be part of the record and such records shall
be public records." They had never been denied one before,
but in this case, they could not get it—not from the justice of
the peace, who was supposed to have a copy, nor from the
district clerk, who was supposed to have one, nor from the
district attorney nor from the judge, not from anyone in the
courthouse. So far as they could find out, Jim Keeshan had
cornered every copy in Conroe and he would part with none
of them.

Don Brown tried to outflank Keeshan by going direct to
Dr. Jachimczyk, the medical examiner in Houston who had
performed the autopsy. Brown knew him slightly from law
school. But when Brown called him, the doctor claimed that

he had performed the autopsy on Cheryl Fergeson not as a public medical examiner but as a private physician hired by Montgomery County and therefore that his report was private. Brown became heated. He got nowhere and suspected that Keeshan had gotten to the doctor before him.

Finally, Morris and Brown compiled a stinging motion in which they accumulated all of the facts and all of the law and submitted it to Judge Lee Alworth with the threat of an appeal to a higher court.

On October 3—a full forty days after the autopsy—the judge finally conceded that Clarence Brandley's attorneys should be allowed to read the report.

It was all they had. Despite Ray Reeves's small victory on September 25, the district attorney had still not handed the attorneys any of the evidence which he had been ordered to provide: no transcript of Brandley at the grand jury, no copy of his statement on the day of the crime, no photographs of the scene of the crime, no clothes from the dead girl, and none of the other scientific evidence that Keeshan had promised to release.

On October 10 Keeshan finally told Don Brown that he would hand over the clothes and the scientific evidence. On October 15—twenty days after the court's order—Texas Ranger John Wesley Styles collected a plain brown box from the Department of Public Safety's labs in Austin and drove it up to Dallas, where a scientist named Irving Stone was prepared to study its contents for the defense.

The box was full of mysteries. For a start, there was no rape kit. It was standard procedure in every county in the state of Texas that when a woman was raped, the police and the doctors made up a kit of physical evidence—especially any swabs of semen—and kept it for any subsequent trial. The semen was key evidence, and it was particularly attractive to any defense attorney because its potential to help was much greater than its potential to harm. If the semen matched the blood group of the defendant, that merely meant he was one of millions of men who might have committed the crime. But if the semen did not match his blood group, then he was innocent and the defense was home free. But there was no rape kit in the box. No swabs. No semen. And no chance for the defense to be home free.

Other things were also missing. There was supposed to be a yellow gym mat that the girl had been lying on up in the

props loft. Perhaps it would have shown some semen stain.
But it was not to be found. And then there was the girl's
underwear. It was there, but a small patch in the front that
had been stained with semen had been cut out.

It was very mysterious. Strangest of all was the pubic hair—
or rather, the lack of it. When Don Brown was told the contents
of the box, he thought it was surprising that the police had not
taken samples of Brandley's pubic hair. His sample of head
hair was in the box, but no pubic hair. At first Brown assumed
it was just another example of Captain Monty Koerner's slop-
py work, until he mentioned it to Clarence Brandley. Brandley
vividly remembered the nurse with her tweezers plucking out
his head hair and his pubic hair. Brown rummaged around in
the case papers and found that Brandley was right. The pubic
hair was listed. But it was gone.

It was another mystery. Morris and Brown set out to find
an explanation.

Lorna Hubbell was still looking for clues and sending
reports to the attorneys. Finally, she was beginning to find
some that had not been swept away.

She spent a morning speaking to a man named David Harris,
who had once worked at Conroe High as a janitor and was now
one of Mallie Davis's assistants, supervising the janitors for all
the schools in Conroe. She found him very impressive. He was
a tall, heavily muscled black man who had fought in Vietnam
and who appeared to be highly educated. He played the violin
and the trumpet and spoke Swahili and English that had no
trace of a Texas accent.

Like everyone else, he had originally refused to talk. He had
been frightened of losing his job, and he had been explicitly
ordered by the school superintendent not to talk to anyone.
But Brandley's girlfriend Beverley had gone to see him, and
finally he agreed to talk because he had something to say.

He believed Icky Peace might have killed the girl.

He had a low opinion of most of Brandley's coworkers.
He said Acreman was an underminer, always complaining
and trying to cause trouble. John Sessum, he reckoned, was
certainly a drunk and also a racist. Sam Martinez might be
OK, but in his view, Icky Peace was psychotic and capable
of just about anything, rape and murder included.

Harris said he had personally seen Peace showing off a
pearl-handled gun in the school. He had also seen Peace

brandishing the identity card that was supposed to show that he was working for the police as an undercover narcotics agent. Harris knew it sounded crazy, but he had seen the card and talked to Peace about it, and he believed him. Peace had even offered to recruit him and told him some senior officer would be in touch with him. Peace could easily have used that card to trick the girl into going with him into the auditorium.

And Harris had information about the auditorium. In the first place, he said, it was common for doors to be left open. Some of them were broken and had never shut properly. So it was nonsense to claim that Brandley was the only person who could have gotten in there to hide the body. But more than that, he knew that Peace had a set of keys to get in there. He was not supposed to have, but during the past summer he had been issued a set and had then failed to return them. He claimed to have lost them.

After six weeks on the road Lorna Hubbell could barely believe her ears. This slotted together with what she already knew. Peace was now a prime suspect.

Harris also gave her an account of the way the police were treating witnesses. He said he had been visited by the Texas Ranger, Wesley Styles. "He has a big stomach, a big head, and a narrow mind," he told her.

And Harris had been in the high school one day, about a week after Brandley's arrest, when the ranger had been questioning Icky Peace, walking him up and down the hallway. According to Harris, the ranger had been coaching Peace, rehearsing his story with him and then recording only the final version.

Finally, Harris believed he was being harassed because he was not cooperating with the police. A cleaning woman up at the high school had recently reported that she had been raped in the grounds of the school. She said she had been attacked by a white man, but that had not stopped the police from arresting one Mexican and three black men, including Harris himself. Even now, after spending the morning talking to Lorna Hubbell, he was nervous about being seen with her. If the police heard that he was dealing with white people, there could be trouble. He said he would stay in touch through Beverley. It was safer that way.

Buoyed by her success, Lorna Hubbell made one more attempt to get to the white janitors. She drove out east of Conroe, toward Cut and Shoot, and after an hour of tracking up and down and checking out mailboxes, she found John Sessum in a trailer. David Harris had told her that according to the records in his office, Sessum was thirty-nine. But he looked much older. His face was deeply lined, and his body was bowed. His clothes were dirty. She did not need to be told he was a drunk; she could smell it.

Away from the school, he was willing to talk to her. She needed to know what he had told the police so that she could try to solve one of the biggest mysteries in this whole mysterious case: how the police expected to be able to convict Brandley. Sitting hunched up outside his trailer, scratching frequently, Sessum explained that he and Gary Acreman and Sam Martinez had finished laying out the tables and chairs in the school cafeteria and wandered into the hallway to wait for Brandley. They had seen this girl come along and walk up the steps to the rest room at "Sesame Street." They had noticed she was blond and pretty. Then Brandley had come along the hallway carrying some rolls of toilet paper in his hand and had sent them across to the Vocational Building and left them all waiting there for some time before he came across with a key. That was it.

On the face of it that meant nothing. It all depended on timing. The janitors might have had time to drag the girl into the auditorium and kill her before Brandley got there with his toilet paper. An outsider—or even Icky Peace—could have caught her coming out of the rest room after Brandley and the other janitors had moved on and then killed her while Brandley was smoking in his office and the others were in the Vocational Building. Or Brandley could have had time to kill her himself if he had waited for the white janitors to leave and then had cornered her in the rest room. It all depended on timing, and nobody Hubbell had spoken to seemed to be sure of any of the timing in this story.

Sessum started to drift off, rambling on about his wife, who had divorced him, and all the fights he had been in and how he must have a thousand different stitches in him. He also refused point-blank to give her a formal statement. Lorna Hubbell left him and went off to find Gary Acreman. Her luck stayed good, and when she cornered him at the high school, he also agreed to talk.

To begin with, he was fine. He went over the events of that day, just as Sessum had. But when Lorna Hubbell told him that she had already spoken to Sessum, his mood shattered.

His hands started to shake. He could not sit still. He was smoking as if he couldn't breathe without nicotine.

He kept saying: "What did John say? What did John tell you?"

He, too, refused to give her a formal statement. Clearly, he was hiding something. And he also obviously believed John Sessum was hiding it, too. Neither of them was ready to say what it was.

Just like Ray Reeves before them, Morris and Brown had given up hoping that Jim Keeshan was going to play fair.

On November 13, 1980, they went back to court, just as Ray Reeves had, to try to compel the district attorney to cooperate with them. He had still not given them the rest of the evidence he had been ordered to hand over on September 25—fifty days earlier. They still had no transcript of Brandley at the grand jury nor any copy of his statement on the day of the crime nor any photographs of the scene of the crime.

In court Keeshan was suave and charming. Ignoring the long delay, he stood up at the beginning of the hearing and asked to speak first. "May I make a brief representation to the court?" he asked politely. "Most of these matters are all available, and the state is prepared to voluntarily turn them over to the defense attorneys. If they are willing to come down to my office and not take up the court's time, I will be glad to convey all these matters."

Don Brown rumbled under his breath that Keeshan made it sound as if this were the first time the defense had asked him for any of this stuff. He asked the judge to order Keeshan to produce the evidence in court now. The judge brushed him aside. Morris and Brown then explained that there was more evidence that they needed. They explained their needs, one by one. One by one, Judge Alworth brushed them aside.

It had become vital to sort out their suspicions about the white janitors. Judge Alworth had already refused to order Keeshan to hand over the statements they had made to the police. None of them would give a statement to the defense, and although they had now started to talk, none of them had done so in any real detail. All of them claimed that they had been told to keep their mouths shut.

Morris and Brown asked the court to order the white janitors to give a deposition of facts to the defense. They said this was essential if Brandley was to get a fair trial. Keeshan and the judge said no.

Morris and Brown pleaded that at the very least the court should order the white janitors to provide samples of their blood, hair, and saliva. The attorneys still found it inconceivable that the district attorney had not done this himself. They now knew from their scientist in Dallas, Dr. Irving Stone, that the rumor about a white man's hair being found on the girl's body was true. It was a reddish brown hair. It had been on the girl's inner thigh. It was a vital clue. Samples from the white janitors were equally vital if they were to be able to make sense of it. Keeshan and the judge said no.

They asked for the notes that the high school students had written for the police about the day of the crime, for a list of witnesses who had spoken to the state about the crime, for a transcript of the whole grand jury hearing. Keeshan and the judge said no.

Morris and Brown then closed in on the mystery of the missing rape kit. Keeshan shrugged them off as if he had no idea what they were talking about. "There is absolutely no other evidence in the nature of semen in my possession or in the Conroe Police Department's possession or in the Department of Public Safety's lab's possession or, to my knowledge, in the pathologist's possession."

Morris and Brown were dumbfounded. What in hell were these clowns doing? If that was true, then the state was either so dumb that it had failed to gather some of the most vital evidence in the inquiry or so corrupt that it had deliberately destroyed the evidence in case it might help Clarence Brandley.

Brown tried to find out what had happened to the missing patch from the dead girl's underwear. He was told that it had been used up during tests that had failed to disclose anything conclusive about the semen. Brown turned to the judge and asked him to order Keeshan to produce either the semen or the results of any tests that had been conducted on it. Judge Alworth interrupted him. "I believe the DA has already told you that he has no such sample, Mr. Brown. How can I order him to produce that which does not exist?"

That was it. No question of this judge's ordering an inquiry or castigating the DA or the police.

Brown called Monty Koerner, the captain of detectives, to the witness stand. He shrugged and stammered and said he had no rape kit and had never asked for one. For Morris and Brown this was too much like the Keystone Kops, even for Conroe. These cops might be dumb—just the other day two of them had driven into town with their uniforms in tatters because they had tried to capture an escaped lioness without any backup—but this kind of stupidity bordered on corruption. They refused to believe that there were no semen samples, that there was no scientific evidence that might prove Brandley's innocence. Brown had only one option left.

During the lunch break he called the medical examiner, Dr. Jachimczyk. Surely he could help. If the police had really not asked for the swabs, they must still be in his lab. But if the police had asked for them and taken them and thrown them away, then the doctor would be able to testify that they were lying. But Jachimczyk did not see it that way.

"Oh, gosh," he told Brown on the phone. "That case was back in August. That's more than thirty days ago. I throw everything away after thirty days."

Brown's temperature started to rise. "What? On a rape-homicide? You throw everything away? Just throw it away?"

"Well, I don't have the room to keep everything here."

"But didn't you give it to the police?"

"If they ask me for it, I give it to them."

"Well, did you give it to them on this occasion?"

"I don't know. I couldn't say. I just identified it as human semen."

"Yes, but, Dr. Jachimczyk, we're trying to identify which human it belongs to."

It was no use. Brown found it all hard to believe. Here was a professional medical examiner, highly experienced, indeed, one of the most experienced in the country, who threw away the most important medical evidence in a rape-homicide when the trial was still pending. Here was an experienced and intelligent district attorney who claimed not to have noticed that this evidence was missing when all the material was sent to the Department of Public Safety labs a few days after the crime.

Brown did not believe a word of it. He believed Keeshan was a ruthless careerist who was going after a poor black janitor with nothing but circumstantial evidence and did not want any evidence that could get in his way—not the autopsy report or the semen samples or the hairs from the white janitors or even the statements of witnesses. They were maintaining a blind focus on Clarence Brandley. He believed that this whole prosecution was dedicated to stringing up the nearest available black man and that what was happening in that courthouse was damn close to a conspiracy. But what could he prove?

And there was one more mystery that he was afraid they might have cleared up: the missing pubic hair. There was still no sign of the original sample that had been taken from Brandley on the day of the crime. Morris and Brown had arranged for Brandley to provide a new sample. In the meantime, their scientist in Dallas had reported to them that the reddish brown white man's hair was not all that had been found on the girl's body. There were also several Negro hairs. They appeared to have been forcibly removed from their owner.

But what could they prove?

Morris and Brown's day in court was not yet over. That afternoon they returned to Judge Alworth's courtroom to fight for an issue on which they believed they were so completely in the right, and Jim Keeshan was so obviously in the wrong, that not even the Montgomery County Courthouse could deny them justice. They wanted Clarence Brandley released on bail.

As soon as Morris and Brown had got a grip on the case, they had fired off a motion demanding a court hearing at which Keeshan would have to prove that Brandley had breached his probation by murdering Cheryl Fergeson. The law said the hearing must take place within twenty days. If Keeshan did not come to court within the twenty days, then Brandley would again be entitled to bail.

Their motion had gone into the courthouse on October 3. A few days later Judge Alworth went off elk hunting in Colorado without setting a date for the hearing. The twenty days passed. Morris and Brown had still heard nothing. Brandley was now entitled to be released on his thirty-thousand-dollar bail, but he was not. So on October 24 Morris and Brown fired off yet another motion. This one was a writ of habeas corpus, the traditional legal device for lawyers to prize their clients out of the jailer's grip. They quoted the law, which declared that this writ must be heard "at the earliest practicable time." In the courthouse Judge Alworth, who had by now returned from his hunting trip, agreed to consider the matter on November 13, nearly three weeks later.

Like many big men, Don Brown maintained an air of gentle courtesy, but under pressure he was capable of exploding with mighty force. Now Brown was beginning to get mad. So far as he could see, the state was playing games with them. Keeshan did not want to prove that Brandley had breached his probation by murdering Cheryl Fergeson because he would have to disclose the evidence he had collected. Nor did he want to release Brandley. So he did neither, and never mind the law. Brown said the state had no right to leave Brandley in jail without a hearing and there was no damned way that November 13 was the earliest practicable time they could get to court. He could see Keeshan's game: he was playing for time, trying to get Brandley tried for murder before the defense ever had a chance to hold a hearing on his bail.

Brown and Morris reached for the big gun and went to the Court of Criminal Appeals in Austin, the highest criminal court in the state of Texas, and asked for a writ of habeas corpus. By Thursday, November 13, when Judge Alworth was finally due to consider Brandley's freedom, everyone in the courthouse knew that the judges in Austin had heard details of the case. Everyone knew that they were due to make their decision in a few days, and everyone understood the message: If Conroe did not put its own house in order, then the judges in Austin would do it for them.

Morris and Brown heard that Judge Alworth was furious with them for trying to cause him embarrassment. They didn't mind that; the main point was that the courthouse had failed to give Brandley his hearing within twenty days. That meant the court could not revoke his probation. So now, the law said, he could be released on the thirty-thousand-dollar bail that had been set back on September 5.

That morning George Morris and the third partner in the firm, Nat Davis, went over to the sheriff's office to tell him that they had raised the thirty thousand dollars for Brandley's bail bond, using their own property as collateral, and that they wanted to make sure that there would be no hitch in releasing Brandley once Judge Alworth had finished his hearing. The sheriff, Gene Reaves, did not seem pleased to see them.

"I'm not gonna let him out," he said. "I don't care how much bond you post."

Morris, who knew the sheriff as an old-fashioned East Texas racist, suggested that he would have to obey the court. The sheriff scowled, and Morris and Davis went off to court, marveling at the idea of a lawman who so openly defied the law.

That afternoon in court Keeshan fought to keep Brandley behind bars. But Don Brown said the facts and the law were cut-and-dried: there should have been a hearing on Brandley's probation within twenty days of their asking for it; there had been no hearing; Brandley had to be released. He told the judge that the court in Austin would be handing down a ruling on the issue within the next week.

In Brown's eyes Alworth was not as bad as some of the other Conroe judges. Brown knew the judge had a reputation as a bad-tempered, overbearing son of a bitch, but at least he knew his law and was capable of upholding it. Just the other week he had enraged the rest of the courthouse people by throwing out the confession of the man who was accused of killing a twelve-year-old girl after hearing that the interrogators had threatened to feed the man maggots from the dead girl's body! Not every judge in Conroe would have done that.

That was what Brown was betting on: that Alworth knew the law was clear and that there was no point in pretending anything different with the Court of Criminal Appeals waiting to pounce. A stony-faced Alworth agreed that Brandley should have his probation back and that if the state tried to revoke it again, he should be allowed out on bail of only one thousand dollars until a hearing took place. In the meantime he could be released on bail of thirty thousand dollars.

Brandley's family wept and cheered with relief. After eleven weeks of doubt and confusion, Brandley would be released that evening. Don Brown felt a bitter relief: Brandley might now have his freedom, but he had been denied it for eleven weeks by trickery and prejudice. And even now, after the judge's ruling, Brown was not sure. He knew Sheriff Gene Reaves. He could be a mean old boy. It looked as if he had been telegraphing his punch that morning. So before the hearing ended, Brown asked the judge if he would agree to stay in the courthouse in his chambers so that he would be available in case there was any problem with the sheriff. Alworth agreed. Then he gave Brown a withering stare and swept out of court. Morris and Brown might have won, but they had made an enemy out of the judge by threatening him with the court in Austin.

*   *   *

Brown led George Morris and Ray Reeves off to talk tactics in one of the jury rooms where there was a little coffee bar. Most of Brandley's family followed. So there were plenty of witnesses there a few minutes later when Judge Alworth followed them in.

At first the judge said nothing, just poured himself some coffee. Then, with his jaw muscles bunching in his cheeks, he walked toward the huddle of defense lawyers.

"Don, so that you will know where you and I stand, I want you to know that I ruled the way I did because the law says I have to. But I do not appreciate a lawyer doing what you did."

His voice was loud. Everyone stopped talking to watch.

The judge was accusing Brown of deliberately asking for a hearing on Brandley's probation just as he was going off on his vacation in Colorado. Brown was starting to explain that it had nothing to do with that, but the judge was already on his way to the door, where he turned. "And furthermore, I do not appreciate some of the words you used in the petition that you filed with the Court of Criminal Appeals."

Brown muttered that that was fine.

The judge jabbed a finger across the room at him. "You are going to regret those words," he shouted. "I guarantee that you will answer for them when this case is over."

Brown, who had never seen a judge behave this way, looked back at him and said: "That's all right with me."

Now the judge was white-faced. "You are going to eat those words," he yelled, his voice whipping past the dazed spectators, "because I am going to stuff them down your damned throat!"

Then he was gone.

"OK," said Brown.

It was only half an hour later that George Morris headed up to the fourth floor of the courthouse to deliver the thirty-thousand-dollar bond that was to secure Brandley's freedom. Outside, Minnie Ola Brandley and the rest of the family waited. Less than five minutes later Morris returned without Brandley. The sheriff had kept his promise. He was not interested in the bond. He did not care what the court had ordered. He did not give a damn what the law said. He was not going to let the nigger go.

Mrs. Brandley started to weep.

Morris and Brown were outraged and immediately stormed up to Judge Alworth's chambers. Alworth had promised he would stay there to make sure Brandley was released. Brandley was now being held captive illegally. They would just have to ask the judge to intervene directly to force the sheriff to obey the court. But when the two attorneys arrived at the judge's chambers, they found he had abandoned his promise and gone off for the weekend.

Morris and Brown agreed that promises did not count for much in the Montgomery County Courthouse and trudged back across the courthouse square to their offices with their useless bond. In all their years of dealing with small-town prejudice, they could not remember a more brazen abuse of power.

The Brandley family, all downcast, went slowly home across the tracks to Dugan.

The black man stayed behind bars.

For four days the defense camp was paralyzed while it waited for Judge Alworth to return from his long weekend and enforce the rule of law in Conroe. Friday, Saturday, and Sunday passed, and then when the judge finally returned to the courthouse on Monday morning, he announced that he was too busy to consider the matter until the evening. In the meantime, news of the row rolled around the town, harming Brandley at every turn.

Keeshan was quoted in the paper expressing his surprise that the judge had agreed to let Brandley keep his probation, and the sheriff baldly declared that he had personal reasons for defying the court. "I just don't think a man like the accused should be on the ground," he told the *Courier*.

Judge Alworth finally agreed to consider the Brandley case in his chambers at five-fifteen on Monday afternoon. It was a tense meeting. Don Brown was there with his partner Nat Davis. Keeshan was there with Sheriff Gene Reaves by his side. Judge Alworth opened the meeting by asking the sheriff if the bail bond was sufficient.

"Sure. The bond's sufficient. There's no problem with that."

"So why don't you let him out?" asked the judge.

The sheriff looked straight back at the judge and said: "Because that little nigger don't belong on the ground."

Brown exhaled sharply and resisted an urge to cuss the sheriff out there and then as a racist who was not fit to wear a badge. The judge was still talking. "But, Sheriff, that is not sufficient reason."

Now Keeshan intervened. Brown sat in silent horror and heard the DA say: "I agree with the sheriff. That little nigger doesn't belong on the ground."

Judge Alworth seemed not to notice their language, but he held his line. Brown guessed he did not want to be threatened again with the judges in Austin. The judge said that if Brandley could put up the thirty-thousand-dollar bond, there was no lawful reason to keep him in custody. "I'm ordering that if that bond is sufficient, the prisoner be released," he said.

Keeshan was not happy. "If you're gonna do that, I ask that the amount of the bond be increased."

"Jim, I can't do that," said the judge. "We had a hearing on that, and you didn't choose to put on your evidence so that I could find that there was proof evident that he committed this offense. I'd have to conduct another hearing to raise the bond."

"That is correct," said Keeshan, his eyes fastened on the judge.

This was too much for Brown. Keeshan had made a deal with Ray Reeves that he would not press for a high bail bond. It was bad enough that he had tried to bypass that deal by revoking Brandley's probation. Now he was going right back and breaking the deal in two, pushing for a higher bond.

"We've had the hearing," said Brown in his deep bass voice, "and we have the judge's decision. I suggest we just go up now and get him out."

It was already five-thirty. Keeshan could not mount a hearing that evening. He lapsed into silence.

The sheriff, too, appeared to be accepting defeat: "They'll be feeding them now in the jail and trying to get them put away to bed. How about y'all come around in the morning to get him, about nine?"

Brown guessed that the sheriff was trying to save face. He didn't want to cause any more problems.

"OK," he said. "We'll be there at nine in the morning tomorrow."

After all, he thought, what difference could one more night make?

*   *   *

The very next morning, Tuesday, November 18, 1980, shortly before nine o'clock, two deputies came to Clarence Brandley in his cell in the county jail on the top floor of the courthouse. They told him his attorneys were making bond for him.

They let him gather his few possessions from the cell. They marched him along the corridor, took his photograph and his fingerprints, filled in some paperwork, and told him to wait for his attorneys. Downstairs, in the first-floor lobby of the courthouse, Don Brown, George Morris, and Nat Davis were standing waiting for the elevator to take them up to the cells when Sheriff Reaves came by. He seemed a lot more relaxed and stopped to chat with them about the weather and one thing and another.

Just then Jim Keeshan's secretary, Kathy Olson, came up with an envelope and handed it to Don Brown. Brown was explaining to the sheriff that they were on their way up to the cells with their thirty-thousand-dollar bail bond to get Brandley released. The sheriff nodded. Brown was starting to open the envelope as the elevator doors slid open to let them in. All three lawyers were in the elevator, and the sheriff was just nodding good-bye when Don Brown exploded. "That son of a bitch!" he shouted.

The envelope contained a motion from Jim Keeshan to raise Brandley's bond to seventy-five thousand dollars—and an order signed by Judge Lee Alworth that morning agreeing to the increase. How the hell could they do that? They hadn't even had a hearing. It was just plain illegal. The sheriff retreated. Brown thrust the papers into George Morris's hands and told Nat Davis what they contained. By the time the elevator reached the fourth floor, three very angry men walked out.

Back in his cell Clarence Brandley was angry, too. He felt as if the state wanted to torment him before they killed him, by dangling his freedom in front of him—just so he knew that no matter how close he got, he could never have it back.

As soon as they had finished telling Brandley the bad news, the attorneys returned to their office to take a step that they had resisted but that now seemed inevitable. They would force Judge Alworth off the case by recusing him—filing a formal motion complaining about his behavior and, if necessary, holding a public hearing to prove that he should be removed.

They had not wanted to. No attorney wants to make an enemy out of a judge. But it had gone too far. That morning Morris and Brown sat down together and drafted a damning indictment of the judge's performance.

They accused him outright of bias and prejudice. They complained that he had refused to let Brandley defend his right to probation within the twenty days allowed by law and that he had refused to hear Brandley's writ of habeas corpus in good time. They said he had displayed "a generally sarcastic and intimidating demeanor" toward them and had shouted abuse at Don Brown. And they raised the issue that had made their blood boil: the sudden hiking of Brandley's bail bond to seventy-five thousand dollars.

They were outraged that Keeshan and the judge had decided to do this behind their backs. There had been no hearing, no chance for Brandley to put his side of the story. They had not even tried to contact the defense team. Raising Brandley's bond like this was a breach of Keeshan's deal with Ray Reeves, a violation of Keeshan's code of conduct, a flagrant contradiction of the judge's own ruling that Brandley should be released on a thirty-thousand-dollar bond, and a denial of their agreement the previous evening that Brandley would be released at nine that morning. It also drove a horse and buggy through Clarence Brandley's civil rights. They were outraged.

Keeshan, it seemed to them, had just gone in to see Alworth as one good ol' boy to another, trying to find any way they could to keep the nigger in jail. Keeshan had produced a motion that was full of holes. It was not even sworn. Keeshan had even tried to pretend that since the thirty-thousand-dollar bond had been set on September 5, he had learned of new evidence that Brandley was a threat to public safety: the supposed rape of Pokey Smith. Morris and Brown knew that was dishonest. Not only had Smith withdrawn her allegation, but also Keeshan had known all about her on September 5. He had used her story two days earlier at the grand jury hearing. He was simply pretending that it had come to light more recently to give a phony justification for raising the bail bond. As far as Morris and Brown were concerned, Keeshan was nothing but a snake—and a racist snake, too—and this whole motion was the purest horseshit.

Keeshan had wreaked the maximum possible damage with his motion to raise the bond to seventy-five thousand dollars.

Clipped to the back of the motion was a copy of Pokey Smith's statement to Ted Morgan. It was a powerful story: Brandley had abducted her at gunpoint, beaten her with a stick, and raped her four or five times, and he had done the same thing on other occasions to her sister and to one of his own sisters.

There was no indication that Smith had now withdrawn that statement, and by filing it publicly with his motion, Keeshan had instantly advertised its contents to the press, which could be relied upon to reproduce it with yet more prejudice to Brandley.

Morris and Brown poured their feelings into their demand for Judge Alworth's recusal. By midday they had dropped their bombshell in the courthouse. Later that afternoon Judge Alworth replied with a couple of his own.

First, he voluntarily stepped down from the case. In doing so, he issued a statement in which he rejected the charges laid by Morris and Brown. He had not been denying Brandley a hearing. He had been away elk hunting, and then he had been too busy with other cases. He claimed he was entitled to raise Brandley's bail bond. He agreed that he had made aggressive remarks to Don Brown, but this brought him to his own reason for standing down.

"I have a great dislike for Don Brown," he said, "whom I find to be the most completely obnoxious individual it has ever become my displeasure to know and I certainly conveyed that thought to him in my remarks. Unlike Will Rogers, who never met a man he didn't like, I can only say that Will Rogers never met Don Brown."

Morris and Brown were relieved to see the back of the judge. But even as he left, they admired his clever footwork. By identifying "obnoxious" Don Brown as his reason for stepping down, he avoided the embarrassment of a recusal hearing without having to admit any of the complaints made against him. But Judge Alworth was still not finished.

Having stepped down, he next had to contact the administrative judge who covered Montgomery County, Max Rogers, and ask him to appoint a replacement. But Judge Alworth went a little further: he contacted Rogers and told him that he himself would find a replacement.

He picked Judge Sam Robertson, Jr., of Houston.

"The son of a bitch," said Don Brown when he heard. "Sam Robertson is the most prosecution-minded judge in the whole area. That Lee Alworth has malice in his heart."

Jim Keeshan wanted to start the trial. The courthouse set a date. Clarence Brandley would go on trial for his life on Monday, December 1, 1980.

After Judge Alworth stepped down from the case on Tuesday, November 18, Morris and Brown had less than two weeks to prepare for trial. They still lacked basic information about the case, and their client was still trapped in jail, unable to help them.

The two attorneys went to a bail bondsman, who specialized in lending money for defendants who were trying to make bail. Despite the Brandleys' poverty, they succeeded in borrowing seventy-five thousand dollars to make the new, higher bond that Keeshan and Judge Alworth had arranged. They could still get Brandley out of jail before the trial. But before they could do that, they had their first encounter with the new judge.

On Wednesday, November 26, Judge Sam Robertson, Jr., came to the courthouse in Conroe to hold his first hearing in the case of Clarence Brandley. First, he wanted to discuss three procedural motions, known as motions in limine, which Don Brown had filed. They were designed to prevent the state from referring to Brandley's conviction for possessing a sawed-off shotgun, to Pokey Smith's claim that Brandley had raped her, or to any suggestion such as that which Keeshan had made to the grand jury that Brandley suffered from some obsessive desire to have sex with white women. Brown said any reference to any of these would be highly prejudicial, even if the judge then told the jury to disregard them. "That would be throwing the skunk in the jury box and taking the skunk out, but leaving the smell there," rumbled Brown. Keeshan agreed not to mention any of them without first consulting the judge.

Then Jim Keeshan filed a new motion, asking to revoke Brandley's probation.

Morris and Brown could hardly believe it. Keeshan must have heard that they had got their seventy-five-thousand-dollar bond. This had all been dealt with. Even Judge Alworth had admitted—with a little pressure from the court in Austin—that the state had lost its right to revoke Brandley's probation by failing to hold a hearing within twenty days. And he had also ruled that if the issue ever rose again, Brandley could be released on one thousand dollars' bail until the DA came to court and proved that he had breached his probation by murdering Cheryl Fergeson. But Keeshan was trying it again.

Morris and Brown fired back their own motion calling on the judge to stop the district attorney from harassing Clarence Brandley with his attempts to revoke his probation.

Brown led the new judge through the whole saga, calling himself as a witness and then Jim Keeshan and finally the sheriff, Gene Reaves, who now claimed that he had refused to release Brandley because the signatures on the bond were faint. Brown pleaded with the judge not to revoke Brandley's probation, not to uphold the seventy-five-thousand-dollar bail bond, not to sweep aside their few hard-won legal gains. His speech was long and detailed and sometimes passionate. Judge Robertson listened in silence.

First, the judge agreed that Jim Keeshan could file his motion to revoke Brandley's probation. So Brandley had again lost his right to bail. Then Robertson dismissed the idea that Brandley was entitled to a thousand-dollar bond while he waited for a hearing on his probation. "I am not going to set bond on the basis of what Judge Alworth said he would do." So Brandley had lost the escape route that had been guaranteed him. Then he agreed to uphold the seventy-five-thousand-dollar bail bond. That no longer mattered since Brandley could not now have bail at any price, but it rubbed salt in the attorney's raw wounds.

Brandley dropped his head. Brown slammed his files shut and clenched his fists in anger. This was not even remotely fair. This was old-fashioned redneck justice.

Hour after hour George Morris and Don Brown sat up in their smoke-filled cave overlooking the courthouse square, talking to Lorna Hubbell and Ray Reeves and the Brandleys, shuffling the few facts that they had managed to gather, trying somehow to put together a coherent picture of what had happened that Saturday at the high school.

The autopsy report and the scientific evidence from their expert in Dallas had turned out to contain hidden treasure.

There was the mark around the girl's neck, left by whatever she had been strangled with. It was four and a half inches wide and one and a quarter inches high. It was the last measurement that mattered. Brandley was worried that Keeshan was going to use his mistake at the grand jury hearing to make out that he had used his belt to strangle the girl, even though he had not been wearing it on the day of the crime. The autopsy report put an end to that: his belt was one and a half inches high and could not have left such a narrow mark. As confirmation, his belt showed no traces of the dead girl's skin tissue. His work knife, which had been seized by the police, had no fibers from the girl's clothes, even though the killer had cut some of them from her body. And none of the fingerprint testing on the girl's body and clothes revealed any of his prints.

There had been a point, soon after they had first taken the case, when Morris and Brown had not known for sure if Brandley was inocent. They had asked for all these tests, knowing that if they had found anything, it would have been devastating. But they had found nothing. Now they began to feel strongly that their client was innocent. It was not just the striking absence of any evidence to link him to the crime. There were also now clues that clearly pointed away from him.

The most important, they believed, were the numerous hairs on the dead girl that could have nothing to do with Brandley since they were not from a black. If only Keeshan had allowed them to take hair samples from the other janitors or from anyone else, they might have been able to crack the case. Even so, the white man's hairs must surely raise real doubt about Brandley's guilt. How in God's name could Keeshan explain them away?

But there were also the two hairs from a black. They were giving Morris and Brown a headache. They were more than ready to believe that they had been planted. They had fought the courthouse long enough to believe that if the people over there persuaded themselves that they had got the right man, they would plant evidence and never suffer a moment's bad conscience about it. The trouble was that the defense attorneys could not prove anything, and if they started waving that allegation about in court without any proof, they would surely alienate the jury—particularly a Conroe jury trying a black man. That could only damage Brandley.

Then there was a group of clues that caused endless speculation up in the smoke-filled attorneys' office. First, there were the girl's fingernails, which were unbroken and showed no trace of her attacker's skin or blood underneath them. Then there were strange bruises on her upper arms and on her palms at the base of both thumbs, and finally there was the eerie indentation on her back in the shape of her crucifix.

After great debate Brown put the clues together and concluded that the girl had been attacked by two men, not one: her hands had not been free to scratch; she had been held down on her back, the crucifix pressed into her skin, with one man raping her while the other crouched behind her head, held her arms back over her head, and possibly even knelt on her palms, bruising her as he trapped her. The clues did not fit the theory of a one-man attack, no matter what color he was.

Finally, there was the whole cluster of clues around Icky Peace. And this, they concluded, was their strongest single line of defense.

So far as they could see, they were facing a case of circumstantial evidence. For weeks they had waited in dread of hearing that Keeshan had produced some devastating breakthrough. But there was still no sign that he had anything more than circumstance. Keeshan would say Brandley was alone near the rest rooms at the time that the girl disappeared, that he was the only one with the keys to the auditorium, that he knew about the props loft, and that he had been missing for at least half an hour. The classic defense against a circumstantial prosecution like that was to come up with a reasonable alternative. All the defense had to do was show that there was another suspect against whom an equally good circumstantial case might be built. They did not have to prove that another suspect had committed the crime, only that an equally strong case could be made against him. If they did that, they would win. That was the law.

And although they did not believe that Peace had committed the crime, the circumstantial case against him was demonstrably stronger than it was against Brandley. Just like Brandley, he had been alone—supposedly buffing the floor in the teachers' lounge—at the time that the girl disappeared, he had keys to the auditorium, he knew about the props loft, and he spent more than an hour out of sight of the other janitors. In addition, he had a strong motive in his problems with women, the right means in his gun and his narcotics card, and furthermore, unlike Brandley, he admitted he had been having nightmares and anxiety attacks about the crime.

It was frustrating to push a theory they did not believe. But that was the direct result of the other side's activity. If Captain Koerner had not allowed the high school cleaners to sweep away all the clues after the crime and had not lost or destroyed the semen swabs, if the Texas Ranger had not gone around threatening witnesses, if the district attorney had not kept a blind focus on the black janitor, it all might have been different. But Morris and Brown had to face the fact that they had only fragments of the truth to work with.

There was one other thing they had to face: they appeared to have removed a bad judge from the case only to have him replaced with another who was even worse. All Brandley needed to become a free man was a fair hearing. Morris and Brown did not believe that Judge Sam Robertson, Jr., would give them one.

For the second time in only eight days they would have to try to recuse a judge. Chain-smoking over their word processor, they constructed a legal torpedo. Its thrust was straightforward: Judge Roberston had endorsed the sins of his predecessor and was therefore just as biased and prejudiced as Alworth had been.

"Sam Robertson, Jr., has demonstrated by the foregoing actions that he cannot be fair and impartial to this defendant," they wrote. "He has arbitrarily and illegally deprived the defendant of his liberty."

But unlike his predecessor, Robertson refused to step down. So on December 1, it was not the trial of Clarence Brandley that opened in Conroe but the recusal hearing of Judge Robertson, staged in front of a regular Conroe judge, Lynn Coker.

Brown rehearsed his argument and the injustice that had been handed down to the black school janitor. He put Judge Robertson in the witness box and challenged the contention that he could be a fair and impartial judge. Robertson said he could be.

Brown boomed out his demand for justice for Clarence Brandley. "We know he has had no due process up until now. Is this man going to have due process for the rest of the time that he is going to be tried for capital murder?"

Judge Coker listened in silence. Then he agreed to let Judge Robertson stay on the case. The trial could start immediately.

It occured to Don Brown that times had indeed changed in East Texas. Once it had been common practice for lynch mobs to collect money to pay the bail bond of some nigger they wanted to get their hands on, so they could get him out of the courthouse and put him to death. Now all that had changed, and a black man in trouble was denied his bail and trapped under lock and key. But that was where the real danger was, for now the lynch mob was inside the courthouse.

make to collect money to pay the bail bond . . . . they wanted to get their hands on as they came out of the courthouse, and get money back . . . . not until it's proven innocent . . . .

[text partially obscured in top margin]

Chapter Four

Bill Srack was not a Conroe man. He had been born in Oklahoma and had grown up in Houston and spent most of his working life there, running around with a clipboard and a hard hat, managing construction projects for an oil company. It was only ten years since he had sold his house in Houston and bought a plot of land in one of the new satellite communities, River Plantation, to the south of Conroe. It was a green, sculptured landscape with a golf course and the deliberately quaint feeling of an old English village about it. He and his wife had designed their own house and moved in permanently in 1971. They liked it.

Bill Srack had never visited Dugan and never intended to. He was not concerned with civil rights or integration and was happy to vote Republican at elections and mind his own business in the meantime. He had never heard of Clarence Brandley, and though he was dimly aware that there had been a murder at Conroe High, he had not followed the case and he had no interest in its rights or wrongs—until Tuesday, December 2, 1980, when he was called to the Montgomery County Courthouse for jury duty.

The truth was that he had been called before, two weeks earlier, and he had done something quite out of character. Even though he had written it in his calendar and made a mental note of it, he had completely forgotten to go to the courthouse, and he was on the other side of Houston that day before he realized his oversight. He had apologized to the court and been called, instead, for the first week in December.

His wife, Lajewel, a religious woman who regularly attended a Bible study group in Conroe, said that that was no accident, that was Providence and God had wanted Bill on the jury in this murder trial. And when he set off that Tuesday morning to answer his jury summons, Lajewel went to her Bible study group and told its members, who agreed that they would all pray for him to be selected for the jury if that was what God wanted and for him to have wisdom to discern the truth and strength to stand up for it.

For his part, Srack would just as soon not be selected. He had already served on four juries down in Houston, including two federal cases, and he was beginning to feel as if he had done more than his fair share for the community. But there was no stopping it. In the second-floor courtroom each of the fifty prospective jurors was given a number. He was number two. The first juror was questioned and rejected because he said he had already made up his mind about the defendant's guilt. Srack stood up and said he knew nothing about it but would do his best to follow the evidence. He was the first juror chosen.

Conroe was still stricken by the schoolgirl's murder.

In the three months since her death, it seemed, there had been one outrage after another in the town. Someone had taken a high-powered rifle and shot up some of the stores near the courthouse, just for the hell of it. Someone else had broken into the church on Hillcrest Drive and stolen all the musical instruments.

Up in Willis, ten miles north of Conroe, Montgomery County sheriffs had arrested a man for repeatedly sexually abusing a nine-year-old boy. "There are more reported cases of sexual abuse of children than there have been ever before," said the arresting officer, Richard Reyna.

A woman was abducted from a convenience store on Route 105 and brutally raped. A schoolgirl in Cleveland was assaulted and strangled and left for dead. A woman in Porter was raped by a man to whom she had given a ride in her car. A female cleaner was attacked and raped on the grounds of Conroe High. A maintenance man was missing from Runyon Elementary School, and the police said he had been molesting a young girl there. A Conroe minister had been indicted for stealing from two old ladies in his congregation.

The Brandley case was never out of the paper. It had been on the front page every day for two weeks after the murder: pictures of Brandley, details of his past, speculation about his guilt. Every time there was another twitch in the case, it was back on the front page. The Montgomery County Rape Coalition was up in arms. It set up a panel with eight expert speakers to advise the county's women on how to protect themselves. It was calling up volunteers and training them to inspire more vigilance. Sergeant Berle Johnson of Conroe's Crime Prevention Office started running rape prevention workshops to meet the demand. The Conroe YMCA announced free classes in rape prevention, to be held during daylight hours. "The next rape could be you," the *Courier* warned its readers.

The town had elected a new sheriff to replace Gene Reaves, who was retiring at the end of December after twenty years. The new man, Joe Corley, promised to be tough on criminals, to make this town safe again, and no messing around.

But there was no easy cure for the fear. There was only the chance of punishing the guilty—with death, ordered by a jury, sanctioned by a judge, and welcomed by all.

The stricken town looked to the courthouse.

It was Monday of the next week, December 8, before Bill Srack was called back to the courthouse. The whole of the previous week had been consumed by arguments about who should sit on the jury. It had been a bad-tempered business. The defense had been trying to ferret out anyone who had already formed an opinion against Brandley. Some jurors admitted they thought he was guilty because they had read it in the paper; one or two even admitted they thought he was guilty because he was black. But Judge Robertson had complained that the defense was taking too long and was playing with the jurors. Morris and Brown thought the judge was trying to do Jim Keeshan's job for him, making objections to their questions, ruling against them all the time, and even interceding to defend jurors who admitted they were prejudiced. Keeshan, for his part, seemed to be determined to stop any black person from getting on the jury. He challenged some of them because they admitted they did not believe in the death penalty. Others he removed with a peremptory challenge, which needed no explanation. The judge allowed him to do it, and the result was clear: a jury of nine men and three women, all of them white.

Now, on a warm, cloudy morning, when all the rest of the world seemed to be in a state of shock about the murder of John Lennon in New York, Bill Srack climbed into his half-ton blue pickup, drove north a few miles up I-45, swung off onto Frazier Street, parked at the First Baptist Church, where he and his wife worshiped every Sunday, and walked across the street to the imposing white building that rose like a temple over the square.

Srack was in somber mood. He knew he was going to be dealing with murder and rape and with a defendant whose life was at stake. It was going to be a serious trial. He could not imagine a more serious set of circumstances, and he deliberately tried to prepare himself mentally for what lay ahead, clearing his mind, telling himself that all he had to do was be honest and fair. He believed he could do it. He had a mind like a trolley track, which went straight to the point without distraction. Sometimes it was a little short on humor, but it was always logical and clear. He was certainly not about to be swayed by any feelings against Brandley because of his color. The truth was that he had had his troubles with black people. They were the reason he had uprooted his wife and three children and left Houston. Black families had started moving into their neighborhood in the south of the city, and it seemed to Srack and his family that the area had started going downhill fast: more litter in the streets; more crime. He was no racist, but he was happy to live in a white neighborhood like River Plantation.

Srack found his way to the jury room, where most of the others had already gathered. He did not know them. Some of them introduced themselves.

On the other side of the courtroom, in the office where Judge Lee Alworth usually ran his affairs, the small, bespectacled figure of Judge Sam Robertson, Jr., was making his final preparations. It was a familiar routine. He had been prosecuting criminal cases for nineteen years with the district attorney in Houston before his appointment as a judge two years earlier, on January 1, 1978. His critics said he had spent too long in the DA's office and was too prosecution-minded. That kind of criticism had never been known to worry Judge Robertson.

Down on the first floor Jim Keeshan and his assistant, Jerry Winfree, were checking their paperwork in the district attorney's office. This was an important case. Conroe did not elect its district attorneys to allow black rapists to run around murdering young white girls. But it was not going to be easy to put the evidence across. And it was all slightly complicated by the fact that this was really two hearings rolled into one: the jury had to decide beyond reasonable doubt if Brandley was guilty of capital murder and the judge also had to decide if it was more likely than not that Brandley had breached his probation by committing a murder. It meant that even if the jury decided to acquit Brandley, the judge could still make him serve his three years for breach of probation.

In the courtroom above them, spectators already lined the public benches: white men in faded denims and battered baseball caps; a knot of anxious white faces belonging to the dead girl's relatives; a second knot of anxious brown faces belonging to the Brandleys; some black ministers and observers from Houston civil rights groups, drawn to the courthouse by rumors that a black man was being railroaded; everyone gently murmuring speculation, exchanging opinions, confirming foregone conclusions.

On a solitary chair at the front of the court sat Clarence Brandley, wearing his blue Sunday suit. He looked around at the white faces, lined up in rows like gravestones: the white jurors; the white district clerk with her bright red nails; the white reporters with their notebooks; the white deputies at the door. All he could do was hold on to his hope and fight the fear that was battering his insides.

At a long wooden table at his side, just in front of the judge's raised dais, sat the defense team: George Morris and Don Brown, occasionally leaning toward each other to swap whispers; Ray Reeves sitting apart, working a pinkie finger into his ear. Despite the futility of their struggles since they had come into the case, they were feeling good about their defense. Just so long as that judge didn't try to screw them again.

Now, on the other side of the defense team, at a second long wooden table, Keeshan and Winfree took their seats.

Just before nine o'clock Sam Robertson swept into the room, and the case of the *State of Texas* v. *Clarence Lee Brandley* began.

Brandley sat still and silent. People he had never seen before started to act out a strange ritual. Its language was foreign. Its form was alien. It was all about him, yet he seemed to have no role in it. The white people in the jury box solemnly swore that they would a true verdict render according to the law and the evidence submitted to them, so help them God. The white clerk with the long, glossy strawberry-colored fingernails stood up and said that the grand jury—duly selected, impaneled, sworn, charged, and organized—had indicted a defendant for having, on or about August 23, 1980, intentionally caused the death of Cheryl Fergeson by choking and strangling her by means to the grand jury unknown in the course of committing and attempting to commit the offense of aggravated rape of the said Cheryl Fergeson. From time to time people mentioned Clarence Lee Brandley, the name he had grown up with.

A tall gray-haired man with a deeply lined face, the father of the dead girl, was stooped with grief. When he tried to describe how he had last seen his daughter, through his kitchen window as she drove off one Saturday morning with her blond hair catching his eye, his face crumpled, and he had to stop to clear away his tears. Schoolteachers came and told how the girl had disappeared and they had started to worry. Girls who had been playing volleyball remembered searching the school. Policemen talked about calls they had received over their radios and then about the calls they had made to bring in the detectives when the dead girl's body was found. From time to time, they mentioned Brandley's name.

The white volleyball coach from Conroe High said Brandley had told her to keep everyone away from his end of the building. He didn't remember that. They said he had helped with the search and then taken the police to the body. Nobody said he was guilty of anything. Not so far as he could see. Then the four white janitors came and told their stories. Each one said pretty much the same as the others. Brandley could not see how any of it meant that he had killed the girl. Not at first.

They told the plain facts about right: all of them getting to the school around seven-thirty, Icky Peace going off to buff the floor in the teachers' lounge while Acreman, Sessum, and Martinez set out the chairs in the cafeteria, how they all waited around in the hallway till Clarence came along with an armful of toilet paper rolls. They all agreed that Acreman had said something about a girl's being in the rest room and that Brandley had sent them all over to the Vocational Building, where they had waited for some time before he came over with the key to the door. It was all true enough. Brandley remembered it clearly. It was Gary Acreman who started to worry him.

He slouched in the witness chair with his hair all slicked down and his long, thin legs spidering out across the floor, fidgeting all the time and talking in that whining voice with the East Texas twang in it. Right away he said something that set Brandley thinking. It was nothing important. It was just that he claimed that they were friends: "Me and Clarence worked together and we got along real good and he had even bought my lunch for me." Who was he trying to kid? Acreman had never liked him, never liked a black man's being over him, and never made any secret of it.

Then he started to say some other things. None of them was that big on its own. All of them put together did not really add up to anything. But they were not true, and that worried Brandley. For example, when he was talking about how they all waited in the hallway for Brandley to come and give them another job to do, Acreman said that he reckoned he and the others had started their wait around nine-fifteen and had been standing there for a full fifteen minutes before they noticed a girl come walking down the hallway, turn up the little staircase about fifty feet away from them, and go up into the "Sesame Street" rest room.

Brandley winced. Why was he saying the girl went down the hallway at nine-thirty when all the teachers and volleyball players had agreed that it was nine-fifteen? Acreman had somehow lost fifteen minutes. And another thing: those white janitors had not been fifty feet away from "Sesame Street"; they had been right there on the staircase. They had to have been. Acreman himself said he had been able to read the girl's name on the back of her belt: CHERYL.

Brandley had no time to think about how all this mattered before Acreman said something else that was not quite right. According to him, Brandley was following along right behind the girl, walking just ten feet behind her as she came down the hallway. Brandley knew he had never seen that girl alive, that the first time he laid eyes on her was up in the little props loft when Icky Peace screamed and then he saw her lying there, naked. He had never seen her going down any hallway. Still, it didn't mean much. It surely didn't mean he had killed her.

Acreman carried on talking. "I told Clarence there was a girl in the rest room, and he said he wasn't going to go in there."

That was true. He had gone down there to put new rolls of toilet paper in the boys' rest room. He never did go in the girls' rest rooms. Acreman recalled how Brandley had sent them all over to the Vocational Building and how they had waited there for some time before Brandley finally came over with a key to open the doors. That was all true, except for one other little thing he added: "Clarence had a white towel around his neck which I had never seen him wear before."

What was he talking about? Brandley couldn't remember any towel, but he did remember how the DA had been on at him about a towel with the grand jury, trying to make out he was carrying one. Acreman was playing some kind of game here. He had always been a sly one, always mouthing off. What was he trying to do? It was as if someone had got to him and told him to nail Brandley to the crime. Acreman hammered once more. "Clarence seemed to act kind of strange," he said. "He seemed to act strange like he wanted us to go, so me and John Sessum went and got my truck and took off. Brandley could feel his heart thumping. Acreman was out to get him here. There was no telling why, but Acreman was taking every chance he got to point a finger his way.

Still, Brandley couldn't see where anyone could say he had killed the girl. No way.

In the jury box Bill Srack watched carefully. He did not like the look of Gary Acreman. He was cocky. He was nervous. Srack watched his little eyes twitching all around the room, now at the floor, now at the ceiling. Srack was not at all sure that Gary Acreman was an honest witness. It was not just his manner. Sam Martinez had been very tense, and John Sessum was even worse—so nervous he was almost incoherent. It was something more subtle than that.

Srack pushed the facts a little farther down his trolley-track mind and finally came to a conclusion: all these white janitors were telling the same story, not just in general shape but in all its essential details and particularly in any detail that tended to make Brandley look bad. They all said the same thing. But real people, honest people, didn't do that. Honest people recalled all kinds of different things and, with the best will in the world, gave different versions of the same events. But these white janitors were all agreeing about who had arrived at what time at the school, all agreeing that Brandley was the only one with keys to any of the doors, all agreeing that Brandley had been walking right behind the girl, all recalling that Gary Acreman warned him that she was in the rest room, all rehearsing the same sequence of events in which they moved away, leaving Brandley alone and unobserved, and which ended with Brandley's returning and all of them noticing that he had a towel around his neck and all of them thinking that he seemed nervous. It was too pat. It was not real.

The more he thought about it, the more convinced Srack became that the white janitors had put their heads together and agreed on a story. But there was something wrong with that, too. To Srack's mind, these white janitors were obviously unintelligent men. Sessum, in particular, looked like a complete derelict. These men were not sharp enough to have put their heads together and agreed on a story. They had to have had some help. Somebody had gotten them all together and helped them sort out the story.

On the defense bench Morris and Brown had arrived at the same conclusion. This was the first chance they had had to question these white janitors. They began to see more of how the police and the Texas Ranger had been acting. They discovered that Gary Acreman, John Sessum, and Sam Martinez had all made two statements. First, they had been down to the Conroe Police Department on the Monday after the crime, while Brandley and Peace were in Houston taking lie detector tests, and had put their stories down on paper.

Then, five days later, on the Saturday immediately after Brandley's arrest, they had all been taken back to the high school by the Texas Ranger, Wesley Styles, and walked through the hallway, reenacting the day of the crime. After that they had made another set of statements. And they had changed their stories. It was their second version of the story, compiled after their walk-through with the ranger, that contained all the details that were causing the defense trouble.

In their first statement none of them had suggested that Brandley was the only one with keys to the auditorium, or that the girl had appeared at nine-thirty, or that they had been standing at least fifty feet away from "Sesame Street" when the girl arrived, or that Brandley later had a towel around his neck, or that he was then acting in a nervous fashion. But after their walk-through, the three of them agreed that all these details were correct and even used the same words and phrases to describe them. And it was not just that they were adding damaging details to fill holes in their first version. They were completely contradicting themselves. Both John Sessum and Sam Martinez had said originally that the girl had come down the hallway behind Brandley, but after their walk-through they all agreed that the black janitor had been following the girl. In their original statements they guessed Brandley had left them waiting outside the Vocational Building for as little as five minutes. Now they all agreed he had left them for forty-five minutes.

George Morris did his best to put pressure on the white janitors, to point out all these changes and to try and make them admit that they had been coached by the Texas Ranger. At one point John Sessum started to say he had been scared by the ranger. But Morris could not break through. It left Morris and Brown with a frightening picture of a town in which the investigation of a crime was stood on its head. First they arrested a man, and then they started work. It was only after Brandley had been arrested that the ranger extracted these damaging details from witnesses, just as it was only after the arrest that Ted Morgan was sent down into Dugan to find some dirt to justify what they were doing.

Bill Srack was impressed by only one of the white janitors, Icky Peace, who seemed to have more poise about him than the others despite the fact that he admitted to being illiterate and to having attended a special school for those with learning difficulties.

The little fat janitor with the squeaking voice started his evidence by following the well-trodden path through the day of the crime. Then he came to the time when he and Brandley joined the search for the missing girl, checking the lobby doors and then going into the auditorium, where, he said, Brandley had told him to go up and check in the props loft over the stage.

According to Peace, he had taken a quick look and come straight back down. He said Brandley had then sent him back up to look properly. "I went back up there and started moving stuff around, not looking real good, but I moved a few things around." He had come down again, he said, without finding anything, and the two of them had then gone off around the school, looking in the gyms and out on the football field before coming back to the auditorium, where, he said, Brandley had sent him up to the props loft yet another time. "This time, I did look. I just got disgusted and I just decided I would go ahead and look real good. I started moving boards around and everything and then I picked up this sheet of plywood. . . . I saw the girl laying there. . . . I screamed and called his name. . . . He ran over to where I was at. He just said: 'Oh, my God. I'll go get the police and you stay here.' "

Srack could see the point plain enough. The state was trying to suggest that Brandley knew the girl's body was there and wanted it discovered by Peace. He could see some of the other jurors nodding their heads knowingly. But why, Srack wondered, would a killer go to so much trouble to conceal a body and then, one hour later, go to such trouble to uncover it? The truth might just as easily be that it was Peace who had hidden the body and that he was deliberately avoiding uncovering it until Brandley made it impossible for him.

Anyway, Srack wondered how he would have handled someone like Peace himself if he had been in Brandley's shoes, working as a supervisor; if you sent a man to do a job and he failed to do it, you had to send him back and keep sending him back until he did it right. That was what a supervisor was for.

Now Srack watched as the defense tried to make a very different point about Icky Peace. As George Morris questioned him, Peace started to reveal some strange things about himself.

Morris asked him about the police searching his car on the day of the crime. "Did you have a gun in it?"

"Yes, sir. I just forgot about it being in there. I had just got it fixed."

"Did they also get a club out of your car?"

"Uh. Yes, sir. It was a souvenir at the school where I used to work at, the kids all made it and gave it to me."

"Have you ever showed that gun to David Harris?"

"I showed it to him once."

"Was that in school?"

"No, sir. It was a picture that I showed him."

"Isn't it a fact that you carried that gun underneath your billfold?"

"No, sir."

"You didn't show David Harris that gun while you were working on the job there at the school?"

"I showed him a picture of it."

"Do you have a card showing you to be a narcotics agent with the name Four Seasons written across it?"

Srack was watching Peace's face closely. Peace seemed to be making this up as he went along. Had he been showing off a gun in school or not? What was he doing with a gun and a club? There was something about this story that was just not right. Srack could see that the defense was driving at something. Suddenly, his thoughts were interrupted. It was the judge, barking at George Morris. "Counsel, what does that have to do with this?"

"I think I can connect it up, Your Honor. If it please the court, I would like to be able to show—"

But the judge barked again. "Members of the jury, I'd like you to step back into the jury room."

Puzzled, Srack allowed himself to be shepherded out of the courtroom with his fellow jurors.

Brandley watched them go. He had not been enjoying Icky Peace's evidence one bit. It was just the same as Acreman. Like this business about his repeatedly sending Peace up to the props room. It couldn't be true. The first thing that he and Peace had seen when they left the Vocational Building to go lock up the main building was a cop car, sitting there. The cops themselves said they had not got to the school until eleven-forty. The girl had been found at about eleven-fifty. There was no way they could have straightened out the cafeteria, searched the auditorium, gone off on Icky Peace's grand tour of the school, and then come back and found the body in only ten minutes.

But why was Peace saying it? Maybe he was just scared the police were going to lay the crime on him if he didn't point the finger at someone else. He always had been good at talking himself out of trouble. Brandley knew he was lying about the gun he had been showing off in school. All these little lies were adding up. And now this judge was acting funny. Every time George Morris opened his mouth, the judge seemed to snap at him.

As the jury disappeared behind a closed door, Morris started to explain that he was trying to show that someone other than Brandley could have committed the crime. "We would like to show another reasonable hypothesis as to—"

"First let the jury retire," said the judge in a tone that suggested he was dealing with a disobedient brat, "and ask him some questions."

"Oh, I thought you wanted to know the purpose."

"No, sir. I am not going to permit this. I am not going to permit questions to be asked of this witness that don't have anything to do with any matter that is on trial."

Morris opened his mouth to say that the fact that Icky Peace might have killed the girl was all that mattered. But he thought better of it and started to ask Peace if it was true that he had originally been a suspect.

"Did they tell you that you were a possible—"

The judge barked again. "This is not what the jury retired on. Ask him the question that you asked him, that I had the jury retired on."

Morris started again, asking Peace whether he had been in the habit of showing people, including David Harris, an identity card that claimed he was a narcotics agent with the code name Four Seasons.

"I showed the whole crew a bunch of cards."

"I'm talking about a particular card showing you as a narcotics agent."

Peace then launched into an explanation that involved a toy city that he said he played with at home with his little nephews and nieces. It was a hobby, he said, and to make it more real, he had had made some plastic ID cards complete with his photograph. "I have a whole bunch of them made up—doctors and lawyers and druggists and FBIs," he said. "I'm head of the narcotics division of my play city."

Had he ever shown his narcotics card to David Harris and asked if he would work undercover for him? Peace said no. Morris moved in for the kill; he was damn sure Peace was lying and if he could just draw him out and—

But the judge barked again. "All right, now, hurry up. What is the materiality of this?"

Morris sighed and tried to explain. "I am demonstrating to the jury that this man also could have committed this offense. It would have been very easy for him to induce some little girl, 16 years old, by showing her a narcotics card to get her to go anywhere with him. And I think it is admissible."

The judge shook his head. "I am not going to permit this witness to be questioned about this matter in front of the jury. Bring the jury out."

Morris took a deep breath, shook his head, and sat down.

Brandley watched in silence as his best shot was stolen from him.

Bill Srack came back with the rest of the jury and tried to figure out what he had missed. It seemed to be important. But it was clear that they were not to be told.

The Reverend J. J. Roberson had traveled up to the courthouse from Houston, where he was the pastor of the Mount Hebrew Missionary Baptist Church. He was concerned by the rumors he had heard about a railroading. Now, as he looked around this courtroom, his heart felt heavy. Not that it was any surprise to him. He knew all about Montgomery County. He remembered a particular time, back in 1955, when he was a younger man, and he had bought himself a brand-new Mercury and driven it up through Montgomery County. The police had stopped him in Conroe. He had not committed any crime. So he had asked them, "Why did you stop me?"

And they had told the young minister to his face, "Any nigger that comes through Conroe driving a '55 Mercury is gonna get stopped."

It seemed to him that twenty-five years later the atmosphere was still the same. Every time any black person got up from the court and went outside, one of those white deputies would get up and follow him. Not say anything, just follow him. The deputies were even following black people into the rest room. All around the court, on the white faces, the minister could see the same look—an angry, hateful look. And he was not just talking about a few redneck spectators. He meant the white people who were running this court. They all had the same look. And that included the judge.

This was a white man's court.

As the trial progressed, Morris and Brown retired as often as possible to the Iron Horse across the street from the courthouse to discuss each day's events. They agreed that they were happy enough with the way the trial had started, but they were worried about the judge.

"Anyone would think he was working for the prosecution," grumbled Brown. "He's not even waiting for Keeshan to make objections. He's just coming out and doing the DA's job for him."

Ray Reeves had started keeping a note of every time the judge did the district attorney's job for him. The writing on his notepad was getting bigger and bigger as his anger at the judge's behavior got the better of him.

The crucial test would come when the defense tried to put on its own witnesses to outline its theory about Peace, and Morris and Brown both had seen something that worried them greatly: Keeshan slipping into the judge's office on his own.

It would be totally improper for the judge to start discussing the case with one side while the other was excluded. But after both had seen Keeshan disappearing into the judge's room and closing the door behind him, Morris and Brown had complained and asked if they could join in these meetings. The judge had told them that the meetings had nothing to do with the case. Keeshan was just in there talking about other things, never even mentioning the trial.

"Bullshit," said Brown.

"Damn right," said Morris.

For three days Bill Srack listened to Jim Keeshan as he paraded his witnesses. Some of it was worrying. Some of it seemed to him to be irrelevant. Some of it was plain embarrassing, like the evidence of E. H. Hoffmeister, a fingerprint specialist from the Department of Public Safety in Austin. Mr. Hoffmeister had no fingerprint evidence of any significance to offer the court, but he had a sorry story to tell. He said, for example, that he had not been able to take any prints from a wad of paper that had been screwed up and possibly used to gag Cheryl Fergeson because the police had failed to pass it to him. He added that he might have been able to take prints from the girl's body if the police had given him access to it soon enough after her death, but the police had failed to do that. He had, however, found one fingerprint on the trash bag in which the dead girl's clothes had been found—that of a detective who had not bothered to wear gloves while he handled the evidence.

Srack found even less comfort in the evidence of the short, hefty captain of detectives, Monty Koerner. Koerner told the court proudly that he had been a law enforcement officer for fifteen years and captain of detectives for the Conroe Police Department for nine of them. He explained how he had set about tackling the crime. On the day of the murder he had ordered one of his sergeants, "Woody" Allen, to take photographs of the scene of the crime and of the people who were there.

"What about those photographs?" he was asked. "What happened to them?"

"The—Sgt. Allen had the uh—wrong setting on the camera. And the film did not come out."

At the defense table the attorneys grimaced.

Had they tried to develop the photographs? Not exactly, said the captain. They had taken them to Fox Photo. The defense attorneys laughed out loud. Fox Photo? Not the FBI in Houston or the DPS lab in Austin or even the Montgomery County Sheriff's Department? Conroe's captain of detectives had allowed his scene-of-the-crime photos in the biggest rape-homicide in the history of the whole town to be taken down to North Hills Shopping Center and chucked into the Fox Photo deposit, to which little kids took their happy snaps of family pets to be developed? That was so, said the captain.

The defense attorneys shook their heads in wonder.

The captain was asked about the autopsy on the dead girl. Yes, he had been there. Yes, he had been investigating rapes for some ten years now. Yes, he knew what a rape kit was. And yes, he knew that swabs of semen collected from a rape victim could reveal the blood type of the rapist. But no, he had not collected the swabs and washings that contained the semen collected from this girl's body. He had thought that someone else was going to do it.

Srack sighed.

Srack found little to reassure him in the testimony of Joseph Jachimczyk, M.D., J.D., forensic pathologist, attorney at law, chief medical examiner for Harris County, and medical examiner upon request and upon payment of the appropriate fee for Montgomery County. Srack listened respectfully to the portly medical examiner with the owlish face as he outlined his findings that Cheryl Fergeson had died of asphyxia caused by ligature strangulation and that she had been the victim of a sexual attack and his belief that it would have taken at least thirty seconds for her to lose consciousness and at least three minutes to die.

The doctor disclosed that the girl's bladder was completely empty and said that this was striking since a bladder filled with urine at the rate of two milliliters a minute. The district attorney said this proved that she had been attacked as soon as she had tried to leave the rest room—timing that tended to point to Brandley as the attacker. The defense suggested that if Brandley had attacked her as she left the rest room, then in the three minutes it had taken her to die, her bladder would have accumulated six milliliters of urine, so Keeshan must be wrong. It seemed to Srack to be more likely that the girl's bladder had emptied after she was dead when her muscles relaxed and that its emptiness told them nothing at all about when she had died. He was surprised that the doctor had not suggested it himself.

The doctor also said that the girl's hymen had still been intact, even though the presence of semen showed she had been raped. Srack assumed that meant her attacker had simply failed to penetrate her, but the doctor had a more disturbing theory. It suggested to him that the girl had been killed and then raped when she was already dead, and that her hymen had been so relaxed in death that it had not broken. Some of Srack's fellow jurors stared at Brandley with deep revulsion.

Srack was not impressed, but his respect for the doctor's evidence began to crumble completely as Jachimczyk was led through the sensitive question of the missing swabs. At first the doctor declared confidently that he had passed the swabs to Captain Koerner during the autopsy. Then he backtracked and said it was possible that he had not. Then he said he would have given the captain anything he had asked for. He could not be sure.

The point was rubbed in by Sally Williams of the Forensic Science Institute in Dallas, who specialized in analyzing body fluids for the police. Don Brown asked her if it was unusual to have no vaginal swabs from a rape victim.

"It's not only unusual," she said. "That's the whole purpose of doing the examination."

Srack despaired. There was no way of knowing whether this was foul-up or conspiracy. It was certainly no way to run a murder inquiry.

Brandley did not know what to believe. All this mattered. The lost fingerprints might have identified the guilty man. The photographs the police had messed up could have shown that he was not carrying a towel around his neck and that he was not wearing a belt—or carrying anything else that they might try and say he had used to kill this girl. The swabs were even more important. The swabs could have blown the lid off the whole case. It seemed more than just bad luck that they had all been lost. Lost and gone forever. And there was more bad luck with the judge.

Before Captain Koerner retreated from the witness chair, George Morris tried to get him to admit that there were some similarities between the rape of Cheryl Fergeson and another rape in the town, one in which a man who had no connection with Clarence Brandley had been identified as the rapist. Could there not be a link? Was this not a reasonable hypothesis to put to the jury? But the judge sent the jury out of the room. Then he listened to the evidence and announced: "There will be no reference to this in front of the jury."

Srack was still waiting for the state to land its big punch. So far, it seemed to him, it had been swinging hard but never making contact. Even if he supposed the other janitors were all honest, and he doubted that, all the evidence meant was that Brandley could conceivably be guilty, that he had had the time to commit the offense. But that did not seem to Srack to be anywhere close to proof beyond a reasonable doubt that Brandley had really done this thing. What other evidence was there? Icky Peace said Brandley had kept sending him up to the props loft. Maybe, maybe not. So what? It still did not prove a thing. The state was trying to say that Brandley had been the only one with a key to the auditorium, but Srack had worked in places like this where keys were given out and soon got left with all kinds of people who shouldn't have them, and this school, as far as he could see, hadn't changed its keys since Methuselah. Anyone could have gotten into the auditorium. The fact was that there was not enough circumstantial evidence to pinpoint Brandley, and so far there had been nothing—no fingerprints, no photos, no swabs— nothing that linked him with this crime.

Morris and Brown launched into the scientific evidence, try- ing to alert the jury to the clues they had found in the autopsy report and to their experts' work. Keeshan fought back.

The jury was told that the line across the girl's neck was too narrow to have been made by Brandley's belt. The defense attorneys sat, mute in disbelief and admiration, as the district attorney took Brandley's leather belt in both hands, stretched it with all his strength, and suggested that if it were pulled with maximum force, its width would be reduced by the tension so that it might, after all, fit the line on the girl's neck.

The jury was told that scientists for both sides had studied Brandley's belt and his knife and all the girl's clothes and found nothing—no fiber, no skin tissue, no fingerprint—that could conceivably tie Brandley to the murder. It was only then that the defense finally understood the importance of the towel that all the white janitors now remembered seeing around the black man's shoulders. Of course, he had used it to wipe away all this missing evidence.

Then they came to the hairs.

Keeshan called his expert, Tony Arnold, who worked at the DPS lab in Austin, and the defense called Dr. Irving Stone, its expert from the Forensic Science Institute in Dallas. They had examined thirteen different hairs or fragments of hair that had been found on the dead girl's body or clothes. Both men agreed that you could never be too sure about hairs: you could sometimes say that a hair came from a black or a white person, but you could never show a definite link between one particular hair and one particular individual.

Two of the hairs, they thought, could have come from the dead girl. They had compared the remaining eleven with the samples they had been given from Clarence Brandley and Icky Peace. Eight of the hairs had no resemblance to the samples from either man.

The defense quietly cursed Keeshan for his blind focus on Brandley. Why had he refused to test anyone else's hair? Still, those eight hairs should be powerful evidence for the jury, they thought. They were eight clues to the real culprit.

Those in the courtroom pored over the origins of the remaining three hairs. Two of them had been rescued from the girl's inner thigh by the detective who had stashed them in his cigarette pack. One was black, and the other was reddish.

The black hair, according to Keeshan's expert, could have been one of Brandley's pubic hairs. However, the defense expert said it was not a pubic hair at all, never mind being one of Brandley's. Morris and Brown had no idea what it was—whether it had been taken from Brandley and planted or whether it belonged to one of the black volleyball players or even the dead girl's boyfriend, who was a black-haired Hispanic. But the confusion between the experts gave them plenty of room to dismiss the hair as real evidence.

The red hair from the girl's thigh, according to Keeshan's expert, could have been one of Icky Peace's pubic hairs. Morris and Brown were delighted to hear that, but their own expert disagreed. He thought it was a pubic hair, but he believed it probably belonged to someone other than Icky Peace. He could not say who. For Morris and Brown, this red pubic hair was a powerful reason to find Clarence Brandley not guilty. There were also two other hairs on the girl's thigh that could not be linked to any known suspect. But the district attorney had an answer. He suggested that while the dead girl had picked up the black hair in the course of being raped by Clarence Brandley, she must have picked up the other three from a toilet seat. Morris and Brown thought this was a desperate argument since it meant the girl must have been lying across the toilet on her abdomen.

The final hair had been found in one of the dead girl's socks. Keeshan's expert said it probably came from a black person and had some similarities with Brandley's. The defense expert said that he could see no difference at all between this hair and Brandley's, but before anyone in court had a chance to think that he might be offering a conclusive clue, he explained that all that he meant was that "there is a number of people in the population from whom this hair could have come and it's not just one person."

Did that mean, asked Don Brown, that he was merely putting Brandley into a segment of the general population who could have committed this crime?

"No, sir," replied the expert with searing precision. "It just puts him in a segment of the population that could have gotten the hair on that sock."

The Reverend C. Anderson Davis had also traveled up from Houston to witness the trial of the black janitor. He worked for the Baptist Ministers Association, and he wanted to observe the quality of justice in this courthouse. He was not impressed. It was not just the judge with his hostile attitude and his way of talking down to black people who dared make a sound in court or the atmosphere in the room. What most disturbed the elderly minister were his conversations with a Montgomery County deputy. The deputy never went into any detail, and if he had not been such a reliable source, the minister would have paid no attention at all, but the one thing that this deputy kept coming back to was that this trial was rigged.

Late on Wednesday afternoon, December 10, 1980, after three days of evidence, Jim Keeshan declared that he had completed the state's case. For a moment Morris and Brown were confused. They had never quite shrugged off the fear that Keeshan had some secret weapon to throw at them. The fear had dogged them ever since they had taken the case. But now Keeshan was sitting down. That was it. There was no secret weapon.

George Morris immediately hauled himself to his feet and invited the judge to instruct the jury to find Brandley not guilty.

With the jury dispatched to its room, George Morris put the argument. "I'd like to state to this court that there is a difference between possibility and probability, and that even though it might be possible for this defendant to have committed this crime, it's also possible that other people might have committed this crime. The probability is great that other people could have committed this crime."

Morris tried to make the judge focus on the law covering cases of circumstantial evidence and, in particular, on the need for the state to exclude all other reasonable hypotheses, leaving the guilt of the defendant as the only reasonable explanation for the crime. He pointed in particular to the hairs which had been found on the dead girl and for which no owners could be found.

"It gives rise to the proposition that somebody other than this defendant could have committed this crime," said Morris. "Your Honor, since the court knows the law on circumstantial evidence, we feel that there is another hypothesis, there is another theory—that somebody other than the defendant could have committed this crime. We feel that because the State has failed to exclude every other reasonable hypothesis that this defendant is entitled to that law—and that law should be an instructed verdict."

Morris believed he was right. Yet it was no surprise when the judge, without pausing to hear any further discussion, said: "All right, sir, your motion will be denied. Mr. Morris, it is a fact issue to the jury."

Morris and Brown were not too worried. Brown, in particular, had gone over all the evidence thoroughly. "No reasonable jury could possibly convict anyone on this evidence," he kept saying. "The state has not made its case. It's as simple as that."

When the defense opened on Thursday morning, Morris and Brown had a simple strategy. All they wanted to do was to

show that someone else could have raped and killed Cheryl
Fergeson. Their best suspect was Icky Peace. Their best theory
was that he had used his ID card to pretend to be a narcotics
officer; he had stopped the girl and told her he wanted to
question her in the auditorium, where he had used his gun
or his club to subdue her before raping and strangling her.
They did not know whether it was true; but they knew it was
at least as reasonable as the state's case, and it was enough to
cut Brandley free of the flimsy web of circumstantial evidence
that Keeshan had tried to throw around him.

Their first big witness was David Harris, the black Vietnam
veteran who helped supervise all the janitors in Conroe's nineteen schools. He had become a key figure for the defense. For
a start, he could tell the jury how he had personally seen
the Texas Ranger, Wes Styles, coaching Icky Peace in his
evidence at the high school. But as soon as Don Brown asked
Harris to describe what had happened, Jim Keeshan leaped to
his feet.

"I would object to hearsay, Your Honor."

"Sustained," said the judge.

Brown was openmouthed. "Your Honor, we are asking—"

"I have ruled, counsel, I'll hear you in the absence of the
jury on what your contention is, but I have ruled on it."

George Morris tried to help. "I don't believe this would be
hearsay. Mr. Peace is already—"

"I have ruled, counsel, I have ruled. I have told you I would
hear it in the absence of the jury if you want to argue the point.
Now move along."

Brown struggled on, trying to explain that they wanted to
warn the jury that Peace might be lying. "Your Honor, we're
not offering this to the proof of any facts. We're offering it
for the purpose of impeachment."

The judge glared at him. "Counsel, do you understand me
when I say I have ruled?"

Eventually, the judge sent the jury out of the room, listened
to Don Brown, who was barely suppressing his desire to bel-
low like a bull, and told him he could not put this evidence
before the jury.

But that was not the end of David Harris. He could also
testify that Icky Peace had carried a gun in school and
had posed as a narcotics officer, and he could vouch from
his own experience that Peace made a convincing job of
it. This, too, would show that Peace had not necessarily

been telling the truth when he was in court earlier in the week.

The jurors were back in their seats. Don Brown had settled Harris into his evidence and was just bringing him around to the big questions when—without any hint of an objection from Jim Keeshan—the judge intervened and sent the jury out of the room again.

Brown tried to persuade the judge to allow the evidence. With the jury out of the way, he asked Harris to tell his story. Harris was clear that Icky Peace had shown him a pistol in the school, not a picture of a pistol. He recalled, too, how Peace had shown him his narcotics ID card with the code name Four Seasons.

"Did he say anything about this was part of his play city or play world?"

"No, sir."

"Did he inquire of you as to whether or not you wanted to participate in narcotics work?"

"Yes, sir."

"What if anything did you tell him when he inquired of you if you wanted to participate?"

"I told him to let me think about it."

Brown was pleased. This was a direct contradiction of what Peace had told the jury. If he could just show the jury that Peace was a liar, the jurors might not only discount anything bad he had to say about Brandley but might also see that perhaps he had some reason for lying, including the possibility that he was trying to cover up his own guilt. Brown started to draw out more detail from his witness, but the judge intervened.

"Is there any other evidence other than just this? All this doesn't have anything to do with any matter here before me."

Jim Keeshan stood up and asked if he could put some questions to the witness.

"You can ask him a couple, but as far as I'm concerned, I've heard all I need to hear. If you want to, I'll let you ask him."

"I won't ask him, Your Honor," said Keeshan.

With that, the judge dismissed the witness. "I'm not going to permit this in front of the jury."

Brown tried to plead with him, saying he was offering the evidence to show that Icky Peace might have lied to the jury.

"Your offer is refused," barked the judge.

The defense had lost its first big witness.

Brown and Morris were not beaten yet. They had other witnesses. They called Officer Wayne Kremenak, one of the detectives who had searched Icky Peace's car on the day of the crime. The gun and the club were not all he had found.

But the judge said this was not for the jury. So once again Don Brown found himself questioning his witness in the absence of the jury in an attempt to persuade the judge to allow the evidence into the case. Brown went straight to the point.

"Did you recover any pictures from his car of nude women?"

"No, sir."

Brown straightened up his considerable bulk and looked the officer straight in the eye. "You don't recall recovering any pictures of nude women from his car?"

"No, sir, I don't."

Brown was not going to let him go. "Are you saying you didn't recover any pictures of nude women or you don't remember whether you did or not?"

"I don't believe I recovered any pictures of nude women."

Brown was still not persuaded. "Did you recover any pictures of nude people of any kind?"

"There were some on the dash of the car."

At last.

"These were nude pictures of people?"

"Yes, sir."

"And they were women?"

"Women, I believe."

"Then you do remember there being some nude pictures in his car."

"Yes, sir."

The detective went on to recall that there were two pictures of naked women pasted to the front of the dash of Icky Peace's car. He believed they were drawings cut out of a magazine.

The judge made no move to reprimand the officer for trying to mislead the court. Brown let it go. All he wanted to do was to get this in front of the jury, so that they would see that although this strange little man might seem like a child, he had some advanced adult obsessions.

But the judge said: "There will be no mention of this to the jury."

Then he warned the attorneys to behave themselves and told Brown to call his next witness.

Morris and Brown were beginning to worry.

As Bill Srack shuttled back and forth to the jury room with his fellow jurors, a troubling idea began to form in his mind. After serving on four other juries, he believed he knew a little bit about how judges should behave. He understood, too, that there was some evidence that a jury could not hear, things that were prejudicial or inadmissible for some technical reason, but this judge seemed to be blocking the defense for the wrong kind of reason. It appeared to Srack that the judge was being unfair, as if he were on the side of the prosecution. He did not even seem to be hiding it; it was more as if he were deliberately trying to show the jury that he believed that Brandley was guilty. His whole demeanor, as well as his rulings, was hostile to the defense. That troubled Bill Srack.

He had been around courts enough that he could see what was happening and not to be swayed by a judge doing something like that, but he was not so sure about some of the other jurors. They might just decide that if the judge thought Brandley was guilty, then it would be all right for them to think so, too.

Clarence Brandley was determined not to lose his hope, but he was finding it hard.

Each morning two white deputies came to his cell and led him out in chains. Before they got to the courtroom, they would pull out their keys and release the locks because the jury was not supposed to see that he was a prisoner. It made no difference to Brandley. OK, so he could move his hands around some. He was just as trapped all the same.

He watched the judge and the way his face seemed to go as red as a brick any time Morris or Brown dared to stand up to him, and he watched the people on the public benches in the courtroom and he saw the way they stiffened and shifted away any time a black person came and sat down next to them. Black people were treated like intruders in this courthouse. It was as if black people came to court only as criminals.

Each day, before the hearing began, Brandley's family and friends stood in a circle in the hallway outside the courtroom and joined hands and prayed for justice in America. Brandley found it hard to pray or to hope. Today, especially. Today he had to get on that witness stand and give evidence in that courtroom. He had to stay cool.

George Morris had told him that he was going to ask just a few simple questions to start with and then leave it to the prosecution to set the pace.

Brandley sat with his hands folded in his lap, trying to concentrate on Morris and to ignore the unyielding stares that surrounded him. Nothing at school or in his work had ever prepared him for this. It was as if he were talking for his life.

Morris led him through the facts of his life for a few minutes. Then he asked him: "Clarence, do you believe in God?"

"Yes, sir."

"Clarence, did your mother raise you—"

Keeshan was on his feet objecting. He never explained why. The judge sustained the objection. Brandley thought that was no surprise.

"Clarence," Morris persisted. "Do you know right from wrong?"

"Yes, sir."

"Clarence, I ask you: Did you commit this murder-rape that you have been charged with?"

"No, sir. I did not."

George Morris sat down. Brandley saw Keeshan's assistant, Jerry Winfree, rise to cross-examine him. Winfree was a short man with a barrel chest and an untidy mustache. Brandley hardly knew him, yet here he was dissecting the tiny details of a day in his life, a day he could barely remember. For chrissake, he had been half asleep all day. He'd never known people were going to want to know every move he made. If he had known, he would have written it down.

Winfree started asking him about the white lady, the Conroe volleyball coach, and how he was supposed to have told her to keep everyone away from his end of the school. As if he were already planning to murder someone up there. He knew that's what the prosecutors were trying to say. But he had never said any such thing. Why would he? Anyway, no white lady teacher was going to take orders from some no-account black janitor. So he told Winfree it had never happened.

Then Winfree started on at him about where he had been while the white janitors were waiting outside the Vocational Building.

Brandley told him: "I sat down and smoked a cigarette and listened to the radio."

Winfree paused for a scornful moment. "How long did you smoke the cigarettes there in the office?"

Brandley could not remember. He had had no watch. He had not been interested. "I would say . . . I couldn't say how long. I couldn't give you no time, how long it took me. I stayed in the office maybe fifteen to twenty minutes."

"How many cigarettes did you smoke?"

"I smoked one."

"What made you decide to get up and go on over to the Vocational Building?"

"I decided it was time to go on over because the main reason I didn't proceed right on over—I wasn't in no big hurry. We had to try to make at least half a day."

"You wanted those janitors to just kill some time in front of that Vocational Building then?"

"That was normal."

Brandley could see Winfree did not believe him. But what did some attorney from the DA's office know about a janitor's life? What did this jury know about it?

Winfree started pressing him on his movements and the timing of his movements. Brandley felt his memory collapsing. He could not even remember what all the other witnesses had been saying, let alone what had really happened.

He said he had gone down the hallway and seen the white janitors standing by "Sesame Street" soon after ten past eight— at least an hour earlier than anyone else's timing. He said he had started searching for the girl at ten o'clock and not found her until twelve.

Winfree gave him that scornful look again. "So you are now testifying that from ten until twelve—for two hours—you and Icky looked solid for that girl?"

Brandley shook his head, lost between anger and helplessness. "I am not saying we didn't look for no two hours. I'm saying that if that was the time, then undoubtedly I am mistaken with my times."

Winfree got him to describe exactly what he and Peace had done during their search for the girl and then dug at the same sore point. "So it took two hours for you to do this—what you have just described?"

"No, sir," said Brandley, his frustration building. "It didn't take no two hours."

Winfree dragged him back and forth across the events of that morning, tearing him to shreds with time.

Bill Srack was beginning to despair of ever hearing anything persuasive in this trial. The prosecution case had been a shambles. Now the defense was being ruled out of court by the judge, and its one star witness, Clarence Brandley, seemed to him to have nothing helpful to say in his own defense. It was all very well that Brandley was saying he was innocent. Anyone who was accused of capital murder would say that, but so far as Srack was concerned, he had said nothing to clear his name.

Morris and Brown were also unhappy with Brandley's performance as a witness. He had rambled on too much and got all his times in a mess. They knew he was nervous—after all, he was charged with a capital murder—but he seemed dishonest. He looked like the "bad nigger" the jury was expecting him to be. And it had done him no good to challenge the white volleyball coach about whether he had told her to keep everyone away from his end of the building. It would have been fine to admit that he had said it to her. But he did not remember saying it, so he said what he believed was true. The trouble was that this jury was not going to believe a black janitor over a white teacher. Not in Conroe.

They had to press on with their chosen strategy, somehow to get that jury to understand that the circumstantial evidence was just as strong against Icky Peace as it was against Brandley. They had one last witness who could bring the point home: the private investigator, Lorna Hubbell.

But the judge did not like it. Once again Don Brown found himself pleading: Icky Peace had told Lorna Hubbell a number of things that he had then denied to the jury. The jury needed to know that Peace might be lying. And some of the things he had said to Lorna Hubbell suggested he had something to hide. The judge agreed that he could once again rehearse his witness's evidence in front of him in the absence of the jury. Brown rapidly took the investigator through her recollection of the day in September when she caught Icky Peace on his way to work and persuaded him to talk a little about the case.

She said Peace had told her that the Texas Ranger had choked him with his necklace, that he had had nightmares since the murder, that he had trouble talking about the case, and that the Conroe police had wanted to hypnotize him because he was blocking out the truth in his mind. Brown told the judge that these were all things Peace had denied in his evidence. Jim Keeshan objected that there was no proper basis upon which to introduce this evidence.

And the judge said: "I sustain the objection and I will not permit her to testify before the jury."

Their strategy had just lost its final witness.

By two-forty on Thursday afternoon, just half a day after it had started to present the case, the defense team was finished. With its three key witnesses ruled out of court, it had nothing left to offer.

Don Brown was in a volcanic mood, barely able to contain an explosion of rage at the judge. Brandley was despondent. George Morris was talking about how bad all this would look if it ever got to the Court of Criminal Appeals in Austin. But this trial was not over, and the one thing that they clung to was that so far as they could see, Jim Keeshan had failed to touch their client.

With the jurors locked away in their room once more, George Morris tried again to persuade the judge to order a verdict of not guilty. He rehearsed the same argument and got the same response.

Judge Sam Robertson said: "Your motion is overruled."

That Thursday afternoon Bill Srack was thoughtful as he drove the blue pickup back to River Plantation. The jurors had now heard all the evidence. Tomorrow they had only to listen to the attorneys delivering their final speeches before beginning their deliberation. In his mind he took each of his fellow jurors one by one and considered how he thought they would vote.

Some of them were easy.

There was one particular group, three men and a woman, none of them very old, who had all hung together and eaten together at the midday break and who seemed to wear the same kind of rough denim clothes and spent a lot of time laughing at the same stupid things. They were a certain type that he knew well. He did not like to use the word, but if someone else had put the word to him, he would have had to agree that they were rednecks. He was pretty sure he knew how the four of them would vote. In their eyes this black school janitor was a guilty man.

But the other jurors, he fancied, might see things his way. He really could not say whether Brandley was guilty or innocent. He did not know. It seemed to him that the whole inquiry had been badly mishandled, and if the authorities had gotten the right man, they had certainly failed to prove it beyond a reasonable doubt. And that was his job: to look for reasonable doubt. It had nothing to do with personal feelings, only logic. That was what he was good at. He could not possibly vote to convict Brandley on this evidence, so it was his duty to vote not guilty, and he reckoned that that was how most of the other jurors would see it.

Just before eight-thirty the next morning, Friday, December 12, 1980, Bill Srack returned to the courthouse. For the next three hours the attorneys heaved and pulled at the jury's sympathies in their final speeches.

The defense assailed the police inquiry. "This was a Keystone Kop investigation," said Don Brown. Why were no semen traces preserved? Why were no fingerprints lifted from the body?

"Clarence Brandley deserved that evidence," boomed Brown.

And what about these janitors and their story? George Morris argued with all his force that they must have been coached by Ranger Wes Styles. There could be no other explanation for the way their statements changed after their walk-through at the school.

What about all these unidentified hairs on the body? Whom did they belong to? Not Brandley. All the experts agreed on that. They belonged to the rapist, to the girl's killer, who had not been caught. Maybe it was Icky Peace. Maybe it was someone else they had never heard of. The evidence did not tell them who it was, but it certainly did not tell them that the killer was Clarence Brandley. They had to vote not guilty.

By the time that Jerry Winfree and Morris and Brown had spoken, Bill Srack was confirmed in his view not only that he should vote not guilty but that at least seven of his fellow jurors would agree with him. Then Keeshan spoke.

Vividly, he described his version of the crime: the black janitor ordering everyone to stay away from his end of the building; the innocent girl looking for a rest room; the black janitor pointing her down the hallway where he could get her on her own and then following her; the black janitor sending the other janitors out of the building and then unlocking the auditorium door and waiting outside the rest room with his belt until the unsuspecting girl emerged, throttling her, dragging her into the darkness of the auditorium, and killing her and raping her and hiding her naked body, then disposing of her clothes, cleaning up with a towel, and calmly going back about his work. Clarence Brandley was the only man with keys, a man who knew his way around the building, a man who was absent, unobserved, when the girl disappeared, a man who owned a belt, a man who would naturally use trash bags to dispose of the dead girl's clothes. Keeshan's passion was rising.

"Doesn't this bear the tracks of a janitor?" he cried. "If you listen to the defense, this could have been the 'Murder of the Rue Morgue' or the 'Phantom of the Opera.' I think if you really use your imagination, you could imagine some ape swinging in through a window to do this." Keeshan paused and then struck. "But this is a janitor! And we know which one, don't we?" Keeshan appealed to the jurors' emotions. "This is a crime against all of us," he shouted. Brandley, he said, was bestial and monstrous. There could be only one verdict: guilty.

As Keeshan sat down, Srack thought he saw tears in his blue eyes. It had been quite a performance. Nothing in it had changed Srack's opinion about how he should vote, but he wondered about some of the others.

Finally, at eleven-forty, Bill Srack and his eleven fellow jurors were sent to their room to reach a verdict. Just as he expected, the group of three men and a woman settled down together at one end of the table, and one of the men, a loud young guy named Joe, began rubbing his hands and grinning. "Let's get that old judge in here," he said, "and get us some cards and some beer and have us a good time."

Srack looked at him sternly and told him the judge would have nothing to do with them until they had finished their deliberations.

By now they were all seated around the table. Srack had found a chair in the middle of one side. To his left was an intelligent-looking man, a teacher, whom Srack had marked down in his mind as a definite ally. To the teacher's left sat the three men and a woman, still snickering about Joe's call for beer, then came the other two women on the jury and the rest of the men around the table to Srack's right, ending with a nervous man with whom Srack had exchanged a few remarks during the case. Srack knew from these conversations that the nervous neighbor on his right wanted to vote not guilty.

They had to choose a foreman. Someone asked if anyone had ever served on a jury before. Srack confessed that he had and added that he had been a foreman twice and did not want to do it again. He turned to the teacher on his left.

"Why don't you be foreman?" he asked. "I'll sit right here next to you and advise you if I can, and we'll see if we can't get through this."

The teacher agreed, and Srack suggested that they should hold a secret ballot to test opinion. Each juror took a piece of paper, marked it, folded it, and passed it around to the teacher, who counted them out into three piles. Four had voted guilty. Srack guessed he knew who they were. But only two had voted not guilty. Srack reckoned that must be the nervous guy on his right and himself. All the other six said they were undecided. It was not so far from what he had imagined.

He suggested that they go around the table, giving each person a chance to explain his or her vote. The teacher gestured to his left, inviting Joe and his friends to speak first. Srack instantly regretted it. All three men spoke bluntly and forcefully in favor of finding Brandley guilty. They pointed to the other janitors as good witnesses, good enough for them, and they agreed that Brandley had no explanation for where he was when the girl went missing. He was guilty. They had no doubt. The three men had set a tone. Anyone who wanted to say Brandley was innocent was now going to be coming uphill, against the mood of the room.

To Srack's surprise, the rough-looking woman who had hung around with the three men said she was undecided. The rest of the jurors started echoing her, mumbling their indecision, until it came to the turn of the nervous man on Srack's right.

"What about you, sir?" said the teacher.

"I think he's guilty," came the answer.

Srack was dumbfounded. This man had told him he thought Brandley was innocent. Srack was sure he had just voted not guilty in the secret ballot. He just did not dare say so.

If only they had gone the other way around the table. Then he himself would have spoken first and explained how they had to vote not guilty. Then the nervous juror might have spoken up for himself, and the mood would have been quite different. It was Srack's turn to speak now.

"I am voting not guilty," he said in a firm voice. The room was still. "And I want to tell you right now that I will not change this vote. I want you to understand that it doesn't matter what happens in this jury room because I believe this is right and I must not change my mind."

There was silence all around the table. Then the teacher on Srack's left spoke.

"I am voting guilty," he said.

Srack hung his head. He had pushed the wrong man for foreman and let the whole mood go wrong. Now he was isolated, the sole vote for not guilty against five who wanted to convict and six who were undecided.

But now they were all talking, some in pairs, some to the room in general. Someone was riffling through the stack of evidence, pulling out pictures of the dead girl. Someone was saying they were not sure and someone else was saying they had to be sure. "Just look at these pictures. . . . You heard them janitors. . . . Poor little dead girl . . . negroid hair. . . . Look at these pictures."

Only ten minutes later—only twenty minutes since they had come into the room—the teacher suggested that they should take another vote. A show of hands, he said. Who wanted to vote not guilty? Srack alone raised his arm in silence. And who wanted to vote guilty? A ripple spread around the table. All of them had raised their hands.

Srack thought of Lajewel at home and the Bible study group and the prayers, and he remembered his oath to find a true verdict according to the evidence, so he tried to explain. About the janitors and the story that was just too pat. And how it made no difference anyway because even if they were telling the truth, it didn't prove Brandley was guilty. It just proved he could have been guilty.

They kept interrupting him. Voices were getting louder. The heat was rising. Srack talked on. About evidence that had been lost and evidence that had been bungled. About hairs that did not prove a thing, except that Clarence Brandley was one of several million people who might have left a hair on the dead girl's sock. And still their voices got louder, shouting sometimes, swearing sometimes. "Can't you see? . . . It's so damned obvious he done it. . . . What's wrong with you, for chrissake?"

And he talked on. About reasonable doubt and circumstantial evidence and about a man's life being at stake here. They shouted, especially the three men at the end of the table. They shouted and slumped back in their chairs and slapped the table in their anger. "Damn it, who do you think done it? . . . All them janitors agree. . . . You only thinking about Brandley. What about that poor little girl?"

Then he heard them. Not shouting. Just leaning back and muttering at each other: "Nigger lover. He's nothin' but a nigger lover. Peterhead. What kind of peterhead is he? He's a nigger lover."

Srack fell silent, a deep despair sinking over him.

The teacher spoke up, suggesting that they write a note to the judge to explain that since noon eleven of them had been agreed on a guilty verdict but that one juror was holding out and would not change his mind. Maybe the judge would say they were a hung jury. But the note came back from the judge's office. "Continue deliberating," he had written.

Now everybody was angry. How long were they going to be stuck in here? A woman said she wanted to do her Christmas shopping. A man said he had left his dog locked in the house and he was worried about it. Someone else had a Christmas party to go to.

Srack said: "Listen. You all can't be worried about parties and dogs. Our commitment is here. There's a man here in life-and-death circumstances. I'm not going to change my mind just to get out of here."

The shouting started again. "What are you? Some kind of professional juror? . . . Brandley done it. He's guilty. . . . How long we got to stay in here? . . . What about that poor little girl? . . . Change your damned vote and get us out of here. . . . Nigger lover. . . . Nothin' but a nigger lover."

Srack gave up talking. He was never going to persuade these people. He himself did not even believe Brandley was innocent. He just did not think he had the right to convict a man on such weak evidence. And that was the beginning and the end of it. It was a matter of plain and simple logic. His duty was to vote not guilty, and no amount of name-calling was going to change his mind.

The jurors stopped while the teacher wrote the judge another note. The same reply came back.

* * *

Outside in the courtroom the defense attorneys were on the edge of a precipice. The tension had been getting steadily worse since the jury retired.

First, Jerry Winfree complained that he had been threatened by a member of the Brandley family. It turned out that Brandley's brother Tim, who considered the whole prosecution dishonest and twisted, had seen Winfree in the corridor and told him, "You need more churching."

Since Winfree liked to think of himself as a Christian—defense attorneys used to say he belonged to "the radical Shi'ite wing of the Protestant Church"—he had taken offense and run to the judge. Morris and Brown had little sympathy for him. In their eyes, he was the kind of white Bible-thumper who thought all black men were naturally criminal.

Then Judge Robertson had done his bit. He had called the attorneys from both sides into his chambers and told them that as far as he was concerned, it did not matter what the jury decided. He had made up his mind that Clarence Brandley had breached the terms of his probation by murdering Cheryl Fergeson. The jury had to come to a decision "beyond reasonable doubt," but all the judge had to do to take away Brandley's probation was to find it was "more likely than not" that he had killed the girl. Even if the jury decided that he was not guilty, Brandley was going to have to serve his three-year sentence for possession of a shotgun.

Morris and Brown were hardly surprised. They had been telling each other all through the trial that the judge was on the side of the opposition. So now he was admitting it. Still, it rankled.

In the corridor outside the court Don Brown broke the news to Minnie Ola Brandley and her family. Brown started to fume about the judge and his rulings. The judge was not even obeying the law, he said.

"But if it ain't the law, why's he doing it?" asked Mrs. Brandley.

"Because," said Brown, his voice quaking with anger, "the judge is a mean and spiteful person."

Brown kept on talking and then went back into court. He never saw the reporter from the *Houston Post* lurking nearby and noting down his every word for the next day's paper.

Amid all the tension, the defense heard that the jury had sent out notes. They saw Jim Keeshan going into the judge's chambers, but they themselves were not allowed in. Ray Reeves cussed loudly that they had no damned right to be discussing notes from the jury without defense counsel's being present—especially if what they had heard was true: that the jury was split eleven to one. If that was one juror voting for the defense, they wanted a chance to call off the deliberation before he got so bullied or so exhausted that he changed his vote. But Jim Keeshan only smiled and said they were not discussing the case at all.

Across the road in the Iron Horse the betting was all one way among the reporters gathered there. If it was split eleven to one, it must be in favor of not guilty. Just for once, they reckoned, Jim Keeshan had missed his mark. The truth was he hadn't put on much of a case. Poor old Keeshan. The reporters started drafting stories about the acquittal of Clarence Brandley.

It was late afternoon now. Srack got up from the table in the jury room and went and sat by himself in a little coffee room off to one side. Behind him he could hear them talking, complaining about being stuck in there, muttering about him, using that same word.

After a while Srack went back in and told the teacher that nothing had changed and that since he did not imagine the other eleven were about to change their minds, they should draft a third note, making it as plain and simple as possible. Srack helped him write it. "Judge, one person on this jury has stated in his mind there was no evidence that suggests the defendant is guilty beyond a reasonable doubt. He will not change his position regardless of our deliberations." The same reply came back.

Finally, at ten-thirty, after nearly eleven hours in their room, the jurors were told that they could leave—but not to go home. They were to be sequestered for the night, taken off to the Holiday Inn, just south of Conroe, sealed off from contact with outsiders, and then returned to their room the next day to continue their deliberations. The other jurors were angry.

By the time they got to the Holiday Inn in their court bus, the other jurors had begun to unwind. Joe and his friends were talking about beer again, though nobody was talking to Srack.

The court ushers shepherded them out of the hotel to the Feed Store restaurant—"Chicken Fried Steak a Specialty."

There they helped themselves to steak and french fries and ice cream and plenty to drink, and all sat down together and jabbered and talked, all except Bill Srack, who could not bring himself to try to cross the great gulf that had opened between himself and these eleven other people.

He took a baked potato and shuffled off to the other side of the restaurant, where he sat in solitude and longed for another day.

Judge Sam Robertson, Jr., had no reason to be happy. In the *Houston Post* one of the defense attorneys was calling him "mean and spiteful," and in the case of the *State of Texas* v. *Clarence Lee Brandley* the jury had run into the sands.

On Saturday morning the judge received a fourth note from the jury, pleading to be released. Finally, he agreed that there was no alternative: this lone juror was not going to change his mind, and this trial had failed to come to a verdict.

In the jury room it had been a desultory morning. The jurors had been locked in there since seven-fifty. No one was even pretending to be discussing the case. No one was even angry anymore. Srack had kept a discreet distance, sitting in the little coffee room, looking out the window, and waiting for this to be over. The others had sat around their table, talking about one thing and another, often not talking at all.

Occasionally, someone—usually the teacher—would try to get them back to the case. But it was never too long before someone—usually one of the three men at the end of the table—said this was a waste of time because they had been through this before and that son of a bitch in there was never going to agree to anything.

Midway through this idle morning one of the men jurors came back into the little coffee room and pulled a chair up to Srack's side. For a moment he said nothing, just stroked his forehead with one hand. Then in a quiet voice, which shook a little, he said: "I'm thinking I might change my vote, might vote not guilty."

Srack looked into his face and saw tears in his eyes.

"Don't do that," he said. "It won't make no difference. They're never going to change their minds. It's OK for me. I work down in Houston, but you got to go back into this town and earn a living. If word gets around that you held out on this jury, you'll be finished. So don't do that."

The juror shook his head and sighed and shuffled back to the jury room.

And that was the truth, thought Srack. A few of these jurors might be nothing more than rednecks and might have that redneck way of thinking about a man like Brandley. But that wasn't the whole story about this jury.

These were small-town people, decent enough people who did not want to be racists or rednecks, who only wanted to get on with their lives without trouble, and they had to go back and live in this small-town community and tell their decent, ordinary neighbors how they voted. How could they go back there and tell them they let this black man go loose among them all again? Who was ever going to forgive them if they did that? If they let this horrible crime go unpunished?

It was not the same for him. He was not a Conroe man. If he was really part of this small town, maybe he would feel the same way. But he was not. So he could understand why they must just want to look away. He could even forgive them for it. In a way they were only bystanders. But he did not have to join them.

Finally, around eleven o'clock, the defense attorneys were told that the jury was being brought back so that the judge could declare a mistrial. It was a victory of sorts, but it was not what they had wanted.

When they learned that eleven jurors had been voting guilty, they felt the hollowness of it all. Don Brown, in particular, felt frustrated that the jury had been even tempted to convict on this evidence. Yet it was better than defeat.

Judge Robertson swept into court, eyed the jurors, fired a few questions at the foreman to confirm that they were completely deadlocked, and discharged them.

Then without pausing he turned to Clarence Brandley. "Stand up, Mr. Brandley. I find you have violated the terms of your probation by committing the offense of capital murder on August 23, 1980. Your probation is hereby revoked. Do you have anything to say why sentencing should not be pronounced against you?"

Brandley looked toward his attorneys. The three of them were shaking their heads and muttering "son of a bitch" to one another. That judge had let Clarence Brandley stay an innocent man for approximately ten seconds. Don Brown looked toward Brandley and lifted his eyebrows in a gesture of helplessness. "A mean and spiteful person," he thought.

Once again Brandley had the feeling he was watching some strange ritual that was only remotely connected with him. He looked back to the judge. "No, Your Honor," he said.

The judge was saying something. "You having nothing said for thereof, it's the order of this court that you, Clarence Lee Brandley, who's been convicted of the offense of possession of a short-barrel firearm and whose punishment has been assessed to be confined to the Texas Department of Corrections for a period of three years, you are to be delivered by the Sheriff of Montgomery County, Texas to the Director of the Texas Department of Corrections who will confine you in the Texas Department of Corrections for not less than two years nor more than three years in accordance with the laws governing the operation of the Texas Department of Corrections and you're now remanded to obey the direction of this sentence."

Brandley guessed he was being jailed.

Don Brown stumbled to his feet again and asked for bail while they lodged an appeal and waited for a retrial of the murder charge.

The judge eyed Brandley again. "Believing that you are likely to commit another offense while you are on bond, if you were allowed one pending appeal—hereby denied."

Then, in case anyone had missed the point he was trying to make, he added: "I am entering the following order denying bail pending retrial of the capital murder case, in that I find proof is evident in that a dispassionate jury would not only find you guilty of capital murder but would assess his punishment at death."

He paused. Don Brown had never heard a more brazen declaration of prejudice.

"The court is adjourned."

The judge brought his gavel down once, hard, with a noise like a trapdoor dropping.

Srack was dazed. He barely understood what the judge had said. The judge's verbal dart about what a dispassionate jury would have done had flown over his head. All he wanted to do was to get home and see his wife and talk to civilized people.

He walked from the jury box and started pushing his way through the milling crowd outside the court. As he left, he heard one of the redneck men being interviewed by reporters.

"I think I can pretty well sum things up," he crowed. "There has been an injustice done."

Obediently, the reporters wrote it down. "Who was it who held out?" they asked. "Which juror?"

"There he goes," Srack heard a voice reply. "There's the little son of a bitch."

The stricken town took the news badly.

At the high school the administrators said they did not care what the jury said: they did not want that black janitor back. Brandley would never be hired for any job where he would be anywhere near schoolchildren, they said. "We would go to court to keep from rehiring him if possible."

The *Courier* printed every word.

The jurors tried to explain that they had done their best. The evidence of the other janitors was most incriminating, they said.

All Conroe read about it in the papers.

Jim Keeshan tried to reassure the town: he would bring this man to trial again. He would do more work, find more clues. He had some ideas he was working on.

Chapter Five

Justice was not a total stranger to the Montgomery County Courthouse. Morris and Brown recognized that the judges and prosecutors who had worked there over the years did not think of themselves as being racist or corrupt. For the most part, they took a real pride in their profession, and day by day they were happy to administer justice with the appearance of reason and fairness, but under pressure—particularly under pressure from the voters—many of those who had been proud to uphold the law glibly brushed it aside. In those moments it was like watching a spoiled child who cannot bear to lose a game, who suddenly complains that all the rules are unfair and that he is the winner, no matter what anyone else says, and just like an angry child the courthouse then defended itself with such openhearted dishonesty that those who watched could only shake their heads and wonder.

The history of the courthouse was riddled with allegations of bribes, vote-buying, ballot-stealing, illegal campaign contributions, and political favoritism. Most of the allegations were never resolved. There was a notorious incident in the 1920s when Conroe's richest citizens complained bitterly about the new, higher taxes they were being asked to pay only to find themselves saved when all the papers detailing their dues simply vanished from the courthouse. Officials explained that they had been blown away by a gust of wind that had left behind only the papers of less wealthy townspeople.

As Morris and Brown prepared to return to the courthouse to save Clarence Brandley's life, they could not help being

worried. This struggle was becoming an eerie repeat of a
notorious case in Conroe's past when pressure on the courthouse people to nail a "bad nigger" had seen the law torn
up and thrown away. It concerned another black man who,
in the summer of 1941, found himself sitting alone in the
same courthouse in the middle of Conroe while angry white
people debated his fate. His name was Bob White, and he, too,
was accused of assaulting a white woman. There were those in
Conroe who remembered his fate, which was recorded in all
its bloody detail in bundles of official papers, and now they
worried about seeing a repeat.

Bob White's family lived and worked in the cotton fields
near Livingston, fifty miles northeast of Conroe. The land
they worked belonged to a wealthy white man named Dude
Cochran, who lived with his wife Ruby and their two boys in
a big house across the fields from the black people's shacks.
Bob White's life began to unravel one hot and humid night
in August 1937.

Dude Cochran was away in Houston. Ruby was in bed
upstairs in the big house while the boys, Joe and Laddie, slept
out on the porch, where the sticky air was just a little cooler.
Ruby had been asleep for an hour or so when she suddenly
snapped awake. She lay still as death. She could have sworn
she heard something, something quite close. She slid her hand
up onto the bedside table and slipped her fingers around the
pistol there.

"Joe, is that you?" she said, and the words were hardly
out of her mouth before she was fighting for her life, the
hard, heavy weight of some foul-smelling man on top of her,
grabbing her hands, knocking the pistol to the floor, swearing,
"Goddamn you, goddamn you," in her face, and then slicing
her fingers with his blade and telling her he'd cut her throat if
she didn't quit struggling. She was afraid to fight, afraid that
if he killed her, he might go down and kill her boys, too. So
she threatened him with something that should have put fear
in her heart.

"Don't you know what them Cochrans will do to you?" she
said, but the gruff voice told her he didn't give a goddamn
what they did to him.

Later, after the intruder had finished with her and slipped
back into the night, Ruby Cochran staggered to her nearest white neighbor to raise the alarm. They called her

brother-in-law Ernest and the sheriff, and when they came, she sobbed out her story to them. Who was it, they asked, who had done this thing to her? She did not know; all she could tell them for sure was it was a nigger.

By the time day broke the next morning, a terrible turbulence had swept across the cotton fields. White families heard of the outrage and cursed the nigger who had done this thing; black families felt a cloud of anxiety sweep over their homes. At the big house Sheriff Roscoe Holliday had found some bare footprints running away down the dirt road and put a bucket over them to preserve them. He had called in the bloodhounds from the Huntsville Jail, and their yelping and howling blew across the plantation like an ill wind. There was a fingerprint man scattering white powder over the scene. There were the Texas Rangers, big white men with leather boots and pearl-handled pistols at their hips, striding around the house, looking out across the cotton fields at the black men.

At the eye of the storm were Dude Cochran and his two brothers, Ernest and Carey, three angry men who knew one thing: the nigger who had done this was going to pay. They set out in their cars to round up as many blacks as they could find in the shacks and the fields, and within a couple of hours they had sixteen of them herded into the yard at Ernest Cochran's house. The law might have said the three Cochran brothers had no right or authority to arrest sixteen black men without a warrant, but no one raised a word against them.

Bob White had left his girlfriend in Houston a few weeks earlier to come up and pick the cotton and stay with his mother, Martha, in her shinny shack a couple of miles down the dirt road from where Dude and Ruby Cochran lived. He knew the Cochrans. He had lived on their land for most of his twenty-seven years.

Bob White was in the fields picking cotton about nine that morning, when Ernest Cochran drove up alongside the sagging wire fence and told him to climb on the car's fender and come with him. He did as he was told and rode back to Ernest Cochran's house, to the yard full of black men.

Bob White's family heard no more than rumors for the rest of that week. All the men had been taken up to the county jail in Livingston. The Texas Rangers were questioning them. There were stories—fearful things that people said were going on in the jailhouse—but no one really knew. It was nine days

before the news came through: Ruby Cochran had listened to
the voices of all the men in the county jail, she had picked out
Bob White, and now he had confessed; he was guilty, and he
was going to be tried and put to death just as soon as it could
be done.

The trial was a sensational event when it opened before
Judge W. B. Browder in Livingston a few weeks later. The
courtroom was crowded. The three Cochran men were there,
stern and subdued. White friends came from all over the county
to see justice done and to stare at the black "animal" who sat
alone in chains at the front of the court. It took less than two
days for the business to be done and for the Livingston jury
of twelve white men to declare that Bob White was guilty and
should be sentenced to death.

The county was ready for him to be hanged as soon as
possible, but Bob White's attorney, J. P. Rogers, who came
from Houston, lodged an appeal. Rogers said the trial had
been unfair from start to finish because of the prejudice in the
courtroom; he said the trial should never have been held in
Livingston, where feelings against the black man were running
so high. A deep fury spilled over white families in the town
when, seven months later, on April 16, 1938, the Texas Court
of Criminal Appeals overturned the verdict and ordered a new
trial in a different venue. J. P. Rogers went back to court in
Livingston, and Judge Browder agreed to move the case. So
Bob White was sent to face his accusers a second time, in
Conroe.

There, on August 2, 1938, a special prosecutor, Zimmie
Foreman, hired by Dude Cochran, paraded his witnesses again.
There was Sol Bergman, the town doctor who had examined
the hysterical victim. "The sperm was plenty active," he said.
"I could tell that it was from some male person." He said he
had not kept any sample of it.

There was Sheriff Holliday, who assured the court that Bob
White had made his confession freely and without duress. "The
nigger was never mistreated in any way," he said.

There were the Cochran brothers grimly recalling the
events of that night and Ruby Cochran tearfully describing
her ordeal.

Then the defense mounted its case and soon ran into trouble: many of its black witnesses refused to testify or claimed
they could remember nothing; J. P. Rogers asked them in
open court if he had not seen them being spoken to in the

hallway by Texas Rangers, but the witnesses said they did not remember that.

Finally, Bob White took the stand and told his story. On the first day, after Ernest Cochran had rounded him up, he was taken to the Livingston jail, and there, he said, sometime after nightfall, some rangers came and led him from his cell, put him in their vehicle, and drove him up into the woods somewhere. They handcuffed him to a tree with his face against the bark, and then they whipped his back with something that he thought was a rubber hose, something that laid deep stripes in his flesh. They whipped him until his shirt was torn into shreds by the blows, he said, so that when they finally took him back to the jailhouse, the sheriff's son had had to give him one of his own shirts to cover him.

Bob White said the rangers had done the same thing for the next three or four nights. Once they made him drop his pants before they tied him to a tree and whipped him. Each time they beat him, they told him that sooner or later he was going to confess, and before they dumped him back in his cell, they always told him not to tell anyone what they were doing to him. Then, around midnight on the eighth day, the sheriff drove him all alone down to the jailhouse in Beaumont. The rangers who had been beating him were there, with the special prosecutor, Zimmie Foreman, and a man who was then the county attorney, Ernest Coker.

All night long, Bob White said, they kept him there, crying on the floor, and every so often the rangers gave him a kicking. At the end of it, Ernest Coker had typed out a complete confession. Bob White said he didn't really know what was in it. He could not read or write. He did not even know whether he had made a cross on it for a signature. He said he didn't know what was happening, although he was sure he had never had an attorney there and no one had told him anything about having any rights. He lifted his shirt to show the court his scars.

Ernest Coker came along to the trial in Conroe and said he had seen no sign of injury on Bob White, and he said he had certainly told White his rights, and he was sure that every word in the confession had come freely and voluntarily from White's own mouth, and all he had done was type it out "exactly as he related it to me." Bob White said that there were words in that confession he had never even heard of and that it was just plain wrong. Even the size of his shoes mentioned in there was wrong. Zimmie Foreman took the stand himself and swore that "nobody did anything to him except to treat him just as nice as they could."

Then J. P. Rogers ordered the rangers and other law officers to stand up at the back of the court, and Bob White pointed to two of the rangers, named Williamson and Davenport, and to a Polk County deputy, Coleman Weeks. They were the ones who had beaten him in the woods, he said.

The sheriff said it was all lies. No one had taken the nigger out of his jail. Ranger Davenport said he didn't think it had happened, but it was hard to say. Then Ranger Williamson came on the stand and admitted they had taken him out so many times that he had lost count, but it had nothing to do with whipping him.

"We took him out of jail to talk to him," he said. "The jail was crowded. There was lots of them in there and we took them out where we would be by ourselves, to talk to him." Coleman Weeks agreed with that.

But Zimmie Foreman was not tolerating any of this. When Rogers asked Bob White if he had recently been injured and White replied "Yes, sir," Foreman jumped to his feet and said it was prejudicial, so Judge Browder agreed to strike it from the record. When White was first asked to identify the men who whipped him, Foreman interrupted. "It could have been John D. Rockefeller," he joked. When he made his final speech, Zimmie Foreman looked straight at the jury and told them that Bob White's attorneys didn't care what had happened to Mrs. Cochran. "As far as they are concerned, their innocent negro should be turned loose," he said.

After three days of evidence the Conroe jury of twelve white men declared that Bob White was guilty, and he was again sentenced to death.

J. P. Rogers launched a volley of appeals. He said that White was the victim of race discrimination and that black people had been excluded from the grand jury and from both trial juries that had dealt with the case. "It has been, was and still is the custom in Montgomery County, Texas to use white men exclusively for jurors to serve in any and all cases," he said in his legal submission. The DA and his officials in Conroe said it was just chance that all the jurors had been white. The judge said it was too late in the proceedings, anyway, to be raising such issues.

Rogers said the confession was involuntary because White had been repeatedly chained to a tree and beaten before giving it and because it had been taken by Foreman and Coker—"both men who were highly prejudiced against the defendant and seeking his conviction." The judge in Conroe said they had been into all this at the trial. Rogers went to the Court of Criminal Appeals, but in March 1939 it turned him down and said there was no evidence of race discrimination and no reason to be disturbed by the court's use of Bob White's confession. So Rogers went all the way to Washington, D.C., to the Supreme Court of the United States.

On March 25, 1940, the Supreme Court reached out to save Bob White. After reviewing all the details of White's eight days in jail and of his confession to Zimmie Foreman and Ernest Coker, the Court concluded: "Due process of law, preserved for all by our Constitution, commands that no such practice as that disclosed by this record shall send any accused to his death."

The Supreme Court ordered a new trial. Back in Livingston the Cochrans were furious. Dude Cochran paid out of his own pocket to send Zimmie Foreman and the Montgomery County DA, W.C. "Cleo" McClain, up to Washington to demand a rehearing, but the Supreme Court stood by its decision. In Conroe Bob White prepared to face his third trial.

The Conroe courtroom was packed with spectators as the notorious case began again on June 11, 1941, with the exhausting process of selecting a jury. Bob White sat in chains at the front of the court with his attorneys. Behind him on the public benches sat the three Cochran brothers side by side. All morning the attorneys questioned jurymen, and by twelve-twenty they had exhausted their supply and had chosen only nine jurors. The court bailiff was just leading the last chosen juror out of the room, the attorneys were just stretching their legs at the front of the court, Judge Browder was shuffling his papers and chewing his wad of tobacco, and Bob White was slumped silently in his chair as usual when Dude Cochran rose quietly to his feet and started to walk forward.

No one even noticed the stony-faced white farmer as he pressed through the little wooden gate in front of the public benches and stepped up to the defense table, up behind Bob White, up behind his black head, and still no one noticed as he drew a .38-caliber pistol from his pocket and shot Bob White dead. The bullet crashed into White's brain from just behind his right ear. He slumped over sideways, spilling blood on the courtroom floor, and he was dead before his body fell out of the chair.

"Don't you know what them Cochrans will do to you?"

For a moment the courtroom was frozen in fear and shock. Then Dude Cochran handed over his pistol to Zimmie Foreman and stood still and cold while spectators surged forward from the benches, leaning forward over the railing to slap him on the back, reaching out to shake his hand, calling out their congratulations. Black spectators who had been sitting at the back of the courtroom vanished quickly. Sheriff Grover Mostyn came running to the court and took Dude Cochran into custody. Outside there was jubilation. "General satisfaction over the killing of Bob White was apparent in the business district of Conroe which is practically all within one block of the court house," the *Courier* recorded.

The jubilation was renewed a few hours later when the white farmer was released from custody on a nominal bond of five hundred dollars.

A week later Dude Cochran was back in the Conroe courthouse, but this time he was the defendant, charged with the murder of Bob White. The trial took less than two hours. Montgomery County DA Cleo McClain led the prosecution by taking the unusual step of urging the members of the jury to find the defendant not guilty. McClain told them that he fully understood Dude Cochran's actions. "It is unfortunate that Mr. Cochran was forced to do that which was done," he told them. "It was his wish that the law handle the matter. In my opinion the guilty party got justice, but it was unfortunate that it had to be at Mr. Cochran's hands."

The district attorney, aided by Zimmie Foreman, read the jury a history of the case that included the full text of Bob White's confession and omitted any reference to his account of the beatings he had received. McClain took the jury of twelve white men to the heart of the matter: "The time has not come in this state when any man, black or white, can assault a white woman and go free by reason of legal technicalities."

The district attorney left no doubt about the course of action he was recommending to the jury: "If I were going into that jury room, I wouldn't hesitate, I wouldn't stand back a minute in writing a verdict of Not Guilty. When you have done that, I say justice will have been done in this case. I ask you to return a verdict finding Mr. Cochran Not Guilty."

Dude Cochran's attorneys thanked the district attorney for his kind remarks, and the jurors retired. It took them less than a minute to make up their minds, and they returned to declare Dude Cochran innocent. The *Houston Post* reported the next day: "The jury's report set off an impromptu celebration in the crowded courtroom, filled largely with friends and neighbors of the Cochran family. Applause had begun when District Attorney McClain finished his argument. Cochran, a slight sun-browned man wearing a tan business suit and high-heeled cowboy boots, was unable to leave the courtroom for nearly 15 minutes after his acquittal. Spectators formed in lines to pass behind the rail and shake hands with him, some still cheering and whistling."

The rejoicing spilled out into the street, and Dude Cochran emerged into the courthouse square to be greeted as a hero. Bob White's body was taken to a funeral home, where it lay unclaimed by his fearful family.

It was Christmas in Conroe. In the drugstore on the courthouse square sprigs of plastic holly appeared in the window and Christmas carols played on the hi-fi system. On the outskirts of town there were Santas in the shopping malls and business was brisk. Clarence Brandley sat in his cell in the county jail. It would be more than a month before he was put on trial again, he had been told, and now that he had finally lost his probation, there was no chance of joining his family for Christmas.

In the office over the menswear shop Morris and Brown talked tactics and returned always to the same point. It did not matter how good their evidence was, how weak the prosecution was, or how hard they tried to overcome the bias of the jury. They were never going to get a fair shot in this trial while Judge Sam Robertson, Jr., was presiding. Robertson had to go.

Even in the quiet days since the trial, he had been giving them a hard time. Morris and Brown had noticed a technical foul-up that had been made in the rush to revoke Brandley's probation at the end of the trial. Keeshan had failed to prove that the Clarence Lee Brandley in the courtroom was the same Clarence Lee Brandley who had been given a probated sentence for possessing a prohibited weapon. It was only a technical point, but Morris and Brown had filed an appeal based on it. And they thought the appeals court might run with it.

But then Keeshan had realized his mistake and had gone to the judge to ask if he could have a new hearing so that he could straighten out the record. Morris and Brown said that should not be allowed because the state had rested its case, sentence had been passed, and they had already filed their appeal. But Judge Robertson had let Keeshan do it.

Then, at the hearing, George Morris had complained bitterly that the state could not go reopening its case and presenting new evidence after sentence had been passed. It was just not proper. And the judge had said the strangest thing: "I doubt seriously, legally, that I have the authority to permit them to re-open, but law is never made unless there is a ruling made contrary to someone, and I will permit them to put the evidence on."

So without even pretending that he had the law on his side, Judge Robertson had given Keeshan his way, and the technical point of their appeal had been destroyed.

At the same hearing Robertson had also announced that he would be presiding over the retrial and ordered it to begin on January 19, 1981. Don Brown said he was more damned sure than ever that Robertson had to go. And he had noticed something that might just help.

By sheer good luck—the first piece of good luck Brown could think of in this case—the state of Texas, in its wisdom, had decided that on January 1, 1981, it would overhaul certain administrative rules affecting the running of its courts, including the right to recuse judges. Brown studied the new rules and found that they made it easier to remove a prejudiced judge from a case. Last time Robertson had beaten them off, but now he might not find it so simple. Brown found Morris in his office looking over the courthouse square. "George," he said, "let's take another shot at recusing Robertson."

"Don, I don't mind if we do."

As Christmas Day approached, Morris and Brown began to wonder whether their luck might not be changing permanently. Their relationship with Ray Reeves had broken down completely. They had told him what they thought of him, and he had given them several paragraphs of Technicolor abuse in reply. Then Morris and Brown had gone to the Brandley family and told them that they would agree to handle the retrial if they were paid a fee and, if it was all the same to them, that they did not intend to share any fee with Ray Reeves. The family agreed, and Reeves was out of the case. Then, as if that were not enough of a Christmas bonus, Sheriff Gene Reaves retired. The *Courier* ran a glowing profile of his twenty years of service. The paper quoted his view that "Some times you kind of think the laws were written for the criminal." It put his picture on the front page. "Into the sunset," the caption said. But good-bye was good riddance, as far as Morris and Brown were concerned. And there was still a little more good luck in the wind.

During Christmas week Morris and Brown held their annual Christmas party. They draped decorations all around their offices, stocked the tables with plenty to drink, called a temporary truce with everyone in the courthouse, and invited all the judges and attorneys and court reporters and even Jim Keeshan to come on over.

The party was swinging. Everybody was having a good time, drinking and yelling and smoking too much. Morris and Brown found themselves jammed into a corner with a group of lawyers, including John Martin, one of Morris's closest friends, a handsome, clean-cut defense attorney who had just been elected to become a district judge in Conroe. Morris and Brown had worked for John Martin's election. They liked the man, and simply out of friendship they had wanted him to do well. But they could also see it would do them no harm to have a friend on the bench in the courthouse. They had put money into his campaign, distributed leaflets, advised him, got sunburned standing outside polling stations, and baby-sat him through election night to daybreak when the last box of votes had come in and given him the most narrow of victories.

Now, amid all the backslapping of the Christmas party, John Martin quieted the conversation for a moment and told the group of lawyers in the corner that he had heard an interesting rumor: Sam Robertson might not hear the retrial of the Brandley case. What was more, said Martin, he had heard that he himself would be in line to get the case. He turned to Morris and Brown.

"I know y'all got a screwing from Robertson. I want y'all to know that if I'm assigned to hear that case, you will receive a fair trial."

Morris and Brown beamed through the smoke and chorused almost as one: "John, that's all we ever wanted."

As soon as the new rules came into effect on January 1, Morris and Brown polished up their motion to recuse Judge Robertson. They read it over, and they liked it. The charge of bias and prejudice ran through the motion like the chorus of a Christmas carol. Before the trial, they complained, Judge Robertson had upheld the illegal seventy-five-thousand-dollar bail bond and overturned the court's promise that Brandley should be released on one thousand dollars' bail if the state ever repeated its attempt to revoke his probation. Judge Robertson had interfered in the selection of jurors, tried to do the DA's job for him, and had then done the same all through the trial, making the DA's objections for him, and capped that by refusing to let the defense present any of its evidence about Icky Peace. The judge had held private meetings with the DA, refused to let the defense take part, concealed the contents of the jury's notes from the defense, and then, when the trial was over, had allowed the DA to reopen the case to offer new evidence. "He has a personal bias or prejudice against the defendant in this proceeding," they concluded. It was strong stuff. They liked it.

Their only problem was that they would have to file the motion at the courthouse, where some Conroe judge would wind up ruling on it—just like the last time, when Judge Lynn Coker had stopped them from recusing Robertson before the trial. They mulled it over and decided it was only fair to let Robertson himself decide what to do. That way they might just be able to persuade him to go gracefully.

On the first Monday of the new year, January 5, Morris and Brown went into their office, took a phone each, and dialed Sam Robertson in Houston.

"We want to know what your intention is about trying the case again," said Morris.

"Well, I've told you I intend to try that case."

They told him about the new rules of recusal, which made it easier for them to get to him, and about their motion, and they read him some of the strongest passages, and then they asked him if he thought they should file their motion.

"I told you I intend to try that case," said the judge.

"Well, that's just fine," said Morris. "We'll go ahead and file this motion."

It looked as though he were going to fight them again.

Two days later Don Brown was reading his newspaper.

"Goddamn," he said out loud. "The son of a bitch stood down."

Judge Sam Robertson, Jr., had announced that he had too many trials competing for his attention and had decided that he would not be able to try the Brandley case.

The next day it was announced that the newly elected Judge John Martin would take over.

The ritual began again.

Brandley sat in the same blue suit, his hands clasped in his lap, and looked around the courtroom. The faces danced before his eyes: the jurors, the attorneys, the clerk with the strawberry-colored fingernails, the jailhouse deputies, the judge, all moving together through the same routine. Some of the faces were different this time, but still they were all the same color.

He had already been sitting there for ten days. While the rest of the world had been watching the new president, Ronald Reagan, being inaugurated in Washington, D.C., he had been staring at the bright white walls and listening to the fans slapping the air overhead.

After ten days there was still not one word of evidence. The attorneys had been scrapping all that time, mostly about who was going to sit on the jury. Brandley could not see where it made too much difference. This time around, there had been four black people called for jury service, and they had sat in court while the jury was selected; but all four of them had been rejected for one reason or another at the request of the district attorney.

Now finally, on Thursday morning, January 29, they were going to start hearing some evidence. Spectators, mostly white, the curious and the concerned, had crowded onto the benches. Some of the men stared at Brandley while they chewed gum. He was glad to see some friendly faces down there, not just his family but people from Houston who had come to show their faith in him. Right in the front row there were two black men bravely displaying badges that announced their support for the National Association for the Advancement of Colored People.

He was glad, too, that they had got rid of that last judge. He had been even worse than the first one. Now his attorneys had told him for sure that this new judge, John Martin, was going to be OK. They knew him. They said he would give them a fair shot, which was all that they needed. That is what the attorneys said. Then Brandley heard the judge speak up: he ordered the two black men to remove their NAACP badges and banned anyone from wearing any more badges anytime during this trial.

Brandley guessed he must have had some good reason for doing that.

Morris and Brown, hunched over a table full of trial papers, were feeling confident. They had a fair-looking jury, and they had managed to get rid of some jurors who admitted to racism and prejudice, though they had had to fight for every inch of ground and they had lost all the blacks along the way. And there was John Martin, their friend, whose election they had fought for, sitting up there on the bench. They had high hopes that he would give them a fair shot, although the truth was that he had already done some worrying things. In some of the pretrial hearings he had been short with them and had ruled against them when he did not need to. Morris and Brown told themselves that he was just trying to prove that he was not in their pocket, that he was independent. That was fine.

Then, during one of the pretrial hearings in chambers, he had gone a little further. Don Brown had been arguing some legal point, bulldozing away at Jim Keeshan, and the new judge had suddenly snapped at him in the meanest of voices, "Brown, shut your damned mouth so Jim Keeshan can talk."

Brown had been so shocked he had walked straight out of the room. It was bad enough to hear any judge address an attorney like that, but worse when the judge was supposed to be a friend. Outside, Brown had recovered himself and gone back in and continued the hearing. Then, when it was over and they had lost the argument, he had turned to George Morris as they left the room and asked him: "What kind of monster have we created?"

They just hoped he would remember his decency and all the times that he had been screwed by Keeshan when he was a defense attorney.

Keeshan sat calmly across the other side of the court from Morris and Brown, dapper as ever in his sharp suit, chuckling with Jerry Winfree and waiting to call his first witness. The defense attorneys knew he had been working hard since the first trial and probably had a few surprises of his own planned so he could win himself a famous victory and salvage his reputation.

The evidence began. To Brandley, it was like sitting on a train watching familiar scenes flash by the window. Questions. Evidence. Cross questions. Objections. More evidence. More questions. The volleyball coaches. The shy young schoolgirls. The times that they did things. The things that they saw. The day of the crime. The day his life got lost. By the evening Brandley had had enough. He was almost happy to see his cell again. The next day, Friday, was a rest day. Brandley stayed in his cell. The attorneys took it easy and worked on their papers.

Saturday the phone rang in George Morris's home. Morris heard the creaking East Texas cadence of a man who said he was John Payne from Houston and he wanted to talk to him about this here Brandley case. He wanted to tell him something about his family and about his brother, Ed.

Morris waited for him to get to the point. This Ed lived out in Grangerland, ten miles southeast of Conroe, and he had a daughter. She was called Cynthia, though she was known as Cindy, and she lived right next to old Ed in a trailer with her husband, and Cindy's husband was a young feller named Gary Acreman.

Morris started to listen. John Payne explained that he and his wife, Marie, had been talking to Ed about this here Brandley case and about Ed's son-in-law, Gary Acreman. And Ed had told them something. According to Ed Payne, Gary Acreman had come home on the day of the crime, very nervous and pacing up and down, saying that a girl had been killed up at the high school.

Morris was now riveted. This was not the story that had been told in court. According to it, Acreman had left school without knowing that a girl was even missing, let alone that she had been killed. He had told the police that the first he knew of the killing was when he read about it in the paper the next day. How could Acreman have known about it on Saturday? John Payne had some of the answer.

According to Ed Payne, Acreman had been real worried because he knew where the dead girl's clothes were. He had told Ed that they were in a Dumpster behind the school. Ed had not known what to make of that, but when it came out a few days later that the police had just found the girl's clothes right where Acreman said they were, his father-in-law got real worried, too.

Morris, hardly daring to breathe, nudged John Payne on into the rest of his story. The way Ed Payne had told it, Acreman had wanted to go back to the school that Saturday afternoon to find the clothes. He never exactly said why he wanted to do that, and he never said how he knew those clothes were in the Dumpster. But Ed Payne could think of only two explanations: either his son-in-law had seen the killer dumping the clothes and he was wanting to cover for him, or he himself was the killer. Whichever it was, Ed Payne was frightened.

Morris saw that this was dynamite. If it was true, it would turn the whole case around. If Acreman really knew the truth about this killing and was covering it up, that was dynamite. Morris took some more details from John Payne, arranged to stay in touch, thanked him, and called Don Brown. The two of them spent the rest of the evening talking like kids at Christmas. They could not believe what they had got here. Goddamn, if they could just get this into court. They had to get to this Ed Payne, get an affidavit from him, get him to come to court and say all this to the jury. Goddamn, it was dynamite. But how would they get to Payne? He seemed to be living more or less on top of Gary Acreman, whose trailer was in his yard. If they went up there, there was no way of knowing whether Acreman would be around or not. If Acreman saw them or if he saw his father-in-law talking to them, that would be the end of it. Acreman would shut the old boy up, might even kill him. They needed to talk to John Payne again, but it was late now. Morris and Brown arranged to meet the next morning, Sunday, in their office.

There they called John Payne, who got his wife Marie on the extension, and they talked it all through again. The story was still the same. The way the Paynes saw it, Ed Payne was crying out for help. He had a bad conscience about sitting on the story, and he wanted something to be done. It was just a question of getting to him without alerting Acreman. Morris and Brown thanked them and talked together some more. Finally, they hatched a plan. They would send someone else up to Ed Payne's place as an intermediary, someone they could trust who would not be known to Acreman and who would do this confidentially. They picked Charlie Hayden.

Hayden had just been elected to the office of county constable, responsible for civil cases involving Montgomery County, gathering the evidence, serving the papers, and so on. Hayden was a young man, but Morris had known him for some time, and he liked him and believed he had a good relationship with him. So Morris called him up and asked if he and Brown could come over to Hayden's office to talk to him about something urgent. Half an hour later the three men sat down together, Charlie Hayden behind his big brown desk, Morris and Brown on the edges of their chairs in front of him.

This was urgent, they said, and it was confidential. This was such dynamite, they said, that if word of it got out, there was no telling what would happen. Did he understand that everything that was said here had to be absolutely confidential? Charlie Hayden said he understood.

George Morris told him their story and explained their difficulty and asked if he would help them by going up to Ed Payne's house and bringing the man back down to the office here so that they could all interview him together. Hayden said he understood what they were saying, but it worried him that perhaps he was being asked to conceal evidence from the proper authorities. Morris reassured him. Once they had interviewed Ed Payne, Hayden would no longer be bound by confidentiality.

"All we're asking is that we get a chance to get this old boy's story first. Then you're free to disclose this to the district attorney. No question. This is all completely legal. But you know what Jim Keeshan's like. If he gets first shot at him, he won't talk. We have to get his story down before Keeshan gets to him."

They chewed it over a little more and came to an agreement: Hayden would visit Ed Payne; Morris and Brown would stay by the phone in their office; as soon as he had got Payne's cooperation, Hayden would call Morris and Brown, and they all would meet in his office for the interview. In the meantime, all of them would hold this in the utmost confidence.

"I got one other thing to do," said Hayden. "Y'all wait by your phone. I should be talking to you about noon."

"We'll be there," said Morris.

Don Brown was smoking far more than he ought to have been. Morris was as bad. It was the excitement. They sat in their office overlooking the courthouse square, talking about the case and swapping cigarettes and trying to get on with some work. Every so often they checked their watches.

Noon came and went. It was one o'clock, and then it was coming up to two and there was still no call. Still, Hayden had said he had something else to do first. They called his office and were told Mr. Hayden was out, interviewing a witness. They smoked some more, called his office some more, and then the afternoon was getting old and the light outside was dimming and they began to wonder what was happening out there. How could it take Charlie Hayden this long just to drive out to Grangerland? They called Hayden's home. No answer. They called his office. No answer there either. It was dark now. They began to feel truly anxious. Could Hayden have screwed them? Goddamn, what was going on?

It was well into the evening and Morris and Brown were knotted with worry before George Morris finally got Hayden on the phone at his home.

"Where have you been? What the hell's going on?"

"The man is not going to cooperate with you."

Pause.

"What do you mean? Why isn't he going to cooperate? What the hell happened?"

"All I can tell y'all is that he is not going to cooperate."

"Did you talk to him?"

"All I can tell y'all is that he—"

"What did he tell you? Why didn't you call us?"

Hayden would only tell them that Ed Payne was not going to cooperate.

A total blank. It had all gone wrong. They could only guess at what had happened, but somewhere out there they had been screwed. And what had they lost? Maybe more than just the chance to get some justice into that courtroom. Maybe they had just lost the chance to catch the bastard who killed that poor girl.

Soon afterward the two attorneys stumbled off into the darkness, split up, and went home to worry alone. All they could do now was subpoena Ed Payne, just like any other witness. But as soon as they filed the papers for the subpoena on Monday morning, everyone in the courthouse, including Jim Keeshan, would know what they were doing. And they would be subpoenaing a witness with no idea of what he was going to say.

Janet Dial was new to the courthouse. She had taken this job only out of friendship for John Martin. He had handled her divorce when he was just an attorney, and she had liked him. She had liked his politics, too. He seemed to be the perfect liberal defense attorney, and to someone like her, who lived and breathed Democratic politics and feminism, John Martin had seemed like a real good guy. So when he became a judge and asked her to come and be his secretary and kind of advise him on politics, too, she jumped at the chance. She thought it would be so interesting to be inside the courthouse, where all the political power in this county was concentrated.

It was not working out quite the way she had expected. Now that he was a judge, John Martin seemed different. He was so concerned about acting the way a judge should. He kept calling her into his office in the morning, asking her whether his robe looked all right. And he was not the great liberal anymore. He was getting to be unapproachable, and they had a bad argument because he started to assume that Dial was going to run around fetching coffee for him. An old defense attorney she knew said that Martin was getting too close to the district attorney.

She was new to the courthouse, so she was not sure how things were supposed to be, but it seemed to her as if John Martin had been caught up by the whole atmosphere of this place—and of the Brandley trial.

Janet Dial thought they were all supposed to be impartial, but the truth was it felt as if they were working on some kind of project to convict Clarence Brandley. She had asked one of the court clerks if she really thought Brandley was guilty, and it was as if she had said something really scandalous. It was all anyone talked about in the courthouse: the Brandley case and how "they" were doing. That meant how the prosecution was doing. No one was interested in the defense. If you were going to work in the courthouse, you had to believe that Brandley was guilty.

The atmosphere was so powerful, and John Martin just seemed to have been taken over by it. The way it had changed him reminded Janet Dial of one of those religious cults that prey on vulnerable people.

* * *

Monday morning, February 2, 1981, the trial continued.

Sam Martinez came and served up the now-familiar story. It seemed so harmless the way he told it: how Brandley had come down the hallway right behind that girl; how he had disappeared for forty-five minutes; how he had been in a hurry to send them all home. It seemed harmless, but it was lethal. Brandley watched Martinez and wondered what could be in his mind. Martinez would not return his gaze.

George Morris tried hard to make him admit that the Texas Ranger had been coaching him in his evidence, but Martinez shrugged him off. Morris did dig one point out of him when he described how the janitors had got bored waiting outside the Vocational Building for Clarence. Martinez said he and Acreman had gone off to the gas station on Route 105 to buy some cigarettes. Martinez had bought himself a cold drink. Then a few minutes later, back outside the Vocational Building, Acreman had gone off alone into the main building. Acreman said he was going to get himself a cold drink from a machine in the teachers' lounge. But Morris wanted to know why if Acreman was really looking for a drink he had not bought one two minutes earlier in the gas station when Martinez had. Martinez did not know. Morris left the little cloud of doubt hanging over Acreman's name.

Doubt was all that Morris and Brown had where Gary Acreman was concerned. Could he be the killer? Or was it just that he knew who the killer was? Or was it all baloney? All day, sitting in court, they were rubbing their chins and chewing their thumbs, wrestling with the problem of how to salvage Ed Payne's story. First thing that morning they had filed subpoenas to call Ed Payne and also his daughter Cindy as witnesses. But they could not just call them to the stand and tell them to recite what Acreman had told them. For one thing, they had no idea what they would say; they might stand up there and say, "Gary always said the nigger done it," and then the defense would be screwed.

More than that, the law just plain did not allow a witness to come out of the blue and start repeating hearsay like that. They would have to go through a legal maneuver; they had to wait for Gary Acreman to give evidence first and ask him if it was true that he had come home on the day of the crime and said all these things. If he said yes, then they were home and dry and Jim Keeshan was wrecked on the rocks.

But if Acreman denied saying all these things, then the law would allow them to call his father-in-law, Ed Payne, and his wife, Cindy, to impeach him, to show that he had been lying. But that was very risky because, thanks to the efforts of Charlie Hayden, they still did not know what Ed or Cindy might say. And Morris and Brown knew that if they raised all this with Gary Acreman in front of the jury and then failed to follow through or, even worse, called witnesses who agreed with Acreman, then Jim Keeshan would wipe the floor with them and Acreman would come out looking like an honest man while the defense looked like no-good rumormongers. It was a tough one.

It came down to a race with time: Morris and Brown had to talk to old Ed and Cindy and find out what they were going to say before Gary Acreman gave his evidence. If Ed Payne and Cindy Acreman were prepared to help, they could throw it all at Acreman in the witness box. If not, it was all lost. It looked as if the defense had most of the rest of the day to play with; there were two policemen waiting to give evidence before Acreman was due, and some legal argument, too.

Don Brown posted lookouts on the courthouse steps to watch for Ed Payne showing up in answer to the subpoena. By the midday break there was still no sign. And Jim Keeshan was starting to do something that jerked Morris and Brown right out of their nervous distraction.

Judge Martin had sent the jury out of the room. Keeshan had called Icky Peace to the stand, and in his mild-mannered and charming way he started to ask him a string of questions that rapidly brought Don Brown to the boiling point.

"During your testimony in the last trial, outside the presence of the jury, Mr. Morris got to ask you some questions about a pistol. As I remember, you had a .25 automatic pistol in your car on August 23. Is that true?"

"Yes, sir," piped the familiar childlike voice.

"And as I remember, Mr. Morris asked some questions as to whether you had a pistol in your pocket on a previous occasion at the school."

"Yes, sir."

"Remember that?"

"Yes, sir."

"Do you remember that you told Mr. Morris that you showed Harris a picture of a pistol?"

"Yes, sir."

"OK. Is it true that you sent your sister to tell me that that testimony was not true?"

"Yes, sir."

Brown shook his head in despair. "Jesus . . ."

"OK. And did you send your sister to tell me that before I found out or anybody found out that that testimony was not true?"

"Yes, sir. I told her to come tell you."

"OK. Did you later have an occasion to explain to me that you did have a pistol in your pocket on a prior occasion, some weeks or months earlier at the school?"

"Yes, sir."

"And did you explain to me that you had showed such a pistol to Harris?"

"Yes, sir."

At last, thought Brown. At last they had got a tiny piece of the truth. Except that it was too damned late for the first trial, when it could have helped Clarence Brandley. And except that Jim Keeshan was still getting it wrong. This evidence had not been outside the presence of the jury. Peace had told the jury on oath that it was only a picture of a pistol that he showed to David Harris. The evidence that was held back from the jury was David Harris's story, in which he said Peace was lying and that it had been a real gun. Judge Robertson had refused to let the jury hear that. Now it was too damned late. The battles at the last trial were already lost. Still, there was something else that was troubling Don Brown, something that might be worth a battle right here and now. He rose to his feet and started putting questions to Peace.

"Mr. Peace, I believe Mr. Keeshan asked you if you sent your sister to tell Mr. Keeshan that you had told a lie about having a pistol at the high school earlier. Is that right?"

"Yes, sir."

"When did you send your sister to tell him? Was it during the trial or do you not remember?"

Brown could see Keeshan stiffen behind his table.

"I don't really remember that."

"Did you, at the time that you said that you showed Harris only a picture of the pistol, did you think that was the truth?"

"No, sir."

"You knew you were lying about showing Harris that pistol then, on the other occasion?"

"Yes, sir."

"Well, did you go right home and tell your sister that 'I lied on the witness stand today'?"

"I went home and told her that I did something I shouldn't have done."

Brown could smell blood here. If this dumb little son of a bitch had told Keeshan the truth while the first trial was still going on and if Keeshan had deliberately suppressed the information, it would be the most improper abuse of his position. It would be disbarment time for James Keeshan. It had nothing to do with this present trial, but Brown pressed on.

"Did you send your sister then to tell Mr. Keeshan?"

"I told her to tell him what it was I said."

Keeshan sat motionless. Peace's eyes were swiveling nervously around the court, trying to work out what was happening here.

"Do you know if that was during the trial?"

"No, sir. I think it was after I went home. I don't really remember."

"It was after you went home, after you testified the first time?"

"I believe it was."

"That day? Do you know if your sister went that day and told Mr. Keeshan?"

"I don't know when she told him. But I had told her that day."

Keeshan had had enough. "Judge, I kind of resent this crap," he said, his mild manner and charm dissolving. "I'm here offering this man's testimony. I asked him to straighten up his testimony. The trial ended in a hung jury and it appears to me that he's trying to show misconduct—"

Brown held his hands up in a gesture of innocence. "No, no, no," he cooed. "We've got an appeal on a revocation of probation growing out of the same facts, and I just sort of wondered."

John Martin intervened from the bench. "Well, let's just confine ourselves to the purposes of this trial today, and this witness."

"Fine," said Brown. "Nothing further."

He could still smell blood.

Keeshan continued to question Peace, laying out his story about the gun and the club and the narcotics badge and the smutty dashboard pictures, trying to persuade Judge Martin that it was not the kind of stuff that should be put before a jury.

In the meantime Brown had received a message that Cindy Acreman was in the building. But she was not the important one. So far as they knew, she had not heard her husband going on about all those things on the day of the killing, but she just might be able to confirm some of the circumstances.

Brown started chewing his thumb again, wondering where Ed Payne was and if he would get to court before Gary Acreman was called and what Jim Keeshan was going to do about the subpoenas, when Keeshan suddenly stopped asking Icky Peace about life in his toy city, turned to Jerry Winfree at his side, and casually asked him an innocent question: "Say, Jerry, what do you think about changing the order of our witnesses a little bit and having Acreman testify now? And then the two policemen?"

They could come back to this argument about Icky Peace later in the day, he said, after the jury had gone home. His only concern, he said softly, was the convenience of the jury.

"I hate to have the jury waiting so long," he explained.

The judge said that would be fine with him. Keeshan said it kind of messed up the order of his witnesses. "What do you think, Jerry?"

"That's fine with me."

Morris and Brown felt their hearts sink. Now they only had a couple of hours to play with. Keeshan was right up to speed. He knew what was going on, all right. There was not much they could do now, just try to keep Cindy Acreman out of the state's clutches and hope that Ed Payne showed up before Acreman finished on the witness stand.

Brown rose to explain that the defense had subpoenaed Cynthia Acreman and wanted her brought in and sworn as a witness and ordered not to speak to anyone about her evidence. Before the judge could reply, Jerry Winfree spoke up.

"You've also subpoenaed another member of the Acreman family."

"Right," said Brown, "but he's not here yet."

Right up to speed.

That Monday afternoon was as tense a time as Morris and Brown could ever remember spending in court. Acreman took the stand and told his story. But all the time they were checking their watches and drumming their fingers and waiting for some word that Ed Payne had answered his subpoena.

Finally, it came: Payne was in the hallway outside.

Keeshan was still taking Acreman through his evidence. There was still time. If they could just check out what Payne was going to say, they could confront Acreman, and if he denied it all, they could bring in Ed Payne and knock him sideways, and then Clarence Brandley would be as good as free.

Brown gathered up his papers and scuttled out of court, leaving Morris to listen to Acreman's evidence. Brown spotted Ed Payne as soon as he got out of the door. He was a strange-looking character, a skinny, scrawny little guy—he looked like a plucked chicken—with gray hair, a pair of heavy dark-framed glasses straddling his nose, and something very badly wrong with one of his legs. It looked as if the whole foot were missing from the ankle down. He was wobbling on a wooden stick.

Brown walked up to him with his biggest grin. "You Ed Payne? Hi, I'm Don Brown. I'm the one that subpoenaed you. We're real sorry to trouble you like this."

Brown shook him by the hand and steered him gently toward a conference room, conscious all the while of the eyes of Conroe policemen screwing into them as they passed. All Brown hoped was that this guy was going to come up with proof.

His hope was soon dead.

As soon as Brown started putting his questions, he hit a wall. Ed Payne shrugged his skinny shoulders and turned down his mouth. No, he didn't know what Brown was talking about. He didn't remember any conversation with Acreman. He never had heard anything about any clothes in any Dumpster. Brown tried to move up a gear.

"We've talked to your brother John. And to Mary. Now they say you told them all this."

"Well, they're lying."

"Now, Mr. Payne, why would your brother lie like that? He told us he wasn't even interested in this trial till you started telling him about all this."

"I never told him nothing."

"Well, why would he say that?"

Payne said he was having a dispute with his brother about some property. This must be some kind of way of getting at him and his family. Brown tried a different line.

"Mr. Payne, you know there's a man's life at stake here. Clarence Brandley is being tried for capital murder. And I don't believe he's guilty of that crime. There's a man may be executed for something he did not do."

"Well, I don't know nothing about it."

Brown did not believe him. He tried some bluff.

"Mr. Payne, you know we're going to have to call you onto that witness stand and put you on your oath. And we can call John and Mary, too, to tell about this. All I want is the truth. But if you get onto that stand and perjure yourself, you're in serious trouble, Mr. Payne."

Payne would not budge. After twenty minutes Brown gave up, told Payne that if he changed his mind, they would like to hear from him, and bade him farewell.

Back in court Acreman was still being questioned by Jim Keeshan. Brown leaned into Morris's shoulder and whispered: "Don't ask Acreman the questions. Payne's going to deny the whole thing. We got to approach this some other way." Morris nodded.

Brown could not remember feeling so frustrated. They had lost the lead. They had been beaten. God alone knew how it had happened, but someone out there had screwed them. Brown tried to calm his rumbling fury.

Now George Morris was cross-examining Acreman, trying to chip away at him, pressuring him to admit that he and the other white janitors had been coached in their stories. Brown could see he was doing a good job, but Acreman was standing up to him. It was pretty much over. Then Keeshan got up and asked a few final questions. The district attorney started to sit down, and then he stopped and lobbed one final query to the witness stand.

"Do you know whether or not your wife and your father-in-law have been subpoenaed by the defense lawyers to be here today?"

"I know they've been subpoenaed," said Acreman. "I don't know by who."

Brown clenched his fists very tight and glared down at the table. That was a piece of dirty, rotten bad faith. Keeshan must have heard from his people outside that Brown had talked to Payne and got nowhere. So now he was trying to tip off the jury, trying to push the defense into calling Ed Payne and Cindy Acreman so that their private problem would become public.

When the hearing ended for the day, Morris and Brown went straight to their office and got on the phone to John Payne and told him what had happened. Payne told them that his brother had lied to Brown. And there was no property dispute between them, he said. He did not know why, but his brother had lied.

Morris and Brown went back to the courthouse and found Jim Keeshan. Brown was seething. "Do you know what this scumbag Acreman's father-in-law has been telling members of his family? Do you?"

Keeshan calmly asked him to explain. Morris and Brown rehashed their story.

"Do you know about this? Have y'all talked to Ed Payne about this?"

Keeshan smiled. "I have had it drawn to my attention that Payne may say something about his son-in-law."

"OK," said Brown. "Will you instruct Wes Styles or one of your investigators to go out and interrogate this man?"

Keeshan smiled and shook his head no. "I feel comfortable with the case as it is," he said. "If Brandley's acquitted, I'll follow it up."

"If he's acquitted?" Brown burst out. "If he's acquitted?"

Brown wanted to ask how Brandley was ever going to be acquitted if people suppressed the truth, and he wanted to ask whether Jim Keeshan had ever read the code of conduct that said his job was not to convict but to see that justice was done, and he wanted to pick him up and shake him. But there was no point. Keeshan had won. They were dead in the water.

The Reverend John Daviss was taking a personal interest in the trial of Clarence Brandley. Nothing that had happened since the day of Brandley's arrest had rubbed out his anxiety that this case had released the worst instincts of Conroe's people, the kinds of instincts he hoped had been laid to rest.

Sitting in court from day to day, Reverend Daviss could not make out this Judge Martin. He had started out all right. Then one day early in the trial Reverend Daviss had been sitting in court when a recess was called and most people had left the room. He had just been gathering his thoughts and getting ready to go when he had seen a whole crowd of people coming through the courtroom heading for the judge's chambers. These had been important people. Reverend Daviss had recognized members of the school board among them and maybe one of the other courthouse judges. They had all trooped into the judge's office and shut the door.

Reverend Daviss never did know what had happened in that office, but it seemed to him that that judge had never been the same again. When he came back into court, he looked as if he had been scolded, and he started coming down hard on Brandley's attorneys. Reverend Daviss did not mention it to anyone. He assumed everyone must know.

Brandley watched the frantic efforts of his attorneys trying to get to the truth. But he didn't know the truth himself and never had. He didn't know whether Gary Acreman knew about the clothes being in the Dumpster or not. He didn't know how Acreman could have known. Acreman surely wasn't no killer. He didn't know why anyone would want to stop all that from coming out in court. Maybe the killer had got to Acreman's father-in-law. He didn't know. The only truth he knew was that he had never killed any white girl. That was just about all he knew.

Morris and Brown told him that even without Ed Payne, it would be OK. They still had their strategy, and they still had John Martin on the bench. But privately Morris and Brown were beginning to admit that their old friend John Martin was slipping away from them. They guessed he was just trying to please this town; perhaps he thought he could walk through the next election if he could send this bad nigger to death row. It was as if he had some kind of private deal with Keeshan that the two of them were working together. They had become a well-oiled machine. Morris and Brown had been fighting for the right to tell the jury everything they knew about Icky Peace. They had won a small victory: they could tell the jury about his narcotics card and about how he had tried to recruit David Harris as an agent. But in everything else Judge Martin was walking in the footsteps of Judge Sam Robertson, Jr.

They could mention the gun and the club that Peace had been carrying in his car, but they could not show them to the jurors so that they could see just how threatening the weapons were. Nor were they allowed to talk about the smutty pictures Peace carried around on the dashboard of his car. Nor could they tell the jury about Peace's set of handcuffs—ideal for restraining the girl. Somehow the police had failed to mention the cuffs in the first trial, but now Peace had admitted carrying them, too. Judge Martin said they could not tell the jury about them either.

While they were struggling to introduce their evidence, Keeshan seemed to be able to pull any stunt he wanted. He wanted to call one of the school officials, a Mr. Collier, to relate a conversation he had had with Peace on the day of the crime. In this conversation, it appeared, Peace had described how Brandley had made him look up in the props loft for the dead girl three times. Keeshan said it was powerful confirmation of Peace's story. Morris and Brown said it was obviously hearsay and could not be admitted. But the judge said Keeshan could have his way. They had objected to some of the pictures of the dead girl, some of which seemed to Morris and Brown to be so obscene and offensive in their violation of the girl's privacy that they were likely to stir up prejudice in the jury. They had asked for them to be held back from the jury since they added nothing except offense. But the judge had let Keeshan put them in.

It was galling. Keeshan was getting so cocky that he was starting to wink and grin at them every time he won another ruling from the judge.

Janet Dial found she got bored with her work, and as often as she could, she would leave Judge Martin's office down on the first floor of the courthouse and go up to the second floor and slip into the big trial. She was sitting in there at the back of the courtroom one day during the first week of the trial. John Martin was up on his dais. The attorneys were bunched around him, arguing about something. She was watching Brandley, trying to figure out what was going on behind his face. Then she heard a strange noise coming from somewhere just in front of her, a sort of muttering. Only it was more like chanting.

She shifted in her seat and saw that the sound was coming from a woman sitting two rows ahead of her, an elderly white woman, statuesque, wearing an old mink that was just on the edge of being shabby and a nice hat and some fancy jewelry. The woman was sitting stiffbacked and chanting in a strident whisper.

It was only a whisper, but it was loud enough now for Dial to make out the words. At first she could not believe them. Then she looked across the aisle at Brandley's mother to see if she could hear it. There was no doubt what the white woman was saying: "Kill the nigger. Kill the nigger. Kill the nigger. Kill the nigger."

Captain Monty Koerner was on the stand. George Morris was cross-examining him. Morris was in powerful form. He had no respect for Koerner, and as a councilman he had tried to get him fired for incompetence. Now he was hitting him from all sides.

At the climax of his attack Morris started challenging Koerner to justify his decision to arrest Clarence Brandley on the Friday after the murder. He made Koerner list all the evidence that he did not have on that day. The ranger's walk-through at the school with the white janitors had not yet taken place. There had been no clues from vaginal swabs, no fingerprints, no report yet on the foreign hairs found on the dead girl's thigh.

Morris looked at him in mocking disbelief. "You went ahead and filed a complaint against the defendant charging him with capital murder?"

Koerner said that he had.

Morris pursued him. What about the knives that belonged to Brandley and Peace? Had he received any scientific reports on them by that day? No, Koerner admitted, he had not. Morris had now got Koerner right where he wanted him. He opened up a new line of attack.

"Were you making daily reports to the administration of the Conroe Independent School District?"

"No, sir. Not every day."

"Not every day. But how often were you making any reports?"

"Officer Williams was coming by and would ask us—he's the chief of their security—would ask how the case was proceeding, but there was no reports made to the school board."

"School was fixing to start the next Monday, wasn't it?"

"Yes, sir."

"Did anybody put pressure on you to get somebody in jail, because school was fixing to start?"

"No, sir. I had no political pressure."

Morris paused to let that sink in, to give the jury a chance to wonder about that. Then he moved in and finished him off.

"Did you have any more evidence on Friday, when the complaint was filed against this defendant, than you had had on Monday?"

Koerner shifted in his seat and asked him to say that again.

"Did you have any more knowledge about this crime on Friday, when you filed a complaint against this defendant, than you had the preceding Monday?"

"No, sir."

"I pass the witness," said Morris, and sat down, victorious. He had taken Monty Koerner right to the heart of this case— to the blind focus on the only black man near the scene of the crime, who had been arrested before they started gathering evidence to fit around him like a noose.

Jerry Winfree stood up to try to rescue the captain of detectives.

"Now listen to the question carefully," he was saying, "and answer yes or no. As of Friday, August 29, 1980, other than the facts that you had learned of this case at that time about what happened at the high school, did you have knowledge of a previous history of this defendant that might have a bearing upon what happened?"

Morris could not believe it. Don Brown was already on his feet, objecting. Damn it, Keeshan had agreed not to go into any of that crap about Jo Ellen Parrish and Pokey Smith. They had a motion in limine all about it. It had nothing to do with the facts of this case, and anyway, both women had retracted their allegations.

Judge Martin immediately told the jury to disregard the question. But the skunk was in the jury box. The attorneys huddled around Judge Martin's desk, whispering their protests and jabbing their fingers. Judge Martin sent out the jury and let the battle begin.

Keeshan spelled it out. "By Friday, they had learned that he had kidnapped and attempted to rape another woman in connection with the possession of a sawed-off shotgun, for which he was earlier convicted. So they had that information as well."

Morris protested that the girls had admitted they were lying and that he had their statements to prove it. Keeshan said it was all George Morris's fault; he had opened the door for this by questioning Captain Koerner's motive for arresting Brandley.

Clarence Brandley sat and watched the attorneys snarling and snapping over his life like coyotes fighting over a kill. The judge was trying to calm them down. He was agreeing that George Morris had been criticizing the captain.

"Counsel had completely emasculated the witness," said the judge.

"True," said Jerry Winfree.

"He had the cords to the testicle running all the way to his counsel table," continued the judge.

"Are we off the record now, Your Honor?" It was Mary Johnson, the court reporter, worrying over her notes.

Don Brown told her to keep writing and turned back in time to hear Keeshan claiming that he was worried that George Morris had made such a bad mistake in cross-examining the captain that Brandley might be able to win an appeal by claiming that he had ineffective counsel.

Brown felt his internal volcano beginning to bubble over and launched into an emphatic appeal to the judge.

"You're hurting my ears," whined Keeshan.

"Well, I don't care," said Brown.

On and on they wrangled, Keeshan saying he had to be able to show that Koerner was justified in arresting Brandley because he had found out about his history as a rapist: Morris saying the information was untrue, irrelevant, and inadmissible.

Finally, Judge Martin ruled in favor of Keeshan: he could ask the question again and get Monty Koerner's answer, but he could not go on from there to explain exactly what Brandley's previous record was. Morris said the damage was done, and this would only make it worse. He filed a motion for a mistrial, and his old friend, John Martin, whose election to the bench he had fought for, turned him down.

One day, during a short recess, George Morris wandered over to Keeshan's table and smiled at him broadly.

"Well, Jim, I knew you'd do it, but how did you do it so quickly?"

"Do what, George?"

"Get John Martin in your pocket."

Keeshan smiled back, his blue eyes twinkling.

As Keeshan unfolded his case, he started introducing new evidence. He called new witnesses from the school to testify that the auditorium would have been locked on the day of the crime. The killer must have had a key. He stressed that the two Negroid hairs on the girl's body were unlike any of the others;

they had been forcibly removed, as if in a struggle. Morris and Brown swept the idea aside, saying you could forcibly remove a hair by ordinary combing or just by running your hand through your hair. Brandley wanted to stand up and shout that a nurse's tweezers would do just as well, but the attorneys did not want to fight a battle about planting hairs unless they could win it. Keeshan called a drama teacher and made much of the fact that one of her students had tied a towel around a pulley rope up near the props loft over the stage and that the towel was no longer there. The implication was clear that this must have been the towel that the janitors said they had seen around Brandley's neck. Morris and Brown were not worried. It was just another circumstantial hint, no proof that a reasonable jury could be moved by.

Then Keeshan pitched his screwball, a black teenager named Danny Taylor who had spent a few days the previous summer working at the high school as a janitor alongside Clarence Brandley. According to Danny Taylor, he had been standing in the hallway one day, just outside the teachers' lounge, when a group of schoolgirls had walked by, and Brandley had said: "If I got one of them alone, ain't no tellin' what I might do."

Morris and Brown were horrified. This could do terrible damage to Brandley. Surely John Martin would stop it. They even had a motion in limine from Judge Robertson that blocked Keeshan from suggesting Brandley had any kind of special sexual interest in white women. But Keeshan said he wanted the judge to remove that block. He seemed very confident. Judge Martin sent the jury away and listened to arguments. Morris and Brown pleaded that the evidence was not true and that even if it had been true, it would be nothing more than locker-room talk, it would mean nothing, it would tell them nothing about what was going on in Brandley's mind on the day of the crime, and it would be the purest prejudice. But the judge agreed that Keeshan could have his way.

Don Brown was furious that after all the times they had been blocked from getting Icky Peace's background into the trial, Keeshan was going to be allowed to put this kind of stuff in front of the jury.

"The evidence is irrelevant," he boomed. "It's immaterial to this case and can serve only to prejudice and inflame the jury against the defendant . . ."

"And unconstitutional . . ." interjected Morris.

"And it is mere speculation as to his intent," added Brown.

But what really worried them was a much deeper point, one that had nothing to do with legal technicalities.

It was the myth that mattered, the myth that black men slavered after white women and longed for any opportunity to abuse them sexually, the myth not only that black men spent every waking hour lusting after white men's women but that they were endowed with special sexual prowess beyond anything that a white man could offer. It was the myth that moved every white man who ever laid hands on a black man and accused him of raping a white woman or attempting to rape a white woman or even just watching a white woman. It was the myth that moved lynch mobs. And the myth could move this jury, this all-white Conroe jury, exactly the same way. It was the most potent poison.

Calmly, Jim Keeshan explained that this was evidence from which an inference could properly be drawn by the jury, that it showed that Brandley was looking for an opportunity to get one of these girls separated from other people. Equally calmly, Judge Martin repeated that Keeshan could have his way.

While the jury was reentering the courtroom and Danny Taylor was led back to the stand, Don Brown went into a huddle with Brandley, trying to find out who this boy was and what this was all about. Taylor started his evidence. George Morris kept rising to his feet to repeat his objections so that at least the jury would know how outrageous he believed this was. The judge kept overruling him. Finally, Taylor said the sentence that Keeshan was looking for: "Brandley said if he got one of them alone, ain't no tellin' what he might do."

All along the jury box, all along the public benches, hostile eyes glared at the black man.

George Morris got up to salvage what he could, taking Taylor back through his story and then, without warning or change of pace, asking: "Now when did you pull a knife on your supervisor?"

Now Jerry Winfree was bouncing up and objecting. There was a brief squabble in front of the bench. George Morris explained that Danny Taylor had attacked the then supervisor David Harris at the school with a butcher's knife, that Brandley had tried to stop him, and that Taylor had been fired because of the incident. To Morris's relief, the judge agreed that they could tell this to the jury since it raised the possibility that Taylor was inventing his story to take revenge on Brandley.

Morris put his questions, but Danny Taylor argued with him. He said that David Harris had attacked him by slapping him and that anyway Brandley had never intervened. The attack on Taylor was weak. It was certainly not strong enough to lift the cloak of the myth that had now been so deliberately draped around Clarence Brandley's shoulders.

Janet Dial did not pretend to know about courthouse procedure. She was new. But she had always thought that the judge and the district attorney were supposed to be separate from each other. The longer she spent in the courthouse, the more she began to think that things were not quite right.

She could see how charming Jim Keeshan was. Most of the time she thought he was probably the most charming person she had ever met. Other times she worried about him, and he struck her as a textbook case of someone who had been emotionally damaged somewhere along the line and had come out with this charming mask to hide behind. But she could see how he was charming John Martin. And somehow it seemed that Keeshan was not just being friendly for friendship's sake. Sitting there in the trial each day, she could see that the judge was ruling more and more for Keeshan and against the defense.

She remembered the judge's odd behavior with the internal phone book, which listed the extension numbers for everyone in the courthouse. When she had first started work at the beginning of January, Martin had taken the book and put plus signs by the people who were all right to talk to and minus signs by those who were enemies. Then, a little while later, he had come back and changed the minus sign opposite Keeshan's name to a plus.

But the thing that most worried her—the thing that just seemed not to be the right procedure at all—was the way that almost every morning before the Brandley trial started Keeshan would come by Judge Martin's office and go in there and shut the door. The defense attorneys never did that. She guessed the defense attorneys did not even know these meetings were happening. To her they just did not seem right.

Most evenings Morris or Brown visited Brandley in his cell after the hearing to talk about the day's events and to plan their strategy for the next day. Brandley kept on at them about the photographs that the police had taken at the high school on the day of the crime. He was sure they had taken photographs of him standing around while they started their investigation, and he was just as sure that those photographs would show that he had not been wearing a belt that day.

"They saying they lost all them pictures," he told them. "I don't believe it. They just won't give them 'cause they'll show I'm telling the truth. I had no damned belt."

When the police photographer, Sergeant "Woody" Allen, came to the stand, George Morris took him once more through his failed attempts to photograph the scene of the crime. The sergeant repeated his evidence from the first trial: that he had taken two rolls of film that day, one color and one black-and-white, and that only a few of the color shots had come out.

Then he disclosed that it was only the color film that he had taken to Fox Photo in the shopping mall—the Fox Crime Lab, as Morris and Brown now called it. He had given the other roll to Officer Wayne Kremenak to develop. And for all he knew, Kremenak still had the black-and-white negatives. Keeshan immediately volunteered that if George Morris was really so interested in these photographs, he would arrange for Officer Kremenak to dig out the negatives.

That night Brandley was on the edge of being happy. He asked Don Brown, "Do you think they know what we're after, why we want them so bad?"

Brown chuckled. "Damn right they do. They're no fools."

The next day of the trial Keeshan called Officer Kremenak to the stand. The detective described how, obeying Jim Keeshan's instructions, he had dug out his old negatives and taken them to the DA's office, where Ranger Styles had taken a look at them and agreed that they might be able to develop the pictures after all. It was not until George Morris cross-examined the officer that he admitted that he was not talking about the black-and-white film at all—only about the color film that the "Fox Crime Lab" had returned to him.

The black-and-white film, he confessed, had disappeared. He could not explain it. It had been in the file along with the color film. He was sure about that. Both rolls of film had been in there. Right next to each other. But now there was only one. The black-and-white film was lost and gone forever. He just could not explain it.

Don Brown could explain it all right. That evening in

Brandley's cell he exploded. "I told you those scumbags knew what we were after. They've destroyed that goddamn film. Clarence, these people are too damned determined to get your ass."

A few days later Jim Keeshan triumphantly presented the court with a pile of glossy color photographs of the high school on the day of the crime. Using the most advanced technology, he smiled, they had succeeded in developing these pictures. A couple of them showed Brandley on the day of the crime. None of them showed his waist.

Keeshan called Ranger Wes Styles, who sat stiff and proud in his uniform and described how he had worked more than five hundred hours on the case. Morris and Brown could see it was good theater. The ranger looked as if he knew what he was doing. A special breed of man. George Morris tried to score a point off him by asking why in all his five hundred hours of investigation he had never seen fit to take any samples of blood or hair or saliva from Gary Acreman, John Sessum, or Sam Martinez to see whether they compared with anything found on the dead girl.

The ranger answered in a firm voice, "I did not because they hadn't been in contact with her. That's the reason."

Morris sighed. He was back in the heart of this case again, back with the blind focus and the grabbing of the nearest black man. How could this big-bellied old ranger possibly know that the white janitors had not been in contact with the girl? Why had they picked on Brandley to give his samples? Even when they found that there were all those hairs on that girl that could not conceivably have come from Brandley, why did they stick with Brandley? But Morris had got into trouble before by pursuing that line, so he had to let it go.

Anyway, something else had surfaced. As soon as Styles started giving evidence, Morris and Brown were entitled to see the offense report that he had written for Jim Keeshan. It made interesting reading.

There was a tape recording, for example, that the ranger had faithfully transcribed in his report, of a conversation between himself and Icky Peace soon after he had joined the inquiry. The little janitor chattered on about how Gary Acreman had come across to the Vocational Building on the day of the crime and told the other janitors that Brandley was fooling around with a girl in the main building and that there were girls' clothes scattered around.

Morris and Brown had no idea what it meant or why the prosecution had never mentioned this apparently important clue. And it was clearly a dangerous statement to start putting in front of this jury. But Peace had never said it in his evidence, nor had Acreman. Morris and Brown wanted the jury to know that these witnesses were not telling the whole story. But Judge Martin said no. "Ranger Styles' investigative report and any investigation that he conducted regarding any interview with Icky Peace is not signed, has not been read by Icky Peace, is not a statement."

Morris and Brown thought it was just uncanny how every time the defense needed a break from this judge, he came up with some kind of procedural objection. He and the district attorney might as well have been partners. Morris and Brown watched glumly as Keeshan started to pull the kinds of tricks that attorneys normally only dream of.

At one point a Conroe High School teacher was talking about keys to the school auditorium. Keeshan smiled politely at her and said: "I believe the evidence will show that Clarence Brandley had a set of keys to the auditorium for about a month before August 23."

The teacher nodded, and Keeshan continued in the same gentle tone. "Did you, before that time, did you ever have anybody raped and murdered in the Conroe High School auditorium?"

Morris and Brown went off together like both barrels of a shotgun. "Objection—irrelevant—immaterial—prejudicial—slurry."

"OK," said Judge Martin. "Sustained."

Keeshan smiled and said he had no further questions.

The maneuver that most deflated Morris and Brown came right at the end of the state's case. They had been waiting for John Sessum to come to the stand. The other three white janitors had already testified, repeating the stories they had told in the first trial. But Sessum was the one Morris and Brown wanted. They thought that Morris had come close to cracking him when he cross-examined him in the first trial, and they hoped that if they could start to pull his story apart, they might get a glimpse of the truth that was being concealed.

All through the state's case they waited for him. With all the legal argument and some extra witnesses that Keeshan called, the state took eight working days to present its evidence. There was still no sign of Sessum. Then, finally, on Tuesday, February 10, 1981, Keeshan rose and turned to the court bailiff.

"Would you bring John Sessum in?"

Morris and Brown sat up and watched. This was not the way that Keeshan usually called a witness. Sessum shuffled into court, chewing his lip and looking unsteadily from one face to another. He looked seasick. Keeshan gestured him toward the front of the court. He was all courtesy.

"Mr. Sessum, would you stop and stand right here, please? May it please the court, this is Mr. John Sessum. We would tender him, at this time, to the defense counsel, and, at this time, state rests, Your Honor."

It was brilliant. Morris and Brown had to admit that it was brilliant. By offering Sessum as a defense witness, Keeshan was destroying their ability to cross-examine him. If Sessum was their witness, the rules said that they could not attack him. They would just have to let him tell the same story as the other janitors with no chance of George Morris's putting on enough pressure to get the truth out of him. And by offering Sessum to them in public, Keeshan was scoring a point with the jury, which would think that the defense had something to hide if it failed to call him. It was brilliant.

While Sessum was sworn in as a witness, Morris and Brown tried to gather their thoughts. Morris stumbled to his feet and asked if they could have copies of Sessum's two statements to the police. That was when Keeshan performed his next maneuver. Since Sessum was now a defense witness, the defense attorneys were not entitled to any statements he had made to the prosecution. "They know this is improper," he scolded.

Morris tried to fight back. He told the judge that it was the defense that had arranged for those statements to be put into evidence in the first trial. That made them defense exhibits. So they must be entitled to them. Jerry Winfree bobbed up and said the state had only lent them to the defense and had never given them away. Don Brown was bubbling over again.

"That case was a mistrial. The revocation of probation has been appealed and those statements—defense exhibits—should be kept by the clerk with all exhibits and they have no right to take our exhibits out of our appeal on revocation."

Judge Martin snapped back: "This court is not concerned with revocation or the prior trial. The witness sits up here. If you want him, fine. If you don't, just dismiss him."

George Morris asked: "Is it the ruling of the court that we will not be given the two statements of Mr. Sessum, any of the statements?"

"Not prior to his testimony," said the judge.

Morris shook his head. "Your Honor, Mr. Sessum is not now and never was our witness. We will pass him back."

"All right," said the judge.

"No questions," said Keeshan.

"Mr. Sessum," said the judge, "you may step down."

Beaten again.

Morris and Brown did their best to fight back. It was extraordinary to see, but after four days of the state's case in the first trial, and after eight more days of the state's case here in the second trial, after the five hundred hours' work by the Texas Ranger, and after all the efforts of the Conroe Police Department, there was still not one witness, or one piece of scientific evidence, or one hard clue of any kind to link their client to the crime. It ought to have been easy to fight this case. All they had to do to knock the state over was to run the case against Icky Peace. They could not see how the circumstantial evidence against Brandley could stand up against it. But it was not that easy. This was not a regular fight. This was Conroe.

Morris and Brown started calling their witnesses, chipping away at the role of Icky Peace, using David Harris to confirm that the little janitor had carried his gun in school and had shown off his narcotics card and even tried to recruit Harris as his agent. Over Jim Keeshan's objections, Harris added that the card Peace had now produced in court was not the one that he had shown off in school. That one had been bigger, and Peace had told him soon after the murder in the high school that he had torn it up.

The defense called a drama student who said he was the one who had tied a towel around a pulley rope up near the props loft. But he said it was not a white school towel like the one the other janitors said Brandley had around his neck. It was a little hand towel students had taken from a motel where they stayed on a school trip one time.

The defense attorneys called a string of witnesses to challenge Keeshan's claim that Brandley must be the murderer because he was the only one present who had a key to get into the auditorium that day. There was talk of damaged doors and doors routinely left open and doors whose keys were borrowed and never returned.

David Harris spoke of the whole set of keys that had been lent out to Icky Peace and never seen again. George Morris urged him to tell more. Harris said Peace had evidently given the missing keys to a man called Clarence Robinson, a white man who had briefly worked as supervisor of the janitors at Conroe High before Brandley was promoted. Over Keeshan's objection that this was hearsay, Morris probed a little further.

"Do you know of your own personal knowledge whether or not Clarence Robinson turned in a set of keys that Henry Peace said that he returned to him?"

"He did not."

"You know of your own personal knowledge that Clarence Robinson did not turn in the keys that Peace said he gave Clarence Robinson?"

"That is correct."

Morris left it at that. The keys were clearly missing. Either this Robinson had them, or, as Morris hoped the jury would conclude, Peace had never passed them on and still had them in his possession.

After little more than a day the defense had made its points. The one thing it had not done was to call Clarence Brandley to the stand.

The two attorneys had discussed it endlessly. Morris and Brown had talked to other attorneys who had watched Brandley's evidence at the first trial and who said that he came across badly and that he had hurt himself by contradicting white witnesses. Brandley insisted that he had only been telling the truth, but in Conroe that could be dangerous. Morris and Brown decided it was better to let the facts they had already produced speak for themselves and not antagonize this all-white jury with the image of a black man calling white people liars.

They believed they had done enough, and they had received an unexpected bonus from one of Jim Keeshan's scientific witnesses, a serologist named Pat Lux, who had examined the dead girl's clothes and the various stains on them.

Brown had been trying to find out about a bloodstain on the dead girl's shirt. It was potentially important evidence. If it was not type O, then it was not Clarence Brandley's blood. The serologist, however, said that she had not tested the stain, so she did not know what type it was.

Brown became irritated and challenged her failure to do the test.

"But these items were all packaged together in one package," complained the serologist. "It's hard to say if that bloodstain came from those socks that were packaged in there . . ."

Brown leaped on her words. "Well, now, wait a minute now. I didn't know you found any blood on the socks. I don't believe you testified about that."

"No, sir. I didn't testify to any of that."

Hardly daring to hope, Brown pushed forward. "Was there blood on the socks?"

"Yes, sir."

"And did you do any testing on the blood on the socks?"

"Yes, sir."

"And what did you find?"

"I found blood group A."

Brown could hardly believe his luck. That was not Clarence Brandley's blood. So whose was it? In Brown's mind there was no doubt: it came from the same person who owned all these mysterious hairs that had been found. Not Brandley. Someone else—the murderer.

There was, however, one problem. The dead girl had type A blood. Yet there was no evidence that she had been knifed or that her nose had bled. She had certainly not got up that morning and put on a bloodstained shirt and socks. The blood had been put there during the attack, and it was the attacker who had put it there. The girl could easily have struggled and given him a bloody nose.

Jim Keeshan fought back. The girl's vagina had been slightly torn, he said. The attacker might have used her shirt, or her sock, to wipe himself, transferring her type A blood onto the clothes. Don Brown found it hard to imagine the attacker doing that to the girl's sock while it was still on her foot, which was where the police had found it. But Keeshan had an answer for that, too. He pointed to a scuff mark on the girl's right shin and suggested that that was the source of the blood on the sock. It was pure speculation, but Morris and Brown feared that, weak as it was, in this courtroom it might suit the jury to accept it.

Late on Thursday morning, February 12, the defense rested.

The court took a brief recess, but before it could move on, George Morris sent a shiver of speculation across the court by announcing that the defense wanted to reopen its case. It had a new witness. It was a dramatic moment, but the tension soon faded. The last-minute witness was a white air-conditioning engineer named Joe McFarland who had been following the case and who had contacted Morris and Brown during the recess to tell them that he had often worked at the school and had found the doors to the auditorium unlocked almost all the time.

Jim Keeshan struck him with the speed of a snake. Had he been there on the day of the crime? No. The day before? No. Had he been drinking before he gave evidence? Wasn't it true that he had been fired by the school? And why had he come forward at the last minute like this? McFarland finally snapped. "The reason I came forward with this information was that I think you're railroading somebody. Everybody had access to the keys to that door."

Morris and Brown knew that McFarland meant well; but he came across like an obnoxious pipsqueak, and Keeshan had just needled him into destroying his own credibility. He sounded as if he were crusading for Brandley.

The defense rested again. It was getting late. Judge Martin sent the jurors home and told them to come back the next day, Friday, February 13, when they would listen to final speeches and then retire to reach their verdict.

Clarence Brandley was ready to be free again. He looked across the room at the members of the jury. He looked at them a thousand times. He had always believed that most people weren't all bad. They were just people. Sure, they were white people, but there was no reason why they should want to blame him for this crime. The jury was not like a judge or a district attorney who wanted to be powerful and wanted to use him. There was no way they were going to accept this evidence. No way they were going to find him guilty. That night Brandley went back to his cell in the county jail and prayed—really prayed—that tomorrow morning that jury was going to set him free again.

At eight-thirty on Friday morning the attorneys began their speeches, following the tracks of the first trial. Jerry Winfree spent forty-five minutes summarizing the evidence from prosecution witnesses. Don Brown rehearsed the scientific evidence, returning again and again to the mysterious hairs that had been found on the dead girl and that had never been traced to anyone, let alone to Clarence Brandley. George Morris attacked the police inquiry, which he said should be written up in a book called *How Not to Investigate a Case*. "They fumbled the evidence. They used poor judgment. And they ignored very important facts. . . . You can't expect the police and the Texas Ranger to find a needle in a haystack. But you can expect them to find the haystack." Morris went back to the autopsy report and raised the theory that two people must have been involved in the attack on the girl. He returned to the unidentified hairs. He argued that the killer had not wanted the body found. He moved Icky Peace to the center of the stage. And he pleaded: "I want you to ask yourselves, 'Where is the proof? Where is the proof?' "

Then it was Keeshan's turn. He moved into a discussion of the evidence that held no surprises for Morris and Brown until he started to remind the jury that Brandley had worked part-time in a funeral home. "Dr. Jachimczyk told you from the medical evidence that it appeared that this girl had been molested after she was dead or unconscious. We know also that the person who committed this offense had to have stayed with the body . . ."

Morris was on his feet. "Your Honor, we are going to object to this. This is inflammatory . . ."

"Overruled," said the judge.

And Keeshan continued. "We know that whoever did this was not repelled by a dead body. Somebody stayed there and took the clothing off that body. Somebody had intercourse with that body, apparently after she was unconscious or dead. It is not just everybody who is going to be involved in that kind of offense. This man was not repelled by the fact that she was deceased."

Don Brown made a mental note that if this jury ever convicted Clarence Brandley, they would go straight to the appeals court and complain about this kind of dirty prejudice.

Keeshan went on, sketching out his chain of circumstances: the path of the janitor; the keys; the Negroid hair; the opportunity; the ability; the motive. Then, pacing up and down in front of the jury box, he moved away from his evidence and started to appeal to something else. He talked about the dead girl, her hopes and her fears, her innocence, and the mark of the crucifix stamped into her flesh. "Cheryl was part of all of us," he cried. He talked about Conroe, a community for families, a community that needed to send out a message, a message that this kind of crime would not be tolerated. A hung jury was no good, he warned. That would not relieve the dead girl's family or help the town.

"It would be a disservice to your community to go back there and decide 'We just can't agree.' I'm going to ask you to help make your community safe and a good place to live. A place where you want your children and grandchildren to grow up, where people can go to a school function without fear that some monstrous person is going to commit an offense like this. And when you reach a proper verdict in this case, when you go back to find this defendant guilty according to the evidence, and you get to go home tonight, I'd like to have you hug your children or whoever you love and tell them you've done something for them today."

Keeshan sat down. The jury had a choice. It could listen to George Morris, asking for proof, or it could heal its town.

Just after two o'clock, for the first time in his new career as a judge, John Martin sent away a jury to reach a verdict in a capital murder case. Before the jurors went, he reminded them that this was a case of circumstantial evidence, and he read them the required rule of law: "It is not sufficient that the circumstances coincide with, account for, and therefore render probable the guilt of the defendant; they must exclude to a moral certainty every other reasonable hypothesis except that of the defendant's guilt."

To a moral certainty.

Just over an hour later the jury came back and said that they had found the black janitor guilty of capital murder.

Clarence Brandley watched the woman with the brightly colored nails come into court to read the verdict. Peggy Stevens. He knew she should not even have been there. She was the district clerk, not the clerk of the court. But she came in and took the verdict from the foreman of the jury and held it in her elegant hands and read out "Guilty" loud and clear. And then she clapped her hands together and smiled.

Brandley saw that smile. It was like pure joy on her face. And the judge was doing the same. Smiling.

Why had they done this to him? He was no murderer. But now he felt as if he could be. He could reach out and grab them and just murder them. Look at them. All over the court they were smiling.

At the prosecution table Jim Keeshan sorted out his papers. He had one last courtroom maneuver to perform: to persuade this jury to order that Clarence Brandley be put to death for this crime.

The jurors were taken away for the night and sequestered, like their predecessors, in the Holiday Inn. On Saturday morning, they returned to the courthouse, where Clarence Brandley's fate now hung on the answers to two questions: Had he killed this girl deliberately, and was there a risk that he might commit more violent acts? If the jury believed the answer to either question was no, he would be sentenced to a lifetime in jail. If the jury believed that both questions should be answered yes, then he would be sentenced to death. The district attorney stood up and set about persuading this jury to say yes twice.

First, he called the former sheriff, Gene Reaves, out of his retirement and asked him what kind of reputation this Clarence Lee Brandley had in the community. "It's bad," came the reply. That was all.

George Morris got up and went straight for the sheriff's jugular. Wasn't this hearsay that he was reporting? Wasn't hearsay most unreliable? Hadn't he himself been the victim of hearsay? Hadn't he been the victim of hearsay in an election campaign when people said he had been stealing gasoline from the county? Keeshan was jumping up and down, objecting, but Morris pressed on.

"You can't really believe everything you hear, can you?"

"No, you sure can't," muttered the sheriff with a face like flint.

Then Jo Ellen Parrish came back, like a bad spirit. Coaxed along by Jim Keeshan, she said that she was a nineteen-year-old girl with a husband and baby son and that one night in March 1979 she had been walking by her friend Mary Zavaba's car when she saw that Mary was being choked by a man she now knew was Clarence Brandley. She had made him stop. Then she had gone with Mary to a drinking club called the Doll House, but Clarence Brandley had followed them there with a sawed-off shotgun pushed down the back of his pants, and he had abducted her and made her wait behind the Doll House until everyone had gone, and he had taken her to his house and made her strip to her underwear and tried to have sex with her. Her husband had knocked on the door, but Brandley had choked her to stop her from crying out. Then he had cooked her a meal and got into bed, and she had run out of the house, wearing her underwear and his coat, and hidden at her friend Lillian's house until the morning. Then she had gone to her husband and told him what had happened, and he had made her contact the police.

Brandley had heard Jo Ellen Parrish was telling some story, but he never knew it was as crazy as this. At least now he understood why she had run out on him that night. If her boyfriend really had come around knocking on the door while he had been asleep, it was no surprise that she had panicked. She must have waited for her boyfriend to go and then worked out this story to cover herself.

Don Brown set out to demolish her story. Parrish soon admitted that she was not married at all. She denied being a prostitute but said she was not sure about Mary Zavaba even though she was her best friend. Brown suggested to her that she and Zavaba had met Brandley and his friend and that she had invented her story of abduction to hide her infidelity from her boyfriend. She denied it and then spoiled her denial by admitting that Zavaba's boyfriend, Ralph, had come looking for Zavaba that night and had dragged her out of the Doll House by her hair and at gunpoint. Parrish admitted, too, that Brandley had not been choking her when her boyfriend came knocking on the door of the house looking for her, and she could not explain why she did not scream for help. Nor could she explain why she had not run away while he was cooking her a meal.

Don Brown showed the jury members the rusty old shotgun and hoped that they shared his view that it could not have fitted down the back of anybody's pants without splitting them in two.

Finally, Brown asked Jim Keeshan to produce Parrish's two statements—the one she had made immediately after this incident in March 1979 and the one she had made eighteen months later, after Brandley's arrest for murder, when Ted Morgan had taken her to the courthouse. He wanted to show how she had embellished this story in the meantime. Keeshan sent someone out to look for the statements. The court waited. Keeshan then reported that the statements could not be found. He could not explain it, he said. He was very sorry. They were gone. Lost and gone forever. Brown was hardly surprised.

He was not surprised either that at the last moment Keeshan changed his mind and decided not to call Pokey Smith to tell her story of Brandley's violent assault and multiple rape. Jo Ellen Parrish had done badly under cross-examination. Pokey Smith was likely to collapse completely and spoil the show. Anyway, in this atmosphere Keeshan did not need any more evidence.

The court broke for lunch. Judge Martin called all the attorneys into his office, and there Morris and Brown witnessed a rare sight. They saw Jim Keeshan drop his guard.

It started with the judge's reporting that a toy pistol had been found in the courthouse. "We have reached a point in the trial where it might pay all of us to be extremely careful and cautious," he said. Everyone agreed, and then, perhaps buoyed by his success in the trial, Jim Keeshan launched into a speech in which he complained that some of the spectators had been unruly, giggling and talking during the evidence, and that some black woman had sat on a white woman's hand. He suggested that police officers should be seated along the front of the public benches, "looking directly down the throats of that audience."

While he was explaining this, he said something that finally confirmed what Morris and Brown had always suspected. It was only a little thing, almost in parentheses as he talked on, but to them it said everything. "I haven't made any announcements to the white people out there," he said, "and I know y'all haven't felt obligated to make an announcement to all the black people."

That was all. Jim Keeshan—the white people's district attorney. He was not going to talk to any black people in court. They had nothing to do with him. They might technically be members of the community he served, but he would speak only to the white people because they were his people. He had simply taken that for granted in talking to them, as he had throughout this trial.

Morris and Brown said nothing. It had already occurred to them that if Clarence Brandley had been acquitted, there were people in this town who would be willing to take revenge on two nigger-loving attorneys. They all agreed that they should take proper security precautions, and they returned to court to finish the day's business.

The two defense attorneys had reached a point where they had just about lost all confidence in justice in this courtroom. Now they had to argue to save Brandley's life, but with this judge and this jury, it seemed to them, there was no rational argument that had a chance of succeeding. If rational arguments had been succeeding, Brandley would never have been convicted. And perhaps that was the thing to work on— the possibility that some of these jurors knew they had returned an irrational verdict, that maybe some of them had a lingering doubt.

Don Brown decided that instead of making the usual attempt to present mitigating evidence and challenge the other side, he would simply appeal to that lingering doubt.

As Brown began his speech, his depression showed through his threadbare attempt to respect the court. Breathing sarcasm, he said: "I will just say that I know that you have heard Clarence Lee Brandley's terrible record this morning, what a terrible person he is. And I'm not going to dignify the evidence they put on this morning by arguing about it. We have argued until we are blue in the face about the evidence in the first phase of the trial with obviously little success. Perhaps Mr. Morris and I just failed.

"I would like to say this: that each of you took an oath on your God that you would a true verdict render in this case, and I am telling you now that under the oath you took in this case, if you believe from the evidence that you have heard beyond a reasonable doubt and to a moral certainty that there is no reasonable possibility that someone else could have committed this crime, you should assess the death penalty—"

Keeshan was interrupting. "Your Honor. Your Honor."

Brown waded on. "—and you know the other alternative if your conscience bothers you at all because of your verdict. Thank you."

Keeshan was still talking. "Your Honor, may it please the court, ladies and gentlemen of the jury, it is not considered professional to attack the verdict of the jury or quarrel with the verdict. . . ."

Don Brown could not believe it. Was there nothing they could do in this case without Keeshan's trying to trip them up? He rose to his feet and insisted he had not been attacking the verdict at all.

"Okay," said Judge Martin. "Over—Let's proceed."

For a moment Brown hesitated. Had the judge overruled him? He appeared to have, but he had swallowed the word. Brown let it pass. He had had enough. Keeshan continued his plea for the death penalty. He commended the ladies and gentlemen of the jury on their verdict. He said Brandley had had his chance to be rehabilitated when he was given probation in 1979. Don Brown objected that this was not an issue. The judge overruled him. Keeshan reminded the jurors of the photographs of the dead girl. "The look of stark terror on her face. It's fair for you to think about the feelings of the father who lost his baby daughter and it's fair for you to think about how you would feel if you lost your children."

Morris and Brown did not think that it was at all fair. For once Brown's objection was sustained. Brown then complained that it was not enough just to sustain his objection when these inflammatory remarks had already been made to the jury. The judge overruled him. Keeshan had finished. The jurors retired.

Three-quarters of an hour later they were back. Just as Jim Keeshan had asked, they said yes to both questions.

Clarence Lee Brandley must die.

Brandley felt nothing. He was numb, physically numb, all over his body. He thought nothing. But a strange thing happened in his head. He saw his life. Just the way drowning people do. Real pictures. Nothing he would ever remember. But it was his whole life, the life he once had.

Reporters crowded around his family. His brother O. T. told them: "I think the state knows who did it and has known it all along. They just wanted somebody caught for it and it's easier to prosecute a black man."

His mother cried quietly on somebody's shoulder.

Then white policemen came and led Clarence Brandley from the court, and he was lost, one black face in a blizzard of white faces, lost like one simple fact in this blizzard of lies: he had not done this thing.

* * *

Don Brown felt sick to his heart. He had never thought this could happen. Sure, he had seen people who appeared to be innocent being convicted by juries. But never in a case like this—where the man's life was at stake. He had never thought it could happen in a death penalty case. And on such weak evidence! He had never thought that jurors could be so indifferent to the oath they had sworn, to find guilt beyond reasonable doubt. But this was not really about jurors. This was about Conroe.

This was about corruption and dirty tricks and about ruthless men who would twist the truth and bend the rules to get their way. This was about politics and power and about ambitious people who would happily sacrifice one innocent man's life in their pursuit of success. This was about a town where black people had always been victims, the town that had killed Bob White in this very courthouse.

Sure, times had changed. Not so long ago a bunch of white men would have done their manly duty and dragged Clarence Brandley out of his shinny shack and hanged him from the nearest tree while the rest of the town turned its back. But not anymore. Now they had to use the courthouse and the law instead of the stout tree and the rope. But the end result was just the same: one dead nigger boy—one big white lie.

HEROES
OF
FAITH

Faith is the substance of things hoped for, the evidence of things not seen.

—HEBREWS 11:1

Chapter Six

High up on a hill, forty miles north of Conroe, in the town of Huntsville, where Sam Houston is buried, there is a building that looks like a shadow in the sky, a giant stockade with a soaring twenty-five-foot red brick wall topped with razor wire. Guards ride shotgun at every corner. This is the headquarters of the Texas Department of Corrections, the biggest jailhouse in East Texas. It is also the home of the Walls Unit, a bright bleached white room with no windows where doctors strap men to gurneys, plug catheters into their arms, run solutions of sodium thiopental pavulon and potassium chloride into their veins, and wait for their hearts to stop beating.

One sunny day early in the spring of 1981 a patrol car from the Montgomery County Sheriff's Department sped northward out of Conroe along Interstate 45 and brought Clarence Brandley to Huntsville.

For Brandley this was the scariest moment so far. He had no idea what to expect. He had never had to deal with anything like this before. He had never even been in jail before all this started. And here he was on his way to death row.

The sheriff's car sped through Huntsville, past the building in the middle of town where the killing is done and out into the desert of empty grass and swamps, to the Ellis Unit, where condemned men are kept until their date to die comes round. A few dead trees rise out of the bayous, their branches bearded with Spanish moss. The sheriff's car prowled through the high red brick gateway and up the long tarmac driveway. To one side there was a work gang, almost like a chain gang: about a dozen black men, dressed in white from neck to ankle, standing in a line, all holding hoes and all hacking the ground in unison, sending little clouds of dust up around their ankles. Beside them white men sat on horseback, resting easy in the saddle, cradling rifles in their laps, chewing slowly on unlit cigars, their eyes masked by the reflecting shades of their sunglasses. Farther up the driveway, over to the left, Brandley saw a firing range.

Then he saw the unit: the high wire fence, the second fence inside that—just as high—the towers at each corner with the shadows of the sentries and their guns, the long, low red brick building with the bars, bars on every window he could see, painted blue.

They took him inside. They stripped him, cut off his hair, sprayed him with powder, put him in regulation all-white clothes from neck to ankle, and gave him a new identity. He was number 680 on death row.

The trial was over.

The *Courier* said: "The guilty verdict ended the Halloweenish atmosphere lying heavily upon the community for the past five months. In less time than it takes to mow the lawn, Brandley was found guilty of one of the most heinous crimes in Montgomery County history."

Yet it was not over.

In River Plantation, a little south of town, in an elegant ranch-style house on a quiet road with the look of an old English village, the phone was ringing. Nowadays it was always ringing. Bill Srack answered it yet again.

And yet again he heard the angry silence and then the sound of breathing before he hung up yet again. It had been happening for months now, ever since that Saturday night in December only a few hours after he had got home from court, desperate for peace. The reporters had followed him from the courthouse. He had sent them away, but that had not stopped them from announcing on the radio and on the television and in the newspapers in Conroe and in Houston that the dissident juror who had refused to convict the black janitor was William A. Srack. So the phone had started ringing that Saturday night.

By Sunday it was ringing so often that he had to take it off the hook. Then he would try to put it back on again, and it would start ringing again almost immediately. Day after day it was the same, even now after a second jury had convicted the man. Mostly, there was just the silence, but sometimes someone spoke. Like that very first call on the day the first trial ended.

Srack, all unsuspecting, had answered the phone, and a man's voice had said: "I'm calling you from Houston."

It seemed a strange introduction. Srack waited. Then his heart sank as the man's bitter voice went on. "You're a nigger lover. You turned that nigger loose. You're a nigger lover."

Srack had started debating with him. "You don't really know what all happened," he said. "I did what I thought was right."

But the man from Houston was not interested. He used those words on him again and hung up. If the callers spoke, it was always those words. Sometimes it would be a man, sometimes a woman who said it. But mostly it was just the angry silence.

Bill Srack was struck by the sheer frequency of the calls as the weeks passed. He could leave the phone off the hook for as long as he liked, but as soon as he put it back on, it would ring again. Within seconds. It made him wonder whether there was some kind of electronic gadget you could rig up that would automatically keep dialing someone's number or whether there really could be that many people out there who hated him that much for what he had done.

He called Jim Keeshan and told him about it. Keeshan said it was outside his jurisdiction but he would see what he could do. Soon afterward the sheriff started sending patrol cars to drive past the house and occasionally knock on the door to make sure he was safe. Then an officer came down from the Conroe Police Department.

He wanted to make a report. Srack told him that the phone rang every few seconds, though it was off the hook at that moment, and told him that it must be some kind of electronic gadget.

"You got any witnesses?" asked the officer.

Srack pointed to his neighbor, who happened to be visiting, and she agreed that she had seen it happen.

"Well, we need two witnesses," said the officer.

Srack asked him: "Could you be a witness yourself?"

The officer agreed. Srack walked over to the phone and replaced the receiver in its cradle. He had just turned to walk back to his chair when it rang. The officer picked it up and listened. The line was silent.

The officer started yelling into the receiver: "Now listen here, you no-account son of a bitch, you got no damned business carryin' on like this. You hear me?"

Then a woman's voice answered: "We gonna get you, nigger lover."

That was no gadget. Srack felt almost awed at the idea that there were real people out there who would devote so much time and energy to persecuting him. The officer hung up and said he would contact the phone company to see what it could find out.

Weeks later he came back and said the phone company had traced the calls and spoken to the people involved. But no one was going to be charged with anything, and Srack would have to get a court order if he wanted to find out who they were. Anyway, the calls would stop now, the officer said. But they didn't—even now that Brandley had been sent to death row. They just became a little less frequent as the months went by.

The case of Clarence Brandley was not over for George Morris and Don Brown. They wanted to get their client a new trial, and so, pushing aside all their doubt and despair about Conroe and its courthouse, they set out once more to appeal to the selfsame people for justice.

They produced a motion. It ran to eleven closely typed pages, and it spelled out twenty-eight different reasons why Clarence Brandley should have a new trial. Their most important point was that there had never been enough evidence to justify a conviction and that the state had failed to exclude other reasonable explanations for the girl's death.

They exhumed the defeats of the last six months: the samples of blood and hair that were never taken from the white janitors; the depositions that were never ordered from them; the secret tape of Ranger Styles and Icky Peace; Brandley and dead bodies; Icky Peace and guns and clubs; Jo Ellen Parrish and her mysterious missing statements; the flare-up over whether Don Brown had attacked the jury's verdict; Keeshan inviting the jurors to put themselves in the shoes of the dead girl's family; the jurors who had never been selected; the objections that had never been sustained; the questions that had never been asked. They added them all up and concluded that Jim Keeshan was guilty of a catalog of misconduct, that he had repeatedly withheld evidence and deliberately misled the jury in order to harm Clarence Brandley. And they castigated Judge Martin and his predecessors for helping Keeshan along.

On February 23, 1981, only nine days after the end of the trial, Morris and Brown filed their twenty-eight different arguments with the court. The next day, they took their motion back and added, recalling the furious row over Brandley's bail, two more points. They filed again on March 13. Six days later they were in court, the same court with the same bright blue carpet and the four gilt fans stirring the air overhead. And there was Clarence Brandley in chains, Judge John Martin on his dais, and there at their side was Jim Keeshan, clean and smart and unfailingly polite as ever.

Morris and Brown had subpoenaed ten witnesses to give evidence about their thirty different arguments. Keeshan immediately attacked them. He wanted to quash all the subpoenas and send the witnesses home, but Judge Martin would not let him. Morris and Brown wondered if their old friend might be ready to fight free of the courthouse crew.

They called their first witness, Oscar Johnson. They wanted him to explain that Clarence Brandley had never had anything to do with dead bodies in his part-time work at Johnson's funeral home and that Jim Keeshan had known that and had been misleading the jury when he suggested that Brandley's work there meant he had some kind of special interest in corpses. Keeshan went on the attack again, insisting that Johnson should not give evidence and that Morris and Brown had no business trying to bring in new evidence after the trial was finished. After a long debate Judge Martin overruled Keeshan, and Morris and Brown began to feel that there might be justice in Conroe after all. Oscar Johnson said his piece.

Morris and Brown then tried to call Ranger Styles. They explained that they wanted him to talk about his secret tape recording of Icky Peace and the fact that Keeshan had known all about the tape and about how it could help Clarence Brandley and how Keeshan had been guilty of misconduct by failing to pass it to the defense. Keeshan attacked again. They should have brought all this up at the trial, he said. It was too late now. Don Brown said they had tried to bring it up at the trial, but this same Judge Martin had refused to let them put the tape into evidence and had refused to let them recall Icky Peace to question him about it. This was their first chance to bring it up. Judge Martin paused and then agreed with Keeshan. Ranger Styles could not give evidence.

Morris and Brown tried to call Icky Peace to talk about the things he had said to Ranger Styles in the secret tape. Keeshan said Peace should not be allowed to give evidence, and Judge Martin agreed again.

Morris and Brown tried to call Gary Acreman to talk about how he had never had to give samples of his blood or hair. Keeshan said Acreman should not be allowed to give evidence, and Judge Martin agreed again.

Morris and Brown watched helplessly as one witness after another was sent away without testifying. Keeshan kept objecting, and Judge Martin kept agreeing. Seventeen times in a row Keeshan objected to the defense strategy, and seventeen times Judge Martin agreed with him. Finally, Morris and Brown tried to call Keeshan himself to give evidence. Keeshan objected strenuously and said he should have to testify on only one issue: his attempt to find Jo Ellen Parrish's statements in which she claimed that Brandley abducted her with his old shotgun and tried to rape her. Judge Martin agreed.

Keeshan then told the court that he and his staff had searched diligently for the woman's statements but had found nothing except a few notes of his own. The defense—still hoping to prove that Parrish had embellished her story at the prosecution's request—asked to see them. Keeshan claimed the defense had no right to see them, and Judge Martin agreed. Keeshan concluded that Jo Ellen Parrish never had made any statement. Then Brown landed a blow. He reminded Keeshan that at the end of the first trial, after the jury had failed to come to a verdict, Judge Sam Robertson, Jr., had revoked Brandley's probation and refused him bail and had later written an order in which the judge explained that one of his reasons for doing this was that "the defendant is presently on probation for possession of a short-barreled firearm, during which offense a female named Jo Ellen Parrish was allegedly raped."

But Jo Ellen Parrish had not given this evidence until the second trial, five weeks later. So Brown wanted to know how Judge Robertson could possibly have known about it—unless Jo Ellen Parrish had made a statement about it that had been given to the judge.

Keeshan started talking fast. He was not sure. Perhaps he had mentioned it to the judge on the telephone when he first took the case. Perhaps the judge had somehow learned the woman's name himself. Or perhaps not. He believed the judge must have asked Jerry Winfree for the name. Or perhaps the judge had just seen the name on the witness list for the trial.

Pressing his advantage, Brown asked for Judge Robertson's order to be put into the record of this hearing. Keeshan objected that it should not be, and Judge Martin agreed. Brown said he would call Robertson to ask him in person how he had learned about Jo Ellen Parrish and her alleged rape. Keeshan objected that Judge Robertson should not be allowed to give evidence. Judge Martin said he would recess for a while to think about it, and then he came back and agreed with Jim Keeshan. Judge Robertson would not be called.

Morris and Brown said they had run out of witnesses. Between them the district attorney and the judge had dismantled their entire case. All they now asked for was a few days to prepare briefs outlining their points of law. Keeshan objected and said the court should rule now, and Judge Martin agreed. Keeshan then argued that there was no reason to hold a new trial. And Judge Martin said he agreed.

Finally, Keeshan asked the judge to pronounce the formal sentence of death on Clarence Brandley. Judge Martin agreed and told Clarence Brandley he would be kept in the Texas Department of Corrections until the Court of Criminal Appeals had heard his appeal, after which a date could be set for his death.

Morris and Brown went back to their offices to lick their wounds. Brandley was sped northward back to Huntsville.

The Brandley case was not over for *Houston City Magazine*.

That spring the magazine ran a story that sprawled across two issues and became a landmark in the case. For the first time someone outside the defense camp with no ax to grind suggested plainly and publicly that Clarence Brandley was being railroaded. And the magazine had new evidence to support the claim. The story succeeded for the first time in peeling a layer off the secrecy that concealed the police and the Texas Ranger and Jim Keeshan as they worked to convict Clarence Brandley. Icky Peace showed the way.

Peace talked to *Houston City Magazine* a few months after the trial. Away from the courthouse and the limelight, the little janitor relaxed and told for the first time how a police officer had turned to Clarence Brandley and told him that since he was a nigger, he was elected to hang for this crime. He went on to say that he had told Jim Keeshan all about this, but the district attorney had not seemed pleased. Peace recalled: "They started shutting doors and everything else and said: 'Don't you dare open your mouth about that. It would help get Clarence off because it would prove you were both threatened. How would you feel having a murderer out roaming the streets?' "

Peace then confessed that he had lied under oath at Brandley's trial; he had been asked if he had been threatened, and he had denied it. He said it had got worse. Jim Keeshan had later warned him that if he ever told anyone about any of this, he would be prosecuted for perjury and could get two to ten years in jail. At the second trial he had been asked if he knew that he could be jailed for two to ten years for perjury, and he had lied and said that was news to him.

The magazine recorded the denials of the district attorney and the Conroe police. But to Clarence Brandley and his family and to George Morris and Don Brown, it seemed like confirmation of what they had always believed: the people in the courthouse had been playing dirty behind the scenes.

They had to fight on, somehow uncover a new witness, retrieve a hidden clue, and throw everything into an appeal to the court in Austin. This was not over yet.

The machine stalled. Brandley sat in jail, waiting for his attorneys to put together an appeal. His attorneys sat in their offices, waiting for the courthouse to produce the official record of his case. The courthouse produced nothing.

Every week or so Don Brown would track down the court reporter whose job it was to type up a transcript of Brandley's trial and put together all the evidence for the official record. Brown liked the court reporter, the cool, elegant—in fact, beautiful—Mary Johnson, who had been hired by Judge Martin. Her hair was so blond it was white, and she wore it in a tight bun, drawn back from her handsome face. She was well into middle age, but every man in the courthouse seemed to be in love with her. Brown and Morris sometimes drank with her over at the Iron Horse. Every time Brown asked her how she was getting on with the Brandley record, Mary Johnson told him that she was working on it. She apologized. It was such a long trial. Brown said he understood. It was not unusual in a big case like this.

Every month or so Don Brown tracked down the district clerk, Peggy Stevens, in the courthouse and explained that they were still waiting for the record, and he filed a motion asking for an extra sixty days to prepare their appeal. The district clerk was not warm and friendly like Mary Johnson.

Peggy Stevens was always immaculately dressed and perfectly poised and entirely polite. She was as sweet as saccharin and just as genuine. She had worked in the courthouse for more than twenty years, ever since she left college, and she looked upon the people who ran it as her family. Jim Keeshan was her favorite boy. Anyone who criticized the courthouse was picking a fight with Peggy Stevens.

Courteously, Peggy Stevens passed the defense motion to Judge Martin, who granted the defense its extra sixty days.

Brandley sat in jail. He wondered how his children were, one hundred miles away in Houston. He missed almost everybody. But he did his best to keep his cool as the months rolled by. August came. He had spent one whole year behind bars. September came. It was his thirtieth birthday—his second birthday in jail. Maybe he would be free by the time the next one came around. Maybe not. Maybe he would die here. His life had stalled.

Brandley's family were becoming desperate with impatience. They had been trying to raise more money to cover the cost of this appeal. It was going to be at least twenty-five thousand dollars. Where were they going to find that kind of money? They scraped out their savings. Tim Brandley had sued his old employers because they fired him for whistling at some girls, and he gave his ten-thousand-dollar settlement to the defense fund. They put the message out far and wide through the black churches and community groups: an innocent black man is being railroaded. They asked for help, and they began to get it. Money started to trickle through, from Conroe and from Houston, even from as far away as Dallas. People heard their preachers talk about this Brandley case, and they reached into their pockets to send a dollar for a good cause. But where was the appeal? What were Morris and Brown doing up there?

It began to seem to the family that the lawyers were not doing enough. Some of them began to say they should never have lost this case in the first place and they should never have let that jury sentence Brandley to death like that. Some of them began to say they needed new attorneys for the appeal.

By the time November came, the family had decided to try something new. They had gathered together the twenty-five thousand dollars they needed, but instead of taking it into the courthouse square for Morris and Brown, they headed southward down I-45 to Houston, to the office of the most famous defense attorney in Texas, Percy Foreman.

In November 1981 Foreman, now aged seventy-nine, was past his prime. His big, broad frame was just beginning to sag with age, his hair was white, his face was like tree bark, but he was still a powerful figure, still able to pummel and pound a witness into submission, still chopping down district attorneys and liberating his clients, still churning out orders from behind his king-size desk, where all the legal papers and the uncashed checks almost buried the sign that warned his visitors DON'T FUCK WITH THE WIZARD.

The Brandleys wanted the wizard. Like anyone else who had ever read a newspaper in the state of Texas, they knew his reputation. He was fearless and completely contemptuous of all forms of authority—particularly district attorneys. He pulled tricks and staged stunts that had never been written up in any lawbook. He got into fights. He was rude, and he was a bully, even to his clients. He often refused pointblank to take a case. But he was a winner. He won cases when other attorneys begged for plea bargains. He had robbed the executioner of so many victims that he had lost count—at least fifteen hundred of them. If he took a case, he would fight until he won it. The Brandleys wanted a winner.

The first Morris and Brown knew of the family's decision was several weeks later, on December 3, when Peggy Stevens passed them a formal notice she had received from Foreman's firm announcing that it was now representing Clarence Brandley.

The two attorneys felt as though they had been slapped in the face. When they found out that the Brandleys had paid their fee to Foreman, they felt as though they had also had their wallet taken. But it was not just a matter of pride or even money. This case now really mattered to them. It had become a symbol of all that they had been fighting against all these years: small towns and mean people; white people and black victims. If ever they had wondered, they long ago stopped doubting that Brandley was innocent. He was the ultimate victim. They believed they could prove it, and if they kept fighting, they could win a great victory. If they were not going to be paid, that was bad news, but they still wanted to fight.

George Morris called Percy Foreman. He knew him from years back, when Morris was fresh out of law school and had gone to work for Foreman briefly in Houston. Foreman was instantly embarrassed—and angry at the Brandleys, who had not told him that other attorneys were still working on the case. He told Morris that they must all work on the case together. They would sort out the fee as they went along. So a new team was born.

In January the stalling finally stopped. And instantly Don Brown knew there was something wrong.

It was January 21, 1982, when he got the formal letter, headed "State of Texas v. Clarence Lee Brandley," from Peggy Stevens. "This is to advise you that the record is complete in the above styled and numbered cause. You now have fifteen days in which to file any objection to said record."

Brown managed to get Brandley sent down from Huntsville to help him check the record. Making sure that everything was accurate was a big job. If there was a mistake, it could cause them trouble later at the appeal. And it was not just the transcript of the last trial, which Mary Johnson had finally finished and which ran to more than two thousand pages. There were photocopies and descriptions of all the exhibits: the precious few witness statements the defense had managed to obtain; the photographs it had finally salvaged; the thirteen hairs and all the expert reports on them; the autopsy report; the dead girl's clothes with their spots of blood; Icky Peace's little armory and his narcotics card. They were all registered and copied into the official record, while the originals were stored safely in the courthouse. They all had to be checked within fifteen days. That was when Brown with his bulldozer mind first became suspicious.

Each day he went over to the courthouse, took the elevator up to the fourth floor, and sat quietly with Brandley in his cell while they both read through papers. Odd things soon caught his eye. Some of the witness statements, for example, had been put into evidence during the first trial when there was a court reporter who always marked her exhibits with little stickers: blue ones for the defense and yellow ones for the state. Brown knew them well. But these photocopies did not show the stickers. Then there was something wrong with some of the exhibit numbers: the photocopy of an exhibit in the record would have one number, but when it was referred to in the trial transcript, it had another. That made no sense. They all were numbered during the trial. How could the numbers have changed so they no longer matched? There was something else, too. A couple of exhibits had not been copied into the record at all. The photocopy of Icky Peace's narcotics card, for example, was nowhere to be seen.

Brown went off to see Peggy Stevens. He told her there was something wrong with the record. "It's like it wasn't made up from the originals or something," he said. "There's something wrong."

Peggy Stevens shrugged and smiled at Brown. "I'm sure I don't know what could have happened," she told him.

"Well, I want the originals."

The district clerk smiled sweetly again. "They are up in the exhibits room, Don. I'll see what I can do for you."

"All right then. I'll come by and have a look this afternoon."

"Sure, Don. I'll be sure and get them for you."

Brown had the feeling he was on to something, but he was damned if he knew what it was.

That afternoon Brown was back in Peggy Stevens's office. The district clerk showed him a box of papers, but as soon as he looked at them, he could tell they were not right.

"These are the same as the copies we've got already," he grumbled. "They got no stickers, Peggy."

"Well, I don't understand that, Don."

Brown shook his head. He was beginning to simmer. He was not sure he understood either, but he had an idea of someone who might. "I've got to go see Jim Keeshan about something in a minute. I'm gonna find out what he knows about this." Brown strode off to pick up some papers and then made his way to the district attorney's office, pondering the mystery, scenting trouble. But he got no joy at the DA's office, just Keeshan's secretary, Kathy Olson, telling him that the DA was not there right now and she really couldn't say when he was going to be available and she was really sorry.

Brown's temperature was now well past boiling. As politely as he could, he told Olson that he knew damn well that they were up to something and he was going to get to the bottom of it. Then he shambled off, cursing Keeshan under his breath.

Don Brown's difficulties were soon the joke of the month all over the courthouse. Everyone was talking about how he had stood in Peggy Stevens's office, raving and raging at her, and then how he had gone and stood outside Jim Keeshan's office, raving and raging at Kathy Olson. In the DA's office they loved it. Poor old Don, they said. Best joke in a long time.

The truth was that not everyone enjoyed the joke.

People in the courthouse knew things, things they had heard in the offices or had read in private papers. They let them go by. They heard stories about Jim Keeshan and the Brandley case, and they put them out of their minds. They knew all about the project to convict Clarence Brandley, but it was not exactly their business. But the truth was that not all of them enjoyed it. Some of them were beginning to feel bad about it. Some of them were feeling it was maybe time to stop being innocent bystanders.

It was only a couple of days after Don Brown's run-in with Peggy Stevens. He and Brandley were still poring over the record of the case, trying to list all the mistakes and missing exhibits. They had less than a week before their work had to be completed. Brown was now convinced that there was something seriously wrong and that Peggy Stevens was deliberately covering up, but he was still trying to find out just what it was. Brown was also trying to earn a living, and every so often he would have to leave Brandley to go down to the courts to represent other clients. It was on one such visit that Frank Robin took him aside.

Robin was new to the courthouse. He was a sharp young attorney, in his late twenties, tall and dark with a clean-cut Superman kind of look about him. He had just been hired out of private practice as an assistant to Jim Keeshan. Brown had dealt with him on a couple of cases and found him personable enough. Now Robin took him into his office and closed the door. He was nervous.

"Look, Don, I'm going to tell you something. But you must hold it in confidence. I'll get fired if this gets out. You understand?"

Brown said he understood.

"I got to tell you this thing." He paused again and then plunged: "You see, the evidence in the Brandley trial has gone."

Brown looked at him. Gone?

"It's gone. Almost all of the original exhibits, so far as I know. I thought you ought to know."

"Well, I've been trying to figure it out. What in the hell happened?"

Now Robin told his story. Mary Johnson had been working on the trial transcript, and she had not gotten around to making photocopies of all the exhibits for the record when the whole lot had just disappeared out of her office. He did not know how it had happened, whether it was accidental or deliberate, but he knew it was a big secret. This had happened several weeks back, around the second week in January, and ever since then the prosecutors had been trying to cover it up. They had agreed that the defense would not be told. Judge Martin was in on it. So was Keeshan, and so was Peggy Stevens. Jim Keeshan and his secretary had been making copies of everything they had in their files and then trying to reconstruct anything that was missing. They had been desperate to throw the defense off the scent. Keeshan had been saying privately that he was going to blame some janitor who worked in the courthouse for throwing everything away. Keeshan had even been out to the garbage dump with Judge Martin and Mary Johnson to dig around and try to find the exhibits, but there was no telling if they had just been going through the motions.

Brown laughed for a moment. He had seen them. He remembered looking out his window several weeks before and seeing the three of them going off somewhere in the middle of the afternoon. He had wondered about it at the time. Now he could just imagine Keeshan and Martin in their sleek suits and Mary with her two-hundred-dollar shoes poking around in some flyblown garbage dump. Still, this was serious. The more he thought about it, the more serious it got.

He thanked Frank Robin and promised he would keep his confidence, and then padded quietly back across the courthouse square to his office to think. There were several angles to this.

First, there was the deceit by the other side. The district attorney, who was supposed to follow a code of ethical conduct, had been conspiring with the district clerk, who was supposed to be an impartial public official, and with the judge, who was supposed to be independent of all sides, to cover up the destruction of evidence. Brown found it hard to believe that this cozy little club had only just been formed. All through the trial and then during the hearing to win a new trial, Morris and Brown had felt they were somehow the victims of a conspiracy. Now for the first time he could prove that the bastards had been working together. Improperly. Unjustly.

Brown could see they were trying to stall him so that his fifteen days for filing objections to the record would be over before he could find out the truth. He remembered Peggy Stevens something like ten days after the destruction of the exhibits primly writing him that "the record is now complete in the above styled and numbered case." That was a lie. And smiling sweetly and saying, "Yes, Don, of course, Don," and promising to get him the originals when she already knew they were gone. Then leaving him standing helplessly outside Keeshan's office.

This was not the first time in the history of Texas that exhibits had been lost. There was an established procedure for both sides to come to court and reconstruct the record. But in the established procedure the people in the courthouse were not supposed to cover up the loss. Why had they done that? Brown could only begin to guess, but it smelled of foul play.

First, the semen swabs from the dead girl. Then Brandley's pubic hair. Then the photographs from the day of the crime. Then Jo Ellen Parrish's statements. Now everything else. All lost and gone forever. How were they ever going to impress the Court of Criminal Appeals with Icky Peace's narcotics card if they could not show it to them so that the appellate judges could see how realistic it was? Or his gun or his club? Icky Peace could now start pretending they were just toys from his imaginary city.

The photographs were gone, too. There was one particular picture of the dead girl that Brown thought was vital. It had been taken in the morgue, and it showed some sort of reddish brown stain on her backside. That stain had not been there in the earlier pictures, taken in the props loft. Brown saw this as evidence that she had emptied her bladder after she was dead, on the way to the morgue, staining herself with her blood in the process. That knocked a big hole in the timing of Jim Keeshan's version of events since it suggested that she had been killed before she went to the rest room, before anyone claimed Clarence Brandley arrived on the scene. Now the evidence was gone.

Then there were the hairs from the dead girl's body. Perhaps they would ultimately prove to be the most important evidence of all—the best clues to the real culprit. Now they were lost and gone.

How many coincidences does it take to make a conspiracy?

Brown went to see George Morris. Then he talked to Percy Foreman's office in Houston. They had to do something about this. The real joke was that whatever they decided to do, they had to go back through the same courthouse to do it.

They moved cautiously. They could not confront the people in the courthouse with their knowledge without running the risk of exposing Frank Robin as their source. Besides, it would be interesting to watch Keeshan and his friends trying to keep up their charade without realizing that the audience had seen through them.

They scheduled a hearing for February 5, 1982, just inside their fifteen-day limit, and filed a straightforward motion in which they listed all the discrepancies that Brown and Brandley had noticed in the record and innocently asked for the originals to be brought to court. At the hearing they listened politely to the other side's poker-faced explanation that it might take a while to prepare for such a hearing. They agreed to wait a week. All that the defense attorneys asked was that Brandley be allowed to stay in jail in Conroe to help them continue to review the record. Judge Martin immediately ordered that Brandley be returned to Huntsville that day.

A week later Judge Martin agreed to give the state a little more time to prepare before having to produce the original exhibits in court.

The defense watched the play. Don Brown was still wrestling with the tactical problem of how to confront the prosecution without exposing Frank Robin. He could not tell how many people knew about this and whether Robin could be identified as the source if Brown went public with what he knew. He was slumped in his office late one afternoon, trying to clear a path through the problem, when his phone rang, and he heard a familiar voice.

"It's Jan."

Jan? It was Janet Dial, Judge Martin's old secretary. Brown had not heard from her for months. She had left the courthouse a few months after the Brandley trial had ended, disenchanted with the atmosphere she had found there.

Janet Dial was not the sort of person who wasted time

making a point. "Don," she said, "Mary Johnson just called me from the courthouse. She's scared to call you direct, but there's some things you ought to know. It's about the Brandley case."

Brown had not confronted Mary Johnson about the flaws in the trial record she had produced. Now he suggested that he and George Morris should meet the two women.

"I don't know if Mary will do it" came the reply. "I tell you, Don, she's frightened of those people in the courthouse. But I've told her that you have to know what's happening. I'll try and get her to come, but we can't meet in town. Someone might see us."

Brown started to take notes as Dial directed him to some godforsaken spot out by Lake Conroe. They were to meet there at seven.

"You won't tell anyone, will you, Don?"

"Don't worry. Y'all be there and we'll meet you. We won't say a word to anyone."

That courthouse was fraying at the edges. Brown hurried through to Morris's office to tell him the news.

It was the kind of night when trees come down on power lines and anyone with any sense stays home. George Morris pointed his old Plymouth sedan up Interstate 45 and peered through the windshield wipers at the lights ahead. He had given up smoking, on his doctor's advice, but that did not stop him from coughing. Brown lit up another Malibu in the passenger seat in what he hoped was a discreet fashion.

They had spent the last hour trying to anticipate what it was that Janet Dial and Mary Johnson could want with them, whether it could be the missing exhibits or something else. This was obviously no social engagement. They just had to wait and see. Twenty minutes out of Conroe, Morris swung off the freeway and headed west down an old farm road that cut a narrow path through the pitch black shadows of the pine trees. The wind was thrashing the rain down onto the windshield. There were no more lights now. Ten minutes down the farm road, Lake Conroe opened up like a black hole on their right-hand side. Then Morris saw what he was looking for, a rectangular patch of asphalt leading down to a jetty at the water's edge. On a spring day it was a peaceful little cove for a quiet picnic, a good place to launch a pleasure boat. On a night like this it was plain scary.

As soon as he turned off the road, his headlights caught the outline of a black Chevrolet, sitting still and dark at the edge of the asphalt. Morris stopped and switched off his lights. For chrissake, thought Brown, what were they doing here? Two men of advancing years playing around like Burt Reynolds. What if it was a setup? Grabbing their jackets to the front of their chests, the two attorneys ducked out of the car, butted their way through the splintering rain, and heaved themselves into the backseat of the waiting Chevrolet. The two women had been trying to smoke themselves out of a nervous breakdown. Brown lit up again, and Morris coughed quietly.

Mary Johnson spoke first. She was plainly frightened—of losing her job or her court reporter's license and of getting into trouble with the courthouse. "You can use what I'm going to tell you," she said. "Just don't use my name." Morris and Brown agreed that they would not use her name unless there was no alternative. Then Johnson poured out the whole story of the missing exhibits. She had to tell them because there was a cover-up in the courthouse. The exhibits had been in a box in her office while she was working on the record and she had come in one Monday morning—she thought it was January 11—and they were gone. She just could not believe it. She was so worried. Then there had been this cover-up.

Morris and Brown, still anxious to protect Frank Robin, pretended that this was the first they had heard of any missing exhibits and encouraged her to tell more.

As soon as she had found they were missing, Johnson said, she had gone to Judge Martin and told him. He had told Keeshan and Peggy Stevens. She had assumed they would try to sort it out with the defense, but instead the judge had ordered her to keep it quiet and on no account to say anything that could leak to the defense attorneys because they would just make a big deal about it.

"Damn right we would have," said Brown.

According to Johnson, Keeshan and the judge had tried to fix it so that the defense would never find out what had happened. They had all agreed together that Peggy Stevens would keep fobbing them off, so they would have time to fake everything they needed to make it look as if they still had the originals. And that day when Brown had been left standing outside Keeshan's office, he didn't know the half of it, she said. The truth was that as soon as he had told Peggy Stevens that he intended to raise this with the district attorney, Stevens had called the DA and the judge to warn them. That was why he had been left standing outside—because Keeshan had heeded the warning and sent his secretary out to head him off. Peggy Stevens had been laughing about it.

Don Brown shook his head in disgust. It was hard to believe that there was really a man's life at stake in the middle of all this. These people just did not give a damn about that black man.

Mary Johnson said that Keeshan had worked out a story to explain everything if they got caught. He was going to say that one of the janitors in the courthouse had thrown the exhibits away by mistake. It was nonsense, she said. The janitors never went into her office. They were under permanent instructions not to go in there. She did her own cleaning. And even if for some reason they had gone in there, they could not possibly have mistaken the exhibits box for trash; Peace's gun and the knives were clearly visible.

But there was someone else who did have keys to her office: Jim Keeshan. Johnson described how her secretary had been working late one evening when suddenly someone turned a key in the lock and opened the door. It was Jim Keeshan with his investigator, Charlie Ray. They had been surprised to see the secretary there and had said something about wanting to make a diagram of the office and that they would come back another time. Johnson was not saying Keeshan had taken the exhibits. She really did not know. She was just saying she never believed a word of this story about janitors.

In the backseat Brown's mind was whirring, trying to figure this out. If it was no accident by the janitors, it had to be either the state or the real murderer. The murderer never could have got into Mary Johnson's office without breaking the door, so it had to be the state. The prosecutors must be worried about losing the appeal and must have figured it would be better to tell the town that they could not stage a retrial than to go to trial and lose.

Now Janet Dial had something to say. She explained that she had been very worried all the time she worked for Judge Martin and how she had felt there was such prejudice against Brandley in the courthouse.

Then she told them the secret that had been worrying its way through her memory for months now: how Jim Keeshan and Judge John Martin had been holding secret meetings all through the Brandley trial and how she knew these were no social get-togethers because sometimes they were still talking as they came out and she had heard them talking together about the Brandley case.

Mary Johnson cut in. She, too, knew about the meetings. "They were kind of rehearsing things," she said, "rehearsing rulings and objections, you know, so that they could get things their way in court."

Morris and Brown swore gently through the smoke. All these years they had worked with the law, believing in what they were doing, believing in the system, believing that even a black man in a white town could get something like justice if they worked hard enough at it. Now this. This was even worse than the missing exhibits. It struck right at the heart of the justice that was supposed to reign in that courthouse. If the judge and the prosecution were colluding, then the whole trial was a charade, just a fancy ritual with a foregone conclusion, and this whole system they believed in wasn't worth a handful of dust. Yet it was no surprise. So many times in the last trial, they had fought and lost and failed to see the reason why.

"Those scumbags," said Brown. "I knew it. I just knew it."

The secrecy that had surrounded the investigation of the Brandley case now had a good-size hole in it. Looking through it, Morris and Brown were torn between disbelief and anger.

The four of them talked a little longer in the back of the smoke-filled Chevrolet and then parted through the storm.

Now they could go on the attack. Morris and Brown spoke to Percy Foreman's office, and on February 16 they fired a new motion into the court in which they said explicitly that "the defense had reason to believe that the original exhibits are missing" and insisted that all the available exhibits should be produced in court. Judge Martin finally agreed that this should happen on March 5. The defense prepared for a showdown.

Before the hearing, however, Frank Robin surfaced again. Once more he took Don Brown into his office, recited his prayer for confidentiality, and then told Brown he had discovered that the district attorney had deliberately suppressed information that he should have passed to the defense during the Brandley trial. According to Robin, the DA had received a call from a woman who said she believed Icky Peace might have killed the girl at the high school. Her reason was simple and personal: Peace had once lived with her family, and when she was eighteen, he had tried to assault her sexually. Keeshan's investigator, Charlie Ray, had taken a statement from the woman, and then the state had buried it. Robin showed Brown a copy of the statement but insisted that he could not keep it.

Brown was no longer surprised by what he heard. Any district attorney in the country knew that that kind of information should have been shared with the defense attorneys, particularly when they were trying to show that Icky Peace was a reasonable alternative suspect. But what could he do with it now? The trial was over. He could not even put it into the appeal, since new facts had to be entered within thirty days of the end of the trial and that time had long passed. They could only store it away and try to find a use for it later. Brown thanked Robin and pledged to cover his footsteps.

Next it was Judge Lynn Coker's turn to break cover. Morris and Brown had never distrusted Coker the way they had most of the judges in the courthouse. He was always affable, and he meant well. His problem, they had always found, was that he did not have the heart to stand up to the courthouse people. He was the judge who had allowed Sam Robertson, Jr., to keep his grip on the Brandley case when Morris and Brown had first tried to recuse Robertson.

Coker came from a family of East Texas attorneys. His father, Ernest, had a fearsome reputation. As a county attorney in the 1930s he took the controversial confession from Bob White that was later rejected by the Supreme Court in Washington. As a judge Ernest Coker later presided over the trial of the police officer who was cleared of murdering Greg Steele. His reputation for toughness and harsh dealings had not prevented Don Brown from recusing him back in 1978. Shortly after that the old man had stepped down, and his mild-mannered son Lynn had been put up to replace him. Lynn Coker had probably never in his life stood up to his father, and now he would not stand up for anything if it was going to cause trouble. Almost shyly he approached Morris and Brown in the courthouse and called them into his office.

"Has anybody told you that the Brandley evidence is missing?"

Don Brown wondered just how many more informants they were going to develop in this courthouse.

"No one has told us officially," he said. "But we've heard scuttlebutt around the halls. We know that Peggy Stevens won't produce the exhibits."

"Well, it's no longer rumor," whispered the judge. "I have it from an unimpeachable source."

"Well, thank you, Judge."

"What I can't understand," Judge Coker confided, warming to his theme, "is how they could carry on like this without telling the defense attorneys. It just boggles the imagination."

"It boggles ours, too," said Brown.

"Anyway, I can't tell you any more," said the judge, who was already scurrying away. "I can't tell you anything officially. You understand."

Early in the morning of Friday, March 5, 1982, a jailer led Clarence Brandley out of his cell in Huntsville. He had been in the cell for a year. It was nine feet long and three feet wide. The front was made of bars, so that he could always be seen by a passing guard. It contained his bed and his Bible and a library book. Brandley had been learning to live on death row. He found he had to fight a little. There were officers who liked to give him a hard time, put him on discipline charges when he had done nothing, that kind of thing. But he could handle it, mostly by keeping his head down and minding his own business. The really big fight was inside himself.

He felt bitter and angry, but he knew he could not let himself feel that way. It would just destroy him, just eat through him like acid. So he tried to get a grip on himself. He quit smoking. His brothers thought that was strange—to quit cigarettes right when he needed them. He made himself fast for one day each week. So he felt clean, and he felt as if he were making a decision about himself. Everything in here was taken away from you, not just freedom but self-respect, too. Every little thing in your life was decided for you: what to watch on TV; when to eat; what to eat; what to wear. But when he fasted, he got a grip.

He taught himself to meditate. He would get up early—not when they decided but when he decided: about four-thirty every morning. And he would read his Bible and sit, calmly and quietly with his eyes shut, and just be easy, try to drain all that bitterness away.

Right now he couldn't say that he was winning the fight. But he sure was trying.

Morris and Brown spent the morning in their office making final preparations for the big showdown. If they played it right at that afternoon's hearing, they just might be able to find out who had taken those exhibits, and that might just take them to the heart of the conspiracy in the courthouse. The phone rang. Brown answered.

"It's Jan."

Morris watched as Brown's face hardened and his intake of smoke increased dramatically. He stopped work and waited. Brown finally hung up the phone and banged his fist down hard on his desk. It seemed that Mary Johnson had just been talking to Janet Dial again. Johnson was terribly upset. She had sat in on a meeting the previous evening between Jim Keeshan and Judge Martin. It had been a late meeting, after everyone else had gone home, in Keeshan's private office. The subject of the meeting had been today's hearing. Johnson said she had watched the district attorney and the judge plotting together to fix the hearing so that the defense would not be able to call any witnesses or uncover any evidence about what had happened to the exhibits.

Sitting right in front of her, the DA and the judge had agreed that as soon as the hearing started, the DA would offer to save time by giving evidence in person about his investigation into the disappearance. The judge would agree, and Keeshan would then explain that after a diligent investigation he had concluded that unnamed janitors had accidentally thrown the exhibits away. He would go on to say that there was no evidence of a criminal intent and that therefore no janitor would be put on trial for anything. Then, when the defense tried to call its own witnesses, Keeshan would object that he had already given all the facts and that the witnesses should not be called, and Judge Martin would agree. So the defense attempt to get to the truth would end.

George Morris was deeply offended. "It's like a banana republic. Except that you probably couldn't get away with that kind of thing in a banana republic."

There was little time to act. The two attorneys quickly agreed that for the third time in the case of the *State of Texas* v. *Clarence Brandley*, the judge had stepped so far out of line that he would have to be removed by recusal. In haste they drafted a motion to remove John Martin from the case. This, too, was quickly achieved since they now had the format for a recusal permanently filed in their computer.

They had no time to revive the long history of their unhappiness with the judge during the trial and the subsequent effort to win a new trial. Nor did they touch on the secret meetings that, Janet Dial had now told them, had been taking place since the judge first took on the case. They simply accused their former friend John Martin of meeting secretly with the district attorney to rig that afternoon's hearing and of plotting for nearly two months to conceal the disappearance of the exhibits—"the clear intent of such conspiracy being to illegally deprive the defendant of an effective appeal."

The two silver-haired attorneys crossed the street to the courthouse, where they found Brandley waiting in the courtroom, and told him what was happening. Brandley smiled quietly and shook his head; how could he not be bitter when people treated him like this?

As the clock in John Martin's court moved around to one-thirty, Morris and Brown felt a terrible weight settle over them. John Martin, once their friend, had sunk so low. The man they had had such faith in had given in to all the corruption in the courthouse and all the lowest and nastiest demands of this community. He had put Clarence Brandley's life in jeopardy. George Morris felt particularly bad. He was the one who was going to have to stand up and confront Martin. They had decided to do it in private, in chambers. It seemed to have helped with Sam Robertson that they had given him the chance to go gracefully without public exposure, and it might make it a little easier on them, too. It was one-forty by the time the judge finally walked into court.

Morris immediately rose to his feet and asked to go into chambers. The judge agreed, the press and the few spectators trooped out, and Morris rose again. Brandley stared unblinkingly at the judge in his robe, as Morris explained that they understood about the missing exhibits and the various steps that had been taken. He paused, and his voice broke a little as he stumbled on.

"We also understand, Judge, that we are not going to be able to put on any witnesses here this afternoon in regard to our motion; that it is all going to be conducted by the District Attorney where he is going to take the witness stand and testify to his investigation and so forth."

Brandley could see the fear creeping over Martin's face. He watched this man who had sat in judgment over him fumble for his pack of cigarettes, his fingers trembling.

Morris trudged on. "We would like to ask the court, so that we can keep out any publicity or anything like that, for you to voluntarily recuse yourself from hearing this matter." Morris paused. "If you don't, then we have a motion in our file right now to recuse you from any further hearings."

He had done it. Judge Martin was speechless, but Keeshan was quickly on his feet. To the astonishment of Morris and Brown, he started confirming their story. Yes, he said, he had been planning to save time by taking the witness stand himself, and he had asked the judge to let him do that. "But as far as you not having the opportunity to put on witnesses, I am sure that was not my intention."

Morris and Brown had learned not to underestimate Keeshan. He was quick. He could see that Morris and Brown were not just guessing here, that they had got some kind of informant, so he was not going to tangle himself up in denials. But he was still fighting, trying to limit the damage.

He had been conducting a criminal investigation, he said. He had no need to go telling the defense about such a thing. And Judge Martin should certainly not recuse himself. He knew more about the case than anyone. Morris and Brown started hammering away at the judge, Brown quoting chapter and verse from the canons of judicial conduct.

The judge finally managed to speak and admitted he was not sure of the correct procedure. Brandley was still gazing at the judge in silent contempt, watching now as he reached for a second cigarette. Suddenly, the judge seemed to feel the condemned man's eyes on his face, and he glanced up and instantly dropped the pack of cigarettes, like an admission of guilt.

The attorneys wrangled on. Finally, the judge decided that he needed time to think. "I might decide over the weekend to recuse myself. I don't know. At this time, I am just going to recess the case."

They agreed to meet again in a week, by which time the judge would have decided whether to step down or face a formal recusal hearing in public. Judge Martin walked briskly out of the room.

* * *

By the end of the week the Brandley case had its fourth judge—affable, ineffectual Lynn Coker. John Martin had never come back to the defense to say that he had decided to step down. Morris and Brown heard about his decision in the corridors of the courthouse and then read about it in the *Courier*, in which the judge claimed that he was leaving the case because he had "personal knowledge of some missing exhibits." Morris and Brown could not remember a case that had generated such bitterness. It was rare enough to recuse any judge, but to recuse three in one case in only eighteen months was unique in their experience.

It was by no means certain that it was worth it. One after another, judges seemed to succumb to the corrupting influence of those in the courthouse and to the townspeople's demands for the black man's life. Lee Alworth had become enmeshed in Jim Keeshan's plot to deny the defense evidence in the case and to cheat Brandley of his bail. Sam Robertson, Jr., had plunged into the same tangle and then more or less joined the prosecution during Brandley's first trial. Now John Martin had been exposed for making secret deals with the DA.

One after another they went the same way. As far as Morris and Brown were concerned, the judges were no different from any of the other good ol' boys who ran this town. The truth was that if they wanted to be reelected every four years, the judges could not afford to be any different. Morris and Brown held out little hope that things would change with Lynn Coker, the courthouse's cowardly lion.

On Friday, March 12, 1982, Lynn Coker sat for the first time in the Brandley case to consider the vexing question of the missing exhibits. He opened the hearing by announcing that some janitors had apparently and inadvertently thrown away the box containing the exhibits, which had now been bulldozed into the ground at the Montgomery County Sanitary Landfill. With the help of Peggy Stevens, Judge Coker started listing the 166 exhibits that were lost and the 143 other exhibits that were not.

Don Brown was on his own in court. George Morris was ill. Now was the time to fight, now that finally, after two months, the defense had been told officially about the loss of the exhibits. Don Brown rose and said it was not good enough for the judge to announce a version of events like this. How could anyone be certain that this version was correct? They needed a public hearing with witnesses and evidence to try to establish the truth. Jim Keeshan objected that there was no need for any such hearing. At that point Judge Coker made his first ruling.

"That's what I think," he said. "I see no reason to have any type of evidentiary hearing in connection with how the exhibits became lost. The fact is, they are no longer present in the courthouse."

Keeshan claimed that it was the state that had suffered from the disappearance because it had to bear the burden of reconstructing the record. He took a swipe at the defense attorney by suggesting that he could not have told them of the disappearance since he was conducting a criminal inquiry and they were among his suspects. Brown insisted that they had a legal right to make a record of how they were lost and that some of the missing originals were vital to their appeal.

"We have nothing on the record that is competent evidence to show that the exhibits were even lost," he said.

"Well," said Judge Coker, "I'm competent and I say they're gone."

"I still object to that because it is hearsay."

"OK," said the judge. "You're overruled."

Once again the truth was being buried. And surely, thought Brown, this district attorney would not be so eager to bury it if he honestly believed that the truth could hurt the defense. No, if Keeshan was not involved in the disappearance of the exhibits, then at the very least he knew something about it that he was frightened of. But Judge Coker was not interested.

The two sides then embarked on a detailed negotiation in which they agreed to correct the errors in the record that had been made by Jim Keeshan and his friends in their hurried efforts to cover up the disappearance of the originals. But there was nothing they could do about the dead girl's blood-stained clothes, Icky Peace's narcotics card or his weapons, the photographs, or the vital hairs that had been left on Cheryl Fergeson's body. They were lost forever—and with them, perhaps, the chance of proving Brandley's innocence.

It was during April of 1982 that George Morris learned he had cancer of the lung. By the summer he knew he was dying. Don

Brown found it hard to imagine working in Conroe without him. It would never be the same. Brown's only hope was that Morris would survive for long enough to see them somehow break through on the Brandley case. Now that they had finally got the official record, they could file an appeal. And it would be a strong one. They could describe the flimsy, insufficient evidence, package up all the bias and all the prejudice, and present it to the Court of Criminal Appeals.

The court in Austin was not always reliable. Its nine judges were elected, not appointed, and had in the past been guilty of allowing their politics to interfere with their judgments. There was obviously a risk that they might think that a ruling in favor of Clarence Brandley would alienate some of their white voters. But this appeal would be strong enough, Brown believed, to cut through any political undergrowth.

The trouble was that Brown was finding it almost impossible to put the appeal together. Morris could not help. Brown himself was still working unpaid and was trying to run other cases through the courthouse to earn a living. Then in July his eighteen-year-old son, Bo, was almost killed in a car crash. That threw Brown off the tracks for a while. He had brought up Bo and his daughter, Celia, alone. Their mother had died when they were children, and now he took time off to help heal his son, whose head, neck, and back had been badly crushed.

Finally, in the fall Brown decided that Brandley was never going to get an appeal unless he took it on his shoulders alone. He stopped all other work and buried himself in his office. After several weeks of solid study he emerged with seventy-five pages of pure aggression. Here was the whole horrible saga: the factual details, the legal arguments, the relevant cases, and the inescapable conclusion that an innocent man had been wrongly convicted and sentenced to death.

He filed it with the Court of Criminal Appeals.

Several months later the court replied. Appeal briefs could be no longer than fifty pages, it said. Brown would have to cut back his argument.

This made Don Brown angry. He knew all about the fifty-page rule. He had been told that all he had to do was file a motion asking to go over fifty pages, and in an important case like this it would be all right. He had done that, and the judges in their wisdom had decided that their bureaucratic rule was more important than the truth about an innocent man on death row.

Brown was not about to give up. He took his seventy-five-page brief to his secretary. "Can we print this a little bit smaller and reduce the margins and kind of run it right down to the bottom of each page?"

The secretary said that was no problem. A few days later the brief had been magically reduced to only forty-seven pages without losing a word. Brown then added a few extra points to take up his full fifty pages and sent a copy off to Percy Foreman for his approval.

In January 1983, a full two years after the trial, the appeal was finally lodged in Austin, where the judges accepted it without comment. Morris, though terribly weakened, saw it on its way.

Two months later Jim Keeshan filed his brief, and the court in Austin rolled slowly into action. It announced that it wanted both sides in the case to travel to Austin to argue their points.

By this time Percy Foreman had passed the Brandley case to his young partner, Mike De Geurin. Foreman and De Geurin were one of the oddest couples ever to grace a courtroom. Foreman was as tough as a tree, a big-boned, barefisted, heavy-handed prizefighter of an attorney. Mike De Geurin, a clear twelve inches shorter, was as gentle as a child, his face almost permanently creased by his impish grin. He was everybody's favorite guy. De Geurin was a boyish blond version of Peter Falk playing Columbo—the same air of harmless innocence and twinkling charm, the same rather deferential stoop, and then the same sudden outbreaks of high-speed insight and lethal intelligence. District attorneys had learned to fear his charm just as they had learned to respect his old partner's aggression. Foreman loved him like a son.

Don Brown and Mike De Geurin agreed that they would go to Austin together to share the arguments. Austin was familiar ground to both men, but particularly to De Geurin, who had worked there as a clerk when he first left law school. Some of the judges there remembered him, if only because he had once ruined their ceremonial exit from the court at the end of a case by secretly locking the door through which they paraded, with the result that all nine judges stood up together, wheeled to the left, headed for the door and then piled into each other, creating a human concertina at the back of the court.

Before they left for Austin, Brown and De Geurin reviewed thousands of pages of transcribed hearings, checked witness statements and scientific reports, talked to Brandley in Huntsville, and finally thought they were ready for anything that the court could throw at them. They hardly dared admit it, but they could not see how they could lose. Even without the missing exhibits, no serious court could ignore this wealth of argument.

The hearing started badly. The judges announced that each side could have only twenty minutes to state its case. Brown and De Geurin took ten minutes each and did their best. Jim Keeshan was there to reply. Despite the restriction on their time, they believed they had done well. De Geurin had never seen a circumstantial case that was so weak, and he doubted if the court had either.

Now they waited.

Brandley waited on death row, a place that had now become scarier than ever. For years no one had been executed in Texas. The U.S. Supreme Court had closed the door at the end of death row and made the executioner redundant. But on December 7, 1982, as Brandley waited for his appeal to be filed, the courts opened the door again, and a young black man named Charlie Brooks was led through it, to the big building in the middle of Huntsville, to the gurney in the brightly lit room and the doctors with their catheters. Brandley would never forget that day.

Charlie Brooks had been on his wing, three cells down, and during recreation periods Brandley had gotten to know him. He had told him all about how he was being railroaded. On the day that Charlie Brooks was taken away, the prison staff had let him come down the wing and shake hands with people through the bars at the front of the cells. He had stopped outside Brandley's cell and told him goodbye and shook his hand. Then, as he was led off, he had turned and said: "You hang in there, man."

It was as if there were some consolation for him in thinking that Brandley, at least, might one day be free again.

Everything changed on death row once Charlie Brooks had gone. Until then everyone there had always believed that the death penalty was finished and that his sentence would be overturned and commuted to life in jail. When Charlie Brooks went, and the state started the killing again, nobody was safe anymore. Nobody knew who was going to be next. Nobody knew what to expect.

Brandley tried to stop worrying about it, while he waited.

* * *

Don Brown waited, too. It was a miserable time.

Frank Robin, his old contact in the district attorney's office, succumbed to disaster. Robin had left Conroe in July 1982 and gone to work for the U.S. attorney's office in Houston. There he had been accused of soliciting a two-hundred-thousand-dollar bribe from drug dealers he was investigating. The Justice Department had been scandalized by the case, and the U.S. attorney general in Washington, D.C., had played tapes of Robin allegedly extracting money from the criminals to President Reagan to stress the need for a war on drugs. Now, in the summer of 1983, Robin was jailed for ten years. Brown wanted to believe it was a mistake.

Then there was his son Bo. By the spring of 1983 he had been climbing back to health and he no longer wore the halo brace around his head. Brown started to hope he would recover completely. Then in June the boy was involved in another car crash, and this time it killed him.

Brown was still reeling from the blow when, two months later, George Morris finally succumbed to cancer.

Now Brown waited alone for the court in Austin.

A year rolled by. It was 1984. Still, there was no word from Austin. The sticky summer heat enveloped Conroe. Clarence Brandley was just approaching the end of his fourth year in jail when a group of people he had never heard of and who had never heard of him dealt him a bruising blow.

The U.S. Supreme Court in a completely unrelated case decided that if a man had a hung jury and was then convicted in a second trial, it was only the most recent trial that should be considered in his appeal. Previously, the courts had always said that both trials should be considered: if the man's first trial ought really to have ended in his acquittal, then it was unfair to expose him to a second trial. Now the Supreme Court had changed the rule.

By doing so, it had wiped from the record the whole history of Clarence Brandley's first trial and the behavior of Judge Sam Robertson, Jr., and it had kicked one of the legs out from under Don Brown's appeal.

Brown cursed their luck and cursed the long delay.

It was around this time that he found himself out on Route 105 in a roadside diner. He was just stopping for a glass of iced tea, and he saw a bunch of Montgomery County deputies sitting at a table, talking and laughing. He went over to say hi, and they showed him what it was they were laughing about—faded photographs of a black man being burned at the stake outside the courthouse in Conroe. Brown glanced at them just long enough to see the boxes and the flames and the white people watching. Then he left and cursed Conroe, too.

Still, the judges in Austin had more important things to do than to consider whether Clarence Brandley was innocent. It was now the spring of 1985. Just outside Conroe a black student who was hitchhiking on I-45 was abducted by four men, who bound him, beat him, and then covered him with tar and feathers before abandoning him in a field. In May, four and a half years after Brandley's conviction, two years since his appeal was filed, the judges finally published their ruling. It was a disaster.

The judges in Austin tore the defense apart point by point and emphatically confirmed Brandley's conviction. At every turn they supported Judge Martin and Jim Keeshan.

The judges not only satisfied themselves that there was plenty of evidence to show Brandley's guilt but added that there was no evidence even to suggest that anyone else had committed the offense. They approved the use of Danny Taylor's claim that Brandley had lusted after a group of schoolgirls. They were content that Monty Koerner had been asked about Brandley's previous record. They were happy with the restrictions on evidence about Icky Peace's armory and about his taped conversation with Ranger Styles.

At one point they considered the moment when Jim Keeshan had accused Don Brown of attacking the jury's verdict by appealing to any lingering doubts they might have. Brown had objected. The judge had started to overrule his objection but had swallowed his words. According to the transcript, Judge Martin had said: "Okay. Over—Let's proceed."

The Court of Criminal Appeals decided that this meant that Judge Martin had not really overruled Don Brown's objection, and therefore that he had nothing to complain about.

The nearest the appellate judges came to conceding anything to the defense was on Jim Keeshan's suggestion to the jurors that they should put themselves into the shoes of the dead girl's family. That had been an error, the judges conceded. But it had been a harmless one, they added, and needed no action on their part.

The defense immediately asked for a rehearing of their appeal. The court refused. It was over.

Don Brown and Mike De Geurin could only guess at the reasons for their failure. Maybe it was electoral politics, and those judges were plain scared of taking on white voters. Maybe it was judicial politics, and they preferred not to join such heated criticism of the Montgomery County Courthouse. Maybe the missing exhibits had harmed the defense. They could only guess. All they knew was that they had been beaten and that Clarence Brandley's life was now in real danger.

The despair in the defense camp was matched by the excitement in the courthouse. The mood there was sparkling. Not only had it won the Brandley case, but Jim Keeshan had been rewarded for his years of service as district attorney by being promoted to a judgeship in a new court that was being created in Conroe.

Before being sworn in by Judge Lee Alworth, Keeshan was praised to the skies in the courthouse, where his supporters boasted that he had won ninety-nine of the hundred jury trials he had fought. Keeshan accepted his new power with modesty. "I intend to be the best kind of judge as I know how," he told the *Courier*.

Judge Keeshan's first job was to swear in his successor as district attorney. The man chosen for the job was Peter Speers III, a lanky, fresh-faced young attorney from Pennsylvania who had settled in Conroe, where he had been working as Keeshan's assistant for three years. Speers had little of Keeshan's sharpness or experience, but it was a popular appointment in the courthouse; what Speers lacked in charisma, he made up in loyalty. He was Judge Alworth's brother-in-law. Peter Speers was reliable.

The excitement did not stop there. Now that the court in Austin had thrown out Brandley's appeal, there was only one more move to make to put the black janitor out of their lives.

On November 22, 1985, Clarence Lee Brandley was led through the corridors of the Montgomery County Courthouse. He was surrounded by armed men. His wrists were cuffed together and locked to a chain that ran around his waist. He was steered through a set of double doors and into a chair.

The room was full of people. Some of them he recognized: Mike De Geurin; Peter Speers; that Peggy Stevens woman with her strawberry-colored nails. Keeshan was there, too, sitting and making small talk with his friends. Brandley could just make out his mother back on the public benches. She was hunched into a ball, crying into her fists. Brown arms held her tight. Now the judge came in. Brandley knew him, too. It was John Martin.

It took only a minute. The words just trickled past him and left no trace. Except for the date. January 16, 1986. Less than two months. The words said that on January 16, 1986, he had to go through the door and be strapped to the gurney like Charlie Brooks so they could finish him off. Brandley tried to show nothing on his face. He did not want to look sad in case his mother saw him.

The judge was trying to make a big deal about how he was not going to have him killed before Christmas. As if he were doing him some big favor by killing him three weeks later. Brandley looked straight into the judge's eye. He did not want to yield to these people. He kept his grip.

As he was led back through the corridors with the chains and the armed men, his mother rose from her bench. Her eyes made out the shape of James Keeshan, and her voice soared over the courtroom like a hovering hawk. "I'm gonna pray for you," she sang, like a slow chant. "I'm gonna pray for you, Mr. Keeshan. How can you kill Clarence for something he didn't do? I'm gonna pray for you."

Keeshan dropped his head and hurried from the room.

Mike De Geurin watched him go. So they had an execution date. He had hoped and believed it would never come to this. It was a sickening moment. And there was something wrong with the way it had finally happened. What was John Martin doing setting the date of execution? He had been forced to step down from this case more than three years ago. This case was no longer any of his business.

De Geurin guessed he could have stopped him from doing it, but he had let him go ahead. It might give them some handle to grab hold of, to get the execution stalled, if all else failed. All the same, it seemed wrong.

In the beginning only a few people in the courthouse knew the truth.

Mary Johnson, the elegant court reporter, knew. She had been sitting next to Judge Martin when the district clerk, Peggy Stevens, had come up, as excited as a schoolgirl at her first dance, and talked to Judge Martin about it. Some of the people who worked in the district clerk's office knew. They had been there when Peggy Stevens had come in and started boasting about it.

Soon the truth was being whispered all over the courthouse. Judge Martin had got back on the Brandley case because Peggy Stevens had asked him. She had no business doing that, but that was how things were in the courthouse. She had a special reason. It was the date. That was what she wanted. January 16. Because January 16 was her birthday. She wanted the black man to die on her birthday. As a gift. So they could all celebrate. She had asked the judge to fix it for her. And the judge had agreed.

Chapter Seven

Mike De Geurin was at home in Houston. It was a Sunday evening, and in among the children's toys and the television, he was shuffling through his paperwork trying to get ready for the Brandley hearing in Conroe the next day.

He was just finishing when the phone rang. It was W. B. Etheridge, a veteran attorney from Conroe who had worked on the courthouse square all his life. He had been born in Conroe. His father had been the editor of the *Courier*. Etheridge had a reputation as a decent man, and he had followed the Brandley case, not just because the whole courthouse was still talking about it but also because he knew the Brandley family. Minnie Ola Brandley had worked for his mother and had more or less raised him. When Clarence Brandley had got into trouble over the rusty shotgun back in 1979, Etheridge's firm had represented him and settled the plea bargain.

He told De Geurin he had read that there was a hearing coming up on the Brandley case. "I just wondered if Peter Speers ever told you about Brenda Medina."

"Brenda who?"

"Brenda Medina," said Etheridge. "She's a client of mine."

"I never heard of her."

"Well, she came to me a while back and told me that her husband had confessed to killing that girl up at the high school. Right back when it happened, he confessed. So I took her over to Peter Speers's office so she could tell him."

De Geurin's mind was spinning trying to get a grip on this. "You telling me that this woman says the murderer confessed to her?"

240

"That's right. She says her husband confessed it."

"And she has told this to Peter Speers?"

"I took her over there. That was several weeks ago now. They interviewed her. Speers didn't tell you?"

"The son of a bitch never said a word."

"Well, I was afraid of that," said Etheridge. "So I thought I'd give you a call."

"And I'm very grateful to you. I can't think of any better way to wind up a weekend than get news like this."

De Geurin paused a moment and then asked the big question. "So who is her husband?"

"He's called Robinson. James Dexter Robinson. He used to work at the school."

De Geurin loved his work. People used to say he won cases because he put his heart out on the counsel's table and let the jury feel the way he felt. It was not a matter of tactics. There were some times when he just got caught up in the emotion of it all. That Monday morning was one of those times.

He left home early to drive to Conroe with Etheridge's words playing in his mind and a tight knot of excitement sitting in his stomach.

Ever since Judge Martin had set a date for Clarence Brandley's death, the defense attorneys had been fighting for time, using the ancient legal device of applying for a writ of habeas corpus to force the court to justify Brandley's incarceration. They had started raising any issue that had not been destroyed by the court in Austin.

De Geurin had brought in reinforcements. He had been working on his own with Percy Foreman, who was now too old to make court appearances and could do little more than lie on the couch in his office, barking orders and playing the wizard. De Geurin had told Foreman they had to get help, and Foreman, irascible as ever, had said that was fine with him as long as De Geurin did not mind paying for the help out of his own wages. De Geurin had agreed, and hired Paul Nugent.

Nugent was an odd addition to the odd couple. Foreman and De Geurin, for all their differences, were both full-time Texans, as happy on horseback out on their ranches or telling tall tales in a bar in the boonies as they were raising hell and bending rules in a courtroom. But Paul Nugent had grown up in New Jersey and gone to law school in Boston, on the other side of the universe, and he looked, sounded, and even thought uncannily like Bobby Kennedy.

Still, De Geurin liked him the very first time they met, down in Galveston in the federal court where Nugent was working as clerk to one of the judges. That job said a lot. A bright, well-groomed, well-spoken young guy like Nugent with a good law degree could have walked into one of those three-hundred-dollar-a-minute law firms in Manhattan and sat there with his meter running, earning a fortune working for some big corporation. But he had ducked out of that and deliberately looked for work out on the edge, where the money might not be so good but the cases would mean something. The fact that he had landed a federal judge as his first employer suggested he knew his law. Plus he laughed at De Geurin's stories.

The first day Nugent walked into his new office, halfway up a skyscraper in downtown Houston, he shook hands with the wizard, hailed Mike De Geurin, and was pointed at the Brandley "file," which consisted of a dozen big cardboard boxes, stuffed with thousands of pages of legal papers. Nugent devoured it all. He had no affection for the death penalty. At college he had taken up public speaking so that he could attack capital punishment. That experience had persuaded him to become an attorney.

Within weeks of the date being set for Brandley's death, De Geurin, Nugent, and Don Brown had put together enough arguments to apply for their writ of habeas corpus. Their strongest pitch had been one of the little nuggets of information passed to Don Brown by Frank Robin: that the DA had suppressed evidence of Icky Peace's once trying to assault an eighteen-year-old girl. They said that this suppression had denied Brandley due process. They had added three more issues: the photographs that had been lost by the Conroe police and that might have proved Brandley was not wearing a belt on the day of the crime; a juror from the second trial who, they had discovered, had been discussing the case with friends while the trial was still going on; the deliberate rejection of any juror who opposed capital punishment, a policy that they said inevitably produced a "conviction-prone" jury.

Peter Speers had fought them, but on January 6, just ten days before Brandley was due to die, the defense had succeeded in winning a stay of execution. Now, six months later, on June 17, 1986, they were preparing to stage a hearing on the four issues they had raised in their habeas corpus writ.

Until now De Geurin had not had much to fight with, but now, as he drove through the outskirts of Conroe, with the knot of excitement still tightening his stomach, he was looking forward to the next round.

He parked on the courthouse square, which was already heating up for another day at melting point, and hurried over to Don Brown's office with his battered briefcase full of papers. He passed old Mr. Gentry's menswear shop on the first floor, now abandoned and empty, and the blown-up black-and-white photograph of a smiling George Morris, which Don Brown had fixed at the top of the stairs, as if Morris were still watching over his old work.

De Geurin had already discovered that Brown's brain was like a gigantic filing cabinet. He had not only an entire library of Texas criminal justice tucked away in there but also the whole history of the case of Clarence Brandley, stretching back over nearly six years now, all dated and cataloged and ready to be retrieved. De Geurin told him all about Brenda Medina and James Dexter Robinson.

"Robinson?" asked Brown. "There was a Robinson came up in evidence."

De Geurin could almost hear Brown's brain clicking and whirring. Then he retrieved what he wanted: toward the end of the second trial, Brandley's old supervisor, David Harris, had talked about a set of keys that were missing. They had belonged to Icky Peace, but Peace had given them to a white man who had briefly worked at the school with the janitors. That white man's name was Robinson.

"The son of a bitch," said Brown. "But he wasn't James Dexter. He was Clarence—Clarence Robinson. But they've got to be connected."

The hearing was due to start in the courthouse. The question was how to use this new information. There was no point in throwing it straight into court without following it up. They needed to find this Brenda Medina, check out everything they could discover about James Dexter Robinson, particularly if he was related to Clarence Robinson and if he could have had those keys to get in and out of the auditorium. If it checked out, it was the best and biggest break they could have hoped for. But it would take time. For today they had to hold back.

Except for one interesting little game they could play with Peter Speers III.

De Geurin had never had any illusions about Jim Keeshan. He had always had a good relationship with him, because he had played along with the whole white man's courthouse and sat around while they all made jokes about niggers. But De Geurin had never trusted him, and he was glad he had been promoted out of the case. He wondered about Speers. The new district attorney had an innocent, maybe even honest, look about him. De Geurin was toying with the idea of trying to talk to him privately, to appeal to some decent streak in him and suggest that they should all work together to save this innocent man. It was only an idea. Now Don Brown suggested that he could test it, in public. They agreed on a plan.

The hearing was before Judge Lynn Coker. That in itself marked a small victory for the defense. Judge John Martin had done his best to take over the case again. After setting the death date, he had continued to act as though he were in charge, ignoring the recusal that had swept him out of court three years earlier. But the defense attorneys did not want him there. They regarded him as a ringleader in the attack on Clarence Brandley and believed that his presence was a guarantee that Brandley would die.

Late one afternoon during the spring De Geurin took a copy of the recusal papers and went to see Martin in his office in the courthouse. Like Morris and Brown before him, De Geurin had known Martin as a defense attorney and had previously thought well of him. He reckoned there was no need to go back to court to recuse him again. He just walked into his office and told him that he had no business in the case. Martin did not take it well.

"All right," he said. "All right. You can get some other son of a bitch to look him in the eye and tell him he is going to die."

"Well, you know you have been recused—"

"All right. All right. You think I care?"

And with that Judge Martin grabbed a large box of Brandley papers from the side of his desk, and with his arms stretched around it, he started heaving himself out of his office, prying open the door with his toe, and then staggering down the corridor toward the district clerk's office with it, muttering all the while: "All right. That's just fine with me. I'm off the case. That's just fine."

At that moment Don Brown happened to be passing. All he saw was the judge in his black robe, red in the face with exertion, straining to hold the box of papers, while he kicked helplessly on Peggy Stevens's door, which had, unfortunately for Judge Martin, already been locked for the night.

Now, with Judge Coker back on the bench, De Geurin prepared. He was not about to telegraph his punch. He played along with the hearing. He raised a new issue about Brandley's trial: the fact that every black potential juror had been excluded by the district attorney. He argued with Speers, who was complaining that things were moving too slowly and demanding a speedy execution. Then, just as Judge Coker was about to close the hearing, De Geurin set his test for Peter Speers.

"One further thing, to keep this from being piecemeal on down the road, I would ask the prosecutor at this point if there is any other exculpatory evidence which has come to their attention in this death penalty case that they are willing to pass on to me so I can add that also on to the writ of habeas corpus?"

Speers shook his head. "Your Honor, that's not our burden. I don't know of any exculpatory evidence—period—in this particular case."

De Geurin had got his answer. The prosecutors were trying to bury Brenda Medina's lead. Peter Speers had just failed the test. He was no different from his predecessor. The judge set a new date for the hearing and told both sides to be ready with their witnesses for July 17. The defense had exactly one month to find the truth about James Dexter Robinson, to loosen the noose around Clarence Brandley's neck.

Richard Reyna grew up tough. His father was Italian, his mother a Mexican-American. He was one of nine children who were crammed into a hole-in-the-wall apartment in a crime-riddled housing project in Houston with one stove and one bed for all the children, the girls on one side, the boys on the other, all head to toe. He got an ass-kicking a day. When he was seven, his father died, and things got worse.

It was not just his toughness that made Reyna a natural-born law officer. He was also street-wise and smart as a whip. People talked to him because he would keep playing parts and pulling strings and teasing them along until they wanted to tell him every secret they had ever had. And like most law officers, he was conservative, an active member of the Republican party, with pictures of presidents on his wall and a basic faith that if the American way of life could rescue him from the ghetto, it could rescue anyone. He believed that by becoming a law officer he could help people who grew up as he had, rescue more of them from the ghetto and its crime.

His only problem was that he became a law officer in the Montgomery County Sheriff's Department in Conroe. He could handle the racism. As soon as he joined the sheriff's department, his new colleagues started calling him Pancho and Chilibean, so Reyna, who had the build of a small bull, told them in all seriousness that if they did that again, he was going to have to tear their tongues out and stuff them up their asses. The problem came from trying to rescue people.

One time a woman from Montgomery came in and said three of her horses had gotten out of their field and gone onto her neighbor's land. The neighbor had just gone ahead and shot two of them—one in the eye and one in the leg. She had complained to the police in Montgomery, but they had done nothing because this neighbor of hers happened to be the mayor of the town. Reyna called him up, and the mayor laughed at him. So Reyna went out and busted him and locked him up and helped the lady from Montgomery. He made himself no friends in high places by doing so. Another time he tried to help a woman who had been beaten up by her husband, who happened to be one of the county judges in Conroe. He came and kicked in Reyna's office door and demanded to see the file. Reyna told him to get his fuckin' ass out of his office and again made himself no friends in high places by doing so. Then there was the businessman who was keeping illegal Mexican immigrants in a filthy shed in Conroe and paying them starvation wages. Reyna put that on TV in Houston, but the businessman complained, that his complaint mattered because he was paying money to the election campaigns of most of the people in high places in Conroe.

It all came to a head in 1983. Reyna was accused of taking bribes. The sheriff and most of his deputies and the district attorney and most of the people in his office all said that Reyna was corrupt. Reyna worked his butt off trying to find out what had happened, and when the case finally came up in front of the grand jury, he produced his own evidence. The grand jury declared that he was innocent and then filed a perjury indictment against the deputy who had pointed the finger at him. But though Reyna was exonerated, Sheriff Joe Corley fired him because during his fight to clear his name, Reyna had spoken to the press without permission. Reyna was out of work at age thirty-seven.

That was when he became a private investigator and revived his dream of trying to rescue people, and that was when he became a permanent pain in the butt for all the people in high places in Conroe. Reyna often worked for the attorneys on the courthouse square, serving papers and chasing down information. He had worked for Don Brown, and Brown liked him. They shared a deep contempt for the courthouse and its ways, and neither of them had any patience with the racists in town. With only one month to get to the truth about James Dexter Robinson, Brown, De Geurin, and Nugent turned to Richard Reyna for help.

Reyna's first aim was to talk to Brenda Medina, but nobody knew where to find her. Not even her attorney, W.B. Etheridge, had a current address, and the district attorney's office was not about to help. All anyone could tell Reyna about her was that she was a fat white woman with jet black hair and at least four children. Reyna got in his car and drove east out of Conroe about five miles, out toward Cut and Shoot, where just about every trailer and every dusty shack had a fat white woman in it with a pack of children around her ankles.

It was July 4. It was hot. Reyna always hated the summer, and this was a bad one. He had only thirteen days before the hearing in Conroe. He started knocking on doors, asking for Brenda Medina. He asked in the stores. He drove up into the hills and stopped anyone he saw. He tried the beer joints, the schools, the churches. If a building had a door, he knocked on it. On July 5, in Midway, about ten miles east of Conroe, some people in a grocery store told him they thought they knew the name and reckoned she lived with a Mexican somewhere close by. Later that day Reyna knocked on the door of a cramped wood-frame house that had more dust than furniture in it, and Brenda Medina answered it.

She was certainly a big woman—at least two hundred pounds and with so many chins that her face seemed to be pushed back at a permanent angle. Two little girls clung to one of her legs like cats on a tree trunk. Reyna always tried to start off calmly with people, so he introduced himself politely and shook her hand and was startled when she replied that he was a son of a bitch.

It turned out that Brenda's mother had once complained to the sheriff's department that Brenda was not looking after her children, and it was Reyna who had had to go and chew her out. Reyna remembered and immediately tried to turn this to his advantage, reminding her how well they had got on and how he had made sure she was never charged with anything. He started talking to her husband in Spanish, and pretty soon Brenda Medina calmed down and started to tell her story. Reyna turned on his tape recorder and let her talk.

She recalled that back in the summer of 1980 she was living with James Dexter Robinson and pregnant with their child. He had been out all day, and she had gone to bed for the night. "Let's see, it was about one o'clock, between twelve-thirty and one o'clock, I guess, in the morning, and he came in, and he woke me up and he told me that he was going to leave.

"And I said, 'Well, that's nothing new because you leave all the time,' and he told me that he had killed a girl, and I said, 'Oh, baloney,' and I turned over, and that was the end of it. He told me, he said, 'No, I'm leaving and I'll tell you, I'll write you, or call you and tell you when I get there where I'm at. If you want to come to be with me, you can' . . ."

Reyna started to nudge her along. Had she asked who he had killed? No. Had Robinson said who it was that he had killed?

"He just said he—that he killed a girl at the high school and that he hid her well enough that nobody would find her."

Had he said where he hid her? "No, he just said that he hid her well enough that nobody would find her till he got out of town. The best I can remember, something about that he was gonna take a bus, and I remember when I woke up at five o'clock, everything he had was gone."

Except for one thing. Later that morning, when she had got up, she had found his tennis shoes still in the house, the ones he had been wearing the previous day. She told Reyna how she had found "little pin drops of blood" on the top of them at the front.

Reyna was watching her closely. She seemed to be telling the truth, but he needed more. Medina told him she had not heard from Robinson again for more than a year. Then he had called from Greenville, South Carolina, to ask about his baby son, and during that call he had asked her if the police had ever found out who killed the girl at the school. She had told him she didn't know; she never read the papers much. She had visited him in South Carolina once, but they had fought, so she had left, and now it was more than two years since she had last heard from him.

She said she was scared of Robinson. He had often beaten her and her mother, and he had threatened her with knives. He had a gun, too. "He was the kinda person that he could look you in the eye and stab you in the back at the same time," she said. Reyna nodded his encouragement. She told him she had never really known whether to believe Robinson about killing the girl. She thought maybe it was just an excuse to leave, so that he did not have to pay child support for the new baby.

She had forgotten all about it until this May, when she was talking to a neighbor whose daughter was about to go to Conroe High, and the neighbor had said she was afraid to let her daughter go to the school alone because of the girl who had once been killed there. Medina had told the neighbor she knew all about that killing because her boyfriend had talked about it to her. Then the neighbor had told her about this black man who was on death row for the crime. That was the first she knew of anyone's being convicted of the crime, the first time she thought maybe she knew something important.

Brenda Medina said that she had no use for blacks herself and that they all should be sent back to Africa, but she did not agree with the death penalty because the Bible says, "Thou shalt not kill." So a few weeks later, when she was in court because she had been accused of stealing some money, she told her attorney, W. B. Etheridge, what she knew, and he had taken her to the district attorney's office, where she had been interviewed by Charlie Ray, the DA's investigator. He had tape-recorded their conversation, and she had agreed to take a lie detector test. That was about six weeks ago, she said, and she had never heard another word.

Reyna turned off his tape recorder, arranged to meet her in Conroe during the next week, and drove home. He was not completely sure about her. She could be telling the truth, but she could just be trying to cause trouble for Robinson.

He felt maybe he was beginning to pick at this knot, but it needed more work. He started reading through all the old trial transcripts. There were twelve days to the hearing.

In the meantime, Don Brown had learned that Robinson had a history of violence and that his latest wife, Berdie, was divorcing him and producing witnesses who said he had often beaten her and had once knocked her out and put her in the hospital for several months with injuries that might have damaged her brain. Even more significant, Brown learned that James Dexter Robinson was the son of Clarence Robinson, who had taken the missing keys, and that both father and son had worked as janitors at Conroe High School in the summer of 1980. Finally, Brown recalled the blood on the dead girl's socks and how he had believed the girl could have given the killer a nosebleed. Now Brenda Medina was telling them that this Robinson had spots of blood on his tennis shoes.

On July 8 Reyna met with Brenda Medina in Conroe and persuaded her to take a lie detector test. To his relief she passed it. Polygraph tests were not foolproof, but Reyna was beginning to feel good about the big woman with the jet black hair. And the more she talked about James Dexter Robinson, the more likely a suspect he became. According to her, he had a history of violence against women, and one day she had come back home early and found Robinson with a girl who she guessed was a prostitute, tied up to the bed, and Robinson and another man had been in the bed with her. She swore the other man was Gary Acreman. She said she was sure because Acreman had been around to their house several times when he and Robinson were working together at the high school.

Now Don Brown asked Reyna to pursue a lead that had been nagging at him for nearly six years: old Ed Payne's story of how his son-in-law, Gary Acreman, had come home on the day of the killing quaking with nerves and talking about the dead girl whose clothes were in a school Dumpster. Brown had never forgotten how he and Morris had been cheated out of the chance of talking to Payne. Now it was Reyna's turn to try to find out what Acreman really knew. It was July 9, eight days to the hearing.

When Reyna arrived at the shabby little house in Grangerland, ten miles southeast of Conroe, he thought it was deserted.

The place looked as if it were still under construction. There was a big hole in the ground, full of water with ducks swimming on it. There was junk everywhere: disposable diapers; fast-food wrappers; fast food; rotting cars. But when he knocked on the door, a small woman in her fifties answered. It was Ed's wife, Billie. She had nothing good to say about her son-in-law. As she told it, Gary Acreman had abandoned her daughter, Cindy, three years ago and never sent a nickel to support their two children. He was emotionally disturbed, she said, because his mother had been seeing three different men before he was born, and Acreman was still trying to figure out who his real father was. Now his mother had died of cancer, and one of his brothers was in jail for stabbing another brother to death in some argument. Billie was not sure how to find Acreman, but she heard he had been drunk at Johnny Dalton's club in Conroe just last week.

Reyna kept her talking, hoping that her husband would turn up, but when he finally heard the sound of a car outside, it was Acreman's deserted wife, Cindy, who stepped out. Reyna did not like the look of her. She was a fat, blank-faced girl with long, lank hair and a clumsy way about her. He had never liked dirty people, not since he was a little boy in the ghetto, but he forced himself to shake her hand and treat her warmly. At one point he even put his arm around her shoulder and let her greasy hair trail along his sleeve. He told her she could help him. She could be like an assistant investigator. He told her he could see she was a good person, intelligent. He was trying to get to the truth, and she could help him do that. Would she like to do that? He gave her a smile that twinkled like an engagement ring, and she said she would try.

She told him what she knew. Acreman had always insisted that Brandley was innocent, she said, and that he had told the district attorney's office several things that should have cleared Brandley, but it had never done anything about them. She remembered something about the girl's clothes being in the Dumpster. Her husband had mentioned it on either the day of the killing or just the next day. One other thing: Acreman was always going on about a towel and about how Brandley had never had any towel that had anything to do with that dead girl. Then, in her new role as assistant investigator, she agreed to try to fix it so that Reyna could interview Payne and Acreman. Reyna thanked her, told her she would make a good police officer, and said he would stay in touch.

Two days later, on July 11, Cindy Acreman brought Ed Payne to see Reyna. They met in a roadside restaurant on the edge of Conroe. In the five years since he had met Don Brown in the courthouse, Payne had become even frailer and had evidently developed cancer in his throat. He now spoke through a metallic microphone that he pressed against his voice box. The combination of the noisy restaurant, Payne's East Texas accent, and the microphone made it impossible to understand what he was saying. They moved over to W.B. Etheridge's office, and there, finally, five and a half years after his brother John had called George Morris with the story, Ed Payne told his tale to the defense. He confirmed every word. Acreman had come home on the day of the crime knowing that a girl had been killed and worrying that her clothes were going to be found in one of the Dumpsters at the back of the school. He had been claiming that he saw a janitor drop the clothes in there, and he had wanted to borrow Payne's truck to go back and get them so he could take them to the DA. Payne had refused and told him that if he had nothing to do with it, he should stay away in case the police caught him with the clothes before he had a chance to hand them over, but Acreman had kept on.

Cindy Acreman agreed and told Reyna that her husband had tried to persuade her to drive him in to the school. He did not want to use his own truck because he was having trouble with it or maybe because he was afraid it might be seen. Ed Payne said he had lied to Don Brown when they met in the courthouse during Brandley's second trial because he was scared of the DA and the police. Even now he did not want to talk about what had happened on that Saturday when Charlie Hayden had come out to see him.

With only five days to the hearing, Reyna spent Saturday, July 12, combing through bars in Houston looking for Acreman. He spent hours sitting outside some hole that Acreman was supposed to drink in, but he saw no sign of him. At home that night he called Cindy Acreman. She was still trying to be an investigator and proudly announced that she had been in touch with her husband and had fixed it to meet him the next day at nine in the morning. Reyna had to be there, she said, and pretend that he had followed her to the meeting. She gave him directions to a roadside store way out in southeast Montgomery County. Reyna said he would be there. He was glad she was not in the room with him. He might have been tempted to kiss her.

*   *   *

Reyna sat and waited. There was no air conditioner in his car. He felt as if he were beginning to melt. He watched the cars flit by on the road. None stopped. He wondered whether this was Cindy Acreman's idea of a joke. Then he saw her, over by the store. And he saw Acreman, too, climbing out of an old Cadillac Eldorado.

As the Acremans talked, Reyna left his car and strode over, took a deep breath, and introduced himself. Acreman looked at him as though his soul had just taken leave of his body and started to tremble visibly. Reyna then calmly added that a young man by the name of James Robinson had made an extrajudicial confession to the murder of Cheryl Fergeson and that he needed to talk to Acreman about it. Acreman's fingers were now quivering so violently that he could not get his cigarette pack out of his breast pocket. Reyna nearly offered to help him but thought better of it.

Reyna explained that he wanted to ask Acreman about some things his family had been saying about him. He flipped on his tape recorder. Acreman, who had managed to juggle a cigarette into his mouth and put a light to it, began to calm down a little. Then he began denying everything that Reyna put to him. He had never said anything to anyone about clothes in any Dumpster. He had never asked anyone to take him back to the school. His wife and his father-in-law were both lying. He never knew a girl had been killed until the next day, when his wife's mother came home with the paper. "I remember that like it was yesterday," he said.

Reyna moved up a gear. "Was James Robinson there that day?"

Acreman looked perplexed. Reyna needed to know. If Acreman confirmed that Robinson was there, then that made Brenda Medina an honest witness, and it made a liar out of Gary Acreman, who had never mentioned Robinson's presence in all these years. It would mean he was truly loosening the knot.

Acreman nodded yes.

"Yes, he was?" asked Reyna, trying to conceal his excitement. "You saw him at the school?"

Acreman nodded again. "Yes."

Reyna paused a moment. He felt as if Clarence Brandley's life were in his hands. He wanted to be sure Acreman knew what he was saying. But as he pushed, Acreman started to

stumble. He said he did not know whether he knew James
Robinson or not. Reyna tried to reassure him that he was
not trying to cause him trouble. Acreman said again that he
thought he had seen James Robinson at the school.

Reyna changed direction. Did he still say he had not seen
anyone throw anything into a Dumpster? Acreman said he
knew nothing about Dumpsters. He had known nothing about
the girl till Sunday. He knew nothing about any of it. Then
Cindy Acreman, still psyched up and trying to be Reyna's
assistant, joined in, reminding her husband that she had been
there and she knew he had tried to borrow her father's truck
to go back to the school.

Acreman frowned at her. "I don't even remember asking—
asking that."

"You did," she said. "I said I wasn't driving."

Reyna reminded him that Clarence Brandley's life was at
stake and asked him whether he really believed his wife and
his father-in-law would lie about him. "You're telling me here
in front of your wife that you didn't ask for the truck to go
back to the school and help the district attorney's office?"

Acreman sighed and changed his story. "Yeah, I was gonna
help the district attorney's office."

That made Ed Payne an honest witness, too. But Acreman
would give no more. The three of them talked on. Reyna
could see Acreman was coming to the end of his patience,
so he steered the conversation back to the crucial issue—
James Dexter Robinson. This time Acreman said he was
sure he knew who Robinson was, and finally he made the
concession that Reyna was waiting for: "He was definitely
there that day."

"He was definitely there?" asked Reyna, still trying to
double-check. "You saw him? What time did you see him?
Do you remember?"

"I seen him that morning."

That was good enough for Reyna. He did not believe for
one moment that Acreman had told him the whole truth, but
he had put James Dexter Robinson in Conroe High School on
the morning of August 23, 1980, and that could be enough to
slip the knot on the noose around Clarence Brandley's neck.

The trick now was to gather more evidence so that Acreman
would not start backsliding and denying the story when they
got him into court. It was time to go see the other janitors.
Reyna had four days to the hearing.

*   *   *

If it was possible, John Sessum's home was even dirtier than Cindy Acreman's. It was not even a real house, just a little wooden shack that had once been painted green, off a back road not far from the Acreman place in Grangerland. There was an unmade bed, a chair, a blackened sink, and one hell of a mess. The shed smelled strongly of urine and also of wet dog. It had no air conditioning, and in the July heat it was Reyna's idea of hell.

He had been tracking Sessum all day, chasing around bars, trying to find his address. Finally, he had found someone who said Sessum had got himself a job bicycling around the back roads, picking up old tin cans and bottles. So Reyna had driven up and down the back roads southeast of Conroe until finally he had seen a shabbily dressed man hunched over a bicycle, pedaling unsteadily down the road. Reyna had stopped him and stood right there by the roadside and told him about James Dexter Robinson's extrajudicial confession.

Sessum had looked at him for a moment. Reyna had been able to smell the beer on his breath and see the grit that lined the creases of his face, his hair matted against his scalp, his skin blistered with sweat, and the old barroom scar over his right eye. Reyna had waited and than watched as this ruined face had suddenly collapsed into an expression of the most complete sadness, and John Sessum had slowly drawled: "I was afeared I should have to take it to my grave."

Reyna had put the bike in his car and driven him home. Now, sitting in this cesspool of a shack, he was beginning to regret it when suddenly, as if some almighty hand had reached down to save his sensibilities, Reyna heard footsteps outside. It was Sessum's neighbor, a woman named Mattie Johnson who had seen Reyna's car and wondered if he would prefer to come up to her house to talk to John. Reyna agreed very quickly. Settled in cleaner and cooler surroundings, Reyna started to question Sessum again on what it was that he did not want to take to his grave. He soon realized that this was not going to be easy. Sessum was confused, his memory fouled by years of alcohol abuse. He was also very nervous. He would not tell Reyna why, but there was no doubt in Reyna's mind that he was worried about something.

He could not or would not say whether James Robinson had been at the school. But he described Gary Acreman's doing something that had never come out at any trial. As he told it,

Acreman had seen this blond girl walking down the hallway toward them as they stood outside the cafeteria that morning, and Acreman had said she looked really good and then started talking to her. Sessum was sure of it: Gary Acreman had been talking to that girl who died. And something else. Just after he talked to her, Gary Acreman had been missing for maybe thirty minutes.

Reyna wanted to know why he had never mentioned this before. Had he told the district attorney? Sessum refused to say. Had he told anyone about this? Sessum nodded slowly and said that he had told the Texas Ranger about Gary Acreman's disappearing and that Wes Styles had told him they had already got their man. When he gave evidence at the first trial, Sessum said, he had traveled into Conroe that morning with Gary Acreman, and Acreman had threatened that if Sessum mentioned anything about Acreman's talking to the girl or disappearing, Sessum would be in trouble. Then the Texas Ranger had told him that he should say that Clarence Brandley had disappeared for forty-five minutes and not mention anything about Acreman's disappearing and that if he said anything different he could go to jail.

Sessum said he did not like niggers. Or Mexicans, for that matter. But the truth was the truth, and it was time to tell it.

Reyna pressed him for more of the story. What about James Robinson? What had Acreman said to the girl? Had Acreman touched her at all? Was Robinson there when Acreman spoke to the girl? What had happened to the girl?

But Sessum would go no further. "That's all I know," he said.

Reyna grinned at him. "I know damn well that's not all you know, John."

Sessum suddenly glared, and Reyna could see for the first time the kind of drunken temper that had earned him his barroom scar. "Well, goddamn, that's all I'm gonna tell you."

Reyna thanked him. He could see the lies crumbling, all the twisted strands falling apart. Still, he wanted more. He had three days to the hearing.

Don Brown had one more lead stored away in his internal filing cabinet, the wife of Sam Martinez. Dolores Martinez had been dropping hints for years about her husband and how he knew more than he was saying about the murder at the school. She seemed to have worked up some romantic feelings for

Brandley. She had been writing to him in jail since way back in 1981 and had started saying things about Sam in her letters. But it was hard to make out. She kept on about dreams she had had. In the dreams Sam was raping the girl and killing her. Brown had never been able to decide whether she was crazy or that was just her way of trying to tell them the truth.

The day after he had seen Sessum, Reyna rose early and by eight-thirty he was knocking on Dolores Martinez's door. She was separated from Martinez now and living in one of the shacks in Dugan. When she came to the door, Reyna had the rare experience of being lost for words. She was like a black version of Brenda Medina, except that she was probably even bigger. Respectfully he started asking her if she would talk about the Brandley case. She seemed reluctant. Just like John Sessum, she was worried. Reyna played an angle.

"I'll probably be seeing Clarence soon," he said. "You want me to tell him I saw you? You got any message for him?"

Her face lit up. Reyna knew he was all right.

She said Martinez had always told her that Brandley was innocent, but he never really explained how he knew that. She had started writing to Brandley to tell him, and the next thing she knew, there was an investigator from the DA's office called Charlie Ray at her front door.

The jail must have told the DA what she was saying in her letters. Charlie Ray said she had to come to the courthouse. She had been very nervous. At the courthouse she had been taken to see Keeshan, and she thought he had a tape recorder in his breast pocket while he talked to her. He had told her not to believe everything she read in the papers and to be very careful of saying things she couldn't prove. Then he had made her go up in front of the grand jury. She had been very frightened by it all and had decided not to get involved anymore. She said that was all she knew, but if there was anything she could do to help Brandley, she surely would.

Reyna left her and drove back across the railroad tracks to Anderson Elementary School, where it took him only a few minutes to find Sam Martinez, going about his business as the school janitor. When Reyna told him that someone had made an extrajudicial confession to the murder, Martinez looked plain scared. Reyna pressed on and told him that there was now a witness who said Acreman had talked to the girl and then disappeared for thirty or forty minutes. Martinez started to nod yes. It was true, he said.

So why had those facts never been reported? Martinez
started to scuttle away, saying he didn't want to talk anymore.
Reyna kept at him. He wanted to know if Acreman had gone
across to the Vocational Building with the rest of them, or
had he gone off alone? Martinez said he was not sure and he
had to get on with his work. He could not talk. What about
when Acreman had gone off to the Shamrock station? Had
Sam gone with him then?

Martinez cracked a little. "No, I didn't. He went by
himself."

Reyna knew that was the direct opposite of what Martinez
had said in evidence. Why had he not said all this before?
Martinez said he was sorry. He had to go. He could not talk.
He knew nothing. Reyna must let him go.

It was July 15. There were only two days to the hearing.

One of Percy Foreman's most famous cases had taken place in
Florida. A beautiful young woman was accused of murdering
her elderly husband. She admitted firing the gun that killed
him. It looked hopeless, but Foreman, who had enough golden
rules to start a small bank, had a golden rule for the situation.
"It's not against the law to kill a son of a bitch," he declared.
Foreman spent the trial talking about the dead man, whom he
portrayed as a vicious bully who had tormented his beautiful
young wife beyond endurance. He told the jury that the old
man had kept a bullwhip that he used to snap at his wife's
feet to make her dance. To reinforce the point, Foreman bought
and borrowed every bullwhip he could find, laid them all out
on the defense table, and constantly played with them, coiling
them through his hands, slapping them on the table, trailing
them on the floor so that by the end of the trial, the jury was
mesmerized by the whips and the image of the bully who
had used them. It voted unanimously to acquit Foreman's
beautiful client.

From experiences like that, Foreman derived his most
important golden rule of all. "Try anyone except your client,"
he used to bark at his partners. Have the jury try the victim or
the police or the scientific experts or the press or the client's
family or friends, but not your client. This golden rule became
more than a mere legal maneuver. It was Foreman's way of
breaking through the flimsy web of rules and rituals that a

district attorney would try to weave around a defendant so that he could get to the moral heart of the case, to all the underlying rights and wrongs, to the real justice that was hidden in the letter of the law.

Mike De Geurin and Paul Nugent had learned this golden rule at Foreman's right hand. On July 17, the eve of the big hearing when they would throw all their new evidence behind their application for a writ of habeas corpus, they sat down with Don Brown and reviewed all that Richard Reyna had brought them. They agreed that it was time to stop trying Clarence Brandley. They now had James Dexter Robinson in the school on the day of the crime and then confessing to a killing. They had Gary Acreman talking to the girl, disappearing without explanation on the day of the crime, and then talking about the dead girl and the whereabouts of her clothes long before he should have known either. They had subpoenaed a line of witnesses to testify to all this on oath.

They knew they were still a long way short of the whole truth, but the cumulative case that these two men had some connection with the crime was far stronger than anything that had ever been laid at Brandley's feet. It was time to put Robinson and Acreman on trial.

There was, however, a technical problem with that, exactly the kind of flimsy rule Percy Foreman loved to destroy. According to the Texas Court of Criminal Appeals, anyone who wanted to use new facts to appeal against a conviction had to produce them within thirty days of the end of a trial. After that, new facts were inadmissible, and in effect, only the legal correctness of his conviction, not the convicted prisoner's innocence, was an issue. All their new information was technically barred by this rule, but they hoped that if they could prove in open court that Robinson and Acreman were guilty, the Court of Criminal Appeals would try to do justice to Clarence Brandley by finding some other reason to release him.

Clarence Brandley had now been in his cell for five and a half years. Nine feet by three feet. Fourteen more men had followed Charlie Brooks through that door. His life now had settled into a steady routine. Nudged along by his mother and by his brother O. T., he had taken to studying his Bible. That helped him with the bitterness. He still meditated and fasted. He often looked back at his old life, the life in the fast lane.

It was impossible to believe that it had been his life. He often thought about that Saturday morning and about the craziest thing of all: if he had not been trying so hard to lead a steady life, he would just have forgotten all about going up to the high school, he would just have lain down with Beverley and stayed at home, and then none of this would ever have happened to him.

He tried to stay up with the news, but it was not easy. Once there had been another guy on his wing who had a paper sent to him every day, and he used to share it. Then he had gone, and now there was no one on the wing who could afford a paper. There were the TVs, but they all voted on what they wanted to see, and the majority ruled. That was just about the only democracy there was on death row.

He had thought a lot about the case until it hurt his head. He could not sort it out. Every time anyone came to visit, he would ask if maybe there was something new. He prayed for God to send him the truth.

One day that summer of 1986 Mike De Geurin came to see him and told him all about the big breakthrough. It was the news he had waited for for so long. He told De Geurin that he remembered Robinson, and his father, too. Then De Geurin leaned right forward into the security screen and told Brandley that this was a most important question and that the answer could make a whole lot of difference to their chances in court.

"Clarence, when you were at the high school that day, did you see James Dexter Robinson. In the school? On that day?"

Brandley knew what he could say and how that might help. But the truth was that if Robinson was there that day, it was news to him. So that was what he said.

"OK, Clarence. That's fine. I'm glad you're honest."

The morning of July 17, 1986, saw a strange scene in the Montgomery County Courthouse. All the way from the back of Judge Coker's courtroom to the bar behind the attorney's tables, the public benches were lined with brown faces, people from Dugan and from the ghettos of Houston who had ventured into this courthouse to see the truth come out, to see a black man win a battle in Conroe. Reporters from all over Texas squeezed in among them. Deputies huddled by the doors, watchful eyes scanning the crowd. In the empty jury box a well-dressed woman with brightly colored fingernails sat stiff and unsmiling. The whole room buzzed with speculation.

Judge Lynn Coker called the court to order, and Mike De Geurin began to speak. He outlined the new lines of evidence and their suppression, and then he challenged the district attorney to open up his file on the Brandley case. "It's time to quit hiding the ball," he said.

The public benches hummed their support.

Pacing back and forth at the front of the court, his shoulders hunched, one hand clutching his notebook, the other beating the air for emphasis, the blond attorney began to raise his voice. "There is no reason at this date for the District Attorney to continue hiding the file from us other than to suppress the evidence that might be inconsistent with Mr. Brandley's guilt.

"This concealment has been going on for five and a half, six years and it's still going on. And it's time for this court to step in and say 'Open it up, let them see the file, let them see what you have left in the file.' "

"Yes, sir," came the voices from the benches.

Peter Speers hopped to his feet. "I would like to say for the record that I resent his allegations."

De Geurin, who was not about to forget how Speers had failed to tell him about Brenda Medina's statement a month earlier, was not impressed. He called her attorney, W. B. Etheridge. But as soon as Etheridge started to tell his story, Speers hopped up again. He volunteered his own version of events, which started with a loud declaration that Brenda Medina was facing criminal charges for stealing money from her employer. De Geurin said he was not interested in Speers's version and continued. A minute later Speers was up again, objecting that Etheridge's story was irrelevant. De Geurin persisted. He was damned sure he was going to record the fact that Brenda Medina had made her statement to the DA and it had been suppressed. But as soon as Etheridge tried to explain what Brenda Medina knew, Speers popped up again, objecting that he was repeating hearsay, and the judge agreed with him.

De Geurin established that Brenda Medina had made some kind of statement to the DA, but when he turned to the fact that Speers had failed to declare this in court a month ago, Speers jumped up again, objecting that this was hearsay and winning the judge's agreement that it should not be mentioned.

The pattern was set. De Geurin called his witnesses. Speers harried them with procedural objections: this information had been covered by the appeal and should not be mentioned; that information came from the first trial and should not be mentioned; this information concerned the missing exhibits, which had been dealt with, and should not be mentioned; this was inadmissible, that was speculation, this was hearsay, that was irrelevant, and none of it should be mentioned. Judge Coker frequently agreed with him. On the public benches there was shaking of heads and mumbling of told-you-so's. Nevertheless, De Geurin followed his lines of evidence through the obstacle course.

Brenda Medina came and told her story of the late-night confession just as she had told it before to the DA's investigator and to Richard Reyna. She added that James Dexter Robinson had a friend called Gary Acreman.

Gary Acreman appeared and agreed immediately and without argument that he knew James Dexter Robinson and that he clearly remembered his being at the school on the day of the crime and poking his head around the door, telling them not to work too hard. That put the cornerstone of the defense case in place.

Don Brown took the stand and tried to build on it. He tried to explain about the telltale hairs from the dead girl's body, which might have proven the guilt of Robinson and Acreman if they had not mysteriously vanished, and about the blood on the dead girl's socks and how that could possibly be linked with the blood on Robinson's tennis shoes, and about how the autopsy report had always suggested that the crime was committed by two people. Point by point, Speers jumped up and said this should not be mentioned, and point by point, Judge Coker agreed with him.

Speers kept on picking at the new evidence about Robinson: attacking Brenda Medina for failure to come forward earlier, challenging Acreman that he did not really remember. ("I remember. I remember," Acreman insisted.)

He had his investigator, Charlie Ray, reveal that school records showed that Robinson had stopped working at the school on July 29—nearly four weeks before the crime. Ray then admitted to De Geurin that he had not tried to question Robinson or any other witness to confirm Brenda Medina's story, nor had he tried to establish whether Robinson had a friendship with any of the other janitors.

Ray declared that there could be no significance in any blood spots on Robinson's shoes since there had been no blood spilled during the crime, and then he conceded that he had personally helped deliver the dead girl's clothes to the DPS lab in Austin so that their bloodstains could be analyzed.

Speers called Jim Keeshan, who said that he had never heard of James Dexter Robinson and that it would not have changed the direction of his inquiry if he had.

A tutting and a sighing welled up from the public benches.

De Geurin was satisfied that despite Speers's hailstorm of procedural objections, he had laid out most of the facts about Robinson and that it must be clear that he was now a prime suspect in the crime and that the district attorney's office had failed to lift a finger to track him down. At the same time, he followed the line of evidence that led to Gary Acreman.

John Sessum staggered into court, grumbling and cursing that he was losing money by being hauled away from his roadside bottles and cans. But he stood by his story and swore that Acreman had spoken to this blond girl in the hallway and had then disappeared for thirty or forty minutes. He insisted, too, that the Texas Ranger had told him not to tell the truth and had threatened him with jail if he did. De Geurin tried to get him to tell more of his story.

Sessum was nervous. "Well, like I said, I've been scared and I'm still scared but I don't know what's going to happen to me."

De Geurin tried to reassure him that no one was going to jail him for perjury. "If this judge were to guarantee you that nobody, no law enforcement officer, can punish you for telling the truth in court—"

Speers was up again. "Your Honor, I will object to that. Obviously, if he's admitted to the court he lied at the first trial, I'd ask the court not to promise him such a thing. If it's a charge for aggravated perjury, if that's what he's talking about."

The judge agreed with Speers. For once De Geurin was happy to be gagged: Speers had just given a loud and public demonstration of exactly how the courthouse had been frightening John Sessum into concealing the truth all these years.

Sam Martinez came and agreed that Acreman had gone off alone for thirty or forty minutes, saying he was going to the Shamrock station. Martinez could not explain why, at Brandley's trials, he had said he had gone with him.

Then Ed Payne limped into court, and with a voice that was twisted out of shape by his butchered throat, he crawled through his story. And for the first time he not only publicly described Gary Acreman's behavior on the day of the crime but also recalled some of what happened one Saturday afternoon in January 1981, during Clarence Brandley's second trial, when Charlie Hayden, the Montgomery County constable, paid him a visit.

Charlie Hayden had taken him to an office, he said. The district attorney had been there with another man, who he thought was a police captain, and he had tried to tell them his story. They had started asking him if he believed Gary Acreman was capable of committing this crime. Payne continued in his strange buzzing voice: "I said No, that he wasn't, that he was scared of everything and everybody. The only way he might commit a crime like this or do something would be with somebody else. Then Mr. Charles Hayden jumped up and said 'That's an angle we haven't thought about.'"

Hayden had gone on to suggest that the crime could have been committed by several white men, acting together. But the district attorney, Jim Keeshan, had not been interested. "No, I've built my case and we know who did it," the DA had told them.

And so, Payne said, he had never told his story. "Keeshan more or less told me to shut up, so that discouraged me in trying to help."

There was an angry stirring on the public benches.

Don Brown sat silently at the defense table as Payne confirmed his worst suspicions about that agonizing day. He remembered the frustration he and Morris had felt as Payne was snatched away from them, their bafflement when Payne came to the courthouse and denied everything, and then their anger when they had confronted a complacent Keeshan about it. Now they were told that it was Keeshan himself who had got to Payne and put the lid on his story. Brown watched intently as Speers called Jim Keeshan to give his version of events. For once Keeshan's footwork was clumsy.

He claimed to believe that the defense had already known Ed Payne's story. After all, he said, it was the defense attorneys who had told him about Payne. Brown shook his head in disbelief; they had not told Keeshan anything until after it had all gone wrong. Then Keeshan slipped up. He admitted he had interviewed Payne before Payne came to the courthouse. But Brown knew that Keeshan was standing time on its head. When Payne came to the courthouse, he had already been persuaded not to tell his story, so, on Keeshan's own timing, he had spoken to Payne before the defense had. Even after acknowledging in open court that he had personally interviewed Ed Payne about his son-in-law, he publicly declared his blind focus on Clarence Brandley: "I don't think I ever considered Acreman to be a suspect."

Once again De Geurin was happy. Any of these witnesses, particularly John Sessum and Ed Payne, might have succumbed to their fear and refused to tell their stories in public; but they had stood up for themselves, and they had stood up to Peter Speers and his objections.

De Geurin swept more quickly through the technical issues. He called Frank Robin from his prison cell to describe how the DA's investigator, Charlie Ray, had come to him back in 1982 complaining that he felt bad because the DA's office was burying information from a woman who said Icky Peace had tried to assault her. Robin remembered clearly thinking that this was the kind of information that should have been handed over to the defense at the trial. Don Brown recalled how Robin had shown him the woman's statement.

Charlie Ray took the stand and said he had really tried, but he just could not remember this statement he was supposed to have shown Robin, and he had really looked, but he just could not find any record of anything of the kind. The statement, if it ever existed, was now lost and gone forever. Jim Keeshan said the same. So did the Texas Ranger, Wesley Styles, when he was called.

De Geurin put Don Brown back on the witness stand and tried to get him to explain about the missing photographs and how they could have proved that Brandley was not wearing a belt on the day of the crime. Speers rained down objections and succeeded in drowning their efforts to explain why they believed Brandley wore no belt and how the missing photographs could have helped.

De Geurin raised the exclusion of black people from Conroe juries. Speers immediately persuaded the judge that this should not be mentioned. All De Geurin could do was to make a bill of exception, a legal device to record evidence for an appeal even though it can have no effect on the outcome of the hearing.

Again he called Don Brown, who recalled that in both of Clarence Brandley's trials every single black potential juror had been removed at the request of the DA and that in all his years in Conroe he had only once known a black man to be selected for a jury and that was when the black juror in question was a policeman.

De Geurin asked him if he believed this exclusion was systematic. Speers hopped up to object, and before he had even explained why he was objecting, Judge Coker had ruled that this should not be mentioned.

De Geurin and Brown, however, had an answer to that. They called Frank Robin back to the stand. De Geurin asked him about the training manuals that were used in the DA's office and about exactly what those manuals had to say about choosing black people for juries. Robin replied: "On jury selection, the prosecutorial manuals recommend that blacks and other minorities be struck because they tended to be more sympathetic to the defense."

There were angry gasps from the public benches.

De Geurin said: "I pass the witness."

Speers said he had no questions. De Geurin and Brown guessed that must be because he had been trained on the same manuals and knew all about them.

After two days of intense work the hearing paused. It was not quite finished. The defense still had a handful of key witnesses to call, including James Dexter Robinson, who was away in South Carolina. They agreed to resume the hearing on August 21.

—

On Wednesday, July 23, Richard Reyna flew to South Carolina. No one on this case was getting paid anything anymore, but Percy Foreman had written a check for twelve hundred dollars of his own money to pay for the trip. All Reyna had was a hired car waiting at the airport and the address of a house in Greenville, where, if Brenda Medina was right, he could find James Dexter Robinson. Reyna had no idea what he was going to say to him.

He was still puzzling about it as he found the house. He drove by a couple of times and then just sat and watched for half an hour. It was early evening, quiet. He believed the guy in the house was a killer. If Brenda Medina was right, he probably had a gun with him. Reyna could not quite see himself just strolling up to the door and calling Robinson a killer to his face. On the other hand, he could not just sit there all night, so before he really knew it, he found himself strolling up to the door and knocking.

The guy who answered the door was short and lightly built, with shaggy black hair and a weird little face, like a pixie or something. He said yes, his name was James Dexter Robinson. He was wearing a dirty T-shirt, and he had a hot dog in his hand.

Reyna started ad-libbing like crazy, telling him he was from Conroe, that he worked for Percy Foreman, that he was looking into the murder at the high school, and that some allegations had been made against him.

The little guy just stared at him. "Yeah?" he said.

"Yeah," said Reyna, running out of lines. "Brenda—you remember Brenda? Well, Brenda says you killed that girl."

The little guy squinted at his feet, and Reyna felt the beginning of an angle to play here. "It looks like they've got it in for you, James. Because Brenda's not the only one been saying these things about you. I talked to Gary Acreman. You remember Gary? And there's some things been said. You see, James, I think someone is trying to frame you."

"Yeah?"

Now Reyna had him interested. "Why did you leave Conroe, James? There's things been said about that."

"I dunno. Needed the work, I guess."

"But when did you leave, James?"

"Seven thirty-one," he said.

"July thirty-first?" said Reyna. "You sure?"

"I remember it like it was yesterday. And I ain't never been back."

If that was true, it meant he had left three weeks before the murder and Brenda Medina and Gary Acreman were wrong.

"How did you leave, James?"

"I flew. Yeah, I flew."

That didn't fit either. According to Brenda Medina, he was supposed to have taken a bus.

They were still standing on the doorstep, and Robinson was still clutching his hot dog. Reyna asked him if he remembered what airline he flew on.

"No, I don't. You wanna come in? Have a hot dog?"

Reyna thought it looked dirty in there, and there was no telling where that hot dog had been, so he declined.

"James, I'm just trying to help you out here. I think somebody is trying to frame you."

"Yeah. It's that goddamn Acreman."

Then Reyna felt it. He felt in his heart that this little guy knew the truth. He knew just what Gary Acreman knew, and he knew that Acreman had the power to blow him away. And Reyna felt he could get him to talk.

"Hey, James, I got an idea here. What about coming back to Conroe, help me clear all this up and sort out that son of a bitch Acreman?"

It took a little negotiation, and it involved old Clarence Robinson's coming out and saying his piece and then James Robinson's repeating that he had left Conroe on July 31. He kept saying he remembered how the high school had mailed him his last paycheck and how he had cashed it in the store down the road from here. Finally, Reyna won out.

Fifteen minutes later Reyna was driving off in his car looking for a pay phone so he could call Don Brown and tell him that the little son of a bitch had agreed to come back to Conroe of his own free will.

Brown, who had just started the complicated process of trying to get a court order to bring Robinson to Conroe, could hardly believe it. "Richard, just get him on a plane. We'll pay for it somehow."

At five o'clock the next afternoon Reyna and Robinson flew into Intercontinental Airport, just north of Houston on I-45. It had been a weird flight. Reyna had decided not to push him anymore, in case he frightened him off, but Robinson had been doing something very curious.

He had kept saying that he wanted to be hypnotized and that that was the only way he could get to the truth because he had blackouts and he had been taking a lot of acid and he did things he could not remember. Reyna, who was already deciding that Robinson was not as stupid as he liked to make out, reckoned he knew for sure what he was playing at: laying out a safety net in case things went wrong in Conroe, so he could plead insanity. This was a little guy with one big guilty conscience.

There were two things that the defense wanted from James Dexter Robinson: a lie detector test and a moment of his time in court to have him placed under a bond to make him come back again from South Carolina and testify at the hearing on August 21.

Friday, July 25, 1986, Reyna collected Robinson from the hotel where he had lodged him overnight, gave him some newspaper clippings from the hearing so that he could see what people were saying about him, and delivered him to the Houston offices of D. Glenn Raney, former military police-man, former Harris County sheriff and now a professional polygraph operator. Robinson was shivering all over.

While Reyna left and drove anxiously around the block, Glenn Raney invited his subject to talk. Robinson explained how he knew nothing about the murder of Cheryl Fergeson. He did not know Gary Acreman at all. And he had left Brenda Medina just because he thought she had probably been going with another man, and he had never heard of the murder until his father told him about it.

Then Glenn Raney wired him up and read him a series of formal questions. All the while he watched the needle scratching out its verdict on the answers.

"Is your first name James?"

The needle traced its line, undisturbed.

"Is your last name Robinson?"

"Yes."

The needle was steady.

"Do you plan to lie to any question on this test?"

"No."

Still steady.

"Did everything happen like you said it did?"

"Yes."

The needle skipped a beat. Something in Robinson's mood had changed. Glenn Raney went back to neutral questions.

"Do you live in Greenville?"

"Yes."

The needle was calm again. Glenn Raney tried another question about the crime.

"Were you actually in South Carolina like you say you were when Cheryl Fergeson was killed at the Conroe High School in August 1980?"

"Yes," said Robinson.

The needle twitched and jumped.

"Do you know who caused Cheryl Fergeson to die at the Conroe High School in August 1980?"

"No."

The needle scribbled out a mountain range on Glenn Raney's graph.

"Were you present at the Conroe High School on August 23, 1980, when Cheryl Fergeson died?"

"No."

The needle calmed down again. Glenn Raney slipped in a neutral question.

"Do you live in South Carolina?"

"Yes."

Needle steady.

"Did you cause the death of Cheryl Fergeson at the Conroe High School on August 23, 1980?"

"No."

The needle jumped again, scratching anxiously at the paper. Glenn Raney offered Robinson another neutral question.

"Can you drive a car?"

"Yes."

The needle was happy again.

"Did you plan with or help anyone cause Cheryl Fergeson's death at the Conroe High School in August 1980?"

"No."

The needle was steady.

"Did you know that a girl was killed at the Conroe High School before your dad told you?"

"No."

The needle was still steady.

Glenn Raney double-checked his equipment and told Robinson that the needle suggested he had lied to some of the key questions, although in fact, the needle seemed unable to make up its mind. He offered him a chance to explain his answers. Robinson started talking. There was one thing that had not happened quite the way he said it had, he agreed. But that was just to do with leaving Brenda, he said. She had not really been with another man. So that must be why the needle did not like his answer.

"But why would you tell a lie about that particular thing?" Glenn Raney asked him.

"I don't know. I just did."

What about whether he knew who caused Cheryl Fergeson's death? Robinson hesitated. "I was thinking, trying to think about whether or not Gary Acreman told me anything about the murder, or maybe said something while we was driving in Gary's truck to the store, to get a Coke, when we was at the school."

Glenn Raney reminded him that according to his version of events, he had left Conroe four weeks before the murder and could not possibly have been with Acreman at the school anytime after the killing.

"Oh, yeah, that's right," said Robinson, who then fell silent.

So had he really been in South Carolina when the murder occurred?

"Well, I thought I was. I thought for sure I was. Well, I don't really remember."

Glenn Raney steered him back to the vital question, which, according to the needle, he had lied about. Had he caused this girl's death? Robinson looked at him and hesitated. Glenn Raney waited. And waited. After a while he started checking his watch, while Robinson shifted and stirred and stared at the floor and still hesitated. When he finally started to speak, by Glenn Raney's reckoning, he had been hesitating for something like four and a half minutes.

"Well, I don't remember," he said.

"What are you saying?"

Robinson started to ramble. "I don't know. I'm just not sure. I could have done it and forgot. I don't remember. No, I couldn't have done it. I'm not that kind of person. I'm innocent. I'm not sure. I'm just not sure."

Had he told Brenda Medina that he did it?

"Well, I don't remember. I could have made those statements to her. I'm just not sure."

When Glenn Raney's report of the lie detector test came through, the defense camp could barely suppress its mood of triumph. It was not just that Robinson had failed the test. Polygraphs were notoriously unreliable and had no legal standing anyway. It was his whole performance. Any reasonable observer of a man behaving like that would have to conclude that he was guilty.

That afternoon Don Brown called Judge Coker and the DA's office and told them the defense attorneys had a witness they wanted to bring into court to be placed under bond. Robinson went along like a lamb and signed an undertaking to come back to court on August 21. As he left the courtroom, two investigators from the district attorney's office took him by the arm and led him away.

It was shortly before the hearing resumed that Richard Reyna called the phone company. An engineer came around and put some gadget on the line and played with it for a while, and then he looked up at Reyna and said: "Buddy, your phone is tapped."

It was about a week before the hearing was due to resume. John Sessum was pedaling slowly down a back road some-where east of Conroe when a car swooped up beside him and two men jumped out. He thought they had sticks. He half jumped, half fell off his bike and ran through the woods as fast as he could go. He could hear the men behind him, running after him. He just kept running, and pretty soon the men stopped and shouted some stuff at him and went away. He waited to be sure they were gone and then crept back out of the woods. He had seen their faces for only a moment. But he knew one of them. He knew Gary Acreman's face all right.

It was three days before the hearing was due to resume, a Monday. Brenda Medina was at home with the children. She heard the car stop outside but thought nothing of it until she heard the knock on the door. There were three men there. She opened the door a little, and the men told her they were from the district attorney's office. They wanted to talk to her about the Brandley case. She let the three men into her house. She soon regretted it. They did not want to hear her story. They wanted her to know that it was an offense to commit perjury. They thought she ought to know that if she went around claiming to know about murderers she could wind up with her ass behind bars. She could wind up having her kids taken away from her.

She said she was only telling the truth. She said she had passed a lie detector test. The two men said they knew all about lie detector tests. They could give her another test and she wouldn't pass that. She'd wind up in jail. The two men wanted to know why she was saying these things. They said she should tell them who had paid her to say these things. Was it that Don Brown? Was it Reyna? Etheridge? Who paid her? How much did they pay her? Did they pay that polygraph operator to say she was telling the truth? She had better tell them everything, or she would wind up with her ass in jail. She could wind up in jail easy—if she went around saying what she had been saying. Then the three men left with their heavy leather boots clumping on the porch and drove back toward Conroe.

The day before the hearing was due to resume, a Wednesday, Richard Reyna was at Houston Intercontinental Airport, waiting for James Dexter Robinson to fly in from South Carolina. Don Brown had paid for Robinson's ticket, and Reyna had come to make sure the little son of a bitch did not change his mind and run away home. They knew they had to watch Robinson. Ever since he had turned up in Conroe, the district attorney's men had been all over him. Reyna had been doing more work, too.

He reckoned he had found a new witness who could knock a fine hole in Robinson's claim to have left Conroe on July 31. Not even the district attorney seemed to believe that anymore. Peter Speers had told the defense that his investigators had traced Robinson's last paycheck. It turned out that he had cashed it not in South Carolina, as he claimed, but in Conroe. On August 5.

Just then Reyna spotted two of the district attorney's investigators standing in the airport concourse. That was no coincidence. Reyna thought there was no point playing around, so he went up and asked them if they were there to meet Robinson. They said that they were and that Robinson had asked them to be there.

It looked as if James Dexter Robinson had changed sides.

On Thursday, August 21, 1986, the courtroom was crowded again. Clarence Brandley and his family and his friends and his supporters and all the press and other bystanders were there to see one man, James Dexter Robinson.

The defense attorneys also wanted to see him. They had arranged and paid for him to come to Conroe, yet they had not seen him since he had been whisked through the airport the day before. They had heard from Brenda Medina about the three men who had come to her house, and they could only guess at what the DA's office had been telling Robinson since they laid hands on him. They now had no idea what story their star witness might tell. They needed the judge's help.

Their problem was that the law did not allow them to attack the evidence of their own witness. If they called Robinson to the stand and he told lies, they would be stuck with them, unless the judge agreed to declare him a hostile witness. Mike De Geurin rose to make the request to Judge Coker, and Speers hopped up. "They are perfectly aware of what his testimony is going to be and I'm aware of no rule that would permit them to bring some guy in from South Carolina to sit there and cross-examine him about something that they already know. I think that's totally improper."

"I think so, too," said Judge Coker. "I'm not going to permit that."

With his hands effectively tied behind his back, De Geurin called Robinson to the stand. It was soon apparent that the DA's men had been very busy. Robinson revealed that men from the DA's office had not only collected him from the airport and spent the intervening time with him but had also previously visited him in South Carolina and warned him that the defense lawyers were "trying to put a hoodoo on him," trying to have him blamed for the crime.

An angry murmur started on the public benches. Robinson suddenly said he wanted a lawyer. De Geurin asked him exactly what he wanted.

"I'd like to have Mr. Speers represent me."

The public benches burst into jeers and laughter. The judge smashed his hammer down on the bench, and the courtroom became quiet enough for De Geurin to explain that the DA was supposed to be an impartial prosecutor. Peter Speers blushed, and Robinson said he would be all right without a lawyer after all.

As Robinson continued his evidence, De Geurin began to understand why this potential murder suspect should want the same district attorney who would have to prosecute him to represent him. According to Robinson, an investigator from the DA's office named Frank Newton had spent two weeks solid in South Carolina trying to prove that Robinson had been there on the day of the crime. Newton had visited Robinson's employers looking for evidence that he had started work there before August 23. He had interviewed his mother, his grandmother, his grandfather, and his friends in search of an alibi witness. He had helped Robinson search through all his personal papers, looking for a ticket from Conroe. All Newton had come up with were some photographs of Robinson at a party that might have been held on August 17, 1980.

Newton had, however, given Robinson an invaluable tip, as De Geurin discovered when he started asking Robinson about his last paycheck, a line of questioning that should have shown that Robinson's insistent claim to have left Conroe on July 31 was a lie. To De Geurin's surprise, Robinson immediately abandoned his story about receiving and cashing the check up in South Carolina and admitted that he had still been in Conroe on August 5 and had cashed the check not far from the courthouse.

"Now, who told you you had done that?" asked De Geurin.

"Well, it was traced down. Mr. Newton told me."

De Geurin asked him when he had told him.

"I think it was yesterday," said Robinson.

In one easy move the DA's investigator had robbed De Geurin of his best chance to prove in open court that Robinson was a liar. But De Geurin was not finished yet. Robinson insisted that he was innocent, but before he left the stand, he took two vital steps toward implicating himself in the murder. First, he dropped the pretense he had maintained with Glenn Raney at his lie test and admitted that he knew Gary Acreman. Then, in an admission that had the whole court bubbling with comment, he conceded that he had told Brenda Medina he had killed a girl. He immediately added that this had nothing to do with the high school, and it was months before he had started working there, and he had said it only to frighten Medina and it was certainly not true.

Having tumbled that far, he tried to stop himself falling the final few feet into the deep hole the defense had prepared for him by insisting, first, that he had never told Glenn Raney that he might have murdered Cheryl Fergeson and, second, that he was certain he had left Conroe on August 6, the day after he cashed his check, and never returned. De Geurin called two witnesses to send him plunging.

First, Glenn Raney came and reeled off his list of law enforcement qualifications. He was not allowed to deliver his needle's verdict on Robinson, but his account of Robinson's performance in his office, and of his four-and-a-half-minute pause after he was asked whether he had killed the girl, provoked such a chorus of sighs from the public benches that De Geurin could not see how the ultimate verdict could be in doubt.

An elderly white man named Reggie Slacum, Richard Reyna's new witness, then took the stand. He explained that he had worked at the high school with James Dexter Robinson because he was one of the regular janitors there, one of those who would have been there on the day of the crime except that he had not wanted to work on a Saturday. Slacum recalled that he had owed Robinson a hundred dollars, and he told how one day Robinson had come around to his house in Conroe demanding his money, which Slacum had been unable to pay him. A few minutes later Robinson's father, Clarence, had come to his house and started pushing him around and threatening to use a gun on him.

That night, Slacum remembered, he had awakened with a sore mouth, and he had had to go to the hospital the next day. It turned out that the sore mouth had nothing to do with his scuffle with Clarence Robinson, but that was the reason he could be so sure of the date when the Robinsons had come to his house. He had his hospital records. He had gone to the hospital on August 21. So Reggie Slacum had no doubt at all that James Robinson had been in Conroe on August 20, only three days before the murder.

Peter Speers attacked Slacum's memory. Slacum insisted. Speers insisted that Robinson had stopped working at the high school at the end of July. "Dexter Robinson wasn't working at Conroe High School the month of August, was he?"

"No," said Slacum, "but he was coming round."

That was not what Speers wanted to hear. "Who told you to say that?" he snapped.

"Nobody," said Slacum.

As Speers sat down, the public benches rippled with applause. Judge Coker told the spectators to keep quiet or he would clear the court.

Slacum then explained to Mike De Geurin that he remembered clearly that Robinson had been in the school just about every day for weeks after leaving his job, trying to sell cosmetics. As far as the defense camp was concerned, James Dexter Robinson had just been pushed over the edge. He had abandoned his first alibi. Now his second alibi is in shreds. Reggie Slacum had put him in Conroe in the week of the crime. Gary Acreman, on oath and despite cross-examination, had put him in the school on the day of the crime. Through his father he had access to the auditorium keys. Brenda Medina, Richard Reyna, and Glenn Raney all said he had made full or partial confessions. Despite all its efforts, the DA's office had been unable to rescue him.

Gary Acreman was not far from the edge. John Sessum and Sam Martinez both now said he had vanished for thirty or forty minutes on the day of the crime. Sessum swore he had been talking to the girl. Acreman's own father-in-law had pointed the finger at him. The defense attorneys knew that there was still a lot of the picture missing, but surely, they reasoned, the next logical step would be for the police to interrogate Robinson and Acreman and for Clarence Brandley to be freed or, at the very least, to be given a new trial.

But this was Conroe.

At the end of the hearing Clarence Brandley was slipped back to death row. In his brief absence two more men had been taken away to be killed. Robinson and Acreman walked free.

Mike De Geurin always found it hard to dislike anyone—even this man Robinson, who had, he now firmly believed, not only committed a vicious crime but also allowed an innocent man to be condemned to death for it. So as soon as De Geurin spotted Robinson outside the courtroom, he smiled, started making small talk, and walked out of the building with him.

On the stand Robinson had said he would have no objection to supplying a sample of his pubic hair to the defense.

"Did you mean that?" asked De Geurin.

"Sure," said Robinson with a smile. "When do you want it?"

"How about now?"

So the two of them stopped by the courthouse door, and while Robinson rummaged down the front of his pants, De Geurin whipped out his cigarette pack and removed the cellophane wrapper. A few moments later De Geurin had the prize safely stashed in his jacket pocket.

"Well, thank you, James," he said, and shook him by the hand. "Very kind."

He drove home to Houston, wondering what Gary Acreman with the sandy-colored hair knew about that reddish brown hair that had been found on the girl's thigh and wondering, too, how things might have been if someone in the courthouse had not had the bad luck or the foresight to lose all the hairs that had been on Cheryl Fergeson's body.

*   *   *

The weeks after the hearing were tense and riddled with rumors. All of them pictured the defense camp breaking through. The attorneys could smell victory but insisted it was too soon to celebrate. Judge Coker, they believed, was finally going to stand up for himself. In his cell in Huntsville Clarence Brandley dared to hope. He had not thought much of Coker. The judge had let Speers have his way most of the time, and he had sat up there, looking so pleased with himself—as if he were having his Sunday lunch, Brandley thought. But now, with all these rumors, he began to believe he could have been wrong.

Immediately after the hearing both sides had sent written legal arguments to the Court of Criminal Appeals, and the judge had sent his own findings. The defense had been preparing to go to Austin to argue in front of the judges there, but nothing happened for months. Then, the week before Christmas, word came from the court. There was no need for anyone to go to Austin. The court did not want to hear any arguments. It was throwing the case out now. Brandley had lost everything, every single argument.

Brandley, his family, and his attorneys could not believe it. They were dazed. De Geurin, normally amiable, was bitterly angry. But they had only to read Judge Coker's findings of fact to see what had happened. The courthouse's cowardly lion had mauled the defense without mercy.

He dismissed the case against James Dexter Robinson for three reasons: Brenda Medina had not mentioned Robinson's confession for six years; Gary Acreman had not mentioned Robinson's presence at the school for six years; Robinson had stopped working at the school twenty-four days before the murder.

He dismissed the case against Gary Acreman for four reasons: the defense knew Ed Payne's story before the DA; the defense had failed to call Payne as a witness at Brandley's trial; the Honorable James Keeshan denied trying to influence Payne; the defense had failed to call John Sessum at Brandley's trial.

Coker also adopted the technical argument, which had been stressed by Peter Speers, that Brandley's innocence was not relevant because of the rule that decreed that new facts must be presented within thirty days after a convicted man's trial.

"Only the legality of the conviction, not the merits, are subject to scrutiny," he wrote.

With equal ease, he wiped aside Clarence Brandley's other finger-holds on life, rejecting the defense witnesses, repeating the evidence of the Honorable James Keeshan and the legal arguments of Peter Speers.

The Court of Criminal Appeals had simply adopted the findings of the Conroe judge and sent the black man back to the executioner.

Chapter Eight

Fifteen hundred miles away from Houston, in the placid old university town of Princeton, New Jersey, on the second floor of an elegant wood-beamed house where Woodrow Wilson once lived, a man was sitting at a small desk in a cluttered room. Apart from the desk and a chair, the room contained a bed and a mass of papers, some piled on the bed, some under it, some on the desk, but mostly sprayed across the floor. On the wall over the head of the bed was a crucifix.

The man's name was Jim McCloskey, and he had just become famous. Not that he had ever wanted to be. He had abandoned all thought of fame or fortune seven years earlier in the fall of 1979, when at the age of thirty-seven he walked out on his well-paid job as a management consultant in Philadelphia. His boss could barely believe it. After all, McCloskey had a good life: a Lincoln Continental; a nice house in a nice suburb; money in his pocket and more in the bank. But he threw it all away. What good is a "good life," he asked, if you feel empty inside? But what really made the boss's jaw drop was that McCloskey announced he was leaving to become a minister.

McCloskey set off along the approved route to becoming a Presbyterian minister by enrolling in a seminary in Princeton to study for his three-year master of divinity degree. The fame came by accident, or maybe Providence, in his second year, when he was instructed that as part of his studies he should take up a project outside the classroom. He decided to visit the inmates of the New Jersey State Prison in Trenton, and there, in the readjustment unit, where the hardest of the hard cases were kept, he met a man who was serving a life sentence and who told him he was innocent. McCloskey listened to him and began to believe him and then began to be moved by his plight. He felt God had led him to this man.

He took a year off from his studies and threw himself into the man's case. He went back to his old business contacts in Philadelphia and raised money. In Princeton he made a deal with an eighty-three-year-old woman, who owned the wood-beamed house that once belonged to Woodrow Wilson, that he would go out and get her groceries every Tuesday if she would let him live rent-free in an empty room on the second floor. He hired an attorney and formed a defense committee, but mostly he went out and talked to people. In back alleys and mean streets where a white man in a suit is usually a cop, people saw the white collar around Jim McCloskey's neck and they talked to him. It took him nearly three years, but he finally succeeded in proving his man's innocence and springing him from jail. He had found his calling.

So the businessman who set out to become a minister also became a private detective, devoted to releasing the innocent from prison. He set up his own organization, called Centurion Ministries after the Roman soldier who looked at Christ on the cross and said, "Surely this one is innocent," paid himself a meager ten thousand dollars a year, and set to work.

Now, in the fall of 1986, the investigator with the clergyman's collar had just engineered the release of his fourth innocent person, a black man named Nate Walker who had been serving life plus fifty years for raping a white woman. McCloskey proved his innocence when he discovered that for twelve years nobody had bothered to test semen swabs taken from the rape victim. He located them, arranged for the FBI to test the blood type of the semen, and proved that it could not have come from the imprisoned man. The case made headlines, and Jim McCloskey became famous.

The phone had been ringing almost nonstop since the Walker case broke: newspapers looking for stories, sympathizers offering support, but mostly relatives of prisoners begging for help. Now, as McCloskey worked at the little desk in the corner of his room, trying to catch up on the paperwork strewn across the bare boards, the phone rang again. The caller said he had just heard about him on TV, and he had got his number from the TV station. He said his youngest brother was due to be executed for a crime he had not committed. The caller's name was the Reverend Ozell Brandley, known to his family as O.T.

McCloskey had learned never to say no, no matter how busy he might be. "Go on," he said. "What's the situation, Ozell?"

O. T. Brandley started pouring out his family's agony: the dead girl; all these janitors; racism; missing exhibits; Jim Keeshan; James Robinson. It was all too much for McCloskey to get hold of.

"Well, I'll tell you, Ozell, I'm just about swamped right now. But can you send me something on paper? Some kind of summary of the case?"

O. T. Brandley said he could. A few days later he mailed him Don Brown's brief for the original appeal with its catalog of pain from Brandley's two trials and a transcript of the summer's hearing with all the revelations about Robinson and Acreman.

O. T. Brandley had never stopped working for his youngest brother's freedom. At first he had concentrated on praying and spreading the word through the Baptist churches where he was a minister. He had tried to interest some of his colleagues at the junior high school in Houston where he taught. None of it seemed to make any difference. One elected politician after another had told him there was nothing they could do. When Judge Coker tore down all his fragile hopes, he was near despair. His respect for American justice sank so low that he no longer joined his students when they pledged allegiance to the U.S. flag each morning. Yet he could not give up. At about the same time that he called Jim McCloskey in Princeton in the fall of 1986, O. T. Brandley also approached the Reverend Don Boney.

Reverend Boney, a man of many images, was well known in Houston. Like O. T. Brandley, who shunned alcohol and prayed before any major decision, he was a Baptist minister. He was an academic in the mold of his father, who had been chancellor of the University of Houston and the only black school superintendent in the history of the city. He was a former TV producer and radio disc jockey, articulate and charismatic, who had spent two years on the road with a rock band. But most of all—and this was what caught O.T.'s eye—he was an outspoken radical, a fiery protégé of Martin Luther King, Jr., and Malcolm X, a champion of causes, a manipulator of the media, an organizer of rallies and boycotts and sit-ins, one of the founders of the Black United Front in New York in 1971, and now Houston's preeminent civil rights activist.

Reverend Brandley showed Reverend Boney newspaper clippings, explained the case and the racism his brother had suffered. Boney said he would look into it. A few weeks later Boney was in touch again. He had consumed every detail of the case, written his own chronology and summary, and prayed about it, and now he told O. T. Brandley that he believed that they should organize a major campaign of popular protest to secure his brother's freedom.

On January 7, 1987, the staff of Governor William Clements looked out of the window of his mansion overlooking Austin and saw half a dozen black people carrying banners and chanting about a man named Brandley. They went on with their work, and the black people eventually went away.

Twelve days later, on January 19, the anniversary of Martin Luther King's birth, the black people were back. But this time Reverend Boney had three dozen supporters with him, carrying banners and chanting. He also had a bucket. Governor Clements thought he had better do something. He did not want these people inside the mansion, so he went onto the steps to speak to them. He assured them that he would ask the attorney general to look into the case of this man Brandley. The protesters were not impressed.

They placed a photograph of the governor on the steps of the mansion and then tipped the contents of Reverend Boney's bucket onto it. The bucket contained manure donated by a cow named Tina, which belonged to a farmer friend of Boney's.

"We are burying your career in bullshit," declared Boney. "All you have ever given black people is bullshit, so now we are giving it back."

The press liked the story, and the campaign got its first publicity.

On February 6, Boney declared a "Day of Outrage" for two reasons. It was the birthday of the man who, Boney said, was responsible for the resurgence of racism in America—President Ronald Reagan—and it was also the day when Judge Lynn Coker was due to announce a new execution date for Clarence Brandley.

This time Boney attracted two hundred people, and they agreed that they would protest not in Austin but in Conroe. Black people in the town could not believe it. Blacks protesting in the courthouse square! It had never happened. Not even in the sixties. Not in Conroe. But Boney promised it was going to happen now, on this Day of Outrage.

In the courthouse people had heard he was coming. All Judge Coker wanted was a quiet hearing. All he wanted to do was to announce when the black janitor was going to die and then carry on with his business. The judge had even suggested that he could do it in a letter to avoid any trouble, but Mike De Geurin had told him that was not good enough. The courthouse came up with another plan.

On the morning of the hearing Montgomery County deputies searched all black people entering the courtroom. They told some of them, including church ministers, that they could not come in. The judge then called the case early and finished before most of Don Boney's protesters could even reach the courtroom. It was a stark event.

The judge sat in his black gown and Brandley in his chains. Brandley's mother wept. The judge's teenage son was there to watch. The judge asked the black man if he had anything to say. The black man looked straight back at him.

"Your Honor, I'm innocent," he said.

The judge looked down at his papers and told Brandley he would die on March 26—in six weeks and six days. In two minutes it was over. Without trouble.

But outside the courthouse angry voices gathered strength, murmuring at first, then rising louder in complaint. This might be Conroe, where black people stayed on their side of the tracks, where young men were burned alive or shot and no one dared protest, but today, for once, they were going to make themselves heard. That was all they were going to do: just raise their voices. Nothing illegal. Nothing violent. Yet in Conroe it was an act of outrageous defiance. Don Boney and his supporters from Houston showed them the way. Anger put their fear to flight. They started to parade around the courthouse. They carried a coffin for Governor Clements to bury his career in. They chanted, "The people united will never be defeated," and "Clarence Brandley, Clarence Brandley." Two men battered drums. Seven times they circled the courthouse, like Joshua at Jericho, their voices climbing in volume as they marched. By the time they came to a halt, they were exuberant.

Don Boney stood on the steps and told the crowd, "This courthouse is defiled. This courthouse no longer represents justice. It represents corruption and hypocrisy. We are not going to tolerate it anymore. We are not going to respect it anymore."

They cheered their defiance. Then Boney deposited a birthday present for President Reagan on the courthouse steps. It came from the same cow, Tina. Boney looked around at the white faces peering out of the windows and the deputies shuffling uneasily on the street corners.

"Are you going to arrest us for putting fertilizer on your courthouse?"

Silence. Nobody moved. Victory.

The protesters, still angry but now determined, moved off home. Just for once the people of Dugan had found their courage, and they had won. Something had changed in Conroe.

On Friday, February 27, 1987, Jim McCloskey flew into Houston. He had passed through the city two weeks earlier and spoken to the Brandley family and to the attorneys and had offered to work on the case. He said he did not want to be paid; all he needed was a room to stay in and a car to drive.

That Friday evening he moved into a room over the garage in the backyard of Paul Nugent's home in a leafy green part of Houston near Rice University. He instantly surrounded himself with piles of paper, the whole six-and-a-half-year history of the Brandley case. All through that weekend he hid in his room, reading and writing notes, emerging only occasionally to shoot baskets with Nugent or play with Nugent's children before diving back into his paperwork.

Saturday was another big day in Conroe. The annual Black History Parade, normally a small, downbeat affair built around a beauty queen, had been turned over to the Clarence Brandley case. Reverend Boney's campaign was now on a roll. Boney had scheduled regular Clarence Brandley campaign meetings every Tuesday night in Houston and every Thursday night in the black college in Conroe. By late February more than 250 people were coming out of their shacks in Dugan to join the meetings. There were speeches, prayers, and hymns. The black people of Conroe, who had finally sensed their power outside the courthouse on February 6, were now ready to fight.

They raised funds not only for the lawyers but also for press releases, statewide mailings, T-shirts, posters, and bumper

stickers to spread the word: FREE CLARENCE BRANDLEY, and
DON'T LET THE STATE OF TEXAS MURDER AN INNOCENT MAN.
They still had to deal with their fear. A Houston minister told
them: "If you are afraid to put this bumper sticker on your car,
then put it on somebody else's."

On Saturday more than one thousand protesters marched out
of Dugan waving banners and chanting Brandley's name, and
crossed the railroad tracks into a deserted downtown Conroe.
Two sheriff's deputies sat quietly in their unmarked car in
the shadow of the courthouse, one using a telephoto lens
to record the faces and the other scribbling names and car
numbers in a notebook. The black people sang: "*Con*-roe,
Con-roe, have-you-heard? This-is-not-Jo-hannes-burg."

A delegate from Amnesty International flew in from Atlanta
to announce that Amnesty was asking its members all over the
world to write to the governor of Texas to demand Brandley's
release. The parade was led by Minnie Ola Brandley.

"My heart is heavy," she said. "I'm happy for what the
people have done, but my heart is sad, knowing that my son
is dying for something someone else did."

That night the demonstrators made all the Texas TV news
shows.

By Monday Jim McCloskey was ready to talk to Clarence
Brandley. He left Nugent's house early and set off in the car
the attorneys had found for him. A big ugly old 1978 Chevy
with red velvet upholstery and miraculously soft suspension,
like a bordello on wheels, it belonged to Mike De Geurin's
mother. McCloskey turned the radio dial until he found his
favorite station, which specialized in 1940s swing music, and
to the gentle sound of Tommy Dorsey and Glenn Miller,
McCloskey struck out northward on I-45 for Huntsville. As
usual he was running on high-octane enthusiasm. He was
itching to see Brandley. He had scribbled out an encyclopedic
list of questions to ask him, which he was still rehearsing in
his mind as the old Chevy cruised up the long driveway and
into the shadow of death row. Twenty minutes later he was
sitting down opposite Clarence Brandley, separated only by a
thick glass bulletproof security screen.

He started with his questions, and two things soon became
clear. First, Brandley could not answer most of them. He did
not know who had killed the girl or what the other janitors had
done or why James Robinson would have been in the school

that day or anything else. This man truly had no idea what had hit him. Second, Brandley was not the way McCloskey had imagined. He had expected maybe some salesmanship or, at least, some venom about Acreman and Robinson, but Brandley just looked him straight in the eye—really straight in the eye—and told him what he knew. McCloskey began to feel moved by him.

He had been warned that he would not get a long time with Brandley. By accident or maybe Providence, he got four hours. When he finally got up to leave, he had almost no answers to his questions, but he had an aching desire to work on this case, to save this innocent man, who now had only three and a half weeks left to live.

It was Saturday, March 7, before McCloskey was ready to go on the road, eight days after his arrival in Houston and just nineteen days before Brandley was due to die. He had spent more time talking with the attorneys, meeting Don Brown and Richard Reyna, burrowing into the papers, listing facts and witness statements. Everyone agreed that the white janitors were the key. McCloskey would go back to them for the truth. Now, on Saturday morning, he and Richard Reyna were side by side in the big Chevy, sailing down a back road ten miles southeast of Conroe, Reyna with his cowboy boots, McCloskey with his white collar, looking for John Sessum.

Sessum was hard to find. He was not in his dirty wooden shed, which was a relief to Reyna. Sessum's drunken friend, T. D., who lived in an equally dirty trailer in the brush nearby, said he hadn't seen him, but he warned them that Sessum was scared. Gary Acreman and some other guy had run him off the road on his bike and chased him through the woods. It was the first Reyna and McCloskey had heard of it. They thanked T. D. and carried on searching.

It was early evening before they finally saw him beetling along the road, hunched over his handlebars, with his body sweated up under an old oilskin slicker and a six-pack of beer planted in his bicycle basket. They gave him twenty minutes to get home and then set off after him, swooping up to his house in a swirl of dust as he was climbing off his bike.

Reyna was all smiles and backslaps as he introduced McCloskey. Sessum hung back like a shy child, squinting at the man in the minister's collar, nodding howdy, and allowing his limp fingers to be shaken before he moved to the back of his bike and peeled a beer out of the six-pack. McCloskey noticed that he had already drunk two beers on his way home.

Standing in the dusk, outside the green wooden shed, the two investigators started talking, taking turns, playing it by ear. They had to get Sessum over some unseen hurdle, some mental block before he would tell the rest of his story. They tried to reassure him that Gary Acreman would not lay a finger on him.

"I ain't worried about him."

"So who are you worried about, John?"

"That sheriff. Gene Reaves. He threatened me that I'd go to jail and all this crap, that I'd get the devil beat out of me." He said Wesley Styles had threatened him, too. Yet the two investigators sensed that this was not the real block. They kept nudging him along. He gave them a couple of beers and yielded a few small fragments: when Acreman was talking to that girl, she seemed scared; he and Martinez stayed at the bottom of the staircase drinking from the water fountain there; then Acreman and the girl were nowhere to be seen; later Acreman disappeared from the Vocational Building for forty minutes and returned just before Brandley came across with the keys to let them in. It all troubled him and gave him bad nights.

The two investigators could see there was a gaping blank space in this story. One second Acreman was talking to the girl. The next she was gone. Something had happened in there. Everything had happened in there. And Sessum knew what it was if they could only get him over this mental hurdle. McCloskey asked him what the girl said when Acreman was talking to her.

Sessum stared at the ground. "I remember she said no."

"Do you remember what Gary said for her to say no?"

Sessum shook his head. He would not look up. "No," he said very quietly.

Reyna tried a new angle, looking for James Dexter Robinson. "Did you see Gary Acreman talking to anybody that wasn't on the work crew that morning?"

Sessum drank his beer.

"Somebody different?" said Reyna.

Sessum sighed and looked away. "Oh, boy . . ."

For a moment Reyna thought he had lost him. Then Sessum started mumbling and sighing. "He had dirty front teeth. . . . I dunno. Might have had no teeth at all. . . . Wait, wait, wait a minute . . ."

"Did this guy talk to Gary in the cafeteria?"

"Yeah, but I can't remember when it was."

McCloskey caught Reyna's eye, and Reyna held up his hand to Sessum—hang on a minute—and strode back to the car.

McCloskey explained. "If we got a picture of him, would you recognize him?"

Sessum nodded at the ground. "He had thin hair, and I think he had it combed to the left side."

McCloskey kept talking. What about when Acreman and the girl were at the top of the stairs, had the guy with no teeth been there then?

Sessum sighed and started slowly talking: "He wasn't right there, but he was on the landing down there. When the girl was coming up, he was down by the water fountain. Then he came up, too."

McCloskey could feel his heart beating. For the first time a witness had put the two prime suspects together with the girl at the moment of her disappearance. They were beginning to fill in the blank.

"Did you ever tell them about the guy with no teeth being there?"

"They didn't ask me."

McCloskey wanted to know more about this police inquiry when no one asked the right questions. McCloskey reminded Sessum of the day, one week after the girl's murder, one day after Brandley's arrest, when the Texas Ranger had walked him through the school with Acreman and Martinez. What had they said to him?

"That's when I was threatened. That Wesley Styles—'You tell them what I want you to tell them.' He wanted me to tell 'em that Brandley did it. And I still say Brandley didn't do it." Sessum paused and drained his beer. "I will tell you this off the record. I believe Gary had something to do with it."

"How about the guy with no teeth? Did he have something to do with it?"

Reyna rejoined them and showed Sessum the picture of James Dexter Robinson. "Yeah, that's him. But I can't prove either one did it."

He was trying to back off again. Had he always believed that Acreman did it?

"I knew after he was talking to her. The same day, when Gary was bringing me home, he said, 'You don't tell any son of a bitch that I was talking to her. 'Cause if you do, your ass is mine.' I said, 'My ass might be yours, but if they ask me, I'm gonna tell them.' "

"Did you ever talk about this to the DA?"

He was looking away again. "You know how tough this has been with me?"

In his gentlest manner McCloskey asked him: "What do you think about when you have a bad night?"

"Like I say, I still think Gary had got something to do with it, and every time I have a bad night, he's right in it."

"In your dream do you see Gary grabbing the girl?"

"I just see him talking to her, and I remember her saying no. Just as loud and clear as we're standing here."

Had he seen Acreman grab the girl and take her off somewhere?

Sessum took a deep breath and slowly blew it out through his yellowed teeth. "That's still a puzzle," he said, slowly shaking his head.

He paused and sighed again, a deep, sagging sigh. "It can put you in—it makes you lose a lot of sleep."

His voice had broken. He was weeping.

They let him recover himself and tear open the final beer can. He seemed to find some new strength.

"I don't give a damn if he is a nigger. I'm not in love with no nigger. Now I want to tell you if he's innocent, I'm gonna fight for him. I guess I'll go back to court."

McCloskey felt a surge of excitement. Then, without another word from the investigators, Sessum went one step further.

"I guess I'd go back to the school there, show y'all what happened."

The two investigators could hardly believe their ears. This was far more than they had ever dared to hope for—a witness to the murder offering to reconstruct the crime for them.

McCloskey said: "Would you have time to do it on Monday?"

"I'll make time."

Now they were really coming close. They had not yet got over that hurdle—whatever it was that pulled Sessum up weeping, whatever it was that had kept him lying all these years. But he wanted to help them. He wanted to tell the truth. They were going to crack this thing.

It was dark by the time they drove away. In Conroe, at the black college on the outskirts of Dugan, they were singing gospel music and selling barbecued chicken to raise more money for the fight.

Monday afternoon, March 9, they gathered in the main lobby of the high school to try to reconstruct the day of the crime. Everyone was nervous. John Sessum looked like a dog that had just had its ribs kicked. Don Brown, who had come along with his internal filing cabinet to check the details of the reconstruction, was smoking impatiently, waiting for an assistant principal to bring them the keys they needed. Reyna and McCloskey were trying to look calm, but inside they were desperate to succeed.

Since their visit to Sessum they had had no luck with other witnesses. They had wasted most of Sunday trailing around the hills outside Cleveland looking for Icky Peace. When they had finally found him, he insisted in his little boy's voice that he was under a gag order and that Conroe High School, where he was working again, would fire him if he talked. With some encouragement from his sister, he had talked a little, describing how he had heard the policeman tell Brandley that he was elected to take the blame and how Acreman had come over to the Vocational Building on the day of the crime saying that they should not worry about Brandley because he was having fun with a white girl over there and there was clothes and chairs scattered all over the place. But Peace was not about to give them any breakthrough, at least not while he thought he was under his supposed gag order.

Ed Payne had been little better. The two investigators had just spent most of the morning with him; they had got him acquainted with McCloskey but had not dug out any new information from him.

And time was moving on. There were now only two and a half weeks until Brandley was due to die. Somehow they had to get John Sessum to unload his story.

As they waited outside the administration office, each pacing a different track in the corridor, McCloskey noticed a small, round figure with a bucket, polishing his way along the hallway window in their direction, rubbing furiously at the glass, frowning with concentration, trying to pretend he was

not at all interested in what they were all doing. It was Icky
Peace, keeping abreast of developments.

"Hey, Icky, how are ya?"

At last the assistant principal came with the keys and led
them down to the scene of the crime, to the rest rooms at
"Sesame Street." They could see the tension building in John
Sessum. They had brought a friend of Reyna's, Peggy Miller,
to act out the part of Cheryl Fergeson, and as she came walking
toward them down the empty hallway from the gyms where the
blond girl in the blue jeans had once walked to the staircase
where they stood waiting for her, Sessum froze with fear. He
could barely speak to tell them he had nothing to say. He just
stood there with his hands buried in his pockets, staring at his
mangled old shoes and shaking his head.

After a while they took him across to the Vocational Building to see if that would help him. Sessum sat on the steps
with his head in his hands. Brown and McCloskey took turns
urging him to talk. Sessum finally found words to speak, but
all he would say was "I can't do it. I can't do it." Finally, they
gave up. They could not get him over this unseen hurdle.

Don Brown went back to his office. Peggy Miller drove
home. McCloskey and Reyna told Sessum they would drive
him back to his bike, which he had left on the edge of Conroe
at the depot where he checked in all his bottles and cans. They
put him in the old Chevy, told him not to worry, and flipped
on the Glenn Miller music. McCloskey made small talk while
Reyna, who was driving, lost himself in thought, trying to cut
through all this crap to see what it was that was bugging this
guy. Reyna was still turning it over in his mind when they
arrived at Sessum's workplace.

McCloskey was talking about the crime again, gently lob-
bing simple questions at Sessum. Sessum was unlocking his
bike, sighing, shaking his head and saying, "That's 'bout all
I know."

But Reyna was beginning to see something, something
that happened by that school staircase all those years before.
"John, you didn't see the murder. But you saw him grab her.
Didn't you?"

Reyna was still not sure what he was trying to get at here.
Sessum said nothing and straddled his bike. "I know it," said
Reyna, "and you know it."

Sessum was silent. Then Reyna finally saw it—the shame
of a derelict alcoholic who wanted to be a brave man. "You

saw him grab her, and you got the hell out of there because you didn't want to be involved in it. That's what you've been trying to live with for the last six years."

Sessum's chin was sunk on his chest, crushed by the weight of his cowardice.

Reyna persisted. "John? John, am I right?"

Sessum looked up. "It ain't been easy."

Now that they could see the hurdle, they started trying to bring him over it. "John, did he grab her by the throat or by the arms?"

"I ain't . . ." Sessum wiped one dirty hand over the grime on his face. "I think he caught her by the arm."

McCloskey pulled him a little further. "Who was with him when he did it? . . . He needed help. . . . Who joined him?"

"The man with no teeth."

Finally, Sessum's memory was starting to unload its story. It came out like water from a rusty tap, stuttering and choking. He told how he and Sam Martinez had been by the drinking fountain at the bottom of the stairs, how Gary Acreman had grabbed the girl up by the rest room. That was when she had screamed no. Then the other guy was there, the guy with no teeth, standing next to them by the drinking fountain, and he had run up the stairs to join Acreman. And he had had something in his hands. It was a belt. Every so often Sessum stopped and cried again, but eventually he got it out.

There were still lots of details missing, but he had told the story—except for one moment he could still not bring himself to recall, the moment his cowardice had been exposed.

McCloskey asked him: "Did she ask any of you guys to help? Did she look down and say 'Help me'? . . ."

Sessum's eyes were closed, his head sunk. Slowly, he said, "I can't answer that question."

"She did, didn't she, John . . . John? . . . She asked you, didn't she, John?"

"Ask Sam."

"All right, John. Thank you, John."

Sessum heaved himself onto his bike and pedaled off, wobbling slightly as he hit the road. The two investigators drove back to Conroe.

The only way to get to Sam Martinez was to set up an old-fashioned stakeout. Reyna had never lost the suspicion that Martinez was involved in this thing, too, and he had been trying to get the janitor to talk ever since he started his inquiry in July the previous year. He had stayed in touch with Martinez's estranged wife Dolores, teasing her about her affection for Brandley, trying to use her to somehow persuade Martinez to talk. But he never would.

The next day, Tuesday, McCloskey and Reyna were outside his home in Dugan, slouched in the red velvet upholstery, listening to swing music, talking about anything to pass the time, and waiting and waiting until their bones ached. It was hard to stay inspired. In the rearview mirror McCloskey saw a young black kid bicycling up the road toward them. For want of anything better to do, he watched him pedal past the car, and so he saw, as the boy rode off down the road in front of them, the message on the little sticker on the back of his bike. "Free Clarence Brandley," it said. McCloskey smiled and felt a little inspiration trickle back. But when Sam Martinez eventually turned up, he was adamant. He would not talk. He had nothing to say. They must leave him alone.

They went back to John Sessum. A storm had blown in from the Gulf. The rain was as thick as sea fog, boiling up from the ground in clouds. Sessum invited them to take shelter in his home, and they agreed. It was a mistake. Both men immediately found themselves gagging in the foul stench, wincing and swallowing. Sessum was very tense. Before, he had always been morose and vague. Tonight he was seething with nervous energy. All the years of guilt and self-reproach were breaking loose in him. He wanted to tell them the truth.

"Y'all wanna beer?" he offered.

The two men accepted and pulled up two metal foldaway chairs from the wall. Sessum perched on the yellow-brown sheets of his bed and started to talk. It was part confession, part thriller, all of it punctuated by gulps of beer and occasional silent lapses.

He wanted to talk about his guilt. "I been thinkin' 'bout it. . . . You don't know how it's been with me. . . . I been through hell. . . . I heard her yell, heard her say 'Help' . . . I feel like . . ."

His voice trailed away. He sat slumped with his can of beer between his knees, and suddenly his whole body was heaving with sorrow and he was crying with all his heart. "I feel like I was the one who caused her death." He was sobbing now. "If I had gone back, maybe I'd a had a chance to save her. They still might have done it, but I'd a been up there, trying. . . . That's what's been eating me up. . . . And I can still see Acreman just as plain as day."

He stopped to suck in air and rub the tears from his face. McCloskey and Reyna told him that it was OK and that he was doing the right thing and he would feel better now. Sessum took a deep breath and started to talk some more, still pausing to gulp his beer and to remember. He looked again at the picture of James Dexter Robinson. "Yeah. He's got those screechy-looking eyes. And he's still got that crease down his face. . . . If I ain't mistaken, that's the man. . . . Yeah, that's the man, because his eyes are still screechy like that. . . . He was going up there, and Sam was coming down. . . . She hollered for help. I don't know how many times. I started up, but Sam stopped me. I couldn't get him out of my way. Sam said, 'You ain't going up there.' "

Determined now to tell his story, Sessum rose from the bed, and using Jim McCloskey as a model, he acted out the grabbing of the girl. Then he talked about Clarence Brandley. Oh, yes, Brandley had come walking along the hallway, just as they all said in the trial, but he was not just ten feet behind the girl. He was ten or twenty minutes behind her. Acreman and Robinson had dragged the girl off to the rest room long before Brandley got there.

"Did they reappear before Clarence came up?"

"Gary did. About the same time. It was ten or twenty minutes."

"Did you hear Gary tell Clarence not to go into the rest room?"

"Yep."

"Do you think she was dead in the rest room with Robinson at that point?"

"I wouldn't doubt it."

Now the investigators could see the details beginning to bind together.

First, there was the girl, walking innocently up those stairs at "Sesame Street"; Acreman trying to talk to her, showing off to the others; Robinson joining in; the two men trying to touch her; the girl crying no; and then this casual encounter turning nasty with each man egged on by the other's presence and the girl being grabbed and dragged into the rest room.

Then, maybe ten minutes later, Brandley had come down that hallway. Acreman was back on the staircase by now—warned perhaps by Martinez. And the black janitor, unaware

of the nightmare on the other side of the wall at the top of
that staircase, had sent the white janitors over to the Vocational
Building, put his rolls of toilet paper in the boys' rest room,
and gone off about his work.

On the way out to the Vocational Building, Acreman must
have blocked the outside door open with the trash can, which
Brandley had later found, so that he could go back to clear
up the crime. That was why he had been missing for thirty or
forty minutes, with or without Martinez. He must have gone
back to the rest room to help Robinson move the girl's body
out of there and into the auditorium, an auditorium that was
easily unlocked with the set of keys that Robinson's father
had given him. One of them had taken the clothes out to the
Dumpster. Then Robinson had left the area, and Acreman had
gone back about his work, already looking for ways to cover
his tracks.

That was when he had done something that now appeared
crucial, something that they now saw was the tiny move that
started the avalanche, something that to a man like Acreman
in a place like Montgomery County was second nature. He
had blamed the black man. He had returned to the Vocational
Building and told Icky Peace: "Don't worry about Clarence.
He's got himself a white girl over there. There's clothes and
chairs all over the place." It must have been almost instinctive.
Blame the black man. Peace had thought he was just kidding,
but he had not known a crime had been committed.

Then when the body was found, it was as if everyone in
Conroe had the same instinct, and the teachers and the students
and the police and the press and the DA and the judges and
all the ringleaders and all the bystanders had agreed that they
should blame the black man, and after a while it had stopped
mattering how many rules had to be broken or how much
evidence had to be lost or how many witnesses had to be
threatened, and so they had taken Clarence Brandley.

Now, in a way that had nothing to do with the filth
in John Sessum's shack, the two investigators felt sick
in their hearts. It was ironic that out of all the people
who had pointed the finger at the black janitor—all the
well-respected officials and all the upstanding townspeople
who agreed that the black man must die—it was a social
reject like John Sessum, a walking failure in everything he
had ever done, who had finally had the courage to break
ranks. Now the important thing was to guard Sessum's

new strength and persuade him to put all this into a statement.

McCloskey said: "Do you know how you can redeem this and especially bring justice and help her father?"

Sessum lifted an eyebrow and asked why McCloskey did not mention the dead girl's mother.

McCloskey shrugged. "Her mother died six months before she was killed."

"Hold on. You just hit something." Sessum paused and scratched his oily hair. "Gary did say something . . . Can't remember all the detail . . . He said something about the girl's mother dying, it was just her and her daddy."

"When did he say that?"

"On the way home that day."

How could Gary Acreman possibly have known that the girl's mother was dead? Suddenly, McCloskey had an image of sheer horror, of the dark rest room and these two animals with the belt, and the little girl on her knees, begging for her life, telling them her mother had died and it was just her and her daddy and how he needed her.

That was maybe the sickest thing of all. This self-righteous mob had been so determined to blame the black man and put him under the ground that they had turned their backs on the real criminals and let these bastards get away with what they had done to that poor girl.

McCloskey explained to Sessum that he must repeat all this to the attorneys. He agreed. The two investigators drove away in silence.

McCloskey and Reyna felt that they had now broken through two vital barriers. They had uncovered what they believed to be the truth. And they had found a witness who was prepared to talk. But they knew it was not enough. Not in Conroe.

The previous year's hearing had taught Reyna that the courthouse would fight forever to keep Clarence Brandley on death row. One witness, one wretched, half-dead alcoholic witness with a bad case of nerves, was not going to be enough to force the courthouse to release its black man. With only two weeks before Brandley was due to die, the defense investigators started an almost frantic search for more witnesses. They tried to find Gary Acreman, but he was working as a truck driver and was out of the state. They went and asked Ed Payne to get a message to him to tell him to contact them, and Reyna saw Cindy Acreman and forced himself to cuddle up to her and ask her to pass on the same message if she got the chance.

They tried Sam Martinez again, but he would not help.

They staked out Icky Peace and spent hours sitting outside the school watching the day go by. Eventually they saw him waddle out into the parking lot and drive off. They chased off after him in the old Chevy and pulled up alongside him at the first set of traffic lights.

McCloskey started waving out the window. "Hey, Icky! Fancy seeing you here! How are ya?"

But Peace did not want to stop and talk. He was still convinced that he was under a gag order. The investigators suspected that this was not merely the work of his imagination and that someone at the school really had told him to keep his mouth shut. Somehow they had to find a break.

On Friday, March 13, 1987, Reverend Boney officially launched the Coalition to Free Clarence Brandley, an umbrella for twenty-five different groups in the area, each of which was now pledged to campaign for Brandley's freedom. Boney called a press conference in a community center in one of Houston's black wards. It rapidly turned into a rally with a small crowd of supporters wearing FREE CLARENCE BRANDLEY t-shirts, cheering, and chanting.

Boney said they were ready to go to jail if that was what it took. Texas's only black congressman, Mickey Leland, announced his support. The president of the local chapter of the National Association for the Advancement of Colored People, Judge Al Green, asked the crowd: "Would Texas allow a white man to be tried by a black judge and jury, in a town that was predominantly black, for killing a black girl?" The supporters jeered their answer.

The press was beginning to move. Both big Houston newspapers, the *Chronicle* and the *Post*, ran lengthy features suggesting Brandley might be the victim of racism. The *Chronicle* interviewed Peter Speers, who announced airily: "The idea that anybody—even the KKK—would be interested in going and trying to frame someone for the murder just because they are black is totally preposterous."

Brandley's supporters were not impressed. They agreed they would once again march on the governor's mansion in Austin in a week's time.

Don Brown opened up a discreet line to the office of the Texas attorney general, Jim Mattox, who would represent the state of Texas if the case ever reached the federal courts and who had the political clout to help them if he chose to. Brown's contact in the AG's office was a young black attorney named Wayne Johnson, whose father had been a labor leader and an old friend of Brown's. Brown asked Johnson to speak to the attorney general to warn him that the defense was hoping to produce strong new evidence of Brandley's innocence and to ask if he would issue arrest warrants for the real murderers since the DA's office would never do it. Wayne Johnson said he would do what he could.

Meanwhile, McCloskey and Reyna had persuaded Sessum to make a formal statement to Mike De Geurin and had arranged to pick him up at his house on Sunday morning to take him into Houston. But when they got there, Sessum was nowhere to be seen. They felt a flutter of anxiety. They started driving up and down the all too familiar back roads, and after thirty minutes they spotted him, picking up old cans in the grass. The Chevy glided up alongside him, and McCloskey wound down his window.

"Hey, John. Where were you, man?"

Sessum kept on loading cans into his sack without looking up.

"John, you're supposed to be coming into Houston with us. You remember?"

"I ain't going."

McCloskey felt his heart sink. It was not so much what he said as the voice he said it in, which was not far from a snarl.

"John, you promised you would come with us. You were going to help Clarence. What's happened, man? What's the matter?"

"I ain't going. Get outta here."

"But, John—"

"Go on. Get outta here."

The two investigators shrugged at each other. "All right, John. Thanks anyway."

They drove off, cursing. Sessum's shame had risen up and swallowed him again. Now they were in big trouble. There were eleven days until the execution. Without Sessum, they could do little more than limp into court and beg for mercy. If they could not get him back, Brandley was a dead man. McCloskey dropped Reyna in Conroe and headed for Mike De Geurin's house to share the bad news. Two hours later he left with a new plan: De Geurin would come with them the next day to try his famous charm on John Sessum.

As soon as Sessum saw the old Chevy burning up to his shack, he scowled. "I thought I told you guys I wasn't gonna talk no more."

They climbed out of the car and introduced De Geurin, who never needed to be asked twice to make a new friend and shook Sessum warmly by the hand. Sessum looked stern and growled: "Y'all wanna come in?"

It was the last thing they wanted to do, but they had to agree. Sessum opened the door of his shack, and his dog, which was normally chained up, pounced out, snarling, with the hair over its shoulders standing up rigid, and leaped at the nearest available stranger, who happened to be Richard Reyna. It locked its teeth into the top of his left leg.

"Goddamn it," yelled Reyna. "Get this son of a bitch off me."

It hurt Reyna, but it helped their situation. Sessum hauled the dog off and cursed at it, McCloskey and De Geurin started chuckling, Reyna cursed some more, but Sessum ended up apologizing and trying to make amends, and it seemed that the ice was broken.

Inside the shack Sessum offered them all beers, turned on an old black-and-white TV set over his bed, and told them to take a seat. The three men settled down while Sessum turned to the grimy sink, where he had some beer cans floating in lukewarm water. Reyna rubbed his leg and checked out the tooth marks in his pants, and De Geurin started shuffling a notebook out of his briefcase. The next thing they knew, John Sessum was rearing up over them like a nightmare, with a twelve-inch butcher's knife flashing in his right fist and his face all red and twisted with rage, and he was screaming at them: "You get the fuck outta here. Get the fuck outta here. Get the fuck outta here."

The knife was quivering in his fist. All three of them started talking at once. "OK, John, OK . . . we're going, man. . . . Don't worry about it . . . stay cool. . . . There's no need for that. . . ."

As they reached the door, De Geurin, following the habit of a lifetime, turned back toward the room, grinned like a pixie, and held out his hand. "Nice to meet you, John."

Sessum switched the butcher's blade to his left hand and solemnly shook the attorney's hand.

"Jesus Christ," said Reyna, "I don't believe this shit."

But once the shock of the moment had passed, they felt the weight of their failure and drove back to Conroe in despair. They stopped by Don Brown's office, and there Reyna decided to try a different approach. He called up Mattie Johnson, the old lady who lived next door to Sessum and who had saved his sensibilities on his first visit to Sessum's shack. He got her on the phone and explained what was happening and asked her to have a word with Sessum for them.

Half an hour later the phone rang in Brown's office. It was Mattie Johnson. Reyna took the call, deadpan, then turned around to the others, clapped his hands together, and shouted: "Holy shit! He's gonna do it. She talked him into it. God knows how. But all we've got to do is be out there again tomorrow."

It was St. Patrick's Day, Tuesday, March 17. The defense team members were feeling strong again. That afternoon, thanks to Mattie Johnson, they would try to interview John Sessum again, and they had arranged to take a video camera so that there would be an indisputable record of his evidence.

In Dallas the *Times Herald* had splashed the story of the Brandley case across its front page under the dark black headline HUNDREDS PLEAD: DON'T LET STATE MURDER INNOCENT MAN. The story disclosed that the case had generated more letters of concern to the governor than any other in the state's history.

By noon the defense was feeling even stronger: Gary Acreman had walked into Don Brown's office, saying he had heard the defense wanted to see him. Brown was in court, but Acreman had waited and then left word with Brown's secretary that he was driving up to Corsicana, 150 miles north of Conroe on I-45, and he would call from there.

At three McCloskey and Reyna set off from Brown's office with Mike De Geurin and Tom Curtis, the reporter who had written that morning's *Dallas Times Herald* story. Curtis wanted the story of Sessum's revelations, and De Geurin wanted him there as a witness to testify that they were not cheating in any way. Don Brown stayed behind, hoping that Acreman would call.

At four John Sessum sat down in front of the video camera and started to talk to Mike De Geurin. He was stumbling and stuttering, he appeared to have been drinking, and he said he was scared; but what mattered was that he was talking.

At five minutes past four Don Brown answered the phone in his office and found himself talking to Gary Acreman in Corsicana. Acreman was curious to find out what the defense was doing and agreed to meet the two investigators. He gave Brown the name and room number of the motel where he was staying for the night. Brown told him to sit tight; Reyna and McCloskey would be there around nine.

At six the defense investigators left Sessum. They felt triumphant. Sessum had told his whole story on camera, nailing Acreman and Robinson to the crime, right down to admitting that he had failed to do anything to help the girl because, as he put it, "I guess I had a little rabbit in me." He had even apologized for attacking them the previous evening. "I'm a hardheaded baboon," he said.

By half past six they were in Don Brown's office, preparing to set off for Corsicana and Gary Acreman. Brown was worried that Acreman might be planning some nasty surprise for them. He had no doubt that Reyna could whip Acreman's ass in a fair fight, but if Acreman had a gun, the unarmed investigators could be in trouble. Tom Curtis had agreed to travel with them to provide the safety of numbers, so while De Geurin stayed behind to talk tactics with Don Brown, the two investigators and the reporter hurtled northward to reach Corsicana by nine.

For McCloskey and Reyna, this was the big prize. Sessum had done well; but he was never going to be an ideal witness, and anyway he knew only part of the story. Acreman was different. If he started to confirm any of their new information, they would surely be strong enough to put the courthouse people to flight. He had already started at the previous year's hearing when he had sworn that Robinson was at the high school on the day of the crime, but he had never talked about the attack on the girl. Somehow they had to get him to fill in more of the picture. The big question was why Acreman would do that and book himself a seat on death row. The question nagged away at them as they sped north. They had still not found the answer when the old Chevy rolled into the parking lot of the Travelers Inn, Corsicana, soon after nine o'clock. But a few moments after the two investigators knocked on the door of Room 211, the problem was solved for them.

Gary Acreman opened the door, and as soon as they caught sight of his face, they saw it: this guy was scared shitless. They decided to give him something to be scared about. They took him across the road to the Holiday Inn and settled him into the coffee shop. Curtis sat a few tables away, observing. Acreman and Reyna ordered cups of tea. McCloskey straightened his white collar and ordered a bourbon on the rocks. Reyna went to work.

He threw Acreman off-balance from the start by telling him that witnesses were changing their stories without letting him know what they were now saying. He told him that finally the truth was coming out and watched his eyes flicker nervously around the room. He started playing him off against James Dexter Robinson, urging him not to take the rap for something someone else had done.

Acreman soon started to move. First, he tried to line himself up with what he guessed other witnesses were now saying. "I'd like to see Brandley get out," he said. "I'd like to see him get out because from day one I didn't think he was the one that done it."

Reyna resisted a desire to slap him in the face and remind him that he was one of the state's main witnesses against Brandley and continued to play him off against Robinson. "Don't protect this guy because he's your buddy."

"He's not my buddy," snapped Acreman, moving a little more to distance himself from Robinson.

Acreman started mumbling about the Vocational Building, and Reyna abruptly told him to forget it. "We're talking about the period of time the girl was looking for the bathroom. That's what I'm interested in."

Acreman's eyes were twitching from Reyna's face to the table. Reyna started to let on just how much they now knew: "Why would they say you went upstairs to talk to her? . . . You talked to her for about three or four minutes. . . . The girl said no, and she started yelling for help. . . . She was grabbed."

Acreman started to shake. It was like watching a replay of his meeting with Reyna the previous summer. Once again he was wrestling with his fingers, trying to get a cigarette into his mouth, and failing hopelessly. Jim McCloskey quietly reached across the table, took the cigarette from the packet, pointed it into his mouth, and lit it for him. Acreman managed to speak. "I didn't see."

"Don't protect that asshole," snarled Reyna. "Let me ask you this. Would all these people lie when they say that they saw you talk to her and saw you grab her, or that you were talking to her and Robinson grabbed her?"

"I don't know."

"Robinson was down there, where the water fountain was, the bottom level. He's already been ID'd as being down there and then coming upstairs with you."

"Not with me. Not with me."

"Don't bullshit us. Just help us."

"I wasn't there with the girl. I left."

"Was Robinson up there?" Reyna stared relentlessly at Acreman, who was now sitting on one quaking hand and using the other to haul smoke out of his cigarette as if it were his dying breath. Reyna jabbed a finger in front of his face. "You know he was there! Did he go into the rest room?"

"I don't know. We left."

"You ain't never gonna get it out of your heart until you come forward. You know you saw Robinson do something up there. Don't protect the asshole."

Then Acreman moved again. "I saw him go up there. I didn't know he did anything."

They had broken through. Reyna and McCloskey could see Acreman struggling to tell the story without putting himself into the middle of it. Reyna kept asking him who had grabbed the girl. Acreman kept shaking his head and then finally said: "Robinson must have put her in the rest room."

They kept up the pressure. "You'll be able to sleep better, man. It's been a nightmare."

"Yeah," said Acreman. "And now it'll be another nightmare."

Reyna and McCloskey reckoned it was time to move on. "Listen now. What we want to do is this. Very simple. We don't want to bother you anymore. We want to get an interview with you. Do it tonight. Take about ten minutes. OK?"

"OK."

McCloskey kept Acreman talking, Reyna went off to get the video camera, Curtis rented a room, and ten minutes later Acreman was settled in an armchair in the room in front of the camera, with a cigarette burning between his fingers. Now he was calmer and more assured. As the camera whirred, he described a scene that confirmed all that John Sessum had told them, with the one exception that in Acreman's version of events, it was Robinson alone who attacked the girl while he was merely an innocent bystander like the other janitors, intimidated and powerless to help. But the details were the same: the same scene at the top of the stairs where the girl was stopped; the same cries of "No" and "Help" as she was dragged into the rest room; the same delay before Brandley arrived on the scene. Sometimes Acreman paused and sighed deeply. Once or twice Reyna thought he was about to cry. Often he rested his head on his hand and simply stared in silence. As the interview went on, he became more and more outspoken about Robinson's guilt. "There's no doubt," he said. He suggested it was no surprise to see Robinson act like that because he had been around to Robinson's house and seen him fighting violently with Brenda Medina. "I mean, you'd think they was gonna have a war."

Toward the end Jim McCloskey in his clergyman's clothes leaned toward Acreman and looked him straight in the eye. "Now, Gary, did you have anything to do with it?"

Acreman shook his head vigorously from side to side. "No. Nothing. I . . ." He sighed long and deep and ran his hand over his eyes. "No." Then his head was back on his palm, and he was silent again.

The investigators did not believe him for a minute. They returned to a theme that had been troubling Acreman throughout the interview: he could not explain why he had told the approaching Brandley that there was a girl in the rest room if the truth was, as he now said, that at that moment he knew the girl was in there with someone who was attacking her.

"Did you think she was a dead girl in the rest room?" asked McCloskey.

Acreman sighed. "I don't know."

"Why did you say 'There's a girl in the rest room'?"

"I don't know that either."

"Because you knew—you knew that James Robinson was in that room with her at the time, didn't you?"

Acreman nodded. Tom Curtis closed in. "So you were trying to stop Clarence from going in there and observing that?"

"I guess in a way I was."

That nailed him. He was never going to tell them he had killed the girl himself, but right there, so far as the investigators were concerned, he had just admitted that he was an accessory to murder.

"Fine," said Reyna.

They switched off the camera. McCloskey walked Acreman back to his room, reassuring him that he would feel better now that he had got it out of his system. Acreman said he did feel better now, and he was glad.

With Acreman out of the way, the two investigators whooped for joy. McCloskey called Mike De Geurin at his home in Houston. It was after midnight now, but De Geurin was still up.

"Mike, we got him. We got him on tape."

"Holy shit, Jim."

And De Geurin had news for the investigators. A reporter had called a little earlier to ask for a comment on the statement from the Texas attorney general, Jim Mattox. De Geurin had had no idea what he was talking about, so the reporter had explained that the attorney had just announced publicly that he believed Clarence Brandley should be given a stay of execution.

McCloskey pointed the old Chevy southward. "That's not a bad St. Paddy's Day," he said.

In Conroe the next morning, Wednesday, March 18, Don Brown strode across the street to the courthouse and filed a formal request for a hearing before Judge Coker so that the defense could win a stay of execution. He then strode back without disclosing what kind of new evidence the defense had found, leaving a dust cloud of rumor and speculation behind him.

In Houston Mike De Geurin opened up new negotiations with Wayne Johnson in the Texas attorney general's office. He explained that he did not trust the DA's office in Conroe to handle the vital new evidence that the defense had now obtained from two witnesses. He wanted the attorney general to see the evidence personally and to take over the investigation of the crime himself. Wayne Johnson agreed to talk to Mattox.

In the community center in Houston's Third Ward, the

Reverend Don Boney called for volunteers for a campaign of civil disobedience on behalf of Clarence Brandley and threw all his energy into the march he was planning on the governor's mansion in Austin that Friday.

In the Huntsville Jail, Clarence Brandley spoke to reporters and said he was hoping and praying for a stay and that he was very happy with the attorney general's statement. "It was delightful for me to hear," he said.

Only Brandley's family knew how desperate he felt. Now only seven days away from his date with the executioner, his face was puffy from lack of sleep, he had lost at least twenty pounds because he was too tense to eat, and he was constantly chewing on the inside of his lower lip.

In Austin, Wayne Johnson went into a huddle with the attorney general and then called Mike De Geurin to tell him that the attorney general would personally meet the defense to review the new evidence within the next twenty-four hours.

Reyna and McCloskey were still looking for witnesses. With two aces in their hand, they figured they might as well go for a third, so with Tom Curtis still in tow they caught a plane for South Carolina.

But the enemy was standing its ground. In the DA's office Peter Speers was being harried by the press. He assured the journalists that Clarence Brandley was "the only man on earth capable of committing that murder." Speers had no idea what the defense had come up with, but he was not worried about any new evidence. Nothing in the state of Texas had changed since the hearing last year, and new evidence could not be introduced more than thirty days after the end of the trial. It did not matter how many new facts the defense claimed to come up with; it would all be inadmissible and could not be mentioned. If Peter Speers III had his way, Brandley was going to keep his appointment with the executioner in the early hours of next Thursday, March 26. When the *New York Times* called him up and asked if he had any doubts about the execution, Speers confided: "I wouldn't lose any sleep over it, except maybe to go to bed later than usual to see that it actually happens."

In the courtroom on the second floor Judge Lynn Coker agreed to hold a hearing in two days, on Friday, March 20.

In the early hours of Thursday, outside a textile factory in Greenville, South Carolina, Reyna and McCloskey closed in on James Dexter Robinson. They knew Robinson was in there, working a shift that was supposed to end at three in the morning. It was dark and quiet. They waited in their rented car for Robinson to walk through the gate. Nothing happened. They were tired and tense. In the backseat Tom Curtis suddenly spoke.

"There's a cop car just pulled up."

The two investigators whirled around, expecting some kind of trouble. They could see nothing. Then Reyna rolled his eyes up and broke into a long, wheezing laugh. There was no car, only a pile of metal pipes by the side of the road, which Curtis in his tiredness had mistaken for the police.

When there was still no sign of Robinson at four in the morning, McCloskey decided to go into the factory. Wearing his white collar, he walked cautiously through the gate and disappeared. Five minutes later he came strolling back, talking earnestly with a small, pixie-faced man, whose face Reyna instantly recognized. As they approached the car, Reyna got out and offered his hand.

"Hey," said Robinson, drawing back, "you never told me he was with you."

Reyna and McCloskey gave Robinson their sweetest talk and told him they did not want to question him. They just wanted to show him the videotapes that Acreman had been making so he could see for himself what Acreman was saying about him. Robinson relaxed and said they could come inside with him while he finished his shift, which had another hour to run. Inside the factory Robinson started scrambling up and down long metal ladders and pouring buckets of dye into giant vats. The two investigators scrambled up and down behind him. Robinson told them he would call his uncle to see if they could use his VCR to watch the video.

But when Robinson came back from making his call, he spoke to a supervisor, who told the two investigators to leave. Back in their car, they saw Robinson walk out of the gate, spot them, and retreat inside again. The next thing they knew, a car was speeding past them with a passenger trying to duck down out of sight. They spun their car around and gave chase, lurching over a thick curbstone and jumping several sets of lights before they saw the futility of it all. Even if they caught up with him, he was never going to talk now. They had to let him go.

In Austin that Thursday afternoon Mike De Geurin sat down

with Attorney General Mattox and explained about the black
janitor and the circumstantial evidence and about all the fragments of information that had surfaced pointing to the guilt of
the two white men. Then De Geurin played him the videotapes
of John Sessum and Gary Acreman—the first eyewitnesses in
the history of the case—each describing the helpless struggles
of Cheryl Fergeson and exonerating the black janitor.

De Geurin could see that Mattox was impressed and asked
him to issue warrants for the arrest of Acreman and Robinson
and to put his own investigators on the case. De Geurin knew
Mattox was a politician, and it was common knowledge that
he was hoping to make a run for the governor's mansion, but
he was not too worried by that. He hoped that as a lawyer
Mattox would see the strength of Brandley's case and that as
a politician he would see the advantage of playing the hero.
Mattox was cautious; he said he would prefer it if the DA in
Conroe would invite him to conduct an investigation, but he
would see what he could do.

That night Reyna and McCloskey flew back to Houston
from South Carolina. Sitting shoulder to shoulder in the plane,
they relaxed for the first time in three days and replayed all that
had happened, the setbacks and the breakthroughs and now the
hope of victory. Before they really knew it, the two of them
were crying their eyes out.

Early on Friday morning, before the courthouse was awake
for the day, an old bus wheezed through Dugan, over the
railroad track, and headed west for Austin, 150 miles away. At
about the same time, outside a community center in Houston,
three more buses set out in the same direction. Reverend
Boney's angry army was on the move.

An hour later the courthouse opened for the day. In the
whole building there was only one subject of conversation:
the newspaper stories that said that two of the white janitors
had changed their evidence and now insisted that Brandley was
innocent. The district attorney asked his investigator, Frank
Newton, to see what he could find out about that.

Soon after ten o'clock a rangy guy with reddish brown hair
drove into a parking lot on Route 105 east of Conroe. It was
Gary Acreman, keeping a date with Reyna and McCloskey.
The two investigators had called him because they wanted to
follow up on some of the things he had told them in Corsicana.

Now Acreman said he, too, wanted to talk about what he had told them. He had been thinking, he said, that maybe there were a few things he had said back the other night that were not quite right and maybe he should be changing a few things. Reyna and McCloskey could guess what had happened: he had had time to worry about whether his new story was going to fit with all these other witnesses he was hearing about.

Reyna spotted an angle. It was too late to change the video, he said, because it had already been sent up to the attorney general. "But if you really want to straighten out your story, well, Jim and I would be willing to help you make another video. We could do it right now if you wanted."

Acreman went for it.

Sitting in front of the camera, Acreman began by repeating without prompting that he had seen James Dexter Robinson grab the girl and drag her screaming into the rest room. No change there. Still, the two investigators were glad he was repeating it; if the DA tried to make out that they had tricked or pressured him into saying any of this in Corsicana, they could now point to the fact that the man had turned up voluntarily and told the same story.

Acreman soon got around to what was bugging him. He recalled how he had gone over to the Vocational Building and started pacing up and down while they waited for Brandley to come and let them in. "And in that time that I was pacing, I seen Robinson come out of the side, back at the main building, and go to the Dumpster and dump a bag in."

"OK," said Reyna. "Do you know what was in the bag?"

"At the top of it, it looked like it was clothes hanging out of it."

Acreman went on to describe how Robinson had then collected a large stack of broken ceiling tiles from the school and dumped them on top of the clothes. He then agreed that he had gone home and told his father-in-law that he knew the girl's clothes were in the Dumpster. Reyna and McCloskey did not believe this man was necessarily telling them the whole truth. They doubted if you could even see the Dumpster from the spot where Acreman said he was pacing. They doubted even more if you could identify the contents of a trash bag at such a distance. The truth, they suspected, was that Acreman was very much closer to that trash bag as it went into the Dumpster and was possibly even carrying it himself. But that did not matter right now. What mattered was that finally he was confirming his father-in-law's story and admitting to having vital evidence that he had failed to disclose in court.

One more thing was bugging Acreman: the trip he had made to the Shamrock station to buy cigarettes and cold drinks with Sam Martinez. He realized now that that had not happened while they all were waiting outside the Vocational Building. That had been three hours earlier, when they had just arrived at the high school, before they even started work for the day.

The two investigators could only guess why he was suddenly shifting his story. But it looked as if he were trying to double the strength of his alibi for those missing thirty or forty minutes. Not only had he been with Martinez, who would swear that they had not been moving the girl's body, but also this whole disappearance of his had happened before the girl was even killed.

Finally, he told them explicitly why he was making these video statements for them. "Because I don't think Clarence Brandley is guilty," he said. "And, well, I know for a fact he isn't."

The two investigators finished the interview, turned off the camera, and thanked him most sincerely for his help.

At noon in Austin all was quiet outside the towering Capitol, which sits on a hill as if in judgment on the city below. The state assembly was in session. The first that anyone heard of the approaching throng was a soft chant, lapping around the edges of the building. "Jus-tice! Jus-tice! Jus-tice!" Several hundred voices sang the word. Then there were shouts. "Stop the racist death penalty. . . . Give justice a chance. . . . Free Clarence Brandley."

There must have been three hundred of them, nearly ten times as many as the last protest in Austin, two long months earlier. There were children wearing FREE CLARENCE BRANDLEY T-shirts, men and women dressed in their Sunday clothes and waving placards, and, most of all, elderly men and women, shuffling slowly arm in arm up the hill. The younger ones waved banners and flags and cheered the Reverend O. T. Brandley and the Reverend Don Boney when they said that they would fight until Clarence Brandley was free and the state admitted its corruption. Black assemblymen came out of the Capitol to join the demonstration.

The crowd demanded to see Governor Clements. The staff in the governor's mansion said the governor was not available. So the demonstrators decided it was time for some of them to get themselves arrested. With the two Baptist ministers, Don Boney and O. T. Brandley, at their head, forty Brandley supporters walked slowly up the steps of the mansion, filed through the door, and, softly chanting "Jus-tice! Jus-tice!" swarmed into the governor's empty office.

At about this time, on a back road outside Conroe, John Sessum was busy picking up rusty cans and dusty bottles when a car spun up beside him and two strangers got out, two men with big leather boots. They stood over Sessum and told him they wanted a word. One of them showed him a badge. One of them said his name was Newton.

They started asking questions. Had he made a tape? What had he said in it? Who had the tape? Did he say Brandley was innocent? Sessum told them he didn't want to talk about it. They asked more questions: the day of the crime; the other janitors; the tape. He told them to go ask Sam Martinez. They said they had. They said Martinez told a different story. They said they might have to make him take a lie detector test. They poked more questions at him. Finally, John Sessum had had enough. He had put up with all this crap from the Texas Ranger and the sheriff once before. But he was not going to be pushed around anymore. He was not going to listen to that little rabbit in him again. So he told the two men with boots to get out of here and quit bugging him or he'd have them arrested for harassment. They told him he couldn't do that. And John Sessum said, "We'll see about that," and walked away from the sons of bitches.

Just before two o'clock three men walked out of a dingy second-floor office in the middle of Conroe, past the blown-up black-and-white photograph of George Morris, down the dusty staircase, and out into the deserted street. It was hot. Nothing moved. No one said a word. Don Brown, Mike De Geurin, and Paul Nugent could feel the eyes on them as they crossed the street—from the drugstore, from the offices over the stores, from the windows of the courthouse. This whole town knew who they were and what they had come to do. They strode in silence up the courthouse steps.

Inside the familiar courtroom the attorneys prepared to present their motion for a stay of execution. For once the court was less than packed. Brandley's family and supporters were in Austin. Brandley himself was on death row. And curiously, Peter Speers was nowhere to be seen. It appeared to have fallen to his assistant, Rick Stover, to defend the courthouse. For a moment they could not understand why Speers was not there. They had been told only fifteen minutes earlier that he was in the courthouse. Then Rick Stover stood up and insisted that they could not hold this hearing without the DA, who, he claimed, was on his way to Florida and would not be back for a week. By which time Brandley would be dead. Don Brown, who reckoned he knew the courthouse people pretty well, thought this was just about the dumbest stunt he had seen them pull: trying to get a man executed by hiding the district attorney. Not even Judge Coker was impressed. Rick Stover had to fight on alone.

The three defense attorneys did not envy his position. Not only did they have powerful arguments that ought to persuade any judge to grant a stay, but they also knew that if they lost here, they could go straight to the federal court, where the attorney general would not oppose them. Mike De Geurin launched the attack. He produced his new application for a writ of habeas corpus and spelled out six reasons why Clarence Brandley should be given not only a stay of execution but also a new hearing. The first and most important, he said, was that two eyewitnesses had now established that Clarence Brandley was innocent. Rick Stover objected that innocence was not a legally admissible issue.

De Geurin then complained of a catalog of past abuse: the secret meetings between the DA and Judge Martin; the plot to conceal the disappearance of all the exhibits; the loss of the most critical evidence, including the semen swabs and the hair found on the girl's body; the blind focus of the investigation, which had opened with the "election of the nigger" and had then been dedicated to proving Brandley's guilt instead of uncovering the truth; and finally, the racist character of the Texas death penalty, which was used disproportionately to punish blacks for killing whites. Rick Stover protested that these issues should have been dealt with before or had been dealt with before and dismissed. There was no justification for a stay of execution and no need for another hearing, he said.

By this time in Austin, Clarence Brandley's supporters had left the governor's office and were once again chanting and cheering on the steps of the State Capitol. The governor's staff had agreed that a small group could speak to the governor about the Brandley case on another occasion. It was not enough, and they said so. They could feel their strength. "Jus-tice! Jus-tice!" Then, at the top of the steps, a man in a suit appeared. He was a black man, an assistant to the attorney general. It was Wayne Johnson. He had a note in one hand, and now he asked for silence so that he could read it to them.

"At two forty-seven today," he announced, "Judge Lynn Coker signed a stay of execution for Clarence Brandley."

Pause. The steps erupted. "Jus-tice! Jus-tice!" Banners waving. Hats flying. Hands clapping. Everybody grinning and chanting.

Now it was O. T. Brandley's turn to ask for silence.

"Father," he cried, and the heads on the steps all bowed, "we thank you for what you have done today."

"Amen, amen," they murmured.

"We thank you for what you will do in the future."

"Amen!" they sang.

"We thank you for making the truth come out, for we know that Clarence Brandley is innocent."

"Amen! Praise the Lord!"

And then they turned and flowed back down the hill to their buses and the road back to Houston and to Dugan, triumphant.

John Sessum heard about the reprieve, and he felt something like satisfaction. He knew he could never bring back the girl, and he could never return to that moment on the staircase and find the courage to stand up and fight for her. But he could stand up now, not just for Brandley but for himself. He could show everyone that John Sessum from the state of Mississippi was a strong man. He could do what was right. He felt something like relief, too; the nightmares had stopped.

Two days after the reprieve, on Sunday evening, his new courage was tested for the first time. He was trying to clean up his act, shave every morning, keep up a better appearance, and he had pedaled down to the Laundromat to get the grime out of some of his old clothes. By the time he came out, it was dark, so he never saw who hit him.

He had his clean clothes tucked into his bicycle basket, and all he was thinking about was getting on home. He had just climbed onto his bike and was pedaling off across the parking lot when some guy—maybe there were two guys—jumped out of a black Ford and knocked him over and started beating him.

It shook him up. It gave him a bad pain in his ribs, all down the left side, and in his chest. He never saw who hit him. But he heard what they said.

"Where's that tape?" He heard it loud and clear. And then again: "Now, will you keep your goddamn mouth shut?"

Then they were gone, leaving him on the ground with his clean clothes scattered.

The defense attorneys guessed it must have been Gary Acreman again or someone from his family; but in the next few weeks there were more incidents, and it began to appear that there were greater forces at work.

Richard Reyna came home to his pin-clean town house on the edge of Conroe, and night after night he found his answering machine stacked with messages: "I'm gonna find you, and I'm gonna kill you. . . . pussyhead. . . . I'm gonna put your blood on me. . . . I'm gonna cut your dick off. . . . Man, you are one dead motherfucker. . . . You're history. You're dead meat." Often it was a woman's voice, shrieking and hissing. After a few weeks he changed his number and kept the new one secret. The calls started again within forty-eight hours. Who could uncover an unlisted number so quickly? He never knew, but he could guess. Then his car tires were slashed, and someone put sugar in his gas tank, fouling the engine and costing him hundreds of dollars. One day, in town, he met a bad cop, an evil bastard, who asked him, "How's that little daughter of yours, Reyna?" He had to tell his ex-wife that Tiffany had better not visit for a while.

Someone threw eggs at Don Brown's car. The burly attorney was not about to be intimidated. He drove around Conroe for a week with the eggs and their broken shells baked onto his car and parked it each day right outside the courthouse, as if to say, "Screw you."

Mike De Geurin came to Conroe for a hearing, parked his car in the courthouse square, and came back to find the gas tank had been filled with metal filings. Who could look at a car parked in the courthouse square and find out who its owner was? De Geurin never knew for sure.

Bill Srack, however, finally came face-to-face with one of his tormentors. Try as he might, after seven years Srack had not been able to forget the Brandley case. Even though the phone calls at his house had more or less dried up now, he still found that just about every day he would catch himself thinking of that lonely time in the jury room. It was painful, but he could not let it go. He collected everything that was written about the case, but he could not bring himself to read any of it. He just piled up the papers and the magazines in a corner and left them.

About this time he applied for a new job in Conroe, as the purchasing agent for Montgomery County, and sent his résumé to the committee of judges who had to make the appointment. Since he had experience and unusually good references, he was not surprised to find himself on a short list of three, and when he discovered that one of his competitors had admitted lying on his résumé and the other no longer wanted the job, his confidence began to build. The job interview soon changed that.

He found himself being questioned by three judges, one of whom was the Honorable James Keeshan. Keeshan led the questioning and rapidly turned the subject to the first trial of Clarence Brandley. Why had he held out against the other jurors? Did he realize that twenty-three other jurors disagreed with him? Did he think he was rational? Did he have trouble getting along with other people? Srack tried to explain, and after twenty minutes of rapid-fire questions about Clarence Brandley, he asked what any of this had to do with the post of purchasing agent for Montgomery County. The interview ended. A few weeks later Keeshan wrote Srack to tell him that the judges had decided to fill the post by making an internal promotion.

There were incidents, too, on the other side of the railroad tracks, in Dugan. On Avenue E, Minnie Ola Brandley received a letter full of ugly, vicious talk. If she had been less than seventy-two years old and if she had not been so weighed down and worn out by Clarence's case, she guessed she might have just torn it up and paid it no mind, but it frightened her. If she had lived in another town, maybe even if she had been down in Houston, she might have felt safe; but this was Conroe, and she knew the kinds of things that went on, so she packed her belongings and moved out of her home on Avenue E and stayed with relations in Houston till things quieted down.

One of the first women in Dugan to come out and support Reverend Boney's campaign, one of those who had ventured into the courthouse square and shaken her fist in defiance, had her windows shot out. A minister who worked on the campaign was run off the road while he was driving just outside town. Some big car came sweeping up alongside him and forced him off; as the car sped away, he saw it had no license plate.

Ed Payne did not escape so lightly. He was driving along a deserted road in the dark near his trailer, ten miles southeast of Conroe, when two cars suddenly swooped up behind him. One of them had lights flashing on its roof. The other, a white Chevrolet like the ones Montgomery County sheriffs drive, sped past him and screeched to a halt across the road, blocking his path. Payne thought he must have done something against the law, so he hauled himself out of the car and started hobbling over to the white Chevrolet, leaning on his walking stick and trying to say howdy through his voice box. A couple of seconds later he realized he had made a bad mistake.

There were men running toward him, men without uniforms, men shouting. He turned and started limping as fast as he could back toward his car, but he was too late. One of them was already on him, kicking him in the legs. He swung around and tried to kick him back, standing on his good leg and kicking him with the bad one. Then another guy punched him in the mouth, split his lip. He was down now, bleeding everywhere, and they were on top of him, and he heard what one of them was shouting at him: "I want you to keep your goddamn mouth shut."

Then the men ran back to their cars and whipped out of there.

Brenda Medina suffered, too. She had gotten up early to drive her husband to work and had fallen asleep on the sofa. Her children were still in bed. Some sound woke her, and immediately it frightened her.

For several days now Gary Acreman had been spooking her. She had run into him in a grocery store, and he had stood there staring at her and turning over a knife in the palm of his hand. Then she had seen him hanging around outside the house. She got up from the sofa to have a look. The next thing she knew, he was inside the house and he had her by the throat and the two of them were fighting like cats. She managed to wrench his hand off her throat, and he started beating her about the head and chest and clawing at her with his fingernails. She fought back and tore his hair out in clumps and hit him in the face. At one point he grabbed hold of her hair and pulled her head down on the couch, and they started shouting at each other, she saying he must have something awfully bad to hide, he telling her she was a whore and a bitch and the nigger was going to pay and she wasn't going to do anything about it.

Then he told her she'd better not tell anyone about this or there wouldn't be nothing left of her to testify.

"Just leave and leave me alone," she shouted. Her three-year-old daughter came running in. He left, knocking the girl over as he went.

Reverend Boney saw the violence spreading and the danger that fear would smother the new courage of the people in Dugan. At a Thursday-night prayer meeting in Conroe he urged them to keep fighting, to fight Conroe and to fight the courthouse and, most of all, to fight their fear. They decided that on Saturday, April 4, the anniversary of the death of Martin Luther King, they would march on the courthouse again.

This time Conroe was prepared. Inside the fire station a riot squad from the Department of Public Safety was waiting with batons and tear gas. Inside the sheriff's department all leave had been canceled, and every available man was ready to go into action. Inside the police station every officer in the department had been called up, and a ten-man SWAT team, dressed in full riot gear, prowled the hallways. On a table in the back of the building, riot guns and extra ammunition were stacked in neat piles.

The people of Dugan, some of them so old and infirm that they used walkers, came over the railroad tracks and headed for the courthouse. Reverend Boney warned them not to give Conroe a pretext to attack them. Their signs said KING DIED SO CLARENCE COULD LIVE. As they marched, they sang and chanted: "We are not afraid." They felt their strength again. They ringed the courthouse, punched their fists into the air, and chanted for justice, then fell silent and prayed. As their fear withered, their defiance grew.

There on the courthouse steps, at Conroe's heart, they dared stage their own act of justice, a people's court. They put the ringleaders on trial. They made one of their number the judge, made Reverend Boney the prosecutor, and appointed a defense attorney for the conspirators; he wore a Ronald Reagan mask to fit the role. Then they indicted six of the courthouse's men: the two district attorneys, Jim Keeshan and Peter Speers; two judges, John Martin and Lynn Coker; the new sheriff, Joe Corley; and the new police chief, Mike Arthurs. They charged them with corruption and conspiracy to murder Clarence Brandley.

They called witnesses, who stood on the steps and told the story of Clarence Brandley and who spoke of racism and fear in the town and of life with the "Montgomery County Department of Corruptions." Then the jury, all three hundred of them with their banners and their flags, voted their verdict, roaring "Guilty" so the whole town could hear, and sentenced the six guilty men to be stripped of all power and banished to the Caucasus Mountains in Russia. They deposited one more message from Tina the cow at the bottom of the flagpole in front of the courthouse and marched back to Dugan, singing and chanting, leaving the riot squads locked in behind their closed doors.

That night, they heard, there were men in robes out by the river, east of town, burning wooden crosses in the dark.

The real fight had started. For the lawyers it was a fight to win the attention of the Court of Criminal Appeals, to which Judge Coker had passed the decision on whether Brandley should have a new hearing. For the courthouse people, it was a fight to save their reputation and the political careers of the ringleaders. For Clarence Brandley it was still a fight for life.

Mike De Geurin landed a public blow to the courthouse when he contacted the FBI and showed them the videotapes, with the result that the Justice Department announced an immediate investigation into civil rights aspects of the case.

The DA's office landed a private blow when it made contact with Gary Acreman. It had spoken to his family and left messages for him to call, and on March 23 he did. He spoke to the assistant district attorney, Rick Stover, who tape-recorded the conversation.

Acreman complained that Richard Reyna had scared him into telling a lie. He had never seen Robinson grab that girl at all, he said. There was no truth in it. "I only seen the man twice that day. The first time I spoke to him. The second time he was throwing clothes into the Dumpster, throwing something into the Dumpster."

This was the moment. Never before in the seven-year history of the case, so far as anyone knew, had anyone claiming to be an eyewitness directly told a law enforcement officer that he could identify the killer, that he had personally seen the killer disposing of the girl's clothes. And never before, so far as any one knew, had a central witness in the case approached a law enforcement officer and admitted to withholding evidence that could have changed the course of the trial. This was the moment.

Rick Stover let it pass.

He told Acreman he wanted to stay in touch with him. "We're going to work with you," he said.

Four days later Stover and the DA's investigator, Charlie Ray, flew to Pittsburgh, where Acreman's new job as a truck driver had taken him. There they interviewed him on video and recorded his statement that he had never seen Robinson attack the girl. They went on to ask him whether Richard Reyna had tricked and scared him, whether Reyna had tried to buy his testimony, whether Reyna had posed as an attorney, and what Jim McCloskey had done. They never asked him once what he knew about the killer and the dead girl's clothes. And they never asked him at all whether he might have been involved himself.

The defense believed it had landed another blow when the attorney general announced that he was appointing one of his investigators, Robert "Duke" Bodisch, to inquire into the case. But the defense people began to worry when they heard that the inquiry was being supervised by an assistant AG named David Hess. De Geurin had already spoken to Hess about the case and found him patronizing and hostile.

The attorney general's investigators began their independent inquiry by setting up a base in Conroe—in the office of the district attorney, inside the courthouse. TV crews and reporters pressed around the office door, jumping on witnesses as they came and went.

Across the street Don Brown watched and started to rumble with fury. What witness was going to finger the killers in front of a TV camera? How were they going to get a confession if the killers were surrounded by people who refused to believe they were guilty? For God's sake, the DA's office was supposed to be one of the suspects in this inquiry. It was obscene. It was nothing but a media circus. Brown was so angry that he called the attorney general's office to complain. The next day the AG's investigators moved upstairs in the courthouse and interviewed witnesses in the grand jury room. Brown was not appeased.

Within days all his fears had been confirmed. John Sessum and Icky Peace reported that they had been interviewed by the AG's team members, who had disputed their evidence and asked them how Mike De Geurin had forced them to change their stories and if they had been paid for their help. Then it was Gary Acreman's turn to meet the attorney general's investigators. They interviewed him in front of a video camera. He told them the same story he had told the district attorney's officers a week earlier. He had never seen Robinson attack the girl, but he had seen Robinson at the school that day: "I seen either him, or somebody that was dressed like him, drop a bag into the Dumpster, and then a few minutes later either the same person or somebody else came out with tile and put it on top of it."

Here was that moment again. After seven years of circumstantial evidence, after thousands of man-hours of complex investigation, after all the controversy and the chaos, here, at last, on video, on the record, was a live eyewitness, someone who had been there at the scene that day, who was prepared to sit down with powerful law enforcement officers and say that with his own eyes he had seen the killer cleaning up the crime. What was more, he believed he could identify the killer. What was even better, he was identifying the same man who had been placed at the scene of the crime by John Sessum, who had spoken to the same investigators just the day before. This was the big breakthrough. Was this man really Robinson? What did he look like? What clothes was he wearing? Where did he come from? For God's sake, what color was he? For a moment no one said a word.

Then the investigators who worked for the attorney general of Texas changed the subject, and the moment was gone again.

They took Acreman through all his story and checked back through its most intricate details—all the precise timings and the exact measurements—but they never asked him again about the killer and the dead girl's clothes or whether he himself might even have been involved.

All through the rest of April, through May, and into June, the fight went on, while the Court of Criminal Appeals in Austin pondered whether or not to grant Clarence Brandley a new hearing at which all the evidence could be reviewed.

The defense kept trying to strengthen its case and made a video with Ed Payne, who repeated the story he had been trying to tell for more than six years. It took Jim McCloskey two months of negotiation to set up the video.

Payne had become scared. Since he had given evidence at the hearing in July 1986, Gary Acreman had moved back with

his daughter Cindy. Payne now had a man he believed was a
killer living on his doorstep, sharing a trailer with his daughter
and his two grandchildren. That started to make him scared.
Then his family all started to take Acreman's side against
him, telling him to shut up or his grandchildren would have
no daddy. But when that gang of men attacked him on the
road that night, he was pushed over the top. He left home
and hid out with his sister Ethel at her place and agreed with
McCloskey that he would not be bullied anymore. So he made
the video.

The defense made a new video with John Sessum, in which
he was clearly sober as well as well groomed and relaxed.

Richard Reyna engaged in a kind of courtship with Sam
Martinez, taking him out to dinner, talking to him in Spanish,
bringing him home, playing the videos of Sessum and
Acreman, hoping he would finally reveal if he was a
witness or an accessory to the crime. Martinez told him a
little. He said it was true that Acreman had spoken to this
girl and that he had disappeared and that Brandley had come
along the hallway some time after the girl had gone. Once he
buried his face in his hands and asked what the penalty for
perjury was. But he never cracked completely.

Reyna and McCloskey tried to get to the truth about Jo
Ellen Parrish and Pokey Smith, but when Reyna went into
the courthouse to read a transcript of Parrish's evidence,
the district attorney's office threatened to arrest him. Inside
the DA's office Reyna saw an old magazine cover about a
crooked businessman. THE SLEAZIEST MAN IN TEXAS ran the
headline. Underneath it someone had stuck a photograph of
Mike De Geurin.

Reverend Boney did all he could to maintain the pressure.
He met the Reverend Jesse Jackson and told him about the
case. He flew to Washington and spoke to the black congres-
sional leader John Conyers. He flew to Atlanta and briefed
Martin Luther King's widow, Coretta Scott King, and the
president of the Southern Christian Leadership Conference,
the Reverend Joseph Lowery, who then traveled to Houston
to speak during an Agitation Weekend when more than a
thousand Clarence Brandley supporters rallied.

The press continued to tear up the case. The *Courier* sent
a reporter to Huntsville to interview the black janitor and then
complained on its front page that he had declined to speak to
her because he claimed her paper had always been prejudiced

against him. The *Houston Post*'s death row specialist, Douglas Freelander, wrote a column describing all the men he had met who went to the executioner proclaiming their innocence and explaining his feeling that they were all liars who were guilty as charged. "For me, the one exception in this limited arena is Brandley," he wrote. "He gives the impression of absolute sincerity."

The publicity began to worry Conroe. County Judge Al Stahl said Montgomery County was developing such a bad reputation that the state was withholding funds. State Representative Keith Valigura said: "Folks in Austin say, 'Hey, Valigura, you've got a heck of a county down there, son.' Montgomery County is a joke. I wish we could take care of that image problem we have."

The courthouse tried to protect their image when they discovered that a team from CBS's "60 Minutes" program was in town working on the Brandley case. They locked the TV staffers out of the building. Then they relented and let them in, but it did nothing to help their image.

When "60 Minutes" telecast its report in April, millions of Americans learned about Acreman and Robinson and the evidence against them and about the black man sitting waiting on death row, and they saw pictures of Jim McCloskey, this Christian detective, shaking his head sadly and saying that "unfortunately, in this county, among law enforcement officers, prejudice runs deep."

The program brought Jim Mattox, the attorney general, out of his neutral corner into the middle of the ring, where he attacked Brandley's attorneys and accused them of "orchestrating the case for publicity purposes." He declared that Gary Acreman had passed a lie detector test, although he had not yet taken one, and challenged Brandley to submit to a lie test himself. The attorney general's office then conducted a campaign of lie detector tests. Gary Acreman, James Dexter Robinson, and Sam Martinez all swore that the stories they had told at Brandley's court hearings were the truth. All of them passed their tests, and the results were leaked to the press. The attorney general repeatedly challenged Brandley to put his own story to the test.

De Geurin was tempted until he discovered that the man who was conducting the lie tests, a former Houston deputy called Kelly Hendricks, was boasting that Brandley was "as guilty as sin." The head of the American Polygraph Association had to write to Hendricks to warn him that he was behaving unethically and was too prejudiced to be working on the case.

Reyna and McCloskey spent the first two weeks of June in Louisiana, where McCloskey had been asked to look into the case of a man named Jimmy Wingo, who was due to die in the electric chair on June 16. They found Wingo had been convicted in a one-day trial on nothing but circumstantial evidence, and they traced a woman who had implicated Wingo in the crime. She told them she had lied. A deputy had threatened to have her children taken away, and she had been so frightened that she had not only lied but agreed to have sex with the deputy. In the forty-eight hours leading up to the execution date, McCloskey begged Louisiana officials to grant Wingo a stay so that they could reinvestigate the case properly. All through the evening of June 15 McCloskey sat with Wingo as the hour of his execution approached, waiting with him for word of a reprieve. Then McCloskey had to leave while Wingo had his head shaved and was fitted with a diaper for when the electric shock emptied his bowels. McCloskey was still waiting for word from the officials when Wingo was killed in the electric chair. It was McCloskey's darkest hour. In the six years he had been working as an investigator, he had never before lost an innocent man to the executioner. He returned to Texas, determined that he would fight even harder.

Everyone who has ever seen a cowboy movie knows that when the lynch mob closes in on the small-town jailhouse and the prisoner is quaking in his cell, the brave hero, armed with nothing but the best intentions, steps out in front of the mob and tells them to throw down their weapons and go home because the prisoner is going to have a fair trial and there is going to be justice in this town.

Not in Conroe.

For a moment, back in March, Brandley had hoped the attorney general might help him. On June 22, 1987, Mattox's office produced a summary of its inquiry. It reviewed each of the six issues that Mike De Geurin had raised in Judge Coker's court on March 20, when he won the stay of execution, from the central complaint that Brandley was innocent back through the history of secret meetings and missing evidence and racial prejudice. The investigators who worked for the attorney general of Texas concluded that all six defense arguments were entirely worthless, and they found no evidence that Brandley was innocent or that any official involved in the case had ever engaged in any wrongdoing of any kind.

The investigators' findings were not published. The report was marked "A.G. Sensitive," and each page carried an instruction that "this report is the property of the Attorney General's office and neither it nor its contents may be disseminated." All the same, Peter Speers told the press what it said.

By chance, Reverend Boney and forty Brandley supporters were in Austin on that day. They went to the Supreme Court and crowded into the lobby outside the attorney general's office. They demanded to see him. They were told he was out of town. At that moment the doors to the elevator opened and the attorney general walked out. Reverend Boney was on him in a flash.

"Don't be a politician now," he said. "Will you or will you not meet with us?"

"You're meeting with me now," said Mattox.

"This isn't a meeting. We want to sit down face-to-face and talk about the issues."

Mattox said he had already talked about the issues, and if they had something to say, they should say it now. Then he walked away with the chants of forty angry people ringing in the lobby behind him.

It worried the defense. They were the ones who had brought the attorney general into the Brandley affair. They had truly believed he would set aside good ol' boy politics, issue arrest warrants, and send his investigators into Conroe to uncover the truth.

Not in Clarence Brandley's case.

Now their only hope was that the Court of Criminal Appeals would reach out a hand to Brandley and grant him a new hearing. The defense could only guess what the odds might be. The judges had already turned down Brandley twice. They had been sent three pages of blistering denials and procedural objections by the courthouse in Conroe. They would know that the attorney general had thrown out all the defense evidence. But surely some of those judges would want to give the defense a chance to develop what it had found, in open court, where both sides could argue about it and the whole community could judge the truth. On good days the defense persuaded themselves that they had at least a 50 percent chance.

When the ruling finally came on June 30, it was splashed across the front pages of newspapers across the state: BRANDLEY GETS A CHANCE AT FREEDOM.

The court had stepped out in front of the mob. Brandley could have his new hearing.

Chapter Nine

The courthouse was not the same. Paul Nugent felt it as soon as he drove into the square. Maybe it was the early-morning mist hanging in the air, which blurred the edges of the stark white temple and rubbed out the rest of the town, leaving the whole place eerie and alien. Or else it was that sound, drifting over to him from the steps of the courthouse, the sound of a woman singing an old Negro spiritual, filling the square with echoes. Or maybe it was the sight, which emerged through the mist as Nugent came closer, of a hundred black people sitting and lying at the feet of the rearing courthouse, staking out their claim on the building and on justice, holding a vigil that had gone on all night, taking turns sleeping and standing guard, as if their vigilance might keep this town at bay.

Nugent crossed the square to Don Brown's office.

It was September 21, 1987, nearly three months since the court in Austin had stepped in. The new hearing was about to begin. Inside the dimly lit office on the second floor, where Clarence Brandley's brothers had first come looking for help seven long years ago, Nugent sat down with Don Brown and Mike De Geurin. No one on the defense team had been paid anything for about five years—the Brandleys had run out of money long ago—but there was no question of stopping the fight. The sounds of protest floated up from the courthouse steps. It was time to consider Percy Foreman's golden rule again: "Try anyone except your client."

For a start they would try James Dexter Robinson and Gary Acreman again. Since the hearing in July 1986 evidence against the two men had piled up relentlessly, and now was the time, the attorneys believed, to go public with everything they knew. But they could go even further. This was no ordinary miscarriage of justice, in which well-meaning law officers were confused by circumstances. This was more like an abortion of justice, in which people who were touched by malice and dishonesty and, above all, by racism deliberately abused the machinery of justice. It was not enough to put Robinson and Acreman on trial. It was time to put the whole courthouse on trial and to expose those in it who had lied and cheated to take an innocent man's life. Yet the indictment did not stop there.

In any lynching there were ringleaders and there were bystanders. The people who ran the courthouse were elected by the whole community. Their behavior was extolled in the pages of the *Courier*. They enjoyed the approval and support of their neighbors. The town rewarded them with power and prestige. They were not alone. They may have been the ones who seized the black man and twisted the facts and threatened the witnesses and broke the rules and packed him off to death row, but there were also those who watched and even a few who looked away. The time had come to put Conroe on trial.

Shortly before nine o'clock the three attorneys crossed the street to the courthouse.

As soon as they entered the courtroom, Nugent felt again how the courthouse had changed. There, on the dais at the end of the room, was a judge who had no connection at all with Conroe. After more than five years the defense had finally kicked Judge Lynn Coker out of the case. Until now they had left him on the bench, believing that he was at least decent even if weak, and calculating that he was better than his more malicious colleagues in the courthouse. But Coker had cut the legs from under them in his findings after the July 1986 hearing, and they had abandoned any hope that he would ever rule in Brandley's favor. They had ousted him easily, simply by telling him that they might have to call him as a witness. In his place the state administrators had appointed an outsider, Perry Pickett. He was just about the most senior district judge in Texas. He had spent thirty years on the bench, mostly in Midland, near the border with New Mexico, where he had also been mayor. Now he was a visiting judge who could be pulled out of retirement to handle particularly sensitive cases. Pickett was an unknown quantity. He was an elderly man, and as far as the defense could find out, he had a reputation as a conservative. It worried them that on the face of it he might be a graduate of the same good ol' boy school of justice that had produced the Conroe judges.

Their first move now—and the first test of the new judge—was to try to get this whole hearing moved out of this court-house with all its memories of injustice, and out of Conroe with all its history of intimidation, to another court, where their witnesses would have a chance to speak without fear. They had submitted a formal motion calling for a change of venue. Today they had to call the evidence to prove the point.

As soon as Judge Pickett called the court to order, Nugent felt the change again. The judge looked down on the ranks of brown faces in the well of the court, and he did not frown, nor did he tell them to remove their FREE CLARENCE BRANDLEY badges, but he said: "Good morning, everyone. We welcome you to the courthouse. We are pleased to have you as our guests."

Nugent felt it again a few minutes later as the first witness began to give evidence. Bill Srack had agreed to talk publicly for the first time about his experiences as a dissenting juror. He was just beginning to speak when Peter Speers hopped up and objected that this was irrelevant.

The judge overruled him.

Srack continued to speak. Speers hopped up again and said that none of this should be mentioned.

The judge overruled him again.

Clarence Brandley, from his seat in the front of the court, watched nervously as, for the first time in his seven years of trials and hearings, his attorneys were allowed to present their evidence.

While Peter Speers sat frowning at his paper work and Peggy Stevens stood imperiously at the back of the courtroom, Bill Srack went on to describe the day a Conroe jury called him a "nigger lover." He told about the hail of phone calls that rained down on his house and the deputy who chose not to prosecute those who had made them, and then he explained how Judge Keeshan had conducted himself when he interviewed him for a job.

The faces on the public benches were set in grim silence.

The Reverend John Daviss, the elderly minister from the First Missionary Baptist Church in Dugan, who had been warned by his friends that he was asking for trouble if he gave evidence, took the witness stand, and in front of the district attorney and half a dozen Montgomery County deputies, he declared openly that prejudice had smothered justice during Clarence Brandley's two trials.

The Reverend Jerry P. Jones, the towering young minister from Pilgrim Rest Baptist Church, followed him to the stand and told the court he was sure Clarence Brandley could never have a fair hearing in this courthouse. Witnesses felt intimidated here, he said. Blacks in Conroe were supposed to be seen not heard. The mayor himself called black people "niggers."

There was a stirring on the public benches. Peter Speers challenged the minister to give even one example of how a witness could be intimidated. Reverend Jones looked down at Speers from the witness stand and said: "One of the things that would be intimidating to them would be you." Speers protested. The minister insisted. Black people would be afraid to tell the truth, he said, in case they or their children were ever arrested and victimized because of their evidence.

"Reverend Jones, I am offended by your remark. What shred of evidence do you have that I have done anything of the sort in the past?"

The minister leaned forward so that he was looking straight into the district attorney's face. The whole room was now stiff with concentration. "I'm very sorry if you're offended by my remarks, but I would like to offend you some more, because I think you are the epitome of everything that is wrong."

Gasps from the public benches.

Speers protested some more: "Reverend Jones, you haven't stated a single fact to support that, and you cannot because it's not true."

Still staring straight into the DA's eyes, the minister replied in a voice that boomed through the court. "All I can say—and I can state this as a fact—is that this is the most prejudiced, biased, racist city in the whole of America. I am out of Alabama and I know that Alabama ain't never been as bad as this."

Speers took to his chair. The deputies shifted in their seats. Judge Pickett gazed down on the court without expression, and all along the public benches there spread a ripple of pure joy.

The defense had one more witness in its effort to prove that there could be no fair hearing in this courthouse, a witness whose evidence it had deliberately held back for the finale. The prosecutors and the deputies and the woman with the strawberry nails all stiffened as soon as Mike De Geurin rose and said, "Call Janet Dial."

Judge Martin's former secretary walked smartly into court with her head raised. The courthouse had frayed at the edges before; bystanders had whispered their secrets to the defense in dark corners. But this was different. Here, for the first time, was an insider from the courthouse without any stain on her character, standing up publicly to tell what she knew. Cold eyes followed her to the witness stand. Would she really do it?

Mike De Geurin asked her if it was just his imagination or was there really an atmosphere of intimidation in the building.

"Well," she said, and paused before plunging on, "I think there is an atmosphere that is intimidating to a fair trial and to any witness that would appear." She paused again and flicked her eyes over to the district clerk, still standing unsmiling at the back of the room. "One of the things I noticed, for instance, was that Peggy Stevens swore us in. And if I'm correct, Mrs. Stevens is to be a witness at some point, and you know, I don't understand why she was allowed to swear us in. It's sort of like she's got some higher status as a witness than possibly the rest of us."

Peggy Stevens glared into the middle distance. Janet Dial now opened the floodgates, and her memories of the Brandley trial came pouring out: "It seemed to me that it was like we worked for a company and, regardless of the fact that there were people who were to play impartial parts in the judicial system—the judge, members of the district clerk's office and all that support group—it was like we worked for the same company as the DA's office. . . . I didn't feel like I could ask any impartial questions. . . . Even though I worked for the judge, I felt as if I was involved in a project to convict Clarence Brandley."

Peter Speers did not know Janet Dial very well. If he had known her better, he might have known that she was not the sort of witness who could be steamrollered. As it was, he stood up and defied her to cite even one occasion when a witness had been intimidated.

Janet Dial calmly recalled the day she had sat in a crowded courtroom where Clarence Brandley was being tried and heard an elderly white woman chanting "Kill the nigger."

Speers shook his head and struggled to bury what he had now uncovered: "This wasn't an elected official or anybody like that, was it? Or anybody involved with the trial?"

"I don't know that that matters. She was not removed from the courtroom."

"Did anybody object to her comments?"

"No. Had I been more experienced or been a little bit more competent in my position, I would have brought that to someone's attention. I know that I did tell people who were more experienced and nothing was done about it."

Speers kept pushing. "The likelihood is that if anybody who was actually concerned with the trial had heard it, there would have been a remark made and a request that she either be removed or at least zip her lip, don't you think?"

"Peter, it happened. You know, I don't really know exactly what you want from me. It did happen. She was not removed and that was the atmosphere in the courtroom."

Speers gave up and tried another line, but it soon became clear that he had still not learned his lesson. This time he challenged Janet Dial to cite even one reason why anyone from the courthouse would now want to intimidate a witness in the Brandley case.

"Okay. I can answer that question," came the reply. Speers then had to stand in silence while Janet Dial explained that courthouse officials were trying to cover up their past behavior in the case. Speers shook his head and defied her to name even one witness who was actually being intimidated.

Janet Dial calmly told him that the court reporter Mary Johnson, who had been caught up in the scandal over the missing exhibits, had been put under pressure not to give evidence and had also suggested that she, Dial, should not testify either. Speers raised his eyebrows.

"Obviously, you're not intimidated by testifying to what you believe is the truth?" he asked.

"I'm not easily intimidated, Peter."

Speers sat down, his lesson learned.

The hearing on the change of venue now rapidly came to a conclusion.

Mike De Geurin summarized the evidence of injustice in the courthouse and in the town. "You have heard the voice of the community," he told the judge.

Peter Speers said there was no proof of any of this, and anyway, technically, the law permitted only "trials" to be moved, not hearings like this, which had no jury.

Judge Pickett looked down from his dais. The whole courtroom was still, each person weighing his or her own hopes and fears. Would this white-haired judge break ranks and abandon Conroe, or would he go along with all the other judges who had handled this case and give the DA his way?

"All right," said the judge in a deep drawl. "The court makes the following ruling: there exists here a volatile and explosive situation, not conducive to the fair administration of justice. I've read the entire transcription of all of the proceedings and there seems to be an atmosphere of fear. The ends of justice dictate that this case be transferred to Galveston County, and it is so ordered. Thank you."

His last few words were drowned in cheers. The rejoicing spilled out into the street, and Minnie Ola Brandley emerged into the courthouse square with tears in her eyes, to be greeted as a hero. Soon the chant began again. "Jus-tice! Jus-tice!" It echoed through the square.

Up on the second floor of the courthouse, in the judge's chambers, Judge Pickett and all the attorneys were looking out of the window at the boiling caldron of cheering and chanting below.

Peter Speers was frowning. His assistant, Rick Stover, kept saying that this was intolerable.

Paul Nugent watched the jubilant crowd surging through the street and nodded. "There's the Constitution of the United States in operation."

News of Judge Pickett's order burned through the county like a flame on a fuse wire. Before the day was out, it had reached the witnesses whose fears lay at the heart of the judge's decision. It gave them hope. The question for the defense was whether that would be enough. Ever since Brandley's reprieve six months earlier, the attorneys and the investigators had been trying to shepherd their witnesses to safety, trying to protect them from physical attack and from official pressure. It had been tough.

*   *   *

All through the summer Icky Peace had been cowed into silence. He was scared, and he admitted it. But the defense still wanted him to talk, not so much about the day of the crime as about the inquiry and the threatening of witnesses.

Three days before the change-of-venue hearing, on Friday evening, September 18, Jim McCloskey made one final attempt to persuade the little janitor to find his courage. The old Chevy climbed up the hill road outside Cleveland, up through the woods to the two trailers where Icky Peace lived alongside his elder sister, Shirley. McCloskey was at his most polite, almost deferential. Icky Peace, however, was in a feisty mood.

He was glad to see McCloskey. He wanted to tell him what had just happened to him earlier that week, on Tuesday. He had been called into the DA's office to talk about this Brandley hearing coming up, and he had been saying to them what he had always been trying to say: that that Texas Ranger had choked him with his medical necklace and threatened to kill him if he didn't do as he was told and that he had gone to Jim Keeshan and told him all about it and he had been told to forget it. But the DA's people had not wanted to hear.

"They told me I was hallucinating," he complained. "They said I was imagining things. And I am not. They said that if I said that in public, nobody would believe me and they could sue me and it would be just my word against them 'cause there ain't no records." And there was another thing, he continued with his voice like a flute. Just that very day one of his supervisors at the high school had threatened him with the sack if he dared give evidence for Clarence Brandley. The supervisor had said something like "Jobs can get lost, you know. We wait a little time, and then you're out of here." McCloskey had never seen the little janitor angry before. But now he was righteously indignant. He had been pushed too far; his pride was hurt. So in his own way he had found his courage. Even so, there was something he still would not say.

"I got a bombshell," he said, stabbing one stiff index finger at McCloskey. "I got a bombshell that'll blow this case apart. But there's only one person I'll tell it to. And that's the judge."

McCloskey was intrigued. He spent the best part of an hour trying to tease this "bombshell" out of Peace. He uncovered all sorts of other half-familiar stories; the officer saying "The nigger is elected"; Acreman saying he had seen Brandley having a good time with a white girl; the police on the day of the crime refusing to let him go home until he had signed their statement. Peace recalled how John Sessum had been lying half asleep outside the Vocational Building waiting for Brandley and interrupting his nap every so often to ask, "Where's that damned nigger?" But he would not part with his bombshell.

Two days later, on the Sunday night before the change-of-venue hearing, McCloskey was back. This time he had Mike De Geurin and Richard Reyna in tow. De Geurin needed to hear Peace tell his story for himself so that he could judge how to handle him in the witness box. And McCloskey thought the attorney might be able to use his famous charm to get a look at the bombshell. It had been raining, and the hill roads were slick with mud, but the old Chevy plowed through them. As they drove into the clearing in front of Peace's pink trailer, they saw a woman standing outside. It was Peace's sister Shirley.

The three men gathered around her and explained that they needed to see her brother again and that they meant him no harm and he had to understand that they just wanted the truth. While they were talking, De Geurin became aware of a strange noise coming from behind him, from the direction of the pink trailer, a wet, squishy sort of noise. He turned around to discover Icky Peace tiptoeing through the mud toward them without his shoes on, his white socks squelching in the soaking soil.

De Geurin grinned and greeted him like an old friend and pretended not to notice his feet.

It was soon clear that Icky Peace did not want to play. The bombshell was his. He would give it to the judge, not to them. De Geurin pushed, but Peace would have none of it. All through his protests De Geurin's eyes kept wandering down to the limp ends of Peace's white nylon socks, which were now soaking up mud the way fresh bread soaks up gravy. The sight stirred something in De Geurin. A name popped into his mind: Trigger.

"Say, Mr. Peace. Look at it this way. You got a problem talking about this thing. I understand that. Now you don't have to talk to me. You don't have to say a word. All I want is the truth. Now I'm gonna ask you a question. And if the answer to my question is yes, I just want you to move your foot there on the ground one time, just kind of

paw the ground one time. And if the answer is no, paw it
twice. Understand?"

Peace looked at him wide-eyed.

"OK, now. You understand what I'm saying? Now, did the
Texas Ranger ever try and threaten you?"

There they stood in a muddy patch in the middle of the hills:
the Tex-Mex investigator and his new partner with the priest's
collar; the blond attorney in the three-thousand-dollar leather
boots; the anxious sister—all standing in a circle staring at the
little fat man's socks.

Peace was still staring straight into De Geurin's face.
Pause. One sodden white sock flapped once against the mud
and fell back into place. Just like Trigger, Roy Rogers's
horse.

So they passed the next half hour with De Geurin asking
the questions, Peace silently pawing the mud with his ruined
sock, Reyna occasionally stuffing his fist into his mouth and
wheezing, "Jesus Christ, I don't believe this shit." By the time
they left, Peace had taken them once again through his story.
But even with the aid of his soggy sock, he would still not
give up his bombshell. It was as if he had found his courage
but was still not sure how to use it.

Peace surfaced once more the next day as the defense team
headed out of the courthouse and across to Don Brown's office
to relish their triumph at the change-of-venue hearing. Richard
Reyna found Peace on the sidewalk, lost. "I can't find my car,"
he was bleating.

"Never mind, man. Come on up to the office. The reverend's
there. And everyone else. We're having barbecue."

Peace waddled along beside him up into Brown's office,
where he took out his false teeth, launched into a barbecue
sandwich, and proceeded to tell his story once more to the
entire defense camp. When he got to the moment a few days
earlier when his supervisor had told him "Jobs can get lost,
you know," Peace waved his bit of sandwich and said he had
told that supervisor that he had been looking for a job before he
got hired there and, if he had to, he'd go and look for another
one now. Then he slapped in his teeth, told the attorneys and
the investigators that he would see them in Galveston, and
strode out of the office.

"Jesus Christ," said Reyna, "that little guy's ready to kick
somebody's ass."

*   *   *

For Ed Payne it had been a long, bitter summer. When his family discovered that he had made a video for the defense, they had renewed their assault on him.

Payne had made the mistake of moving back home, and there his wife Billie, who was afraid for her grandchildren's daddy, started in on him. With his bad leg and his skinny frame, he was no match for her. He complained that she had threatened to kill him if he testified for Brandley and that she had kicked him in the ribs and tried to hit him with an ax. He survived by starting divorce proceedings, only to find the investigators who worked for the attorney general of Texas on his doorstep.

By the time they finished with him, he had withdrawn his story. He now said that Acreman could have been nervous on the day of the crime just because his car had broken down. And he said Acreman could have told him about the girl's clothes being in the Dumpster after it had been reported that the police had found them there. Everything he had told the defense on the video was a lie, he now said. The defense had tricked him into making the video and he had only gone along with it to see how they played their tricks and then Jim McCloskey had made him give false answers and he had had to make three tapes before they were satisfied with the lies he was telling for them, he now said.

Jim McCloskey stayed in touch with Payne's family, including his brother John, who had first approached George Morris in January 1981 to disclose old Ed's story. McCloskey was cruising back from Conroe to Houston late one night, with Mike De Geurin in the passenger seat and Glenn Miller on the radio, when he decided to swing by John Payne's house to see him and his wife Marie. As soon as they stepped out of the old Chevy, a snarling dog came swirling out of the darkness at them.

"Don't worry," said McCloskey. "It won't bite."

De Geurin was no fool. "I'll stay in the car," he said.

John and Marie Payne gave them both safe passage into the house and then began a conversation that soon degenerated into a sort of parlor game.

Every time McCloskey asked them a question, the Paynes shuffled off into their kitchen and whispered together for several minutes before returning with their answer. It took a while, but they finally concluded that the story Ed Payne was supposed to have told the attorney general's investigators was nonsense. They were sure, for example, that he had first told them of Acreman's desire to fish the clothes out of the Dumpster on the day after the murder—twenty-four hours before the police found them. Ed was scared, they said. He had even made a new will, in which he had told everything he knew, and left instructions that if anything happened to him, the will was to be sent to Mike De Geurin. De Geurin immediately saw the significance of that: if the will was hostile to the defense, Payne would hardly want it sent there. After a final conference in the kitchen John and Marie Payne confessed that they, too, were a little nervous. Someone had been following them and sitting in a car outside their house watching them.

In the week after the change-of-venue hearing McCloskey tried Ed Payne once more. He and Reyna spent a day chasing from one relative to another only to find that he was back home again with his wife. The two investigators parked the Chevy down the road from his place and talked. There was no telling what was waiting for them in there. One of the killers lived there. The rest of Payne's family were hostile to the defense. They would certainly have guns. Reyna was ready to go in, but McCloskey persuaded him that, relying on his white collar for protection, he should go in alone.

As he walked slowly up to the house, McCloskey saw a man bent over a car, working on the engine. For a moment he thought it was Acreman, but it was another of Payne's relatives, who nodded him up toward the trailer and went back to his engine. As soon as he walked up to the old trailer, he saw Ed Payne standing there, shaking his head vigorously from side to side. "I can't do it," he said. "I won't do it."

McCloskey put up both hands in a gesture of surrender. "Ed, I'm sorry, but I have to talk to you." Payne gave him a look of deep disgust and led him inside, where McCloskey found to his relief that Billie Payne was out. They sat down, and McCloskey told Payne that he understood the pressure he had been under, that he knew all about the family's problems, that he knew it had been rough with his wife and with the attorney general's men, and that nobody was going to make him give evidence if he did not want to. In his gentlest bedside manner he talked to Payne for an hour and a half.

Finally, Payne squeezed an apology out of his voice box and said he was sorry he had gone back on his story. McCloskey coaxed him onward. "Ed, you know and I know that Clarence Brandley is innocent. We need you to come and tell what you know. I know it's been hard, and I can't say it won't get hard again, but will you do it?"

Payne looked up through his thick spectacles, opened his parched old mouth, and squeezed two sounds out of his throat. "OK."

Mary Johnson was also scared to talk. She refused to meet the defense attorneys. She was afraid of losing her job. She, too, had received a visit from the investigators who worked for the attorney general of Texas and wanted to know all about the missing exhibits. They tried to tell her she was a liar. They suggested she had stolen all the missing exhibits herself. They said she had been dating George Morris and had done it to help him. They gave her a lie test with their regular polygrapher, Kelly Hendricks. He said she was lying, and then they read her her rights. She started talking about Jim Keeshan and Judge Martin and whether they had held secret meetings.

"I know Jim Keeshan is real smooth and all that and may-be he—"

One of the attorney general's men cut her off. "The more important issue," he said, "is that the evidence was in your custody and became missing while in your custody."

By the time they had finished with her, Mary Johnson was completely confused. They had dragged her through the mud. They had not been interested in what Keeshan and Martin had been playing at. They had called her a liar. She was more scared than ever. She begged Don Brown not to make her give evidence.

"I'll be fired," she said. "If you make me testify, they'll fire me. Please don't subpoena me."

But Brown knew that he had to.

Before the hearing resumed in Galveston, the defense studied the thick report that had now been produced by the attorney general's investigators. The defense team waded through it, looking for clues. It turned out to be worth the effort. The attorney general's office defended courthouse witnesses, attacked defense witnesses, and never even bothered to interview most of the ringleaders. It was clear that the inquiry, which had moved into the enemy's camp on its first day, had never left. The investigators disclosed that they had found a new witness. They had never mentioned it to the defense, but the report showed that some four months earlier, just after "60 Minutes" had broadcast its report on Clarence Brandley, a young woman had contacted the attorney general's team.

She had been watching the program, she said, not paying any great attention until this photograph of a man's face had been flashed up on the screen. And suddenly she was back at that high school on the day of the crime, back in the gym where she had been playing volleyball, watching two strange men walking across the room, walking from the direction of the auditorium: two young white men, one with sandy hair and the other with dark, shaggy hair. And she was almost sure that the photograph of one of them was on the screen. It was James Dexter Robinson. It had given her the chills, so she had called the attorney general's people to tell them. Her name was Cheryl Bradford. The attorney general's investigators said they took her back to the school and found that she could not remember the layout of the gym properly. "She does not attach any particular significance to this event," they added.

They disclosed, too, that Icky Peace had given them his most powerful version ever of the moment when a police officer elected Brandley as prime suspect. Peace had told the AG's team that the officer's exact words were: "You're a colored guy. Conroe don't like colored people. So, nigger, you're elected." The AG's team said it was "unable to verify this."

The attorney general's office, however, did something that the defense had never been able to do. It tested the blood of Gary Acreman and James Dexter Robinson. It did not follow that up or even pass any comment on the result. The report simply mentioned in passing that both men were Type A, the same as the blood on the dead girl's socks.

On Sunday, September 27, six days after Judge Pickett's order, Jim McCloskey and Paul Nugent loaded up the old Chevy with legal papers and headed south from Houston on I-45 down to the Gulf of Mexico and over the narrow causeway to Galveston Island.

McCloskey and Nugent could see a great breakthrough at hand, a victory in a little courtroom out here on the edge of the world that would not only free a man but would galvanize the newfound courage of a whole community. They could see, too, the threat of failure: one frightened witness, one twisted piece of evidence, one legal blunder, and they all would plunge off their narrow route into disaster.

The Galveston County Courthouse was alive.

Ever since dawn they had been arriving: the old ladies from Dugan with their flowery hats, the old men with their walking canes, the Brandley family, Reverend Boney, scores of young people with banners, a group from Houston with a gigantic birthday card to celebrate Clarence Brandley's thirty-sixth birthday, church ministers, civil rights officials, reporters, TV crews, attorneys, witnesses, and a phalanx of deputy sheriffs from Montgomery County who had come to run courtroom security and who now blocked the doorway, demanding that anyone who wanted to enter should submit to a metal detector and a manual search. By nine o'clock on Monday morning, September 28, 1987, three hundred people had run the gauntlet of the Montgomery County deputies and filled every space on the public benches in the long, rectangular courtroom. In front of them, on the other side of the wooden bar, the spectators could see the jury box along the left-hand wall, now crammed with reporters, the defense attorneys at their table in front of the jury box, and over to the right the prosecution table. Beyond them were the witness box and then Judge Pickett, an unlit pipe jammed between his teeth, already sitting behind his desk on the raised platform at the far end of the room.

Now a door at the judge's right-hand side opened, and two burly deputy sheriffs led Clarence Brandley into the room and sat him down next to his attorneys. Judge Pickett welcomed everyone to court, and the case of *Clarence Brandley* v. *the State of Texas* began its latest round.

For Brandley and his attorneys this was the day of public reckoning, when all the scraps of information that had been dredged up by Richard Reyna and Jim McCloskey would be displayed for all to see, a day to pitch their evidence not just at the judge, who now held Clarence Brandley's future in the balance, but at the three hundred spectators who saw their own lives mirrored in Brandley's fate and at all the unseen spectators in shinny shacks and ghetto dives across the state of Texas who would track his progress. This was the day to put their case across. They believed the press would help them—all except the *Conroe Courier* and its reporter, Carol Williams.

The star witness of the day was John Sessum. Reyna had done his best to prepare him for his big moment. He had bought him new pants, mended his old eyeglasses, cleaned him up, cut his hair, and kept him sober. Sessum had spent the night in a state of suppressed panic. Right up to the moment that he took the stand, the defense had feared that he might bolt and take refuge in a bottle. But when the time came, he shuffled stiffly into court and took the oath.

He sat there, staring down at his feet, his knees shaking, his voice breaking, occasionally weeping, and he told the world that he had seen two men attack a young girl and that he had turned his back and walked away. He admitted he had committed perjury in all his previous evidence and statements. "I run from people over this for a long time," he whispered, "but you can't run from yourself or your own conscience."

In his faltering voice he choked out his description of the attack and the roles of Gary Acreman and James Dexter Robinson. Then he started to peel the skin off the cover-up.

Acreman had threatened him not only as they drove home on the day of the crime, he said, but also when they drove to give their statements to the police two days later. So he had started lying. When the Texas Ranger took him on a walk-through at the school with Acreman and Martinez, the ranger had threatened him, too. He had tried to tell Styles about how Acreman had grabbed the girl, but the ranger had told him to do as he was told or he would be arrested. The police had typed up a statement, but he had had trouble reading it. "I ain't good on reading," he said.

Watching him, Brandley felt a kind of fire storm in his chest. He was bitter and angry and confused and relieved and frightened and grateful. It was swirling around inside him. All he could do was sit, like a rock, trying somehow to contain it. Sitting right behind him, McCloskey could see the muscles in his back bunched into tight knots of anxiety.

The attorneys were content. Sessum had launched the attack not only on Acreman and Robinson but on the courthouse as well.

The defense had felt less worried about Icky Peace, who appeared to be ready to stand up for himself, but when he came

to the stand, he had only just begun to speak when his courage
flickered and failed him. He looked up to Judge Pickett and
said, "Your Honor, I would like to talk to you privately." The
little janitor and the court stenographer followed the judge into
his office. The three hundred spectators sat and waited and
wondered what was going on. The defense attorneys guessed
this was the bombshell that they had been waiting for. They
bit their fingernails and hoped to hell that Peace was not going
to run out on them now, until some ten minutes later the judge,
with the air of a patient parent, gently led Icky Peace back into
court and told Mike De Geurin to continue.

In a voice that fluttered weakly from the witness stand, Icky
Peace now told his story. The defense attorneys hardly dared
breathe. Ignoring the Montgomery County deputies lounging
in the courtroom doorway, Peace declared that he had never
known what was in the statement he had signed at the Conroe
Police Department on the day of the crime for the simple
reason that he could not read: "I signed a piece of paper that
had a bunch of letters on it, a bunch of words. I don't know
what it said."

He said he had told the police he could not read and asked
them to bring his sister so she could read the statement to him,
but they had refused. They had told him that if he did not sign
that piece of paper, he could not leave. So he had signed. Then
they had retyped part of it and brought it back to him. He had
signed again. He never realized, he said, that the statement he
signed made no mention of the fact that Gary Acreman had
disappeared for some time on the day of the crime. Nor did he
realize, he said, that it did not mention the fact that Acreman
and Martinez appeared to know a girl was missing before
anyone came looking for her. Peace then recalled the moment
soon after he had signed his statement when the police officer
told him about their choice of a prime suspect. "He told me
that I wasn't strong enough or tall enough and that they had a
lot of pressure put on them and Mr.—well, they called him—
Your Honor, can I say what they called him?"

Judge Pickett nodded. "Yes, sir."

"They said that the nigger was tall enough and strong
enough and he was elected."

Peter Speers might have felt three hundred pairs of eyes
staring grimly at the back of his neck.

De Geurin nudged Peace again. "Now, Mr. Peace, did the
officer also say to Mr. Brandley, 'You're a colored guy,

Conroe don't like colored people'?" This was too much for
Speers, who successfully objected that De Geurin was leading
his witness.

Peace had not told the story the way he had told it before,
but the defense was content that he had done his best to tell
it in public for the first time. He had more. A week after the
crime, he said, the Texas Ranger came to see him. "He got
me by the shirt and I don't know if you call it shoving or
pushing, but he got me up against the wall and told me that
I had killed the girl. . . . He had me scared."

Then the ranger had threatened to blow his head off.

Peace said he had told all this to the district attorney, Jim
Keeshan, who had assured him he would handle it. Then he
had signed a second statement without being able to discover
its contents, and he never realized, he said, that this made no
mention of the fact that the Texas Ranger had been threatening him.

"I'm finally telling the truth like I've been trying to tell it,"
he said, "and I'm very glad."

Jim McCloskey, sitting next to Brandley at the defense table,
felt a glow of pride at Peace's courage, a feeling that was soon
mixed with profound relief as the judge instructed his stenographer to read out her transcript of the private conversation he
had held with Peace. It soon became clear that Peace had been
on the verge of desertion and that there had been no bombshell
other than his own fear.

He had told the judge that he felt confused by the defense
attorneys because they kept telling him what questions they
were going to ask and "practically what to say, but not coming
out telling me to say it" and that he felt worried by the district
attorney, who had told him he was hallucinating and there was
nothing to back up his story, and that he was still frightened
of the Texas Ranger as well as being afraid he might get fired
by the school if he gave evidence. The judge had listened and
sympathized and calmed him down, and then the two men had
agreed that together they would go back into court, where
Peace would detonate his precious bombshell, which consisted
quite simply of his finally telling the truth without fear.

Richard Reyna had spent the morning in Conroe, where
he stopped by the courthouse and found Ed Payne coming
out of a hearing on his divorce. Payne seemed buoyant. He
started talking to Reyna about the Brandley case and suddenly

announced in his electronic buzz: "Richard, I'm gonna testify. If you want me to do it, let's do it now." Reyna put him in his car and headed south for Galveston. Payne was still in high spirits and sat beside him squawking his way through a stream of jokes. Reyna could not understand a word and spent the journey trying to nod intelligently and grinning hopefully every time the old man started coughing up his tinny laugh. An hour after arriving in Galveston, Ed Payne was on the witness stand.

As soon as Peter Speers saw him, he objected that Payne should not be allowed to give evidence since he had already told his story at the 1986 hearing. Judge Pickett politely overruled him.

Payne then started to tell his story and added a detail that he had never mentioned in 1986: that his son-in-law, Gary Acreman, had not only quaked with nerves on the day of the crime and panicked about the dead girl's clothes in the Dumpster but also told him that Robinson had been at the school with him. Speers objected that this was mere hearsay. "Overruled," said the judge. Payne described how he had been beaten and how his son-in-law had called him a liar. "I got scars on my hand from his teeth," he said.

Speers lashed into the old man, confronting him with the version of events that he had given to the attorney general's investigators, suggesting that the defense had put words into his mouth and that his whole story was a lie. Payne stood up to him and said that if any of his story was wrong, it was because he was repeating what Gary Acreman had told him. "If I go through life repeating what other people say, I'm bound to tell a lie somewhere."

Finally, Janet Dial strode once more to the witness stand and swore that Judge John Martin and the old DA, Jim Keeshan, had been meeting secretly during Clarence Brandley's second trial to fix rulings for each day's hearing. The two men, she said, were leaders of the "project" to convict Clarence Brandley. The atmosphere had been unsafe and ugly, she recalled.

Jim McCloskey sat at the defense table, glowing with respect for her. He had been in Montgomery County long enough to understand the risk she was taking. She was making powerful enemies by doing this, and they were the sort of enemies who would nurture their anger for years. He could imagine the kind of harassment they would deal in: sneers and innuendos and cold shoulders, the kind of job hassles that Bill Srack had suffered, speeding tickets, slashed tires. Judge Martin had already tried to ban her from the courthouse, despite the fact that it was a public building. McCloskey thought she was wonderful.

On the witness stand now, she was starting to talk about a letter she had written to the *Courier* in which she had tried to alert the town to what was happening—"the fact that most of our arresting officers are white, most of our prosecuting attorneys are white and, in fact, in the Brandley case, the jury had been all white, the judge was white, even the defense attorneys were white. And given the fact that when you go to the grocery store, that there is prejudice, and in the school that there is prejudice, that it was completely unrealistic to think that bigotry could not have taken place, could not have had some influence during the entire Brandley investigation and trial and conviction. And the last thing I said was that a problem is never solved by denial—that as long as everybody was running around saying that each individual that was involved in the case had no shred of prejudice or bigotry, that we couldn't get at the truth.

"It's like we had to acknowledge the fact that this did indeed exist in Conroe, Texas, if we were going to get past that and to the truth."

She said she believed now she could never get work again in the courthouse. Peter Speers hopped up and said that was irrelevant. The judge overruled him.

If it had been permitted, McCloskey would have stood up and applauded as she left the stand.

The defense attorneys were elated. They had seen frightened and vulnerable people standing up and risking retribution for the sake of the truth, and they had opened their indictment against the two suspected murderers and against Conroe and its courthouse. The next morning, when the defense attorneys saw the newspapers, they found that the events in the Galveston court had been telegraphed all across the state. But not in Conroe.

In Galveston the *Daily News* splashed WITNESS CHANGES STORY across the front page and told its readers: "A former custodian at Conroe High School wiped away tears Monday as he testified that he saw a 16-year-old girl fighting the advances of a school janitor—someone other than Clarence Lee Brandley."

The other newspapers and TV and radio stations had taken a similar line. But in Conroe the *Courier* told a different story. Under the headline WITNESSES: FORCE USED IN BRANDLEY CASE, Carol Williams told the town: "Two key defense witnesses gave the indication Monday they had been browbeaten by defense attorneys into changing their testimony to help Clarence Lee Brandley's case."

Icky Peace was the first witness she wrote about. She did not mention how he had signed two police statements he could not read, or how the statements had omitted key evidence, or how the police officer had elected the black suspect, or how the ranger had shoved him against a wall and threatened to blow his head off, or how the district attorney had recently told him he was hallucinating. Readers of the *Courier* were informed only that "Peace, who said he was intimidated by a Texas Ranger, told the judge that the defense had 'told me what my testimony was to be, the words.' Peace said he was told several times what he was supposed to say."

Icky Peace had never said that.

Carol Williams then reported that Ed Payne had sat in court and pointed to Mike De Geurin and said: "They tried to get me to lie for the Clarence Lee Brandley case. They told me what they wanted to hear. Parts of it was a lie. I was repeating what Gary said. If I go through life repeating what other people say, I'm bound to tell a lie somewhere."

It was another phony quote.

In Conroe some things never changed.

Yet in Conroe an unseen tide was turning.

Just as Brenda Medina and John Sessum and Icky Peace and Ed Payne were now telling what they knew after years of silence, so, too, some of the bystanders on the fringe of events began to come forward.

Connie Miller had never said anything to anyone, but she had never forgotten that day when she was in her old office at City Cab and a scruffy young man named Acreman had come in and ended up shouting in her face: "Clarence Brandley did not kill that girl. I know who did. Clarence didn't do it. But I will never tell." She had followed the Brandley case in the

newspapers the same as everyone else. She never had believed
Brandley was guilty. But she had never really considered it her
business, so she had never bothered to say anything about it.

But when she read that Gary Acreman was now trying to
make out that he knew nothing about the killing, that he was
telling the district attorney that Clarence Brandley was guilty,
finally something in her moved. She called up the DA's office
and got the name of Brandley's attorney, and then she called
Don Brown and told him what she knew. Brown wished she
had said something seven years earlier, but still he was happy
to have her evidence. And she was not alone. The City Cab
dispatcher and a man who had been there in the office waiting
for his grandmother had also heard Acreman's outburst, and
they all agreed that the time had come to speak up.

They went to Galveston and told what they knew. Peter
Speers's assistant, Rick Stover, attacked them, complaining
that they recalled slightly different versions of what Acreman
said, ridiculing their delay in coming forward, but the three
of them stood by their stories.

The tide swept forward a woman named Kathy Binford.

She went to Galveston and told the court that Gary Acreman
had once been a truck driver at the place where she worked in
Willis, ten miles north of Conroe, and in June 1979, more than
a year before the murder, he had been caught trying to force
himself on a young white girl there. She said other girls had
also complained about him, so he had been fired.

When she went to court, Kathy Binford was accompanied
by her friend Peggy Riggle, the vivacious telemarketing supervisor of the *Conroe Courier*. To her surprise, Peggy Riggle
found herself on the witness stand explaining that she was the
one who had persuaded Binford to speak up. They had been
watching TV together when the Brandley case came on and
a picture of Gary Acreman flashed on the screen. As soon as
she saw it, Kathy Binford recognized him and told her what
she knew.

Apart from taking her friend to court, Peggy Riggle also
took the story to the *Courier* and arranged for it to interview
Binford. Riggle was upset when the paper never printed a
word. After she gave her evidence, on the fourth day of the
hearing, she stayed in court. She was upset again when she
read Carol Williams's report the next day. She thought it was
biased and inaccurate. So she went to see the editor, and she

told him that she had had just about enough of the *Courier*'s being so prejudiced.

That was on a Friday. On Monday the *Courier* fired her.

Her bosses said it had nothing to do with her giving evidence for the black janitor and nothing to do with her complaining about the paper's prejudice. It was just that they had decided to eliminate her job, they said. Then they made her sign an agreement not to say anything detrimental about the *Courier*.

Gary Acreman looked as though he were dying. The pits of his eyes were blackened and deep. His whole face had hollowed out, and he had a downtrodden, hangdog air about him as he loped into the crowded courtroom. He took his seat beneath the steady gaze of the judge and sat waxen-faced, staring at the floor in front of him. All the attorneys and all the spectators turned to the courtroom VCRs and watched in silent concentration as the image of Acreman's former, fleshier self flickered onto the screens. While he looked away, they saw him as he sat in the motel in Corsicana, smoking and confessing he had lied and describing how James Dexter Robinson had seized Cheryl Fergeson. Then they saw him again, three days later, sitting in an office in Conroe, still smoking and confessing and explaining that Robinson had not only grabbed the girl but had also thrown her clothes into the Dumpster. Finally, he looked up to find Mike De Geurin staring him in the eye.

"Mr. Acreman, that was you on the video, was it not?"

"Yes, sir." Deadpan face.

"You've lost some weight since then, haven't you?"

"Yes."

"But there's no doubt in your mind that was you and those were your words?"

"Yes, sir."

De Geurin paused. There was nothing friendly or affable about him now. "You know James Dexter Robinson?"

"Yes, sir."

"How well do you know him?"

"Not that well."

"By 'not that well,' do you mean you didn't run around with him?"

"No, I didn't do any running around with him."

"Never did?"

"No."

"Drive you to work?"

"Occasionally."

"Ever go drinking with him?"

"No."

"Never?"

"No."

De Geurin hoped the judge would see that for the lie it was. "Ever have group sex with him?"

"No."

De Geurin paced back to the defense table, turned, and asked Acreman whom he had just had lunch with.

"Charlie Ray."

De Geurin pointed to the DA's investigator sitting with the prosecution. "The man sitting here at the table?"

"Yes, sir."

Acreman denied that they had been discussing his evidence. He then admitted that he had made two visits to the DA's office in Conroe in the last week.

"Did you talk about your testimony?"

"I told them what I've been telling them since I talked to y'all."

"How about telling them what you've been telling them since 1980? Or have you changed some of that?"

"No."

"Haven't changed a word?"

Acreman shook his head. "Uh-uh."

De Geurin moved in close again. "Did you speak to the girl at the school?"

"Told her where the restroom was."

"You told her where the restroom was?"

"Yes, sir."

"Now, you didn't testify about that at trial, did you?"

"Yes, sir, I did."

De Geurin spun on his heel and started riffling through papers on his table. "Mr. Acreman, you didn't put that in your statement to the police, did you?"

"I can't remember."

"Are you telling us now you did talk to the girl at the school?"

"Yes, sir. It was in your video, that she wanted to know where the restroom was."

"You did talk to her then?"

"Yes, sir."

De Geurin had found what he wanted in the papers. "Correct me if I'm wrong, Mr. Acreman, but didn't you testify at trial that you were fifty feet away from the area where the girl was, that you never saw her face, you only saw her from behind and that you just happened to see her walking down the hallway?"

"No, sir."

"You didn't say that?"

"No, sir."

"Well . . ."

"Well, I can't remember what all . . . I can't remember what was said in the trial."

"But you would have told the truth?"

"Yes, sir."

Acreman slouched miserably in his seat as the blond attorney paced back and forth before him, now diving for his papers, now striding forward and jabbing the air in front of his face to stress a point. Over and over again De Geurin tied him to the details of what he had said in the videos and then confronted him with the different versions he had agreed to at different times with the Conroe police and the DA's office. Acreman's answers skidded and slid. He pleaded he could not remember. Whether Robinson had been at the school that day, whether it was Robinson who had thrown away the dead girl's clothes, whether the person who threw away the clothes was black or white, whether he had told any of this to the police in 1980, whether he had seen Robinson grab the girl—he could not remember.

"All right," said De Geurin. "Now, when you say on March 20th in the video, that you saw James Dexter Robinson throw the clothes in the Dumpster—did you say that?"

"Yes, sir."

"Sometime since March 20th, you lost your memory?"

"I wasn't sure . . . I wasn't sure about anything really."

"When you say James Dexter Robinson grabbed her, I believe you made a motion with your hands." De Geurin's fingers gripped an imaginary neck. "Grabbing her. Where were you visualizing in your mind that he was grabbing her? What was in your mind? You were going like this. . . ." De Geurin's fingers were clenching the air in front of Acreman's face.

"Nothing."

"You had your hands like that and you didn't have a picture in your mind?"

"No."

"Mr. Acreman, did you say 'I know Clarence Brandley didn't do it'?"

Acreman frowned. "No. I don't think I ever said he didn't do it."

De Geurin reminded him of the evidence of Connie Miller and two other witnesses who recalled his outburst in the City Cab office in August 1980. "Those people are lying that you said that?"

"Yes, sir."

De Geurin went back to his papers. "Then in March 1987, on the video you say 'I know Clarence Brandley didn't do it. He's not guilty.'"

"I don't think I said in them exact words."

De Geurin was flicking through piles of paper, while Nugent and Brown leaned across him to join the search. De Geurin looked back to his witness. "I'll find it in just a moment," he promised. "Exact words. . . . All right, Mr. Acreman, you were asked March 20th, that's the second video that you did, 'Why are you now telling us this?' and you said, 'Because I don't think Clarence Brandley is guilty of it. And well, I know for a fact he isn't.' Now you said that, didn't you, Mr. Acreman?"

"Yeah, I guess."

"Do you want me to show it to you on the video again?"

"No."

"Do you have any doubts that you said that?"

Acreman scratched his hair and shook his head.

"Any doubts in your mind that on that tape, those thoughts, these words came out of your mind?"

"No."

De Geurin closed in on him again. "Mr. Acreman, you know, don't you, that Mr. Brandley is not guilty?"

With something like desperation in his voice, Acreman told him: "I don't know. I wasn't there."

"And you know who did it, too, don't you?"

Acreman shook his head and looked at the floor, as if for refuge. "No, sir. I don't."

De Geurin kept jabbing at his conscience. Why had he said that Brandley was innocent? Why had he held back on the truth in his statement to police? "It still bothers you, doesn't it?"

"No, sir. I don't know of anything I left out."

"Well, you never said you talked to the girl in your statement, did you?"

Acreman stared morosely at his hands.

"Did you?"

"Yes, sir, that was in one of them."

De Geurin pounced back to his table, found his statement, and thrust it toward Acreman. "Take your time," he said with a flick of his hand. "Read it."

De Geurin waited. Three hundred people waited. There was not a sound. "Have you had an opportunity, Mr. Acreman, to read the statement?"

"Yes, sir."

"Do you say in the statement that you talked to the girl?"

"No, sir."

De Geurin was not finished yet. He made Acreman confirm that John Sessum had seen him talking to the girl and that Sessum was now telling the truth about it. Acreman tried to fight back and suggested he had just forgotten to mention it to the police. "That completely slipped my mind," he said.

De Geurin seized the phrase, and stalking up and down in front of the witness stand, he started bludgeoning Acreman with it: "It just slipped your mind that you had talked to the girl a few moments before she was killed? . . . When Ranger Styles was getting your statement after you all walked through the school, it just slipped your mind? . . . And Mr. Martinez didn't tell the police. . . . And Mr. Sessum didn't tell the police. . . . All three of you, it slipped your mind? Is that correct?"

"I guess so."

"Mr. Acreman, were you, Sessum, Martinez afraid you might be implicated in this crime because you talked to that girl?"

"No, sir."

De Geurin paused and asked, as if it were an afterthought: "Was she pretty?"

"I don't know. I guess."

With a look of disdain, De Geurin turned and walked back to his table. "I'll pass the witness."

The muffled buzz of comment had dwindled and died by the time Rick Stover, the assistant DA, stood up to try to rescue Gary Acreman.

Stover reminded him he was on oath and asked him: "Back on the day that Cheryl Fergeson was raped and murdered in the Conroe High School, did you participate in the rape or the murder of her?"

"No, sir."

"Did you see anyone abduct Cheryl Fergeson prior to her murder?"

"No, sir."

Now once again Gary Acreman sat slouched in his seat staring in front of him, while the courtroom was filled with the sound of his voice, first in a recording of his phone call to Rick Stover, complaining that Richard Reyna had scared him into telling lies, and then in a video of his interview in Pittsburgh with Stover and Charlie Ray, insisting that everything he had said at Brandley's trials was still true.

Stover was trying to push a rescue raft out to the drowning witness. All Acreman had to do was stick to the story he had told at the original trials and dismiss everything else as the voice of his fear, brought on by the terror of dealing with Richard Reyna and Jim McCloskey. In his panic Acreman kept flailing at the raft and missing.

First, Stover got him to agree that he had told the truth back in 1980, when his memory was fresh—nobody grabbing any girl; no sign of Robinson—then that he had stood up in the witness stand in July 1986 and sworn on oath that he had seen James Dexter Robinson at Conroe High on the day of the crime. Now was the time for Acreman to talk about the voice of his fear. Stover set it up for him. "Now I'm curious why you testified that you had seen James Robinson at the school on the day of the murder when you have told me that you didn't see him there, and you didn't tell the Texas Ranger that, and you didn't tell it on any of the statements, and you didn't tell it in the first two trials that you participated in."

Acreman shifted in his seat and said: "I . . . I don't know either. I more or less feel that it being that long a time, I . . . I'm not sure what happened that day and as far as that, you know, somebody saying, saying this, or hearing different things about that would make me wonder . . ."

His voice faded and vanished. Stover made no attempt to conceal his own view of the answer. "That's your explanation why, after six years, you suddenly decided to say that you saw James Dexter Robinson at the school on the day of the murder?"

Acreman made another grab for the raft. "Well, not only that, after talking to Reyna the first time, the first couple of

times, whatever, when he first came up to me and introduced
me who he was, like I said, I don't remember ever seeing
ID or anything, credentials or anything, and then he tells
me then, that not to take the rap for anything for something
somebody else done. Then he starts telling me what, who or
telling me who, that somebody had seen Robinson there and
that Robinson was there. . . ."

Stover could see he needed help and held out a hand. "When
he told you this, did you all of a sudden think 'Well, if he says
it, it's got to be true, therefore, I'm going to testify to it'?"

Acreman missed the hand completely. "No," he said.

Stover winced, abandoned the July 1986 hearing, and tried
another approach. Slowly, step-by-step, he brought him up
to his meeting in Corsicana with Richard Reyna and Jim
McCloskey. He got him to explain that he was nervous in
Corsicana because he was waiting to go to court over a road
accident he had been involved in in which another driver was
killed. He got him to recall that Richard Reyna had told him
not to take the rap for the killing at the high school.

"How many times did he say that to you?"

"Once, twice, three times."

"Were you scared?"

"Yes, sir."

"Were you nervous?"

"Yes."

Stover was getting closer to the voice of fear. But Acreman
still had to explain why he had produced such a vivid account
of Robinson attacking the girl if there was no truth in it. Stover
inched a little closer. "What was going through your mind at
that time?"

"I don't know. 'It ain't me.' "

Stover needed more than that. He needed the fear. " 'It ain't
me.' " What do you mean by that statement?"

"I didn't do it."

"Did you think any further than that?"

"Well, I was, I was sitting there, thinking 'Can they make
this stick?' I know that I'm innocent and they're coming at
me with this."

He was still not getting there. Acreman started to say that
he had gone ahead and made this video because Reyna had
insisted.

"Well, Mr. Acreman, I could insist that you saw the assassi-
nation of President Kennedy, I could say that all day long, but

if you didn't see it, that didn't make it true. Is that correct?"
"Yes."

Stover pushed harder. "If I told you that enough times, would I eventually be able to convince you that maybe you were in Dallas on that day and you did see that take place?"

The answer had to be "No, not unless you frightened me the way Reyna did," but Acreman was lost. "I don't know."

"Is it possible?" begged Stover.

"No," said Acreman, missing the raft again.

The defense attorneys had to admire Stover's stamina. He kept on at Acreman to explain how Reyna had scared him.

Acreman kept groping and grabbing. "The way he words things, the way he words things to his advantage . . . I don't know, I don't know how to put it. . . . He was a, uh, type of person who just take you and put you on the spot. . . . Something about him. . . ." Finally, Acreman came up with an idea: "His voice, his tone of voice that he uses."

The words had no sooner rushed out of his mouth than a look of anxiety swept across his face as he realized that the three hundred people who were now looking straight at him had all heard Reyna's voice on the videos.

"The tone of voice that he used," he added quickly, "before the video was made."

Stover was near defeat. "Mr. Acreman, I could use a tone of voice in this courtroom that would scare you right out of that chair, but I don't think it would make you say something that wasn't true, so I don't understand and this judge doesn't understand why you made this video."

It was no good. Acreman was as exhausted as Stover. When they finally got around to talking about the second video he had made with the defense and Stover asked him why he had sat down in front of another video camera and not mentioned that his first video statement was a lie, Acreman looked at him, looked at the floor, shrugged, and said, "I don't know."

Rick Stover gave up and returned to the prosecution table, leaving Acreman marooned on the witness stand with all his words over all the years in mutiny against him.

The turning tide caught Debra Cheney and swept her into court. She lived in a trailer park in Conroe and had once had Brenda Medina and James Dexter Robinson as neighbors. She came forward to tell the defense that she knew Robinson had been in Conroe during the week of the murder because she had seen him on that Wednesday with Brenda Medina at the hospital. She knew it was a Wednesday because she had been taking her pregnant sister to the hospital, as she always did on Wednesdays, and she remembered clearly that it was the same week that they heard about the killing at the high school.

She went to Galveston to tell her story. Peter Speers asked why she had not said all this back in July 1986, when Brenda Medina was giving evidence, why she had taken so long to speak out.

She had no answer—no more than anyone else in the town who had looked away.

James Dexter Robinson had his story all assembled. The loose ends that had jumped out of place during the hearing in Conroe in July 1986 were now neatly tucked away.

He stood in the witness box, with his little elfin face twitching with nerves, and told Rick Stover that he now realized that a whole lot of things he had forgotten about and that other people were talking about had really happened to him on August 5, 1980, two and a half weeks before Cheryl Fergeson was killed.

It was on August 5, he said, that he had cashed his last paycheck from Conroe High. It was on that day that he had swung by the high school one last time, and he was pretty sure he had popped his head through a door and said hi to the janitors he used to work with. It was on that day, too, he now remembered, that he had gone around to see Reggie Slacum to ask him to repay the hundred dollars he owed him. And it was on that night that he had decided to leave Conroe for good—not because he had killed anyone but because he believed that Brenda Medina was seeing another man. That was the truth, he said, now that he had had time to think about it.

He explained that he might have said some strange things when the defense arranged for him to take a lie detector test with Glenn Raney, but that was because Raney had shouted at him and slapped the table in anger and asked him whether he killed Cheryl Fergeson sixty different times. He had not mentioned that at the hearing last year. But now he had had time to think about it. As he told his story, his voice dropped so low that no one in court could hear a word. Judge Pickett leaned forward and made him unhook the microphone from the front of the witness stand and loop the flex around his throat. Paul Nugent wondered at the symbolism as Robinson tightened the noose around his own neck.

Mike De Geurin began to cross-examine him in his gentlest style, persuading him to remind everyone that he had wanted to hire the district attorney as his lawyer. Then he started to turn the screw. He asked him about his former wife, Berdie. "Berdie accused you of beating her up. Are you aware of that?"

Robinson shook his head, all innocence. "No, sir."

"Now, Mr. Robinson, weren't you made aware of the fact that she was put in hospital and claimed that you had repeatedly beaten her?"

"No, sir."

He smiled. It was a mistake.

De Geurin looked at him in amazement. "Why are you smiling?"

The smile vanished. "Because that's a lie."

"Are you telling me, though, that you never heard that before?"

"No, sir, I've never beat her like you're saying I did."

"All right. But you have heard that she said that?"

"Yes, sir."

At last.

"And she's lying?"

"Yes, sir."

Now De Geurin had Robinson where he wanted him. "And when Brenda Medina says you beat her up before, she's lying?"

"Yes, sir."

"Now, Mr. Slacum says that you were in Conroe on the 20th and 21st of August 1980. He knows it for a fact, he says, because you and your father had tried to rough him up."

"No, sir."

"Okay. Is Mr. Slacum a liar?"

"Yes, sir."

"Now, do you know Debra Cheney?"

"No, sir."

"Do you remember going with Brenda Medina to a hospital back in 1980?"

"We went in June."

"Are you saying you didn't go in August?"

"No, sir."

"Positive about that?"

"Yes, sir."

"Now, Mrs. Cheney says she saw you at the hospital in August, in fact she says it was August 20th of 1980."

"No, sir."

"She's lying, too?"

"Yes, sir."

He was all alone. They were all liars. Brenda Medina was a liar for saying he had confessed. And John Sessum was a liar for saying he had grabbed the girl. And Gary Acreman was a liar for saying the same thing.

De Geurin then made him repeat his claim that he had known nothing of the murder at the high school until several months later, when he was living in South Carolina and spoke to his father, who was then still living in Texas. "He called me to ask me how was I doing and everything. That conversation was brought up during our talk."

"And he told you, asked you if you remembered . . ."

"Clarence Brandley."

De Geurin stood in front of him, his head cocked to one side. "Was that the way he referred to him? Is that the way he referred to him?"

"No, sir."

"How did he refer to him?"

"He said 'You remember that black man that was working in the school that was a supervisor?' And I said 'Yeah.' He said well, he had killed a girl."

"You're sure that's the way he referred to him?"

"Yes, sir."

De Geurin's hand darted out to his table and came up with a copy of the statement Robinson had made to the district attorney about his innocence. "I'll let you look at your statement, sir. Read the line to yourself. See if it refreshes . . ."

"I don't want to say that part in court."

"So that's not the way he referred to Clarence Brandley, was it?"

"No, sir."

"Can you go ahead and tell us how he referred to Clarence?"

Robinson glanced at the sea of brown faces and looked down and mumbled the words he had been happy to say in the district attorney's office. "He said, 'Do you remember the nigger at the school?' "

A shuffle spread along the public benches. Now Robinson, too, was marooned not only by the words of all those he called

liars but also by the words of his own father repeated before
three hundred strangers.

As the hearing rolled from day to day, its players developed
daily rituals. Each morning Nugent and McCloskey went to
Gaido's restaurant down by the waterfront to eat breakfast and
talk tactics. They were staying in a beach house on the Gulf
side of the island that had been given to Percy Foreman as a
fee by some former client and was now littered with paperwork
from the Brandley case. Most mornings they were joined by
Don Brown, who was staying at a motel, and Richard Reyna,
who had checked into a block of pseudo-Victorian condos.
Then they all traveled up to court and found De Geurin, who
was staying at the posh Tremont House in the middle of
town, pacing up and down outside, smoking nervously with
a padful of notes under one arm and some new idea he needed
to unload.

The courthouse foyer was always jammed with people. All
the old ladies from Dugan, armed now with pillows to soften
the long day on the hard court benches, stood in line for the
metal detector. The Montgomery County deputies laboriously searched everyone, including the defense attorneys, and
insisted that all the spectators had to leave their little packets
of food and drink outside in the foyer.

Every morning the black people waiting in line watched
Peter Speers's wife flounce by without being searched, drinking ostentatiously from a can of Coca-Cola, which she was
allowed to take with her into court.

Nugent and De Geurin often slipped across the parking lot
to the Galveston County Jail to talk about their plans with
Brandley and to reassure him. De Geurin had bought him a
beautiful new shirt, and every evening Brandley stripped it
off and sent it out to his family, who the next day brought it
back washed and pressed.

Although Brandley was outwardly calm, the two attorneys
could see the tension seething inside him. His fingers shook so
much that Nugent had to help him knot his tie. All his emotions
were running high. He had never been in a jail with young
people before, and he kept talking about how bad it made him
feel to see these young people who thought it was so cool to
live in the fast lane. It made him tearful to talk about it.

Every day in court Nugent played out a minor power struggle with the Montgomery County deputies. He noticed that the prosecuting attorneys had chairs with wheels on the bottom so they could slide effortlessly between their table and the exhibits or the public benches. The deputies slouching at the back of the court had wheels on their chairs, too. But they had given the defense ordinary immobile ones. On the third day Nugent decided to do something about this inequity, so while the deputies stood leaning against the wall of the court, glaring, Nugent sauntered over and took their chairs and replaced them with ones without wheels. Every morning after that, he came into court to find that the deputies had been there earlier and taken back the chairs, and every morning, while the deputies stood sullenly watching, Nugent seized them again for the defense.

Judge Pickett soon became an object of veneration in the court. He arrived early each morning, took his place on his dais with his pipe clenched between his teeth, and quietly watched the goings-on before him. At the beginning of business he bade the court good morning and all the old black ladies chorused "Good morning" in reply. While the attorneys fought and scrapped, he sat calmly, endlessly writing his notes, fielding objections, frequently telling the attorneys, "You're probably right, but overruled." During breaks he remained seated, still watching, and some of the old ladies approached him to strike up a conversation.

Slowly, the defense people began to trust him. They did a little digging and discovered that in his own way he had once had something in common with Clarence Brandley. He, too, had been imprisoned when he hadn't committed a crime. During World War II he had been shot down over the Mediterranean and captured by the Germans. He had then joined twenty-nine other U.S. officers in breaking out of captivity in the escape from a prison train that was made famous as Von Ryan's Express.

Peter Speers's wife soon became an object of contempt. She sat each day in her reserved seat at the front of the court, sipping her Coke, chewing her gum, flicking through *People* magazine during the evidence, sneering derisively at defense witnesses, and occasionally lighting up a cigarette.

At the midday break the defense team hurried back to De Geurin's room in the Tremont House, where the foyer was full of palm trees and piano players, and sat on his windowsill, eating hamburgers and planning strategy. In the evenings they still hung out together, plotting and planning. One evening, in Candy's Italian restaurant, they were in mid-session when Peter Speers walked in with his assistant, one of the investigators from the attorney general's office, and Carol Williams from the *Conroe Courier*. They took one look at the defense team, turned on their heels, and left.

Every day the unseen tide brought new witnesses, who were now ready to peel more layers of secrecy away from the courthouse and the town of Conroe.

Cheryl Bradford, who was now a sports coach, came forward to tell of the two strange men she had seen in the gym that day. But it was not just what she said about Robinson that caught the attention of the defense. The reason they brought her down to Galveston and had her tell her story to the judge was that on the very evening of the crime this girl had been so concerned by what she had seen that she had contacted the Conroe Police Department and told them all about the two white men, and the Conroe Police Department, which had already elected its suspect, had never bothered to follow it up.

Two black ministers walked through the gauntlet of Montgomery County deputies to recall the trials of Clarence Brandley. The Reverend C. Anderson Davis of Houston remembered that in both trials there was "a racist 'nigger' atmosphere where blacks were supposed to stay in their places and you would never have a fair chance when opposing the opposite race." The Montgomery County deputies had made it clear that blacks were second-class citizens. Judge Martin had seemed racially hostile. The minister said he had visited trials all over the United States and had only once seen one that was worse, and that was in Chattanooga, Tennessee, where the prosecution openly used the word "nigger" and said all black people were dishonest and stank. "Now, other than that trial, I've never seen one more racially hostile than the one in Conroe."

Another Houston minister, the Reverend J. J. Roberson, spoke of the anger of white people in the courthouse toward blacks, the cold looks on the faces of the jurors, the surly deputies following black people to the rest rooms, but he explained to the attorneys and the judge: "You couldn't imagine how I felt because you haven't been black one hour."

De Geurin asked the elderly minister if he had ever heard of incidents in Conroe's past when black men who had been accused of assaulting white women in the town had been attacked and killed. Peter Speers interrupted the question three times to complain that none of this should be mentioned. The judge overruled him, and De Geurin asked if the atmosphere in the town had changed since then.

"I imagine the attitudes have changed," the minister replied, "but the atmosphere is still the same."

Don Brown stepped forward and took the stand himself to remember the bitterness of the trial: the belief he shared with George Morris that they might well be attacked if the jury acquitted Clarence Brandley; the all-white court; the chill that spread through the room when the schoolboy Danny Taylor claimed that Brandley had lusted after white schoolgirls; Sheriff Gene Reaves and DA Jim Keeshan sitting in Judge Alworth's office and referring to Brandley as "that little nigger" without a word of rebuke from the judge; the deceit by which Keeshan had tricked Clarence Brandley into appearing before the grand jury and then deprived him of his bail.

There was the former assistant DA, Frank Robin, swearing on oath that Keeshan would have been upset if he had ever allowed a black person to sit as a juror; a sociologist from the University of Texas, Sheldon Ekland-Olson, who explained that his exhaustive research showed that in Texas a black man who was convicted of raping and killing a white woman was five times more likely to be sentenced to death than a normal homicide defendant; and there was Don Brown's law partner, Nat Davis, who swore Don Brown was right in recalling that both the sheriff and the DA had called Brandley "that little nigger."

Then Mary Johnson, the elegant court reporter, came trembling to the witness stand. She was instantly a magnetic sight, with her huge beauty-queen eyes and her white-blond hair drawn back from her face. De Geurin needed her to tell all she knew about the missing exhibits and about the conspiracy in the courthouse to conceal their disappearance. But he knew that she was struggling with a dilemma, torn between telling the truth and remaining loyal to Judge Martin. As he began his questions, Mary Johnson started to cry. For a while the whole room was not so much a court as a theater, and they were an audience, watching this poignant spectacle of a woman at war with herself.

"I'd like to say to all of these questions that I don't recall," she said.

De Geurin grinned his most charming grin. "I know you would."

The blond attorney himself felt the drama of it all. He was confronting her with a moral choice such as she had probably never had to face in her life. She could tell the truth to save this man's life, or she could conceal it and save her job and her position in her community. The fact that she had never met this man and that a well-to-do white woman in her position was never likely to meet him only made the choice more difficult—more pure. She could do right, or she could do wrong.

De Geurin tried to help her by reminding her that he was a close friend of the judge whose behavior he was now having to expose. "It's not easy for either of us, is it?" he said. It was an instinctive move, but it helped move her forward. Slowly, with her handkerchief balled up in her fist, she began to whisper the history of the missing exhibits and all the secrecy surrounding them, rehearsing now in public what she had previously dared say only in secret.

She explained that there was no way those exhibits could have been thrown out accidentally; that as many as twenty-five people in the courthouse were told about their disappearance, but that the defense was kept in the dark; and that she had heard how Peggy Stevens had shown Don Brown a box of fake exhibits to keep him quiet and then called down to Jim Keeshan's office to warn him that Brown was on the warpath. She had decided she had to tell the defense attorneys the truth and contacted them through Janet Dial. In the same way she had decided she had to tell them, too, that Judge Martin and the DA had sat down in front of her and rehearsed a scheme to prevent the defense from calling any witnesses and finding out what had really happened to the exhibits.

De Geurin had to coax each line from her, but as she spoke, he felt an admiration for this unlikely heroine. He could only guess how the courthouse people in Conroe would treat her once they heard what she had done.

As the layers were slowly peeled away, the defense reached the point where it was finally ready to confront the enemy. One by one, in front of the three hundred spectators and all the unseen spectators across the state of Texas, the ringleaders were called to the stand to explain themselves.

*   *   *

Judge Lynn Coker was called.

De Geurin tried to get him to talk about the time he had ushered George Morris and Don Brown into his office all those years ago to warn them of all the activity over the missing exhibits and how it boggled his imagination. The judge said he could not recall such a conversation. De Geurin felt a little anger flickering inside him at this spineless figure who was so eager when he had a chance to get someone to like him and so feeble when it came to standing up for an innocent man. He had never cross-examined a judge before, but he started hounding him for the truth. The judge kept pointing to the hole in his memory.

"Well, Judge. I'm not going to belabor the point. I want to ask you—are you denying that you told Don Brown and George Morris that the evidence was lost, that Keeshan and Martin were keeping it a secret but you thought they ought to know about it?"

The judge shrugged and smiled. "Counsel, I'm not denying anything. I do not recall it."

De Geurin shook his head and turned his back on him. "I'll pass the witness."

Dr. Joseph Jachimczyk, the medical examiner, was called. The court watched him plead that he could not recall what had happened to the missing swabs he had taken from the dead girl, and he could not recall whether he had given them to the police, and he could not recall whether the Texas Ranger had contacted him, and he could not recall whether he had given the swabs to the ranger, and he could not recall whether he had destroyed them himself. But he was sure the swabs no longer existed.

As soon as the portly pathologist had left the stand, De Geurin called a Houston police sergeant who said that he had worked on more than a thousand rape cases and that it was standard procedure to preserve such swabs for comparison with any future suspect and that he could not think of any scientific reason for them to be thrown away.

Peggy Stevens was called, in her immaculate suit and with her manicured nails and her eyeglasses on the end of her fine gold chain. The district clerk of Montgomery County, who was elected by the town to serve prosecution and defense without favor, had an explanation for her behavior over the missing exhibits. She had kept their loss secret from the defense, she said, because the DA was conducting a criminal inquiry into their disappearance, and she had been trained to be discreet about such things. She had certainly not been taking sides with the prosecution and plotting to deceive the defense.

De Geurin watched her sitting there, like a Siamese cat in the sun. Pacing back and forth, hunched slightly forward, he started to probe her claim to impartiality. He soon discovered that her memory was as fallible as Judge Coker's and the pathologist's. He wanted her to remember how she had shown Don Brown a boxful of fake exhibits and then warned Jim Keeshan so he could hide in his office while Brown waited impotently outside. Did she remember showing Don Brown a boxful of fake exhibits?

"I just don't recall it, Mr. De Geurin. I'm sorry. I have racked my brain over all those events. I just do not recall that particular instance."

Had she called Jim Keeshan's office to warn that Don Brown might know what was happening?

"I just don't recall it. No, sir. I'm sorry."

"Could it have happened and you just don't remember?"

"It might have. Like I said, I just don't remember one particular incident like that."

"How about calling Judge Martin and letting him know?"

"No, sir."

"How about somebody on Judge Martin's staff?"

The reference to Mary Johnson was clear. Peggy Stevens had not been in court to hear her evidence. Her memory revived a little. "I may have mentioned it but I don't think I ever picked up a phone and called anybody. I'm sure I probably mentioned it in passing."

It was the beginning of an admission. De Geurin tried to build on it. "I'm talking about mentioning it in passing, if you will, while Don Brown was walking in the courthouse to go talk to Mr. Keeshan, to try to get to the bottom of this problem with the exhibits."

Mrs. Stevens flattened a hand against her chest in shock. "That I mentioned it while Mr. Brown was walking in the courthouse?"

De Geurin persisted. "Well, you said you may have mentioned it in passing that you think Mr. Brown had caught on to the secret. . . ."

"Oh," she said, in a tone that suggested she now understood for the first time what he was asking her.

"And I want to know if you called him and warned him."

"I do not recall picking up a phone and calling anybody. No, sir."

De Geurin could see she was not about to fill the hole in her memory.

Still sitting prettily on the witness stand, she continued to insist it had been her duty to be discreet, and she jabbed at Don Brown, calling him a prime suspect in the disappearance. At the defense table Brown gritted his teeth. De Geurin let her go; he could only leave it to the judge to decide whether she was telling the truth.

Judge John Martin was called. For a moment De Geurin found it embarrassing. This was not just a judge on the stand. That in itself was strange enough. But this was also an old friend, someone he had once liked and respected. For a moment De Geurin wondered whether he might still be the same man he had been pleased to know, whether he might stand up now and help them. De Geurin started gently chipping into his evidence. Was his office on the first floor of the courthouse? "Yes." Was the DA's office on the same floor? "Yes." Did his secretary routinely note all his callers on a notepad? "Yes." Did he have the notepads that his former secretary, Janet Dial, had kept for the period of the second Brandley trial and that would reflect the controversial contacts between himself and the DA? "No."

The judge explained that the notepads had mysteriously disappeared. No other records were missing from his office. Only those notepads for that period of time. He had no idea where they had gone. They were just lost and gone forever.

De Geurin felt his friendship fade. He chipped deeper. "Judge, just for the record, were all the jurors in Clarence Brandley's case white?"

Judge Martin hesitated and said: "Everyone appeared to be white."

No explanation. No apology. De Geurin started hammering home his questions. The more he hammered, the more the judge fell back on the official courthouse version of events.

He had never plotted with the DA to deceive the defense about the missing exhibits. He had asked the DA to conduct a criminal inquiry, and it had to be discreet. He did not recall

Peggy Stevens's warning him that Don Brown was on the track of the truth. He had never known the defense attorneys were worried about it. He had thought the janitors had thrown away the exhibits. He had never held secret meetings with the DA. He had only wanted to be a fair judge. He had never plotted with the DA to rig the hearing about the missing exhibits. He had recused himself from the case only to help his old friends, the defense attorneys. He had never been hostile to black spectators.

The more he denied, the more De Geurin hammered him.

What about Mary Johnson's testimony that he had rehearsed with Keeshan how they would prevent the defense from calling witnesses to find out the truth about the missing exhibits?

"That's incorrect."

"Is the court reporter who testified that that is true, are you saying she's a liar?"

"No. She testified whatever she recalls, counsel. I'm just telling you what I recall. That's all."

What about the secret inquiry into the missing exhibits? Had it been his idea that the defense attorneys could not be told the truth because they were suspects?

"Everyone, counsel, was a suspect. My court reporter, the defense lawyers, or anyone that—the janitors, the lady that typed for Mary Johnson. Everyone was suspect."

De Geurin went for the hole in his story. "Suspects were questioned, weren't they?"

"That's right."

De Geurin ripped the hole open. "Of course, they didn't question the defense counsel?"

The judge sighed. "I don't know. I don't know."

What about his secret meetings with the DA? Had he met with Jim Keeshan in the mornings before going into court during Brandley's trial?

"Absolutely not."

"He never came into your office?"

"Oh, he may have come into my outer office and spoken to my secretary, Jan Dial, or something, but I never had an 'ex parte' meeting with Judge Keeshan about the case while it was in progress."

"Are you calling Janet Dial a liar?"

"I'm not, like I say, talking anything about what Jan Dial might have said. I'm just telling you that I have never had an 'ex parte' meeting with Jim Keeshan when he was District Attorney during the time of the trial."

"Then it's your testimony that he never came into your chambers early in the morning or before the trial started, where just you and he were in chambers together during the trial?"

"That's right."

"Never?"

"Never."

There was no friendship left now. Only the attorney, bursting with passion, hammering in his questions, and the judge, out of place on the witness stand, ducking and denying.

There came a point in the verbal brawl when De Geurin started challenging Martin about why he had never ordered the white janitors from the high school to supply samples of hair for comparison with those found on the dead girl. The judge was saying he could not recall. De Geurin was getting nowhere. Suddenly, somewhere inside the attorney, a dam broke. Words started pouring out of him, his anger gushing over the judge in the witness stand as he flooded him with the details of the truth he was determined to deny.

Just suppose, he said, his finger jabbing at the judge, that within thirty days of Brandley's conviction, he had learned, as the judge in the case, that an ex-janitor had confessed the murder to his girlfriend. And just suppose that two people said this ex-janitor was at the school on the day of the murder, that three or four people said he was in town at the time of the murder, that Gary Acreman said he saw this ex-janitor grab the girl and pull her into a bathroom, screaming and yelling for help.

De Geurin was pounding up and down in front of the judge, his hand beating the air for emphasis, all the fragments of fact and all the years of frustration washing through him. "And let's suppose Acreman further said he lied at the trial that you conducted, and another janitor, that being Icky Peace, testified that he lied at your trial, and another janitor, John Sessum, testified that he lied at your trial and that he saw Gary Acreman grab the girl and pull her into the bathroom, screaming and yelling.

"And let's suppose further that Gary Acreman says 'That's true but it wasn't me, it was James Dexter Robinson'; and let's suppose further that James Dexter Robinson and Gary Acreman both are Caucasian and one has sandy blonde hair and one has brown hair and that you also learned that a volley-ball player had seen two men meeting that general description walking across the boys' gymnasium and out the side doors during the time that it is perceived and projected the young girl was killed, and that the police never called her back, because her information did not appear to be relevant."

The judge sat openmouthed. There was no stopping De Geurin now. And suppose the judge had also heard the evidence of Ed Payne. And the evidence of Ed Payne's brother John. And John's wife Marie.

"And let's suppose further that Gary Acreman admits in court that he lied when he said he never talked to the girl at the school, that he lied to the District Attorney, that he lied to Wesley Styles, that he lied to the Conroe Police and that he lied in your trial.

"And let's suppose further that one of the janitors said that Gary Acreman had told him the day of the killing before anybody was supposed to have known the killing had happened 'Don't you tell anybody I was talking to that girl.' Let's suppose all of that was presented to you . . ."

Judge Martin finally found words to interrupt. "On a motion for new trial?" he said. "I'd conduct a hearing."

"Let me finish," snapped De Geurin, still pacing the floor. "Let's suppose those things came to you, not from defense attorneys, but from somebody else, would you think that would be something the defense attorneys should know about?"

"I would conduct a hearing on all of that, counsel."

"And if those things were established within the time for a new trial, would you grant a new trial?"

"I would conduct a hearing on all of that."

Rick Stover tried to interrupt. Judge Pickett told them to proceed. De Geurin's anger was not to be stopped. His voice was rasping now with effort and emotion. "Would you allow a man to be executed when three of the four janitors that testified at your trial are now being called liars by the District Attorney's office?"

"That's not within my province."

"Let me ask you personally." His finger jabbed at the judge. "Would you allow him to be executed?"

"That's not within my province."

Rick Stover objected. Judge Pickett said Martin had answered the question.

Now Mike De Geurin stopped square in front of his former friend, looking into his eyes: "Judge, why don't you just tell Clarence Brandley and these people you're sorry for what happened?"

Judge Martin just gaped. Rick Stover jumped from his chair, objecting. But De Geurin was already walking back to his seat. "I'll pass the witness."

On the public benches some of the old people from Dugan had tears in their eyes.

The Honorable James Keeshan was called.

He was as smooth and self-assured as ever, sitting calm and poised on the stand, paying no heed to the rows of angry faces, marking out his defense in a firm voice as Peter Speers began leading him through his role in the affair. He claimed no holes in his memory. He did not deal in blunt denials. He simply explained things his way.

Yes, he had ordered Brandley's arrest, but that had nothing to do with race. Yes, he had objected to hair and blood samples being taken from other janitors, but that was because it would have been "a needless imposition." Yes, he had agreed to let Brandley have a low bail bond and then revoked his probation, but that was just standard procedure. Certainly, he had later had that bail bond raised to seventy-five thousand dollars, but he was sure he had invited the defense attorneys to a hearing on the subject. At the defense table Don Brown was tempted to burst into flames at hearing this but restricted himself to a vigorous shaking of his head.

Keeshan was not afraid to admit the faults of others in the courthouse. He agreed that Sheriff Reaves had called Brandley a nigger, but he was sure he had not done so himself. He then explained that although the sheriff had used that word he had many friends in the black community in Montgomery County. There was an outburst of derisive laughter from the public benches.

He had noticed no racial tension and no disturbances at either of the trials. He had certainly not held any secret meetings with Judge Martin. It would not have been possible; he was always far too busy preparing his witnesses, and anyway, he could not have anticipated issues that were going to arise, let alone rehearsed how they would handle them.

He had helped replace the missing exhibits with copies, but he had done that only to test the reaction of the defense attorneys, who were, he said, the only people with a motive to destroy this material. He had never plotted secretly with Judge Martin to rig the subsequent hearing. It was just that the judge and Mary Johnson had come by his office without being invited, and he had suggested that in order to save any embarrassment to Mary Johnson, he could announce at the coming hearing that he believed the janitors were responsible and it was not Mary's fault.

Peter Speers asked him if he had ever intended to deprive Clarence Brandley of any of his rights. The Honorable James Keeshan replied that his aim was "only to do my duty to the best of my ability and without the intent to mistreat or abuse anyone."

Mike De Geurin took him on point-by-point. Keeshan started to retreat. He admitted that since he had an assistant and an investigator to help him, he would have had time to meet Judge Martin before trial each morning, and he admitted that since this was a second trial, he could have anticipated the issues that would be arising.

He admitted that he had never interviewed anyone from the Brandley defense, even though he claimed they were the only ones with a motive to destroy exhibits. He admitted that Sam Martinez's father worked as a janitor at the courthouse and that he had never interviewed him to see whether he might have destroyed the exhibits for fear that his son was involved in the crime. He admitted that he had never previously claimed that his plan for the hearing about the exhibits was designed to save Mary Johnson from embarrassment. He admitted that Peggy Stevens had warned him that Don Brown was guessing the truth, but he could not explain why she would deny that in court.

He admitted, when he was confronted with an official transcript, that there had been disturbances at the trial and that he had personally complained to the judge about unruly behavior and about a black woman who had sat on a white woman's hand and that he had asked for extra security. He first denied and then admitted, when he was confronted with a transcript, that he had told the judge that he would speak to the white spectators in the courthouse about their behavior if the defense attorneys would deal with the blacks.

But on one point he would not move. "It was, and is my belief that Mr. Brandley killed Cheryl Fergeson," he said.

As he left the stand and walked out of court, he was followed by the wordless stares of three hundred people who did not believe him.

The chief investigator for the attorney general of the state of Texas, Robert "Duke" Bodisch, was called. He said that as a result of his lengthy inquiry, he believed Gary Acreman could not have seen the Dumpster where he claimed to have seen the dead girl's clothes being thrown away, that Cheryl Bradford was mistaken in thinking that the two suspicious white men she had seen had come from the auditorium, that James Dexter Robinson was missing only one front tooth at the time of the crime even though John Sessum called him "the man with no teeth," and that Robinson had been at a birthday party in South Carolina that, his family said, took place six days before Cheryl Fergeson was killed.

Mike De Geurin then established that in the course of his lengthy inquiry, Duke Bodisch had never interviewed either of the defense investigators who, according to his report, had intimidated witnesses and encouraged perjury. He had never interviewed Peggy Stevens or Judge Martin about the missing exhibits, and although he had spoken to Jim Keeshan, he had never videotaped the interview as he had with his other witnesses.

When the prosecution tried to put Bodisch's report into evidence, De Geurin objected that its conclusions were politically motivated, and Judge Pickett sustained his objection.

Finally, Texas Ranger John Wesley Styles was called to explain himself.

Wesley Styles walked tall into the court with his Stetson hat and his leather boots and his silver badge hammered out of a Mexican five-peso piece glinting in the light. When he spoke, his voice was a ponderous growl. He began by telling Assistant District Attorney Rick Stover his version of events. He had interviewed all his witnesses in a proper fashion, he said. He believed the white janitors were telling him the truth, he said. He had never threatened any of them, and to mark the point, he produced a tape recording.

At the defense table all three attorneys immediately started to bristle. What was this? New evidence—seven years after the inquiry? Don Brown suspected this was the tape of Icky Peace being interviewed at the Cleveland police station, the tape whose contents had been kept from the jury on the orders of Judge Martin at the second trial. Brown was half right.

De Geurin started asking why Styles had never produced this tape before. The ranger explained that he had thought the tape was lost, but he had just happened to find it in his attic a few days before the start of this hearing.

And how had that come about?

"I just happened to think about it," the ranger drawled, poker-faced.

At the defense table behind De Geurin, Brown was starting to bubble. There was more than one conversation on this tape. De Geurin asked more questions. The ranger explained that this was a tape of his first interview with Peace—at the Cleveland police station late on Saturday evening, the day after Brandley's arrest—but there was also a recording of his conversation with Peace four days later when he walked him through the high school.

Brown shook his head in disbelief. Seven years after the inquiry this came out. The defense attorneys had never before been told that this second tape even existed, never in forty-seven volumes of testimony. They had to show that this had been concealed. De Geurin demanded to see the ranger's report of his investigation. Stover objected. The judge overruled him, and the ranger gave up his report. The defense attorneys flicked through it: there was no mention anywhere of the existence of this recording of the walk-through, an incident that had been the subject of repeated questions and arguments at both trials, particularly because one of Brandley's former bosses, David Harris, said he had seen the ranger walking Peace through the school and coaching his evidence.

De Geurin looked at the ranger in disbelief and pointed at the report. "You did not put it in there?"

The ranger shook his head. "No. I just discovered that a few minutes ago. It's not there."

De Geurin was wide-eyed. "You just now discovered that?"

"It was just brought to my attention. I thought it was in there, but it wasn't."

De Geurin told Judge Pickett: "Quite frankly, I smell a fish, but I'm having a hard time getting to it."

He sat down with Nugent and Brown, and while Styles told Rick Stover that the tapes showed no evidence of his threatening Icky Peace, the three defense attorneys puzzled over why the prosecution should have concealed this for so long. Before they could find it, Rick Stover pointed them to the answer.

The assistant DA started asking the ranger whether Icky Peace had said anything on the tape that was not already mentioned in the statement he had given to the Conroe police on the day of the crime.

The ranger said, "Yes."

The three defense attorneys were all ears.

Stover continued. "Mr. Styles, there is one time during this conversation that Mr. Peace makes reference to a statement made by Gary Acreman, where Gary says that he's been over to the building and he's seen Clarence with the girl knocking some chairs around, words to that effect. Do you remember him saying that on the tape?"

"Yes, sir," growled the ranger.

So that was it. This was not the first time that the defense had heard of Acreman's saying this. Styles had briefly mentioned it in his original report. Icky Peace had told the two defense investigators about it, and they had seen it as Acreman's first lie, the instinctive moment when he started to cover his tracks by blaming the black man. But by producing the tape, the prosecution was drawing attention to its failure to follow up on Acreman's remark, a failure that, in the light of all it now knew about Acreman, seemed so incompetent as to border on the corrupt. If this had been an honest investigation, the ranger should have gone straight from his interview with Icky Peace to Gary Acreman and invited him to come to court and say he had personally witnessed this black janitor raping the white schoolgirl. There would have been no more relying on flimsy circumstantial evidence. Acreman would have been an eyewitness to the crime. But Styles had ignored it. It was his reasoning that excited the defense attorneys' imagination.

In part, they believed, he might have ignored Acreman's remark because it did not fit the official version of events, which had already been laid out in statements and which held that the white janitors had no idea a crime was being committed. If Acreman was saying he had seen it taking place, the official version had to be wrong. But more than that, the defense believed he had ignored it because it would have led the investigation in a completely different direction. If Acreman had truly seen the black janitor raping Cheryl

Fergeson, he would surely have raised the alarm. But he had not done so. Any honest investigator would surely have wanted to nail Acreman and find out why he had failed to cry rape and would, at the very least, have considered the possibility that it was not the black janitor but Acreman himself who was doing the raping and that this was the first move in his cover-up. By ignoring the remark, it seemed to the defense, the ranger had ignored the truth—and kept the blind focus on the only available black man. It was the closest the defense had ever come to proving the malice that it believed was the fuel of the police investigation.

Stover was still trying to sketch out the prosecution's version of events and asked Styles if Peace had dismissed Acreman's remark as "bullshitting."

"That's correct," came the gravelly reply.

"Did you give this information to the Conroe Police Department?"

"No." The excitement at the defense table was plain to see. The ranger added: "Since he said that there wasn't anything to it, that he was just more or less joking about it, no, sir, I didn't."

De Geurin could hardly wait to come to grips with Wesley Styles.

When the ranger had first walked into court, De Geurin had felt a twinge of uncertainty. This was a real-life Texas Ranger. De Geurin was a Texan himself. He had grown up with the idea that a Texas Ranger truly was a special breed of man, someone who brought pride to the state of Texas. He had accepted that idea. The prospect of publicly exposing such a figure had depressed him. But not anymore.

As soon as Rick Stover sat down, De Geurin was up, laying out the ground for his attack.

The ranger told him he had spent five hundred hours investigating the murder and then agreed that Brandley was already in jail accused of murder before he worked even the first hour of his investigation. The ranger told De Geurin, too, that on the very first day of his inquiry, when he walked the three white janitors through the high school, he never warned any of them of their rights because he had already decided that none of them was a suspect.

"Did you let them know, Mr. Styles, that you had already made up your mind Clarence Brandley had committed this crime?"

"No, sir. I did not."

"In other words, you told them they were suspects?"

"No, sir."

"Of course, it was common knowledge. It was on the front page of the *Courier* the day he was arrested, wasn't it?"

The ranger straightened in his seat and in his deepest bass assured De Geurin that he had always been ready to charge anyone who had been guilty of this crime.

De Geurin bounced back at him. "That's the same reason you followed up on this statement that Icky Peace told you Gary Acreman was talking about this girl on the day of the murder before anybody knew she was missing?"

The ranger conceded that he had never asked Gary Acreman about it. He then conceded that he had never asked any of the other janitors about it—or, indeed, he finally conceded, anyone at all.

De Geurin kept at him. "You knew at that point that Gary Acreman had left the Vocational Building twice, at a time when the girl was supposed to be being killed, or the body hidden—during the crucial period of time for your investigation? Is that correct?"

"Yes, sir."

"And you knew that Gary Acreman had at least gone into the school himself during that critical period of time?"

"Yes, sir. . . ."

"By himself?"

"By himself, as far as I found out."

"And you knew he had come back and, according to Icky Peace, told Peace that there was a girl over there with Brandley and they're having fun. You knew that?"

"Yes, sir."

"Are you telling me that because that information came from Icky Peace, that you just disbelieved it from the beginning?"

The ranger shook his head. He sighed. Suddenly, he looked old. "Let's just put it this way. Say I made a mistake and I didn't check it out."

He had cracked. De Geurin moved in on him. "I take it that four hundred and fifty hours later in your investigation you still hadn't checked it out?"

The ranger nodded. "That's correct."

"And that five hundred hours of investigation was all dedicated to building a case against Clarence Brandley, wasn't it?"

Styles lifted a wrinkled finger and pointed it at Brandley sitting below him. "No evidence whatsoever gathered in this investigation or this trial pointed to any other person other than Clarence Lee Brandley."

De Geurin turned on the ranger and, in the kind of tone that mothers use on silly children, told him: "Well, of course, if Gary Acreman knew something about a girl over at the school at the time, it would lead a reasonable person to conclude, I would think, that maybe you ought to go ask Gary Acreman about that?"

The ranger's voice was a surly grumble. "Well, let's say I should have asked him, but I didn't."

De Geurin backed off, but he was not finished with him yet.

"Now you learned, didn't you, Mr. Styles, that the blood that was found on the clothing of the girl was Type A blood?"

"Yes, sir."

"And I take it that you now know that Gary Acreman's blood is Type A blood as well as James Dexter Robinson['s]. Did you know that?"

"If you say so, I'll have to take your word for it."

"Were you interested at the time, Mr. Styles, to see if the other janitors' blood matched the blood that was on the girl's clothing?"

"Let's say I didn't—I didn't have it checked. I didn't check it."

He had cracked again. De Geurin then challenged him over the hairs that been found on the dead girl. The ranger cracked once more and conceded that it would have been a good idea to compare the hairs with samples from the white janitors.

De Geurin asked him: "Would it surprise you to learn that the District Attorney opposed successfully in court all efforts of the defense to compare the scientific evidence to the other janitors?"

"I don't know anything about that."

"Are you aware now the hair has been lost?"

"Yes, sir." The ranger smiled. It was a mistake.

"Why do you smile?"

"Do what?"

"Why did you smile when you answered that, or did I misinterpret it?"

The ranger was not smiling anymore. "Well, I think it's

what all this controversy is over. That's my thought. And I read it in the newspaper."

De Geurin shook his head, more in sorrow than in anger. "Mr. Styles, can you for a moment place yourself in the shoes of Mr. Brandley—just for a moment?" Rick Stover jumped up and said this was improper. The judge overruled him. De Geurin continued. And the words started gushing through him again.

"Just for a moment, Mr. Styles, consider there is a pubic hair, possibly—and most probably—donated by the attacker, and imagine you're accused of being the attacker and that pubic hair is conclusively shown not to be yours and it's Caucasian. . . ." While the ranger sat solemnly in his seat, De Geurin laid out all the evidence that had now accumulated against Gary Acreman and reminded him of the DA's refusal to have Acreman's hairs given to the defense and of his own failure to compare Acreman's hairs. "Now, place yourself in Mr. Brandley's shoes just for a moment. And have the man that we thought in charge of the investigation on the stand, and I ask him, 'Did you learn that the pubic hair had been lost?'—and the man smiled!"

De Geurin's face was a mask of contempt. The ranger said he resented that. Rick Stover objected that it was not a proper question. The judge told them all to take a ten-minute break.

After the break Styles admitted that the tape he had produced to prove that he never threatened Icky Peace covered only thirty-two minutes of up to six hours of conversation and that in the course of the recording he had turned it off and then on again no fewer than thirty-one times. He said he had not realized that Peace had never read his own statement. He had, however, realized that the Conroe detectives had taken a day's holiday on the Sunday immediately after Cheryl Fergeson's murder and done no work on the investigation for twenty-four hours. He said he was not proud of that.

Finally, De Geurin brought him back to the central thrust of his questions: the blind focus of the investigation. "Isn't it true that all of your time was spent building a case against Brandley, a person you had already concluded was guilty?"

Styles raised his wrinkled finger again. "My investigation was for whoever was responsible, and it pointed to him. All the evidence pointed to Clarence Lee Brandley."

"And all that evidence was gathered after he was charged by you?"

"Some of it. Yes, sir."

"Well, all of your work was after he was charged, wasn't it?"

"Yes, sir."

"And the evidence that you were gathering was all circumstantial, wasn't it?"

"Yes, sir."

The ranger then suggested that the scientific evidence also pointed at Brandley. De Geurin recalled Brandley's knife, which had no fibers on it; Brandley's belt, which had no skin tissue on it; the scene of the crime and the dead girl's clothes, which had none of Brandley's fingerprints on them. He reminded the ranger of the Caucasian hairs on the girl's body that could not have been Brandley's and of the blood on the girl's shirt that could not have been Brandley's. "Now, any other scientific evidence that comes to mind that convinces you that it was Clarence Brandley?"

The ranger sighed again. "No, sir," he said.

De Geurin let him go.

Peter Speers seemed to have nothing left to fight with. The defense had waged ten days of pitched battle to seize the ground it now occupied, but Speers never rejoined the fight. Instead, he hovered around the edge of the battlefield, moving only to attack a straggler or turn over some dead issue.

He called two separate witnesses to dispute Icky Peace's claim that someone at the high school had threatened he could be fired if he gave evidence. He called two members of James Dexter Robinson's family to swear that the birthday party at which he had been photographed had taken place on August 17, 1980, and an FBI expert to testify that as far as he could tell, the photographs could have been taken on that date. He called Kelly Hendricks, the polygrapher who had been criticized for his role in the attorney general's investigation, to say that if the defense polygrapher, Glenn Raney, had really shouted at James Dexter Robinson and asked him one question sixty times, that would not be acceptable procedure.

He called Sam Martinez, who swore that he had told the truth in 1980 in his statement to the police and in his evidence at the trial. The defense had never made up its mind about Martinez. It sometimes seemed that he might have been involved in the crime, that he had watched the rape or stood outside while it was going on to make sure that Acreman and Robinson were not discovered. But he had never admitted anything, and neither John Sessum nor Gary Acreman had ever directly implicated him. One thing the defense did know about Martinez was that if its version of events was right, then he must be lying. He must have seen Acreman talking to the girl and the subsequent scuffle, even if he then turned and ran from it, as John Sessum had.

De Geurin set out to prove that Martinez was a liar. Within minutes Martinez had confirmed that Gary Acreman had been talking to the girl in the hallway and then acknowledged that he had never mentioned this in his statements to police or in his evidence at trial.

Martinez would go no further and would not admit to having seen the scuffle, but in his anxiety he insisted that he was not up on the landing where the girl was attacked but down at the bottom of the staircase, well away from the action. He went on to describe, just as he had at Brandley's trials, how Clarence Brandley had walked up the stairs, sent them all over to the Vocational Building, and then gone into a janitor's closet at the far end of the landing. But Martinez could not explain how it had been physically possible for him to see Brandley do this from the position in which he had so firmly placed himself.

The two sides were ready to begin their final arguments, but events intervened. Mary Johnson was still in Galveston. The Brandley case was now under her skin. She was terrified about her job and her court reporter's license. She had done nothing wrong, but she knew she was going to be punished. And she could not stop thinking about those horrible men from the attorney general's office who told her she had failed a lie detector test. She could not believe she had failed it. So she went to see Richard Reyna in his condo. Mary Johnson knew Reyna from the courthouse where he was always padding around, checking on cases or looking for documents. She asked him if he could find out whether she really had failed her lie detector test or whether they had been saying that to frighten her. They started talking.

At first she was just talking about the men from the attorney general's office and how they had treated her like a criminal and tried to humiliate her. Then she talked about everything. Reyna sat, shaking his head in disbelief, as her pride and her resentment at being bullied finally swept away her last loyalty to the courthouse.

As soon as she had finished, Reyna went straight to the phone and called Mike De Geurin. He told him that Mary Johnson had more information, and he outlined it for him.

In his room at the Tremont House, De Geurin listened. "Oh, my, oh, my," he said.

This time the court reporter was in tears before she even took her place on the witness stand. But she was no longer torn between the courthouse and the truth. It took her fewer than five minutes to rip away the final layers of secrecy.

In a room that was wreathed in silence, she took the fragile web of recollections that had been so carefully constructed by Peggy Stevens and Judge Martin and Jim Keeshan around the disappearance of the exhibits and swept it away. She had no doubt, she said, about what Peggy Stevens had been up to when Don Brown was trying to get to the truth. It might have slipped through a hole in the district clerk's memory, but Mary Johnson remembered clearly that Peggy Stevens had warned both Keeshan and Martin that the defense attorney was on to them. More than that, Stevens had run down to warn Jim Keeshan in person, and then, while Keeshan's secretary stood outside telling the defense attorney that she could not help him, Stevens and the district attorney had been hiding inside the office—or even in a closet in the office—giggling together. Mary Johnson said she had no doubt because she had been with Judge Martin a few minutes later when Peggy Stevens had come in, laughing, to share the fun with them.

Where once Don Brown had felt righteous anger at the way he had been treated that day, he now felt only disgust.

The court reporter turned then to her own predicament. She had always said she would be fired if she testified. Now the court reporter explained why she had always been so sure—because Judge John Martin had been making that plain to her for some time. The judge had told her that some people wanted to blame her for the disappearance of the exhibits and that she might be fired if he did not protect her. Then he had told her how worried he was about the Brandley hearing and how he lay awake at nights and how he would always say there had been no secret meetings with the DA. But he had told her he was not going to worry about it all anymore. He was going to leave it in her lap. The court reporter had no doubt what the judge meant. "He was telling me if I would keep my mouth shut on the witness stand about what truly happened, that I'd have a job."

It was already starting to happen. In the few days that had passed since she first gave evidence at this hearing, she said, Judge Martin had sent a message to her attorney that she should not come to work for two weeks. Judge Martin had plans, too, for Mike De Geurin. While Peter Speers sang a chorus of objections, the court reporter explained that in the last few days Judge Martin had come up with a new twist. He was due to pass sentence on a woman who was then being prosecuted by Peter Speers and was being defended by Mike De Geurin's brother, Dick, also a prominent Houston attorney. Judge Martin had been saying that if Mike De Geurin gave him a bad time on the witness stand in the Brandley case, he would make sure his brother's client suffered for it; it would make the difference between whether he gave her probation or a prison sentence.

Now it was De Geurin's turn to feel disgust. He and his brother and his father before him had spent their lives working in the courts of Texas. And now this man—a judge, no less— was ready to intimidate witnesses and abuse his power, fouling everything the courts were supposed to stand for, just for the sake of his own lust for success.

But Mary Johnson was still not finished. She had one more dark secret to share. As she spoke, the silence in the courtroom was finally cracked by shock, a shock that was all the more intense since it was this graceful, beautiful figure, sitting poised in the witness stand, who now disclosed the final ugliness: that Peggy Stevens had arranged with Judge Martin to have the black man killed on her birthday.

Now the disgust spread all along the public benches in a tide of sighs and whispers as the court reporter explained that she had no doubt about this—because her own birthday fell on the same date and they had expected her to join in the celebration.

It was Thursday night, October 8, 1987. After eleven days the two sides prepared to put their final arguments to Judge Pickett. All through the hearing a new and calm confidence had been building in the defense camp. Reyna and McCloskey, who had taken a backseat to the attorneys, went out fishing

together and agreed they had never felt so proud to belong
to a team. For Don Brown, who had once been elected to the
state assembly to fight racism by the people of Galveston, the
hearing had become a kind of homecoming, the fulfillment of
a lifelong mission.

For Nugent and De Geurin, who had decided to share the
next day's final speeches, there was still tension and the nagging knowledge that they were not yet finished. De Geurin,
whose courtroom performances were driven by impulse, found
it hard to decide how he and Nugent should divide up the
material for their speeches. They turned it over for a while,
and De Geurin finally came up with a formula. "You take the
facts," he said. "I'll handle the bullshit."

Nugent went off on his own, pacing for miles along the
beach until the small hours of the morning, trying to clear his
mind, stripping the saga that had now run for more than seven
years down to the skeleton that gave it shape. De Geurin took
to his hotel room, paced his way through a pack of cigarettes,
and filled one of his legal books with scrawled notes.

But when they came to court the next morning, they found
Peter Speers had presented them with one more task before
they could mount their finale. Judge John Martin was back
on the witness stand. The judge, whose face was bruised with
fatigue, explained that Mary Johnson was telling lies. There
was no truth in anything she had said the previous day. She
must want to hurt him, he suggested. Judge Martin seemed
particularly insulted at the suggestion that he had ordered
Brandley to die so that the courthouse could celebrate the
event at a birthday party. He was only doing his duty, he said,
in sentencing him to death. All the time the judge was laying
out his denial, Mike De Geurin was sitting at the defense table,
longing to get at the gaping hole he could see in the middle of
the story.

Stover asked the judge if he had realized that the date
was Peggy Stevens's birthday. "Not really. That's a birthday of several people I know, you know. But it wasn't set
on anyone's birthday. It was probably the most difficult—
one of the most difficult jobs I've ever had as a judge is
to sentence a man to death. And that's not an easy job.
It's a very difficult, onerous burden, and it's certainly not
something that I would do so somebody could have a party
or anything."

Finally, De Geurin got his chance.

First, he pawed Martin into position, inviting him to confirm that he did not enjoy sentencing a man to death. Then he cuffed him a little by persuading him to admit that Peggy Stevens had been in court to see him set the death date, challenging him to recall that Jim Keeshan had stopped his work in another case so that he could be there, too. He pawed him once more by inviting him to confirm beyond doubt that the only reason he had set this execution date was that it was his duty.

Then he clawed the Conroe judge without mercy by forcing him to admit that it was not his duty to set the death date at all: that he had been recused from the case long before, that Judge Coker had been in charge of it, and that he was not supposed to take any further part in the proceedings at all, let alone sentence the defendant to die.

Clarence Brandley watched John Martin retreat from the court, his eyes cast down on the ground. He would not look at Brandley. None of them would. It had been different in the courthouse in Conroe, when they had been sitting up there with all their authority. They could look at him then and tell him he was going to die. But these ten days Brandley had sat here and stared straight into their faces, and none of them had dared look back into his eyes—these people who were supposed to stand for justice.

Brandley wanted nothing more to do with them. He did not even want to think about them. He thought instead about the people who had helped him. Truly, they made him feel humble. Not nigger-humble, bowing and scraping. But humble the way any man—black or white—would feel when he saw people come out and take risks like that for him. His heart went out to Janet Dial and Mary Johnson and Ed Payne and even John Sessum, even though he did still say he was a racist. All he had ever prayed for was that someone would tell the truth. Just tell it like it was. All he prayed for now was that this Judge Pickett would be fair with him.

The courtroom settled down for the final speeches. It was more crowded than ever. All along the back of the court, flanking the judge like bodyguards, there were Texas Rangers, standing with their legs apart and their arms folded and pistols on their hips, staring silently at all the dark faces. They said they were there for crowd control. The defense attorneys thought they were there to bolster their beleaguered colleague, to show who was really boss.

On his walk along the beach Paul Nugent had found the skeleton that shaped the case of Clarence Brandley. Now he tried to lay it out before Judge Pickett and the three hundred spectators: the black ministers who felt intimidated by the white courthouse; the officer who elected the "nigger" suspect; the systematic exclusion of black jurors; the disproportionate use of the death sentence on black defendants; the lone juror who had been hounded as a "nigger lover"; the mayor who said "nigger"; the sheriff who said "nigger"; the district attorney who said "nigger." The skeleton soon became clear to see.

Nugent then fleshed it out: the long trail of lost evidence; the ranger and his blind focus; the white janitors who now admitted they had lied and who had been tied to their lies by threats; the clues that had never been investigated and the questions that had never been asked: the twenty-three jurors in two trials who had joined the project to convict Clarence Brandley. The young attorney sat down to an angry silence.

Peter Speers began his speech by oiling the wheels of justice. "Judge Pickett, I'd like to preface my remarks by saying I've appreciated your patience and tolerance during this rather arduous ordeal over the last two weeks. I think it can fairly be said that Clarence Brandley got a full and fair hearing." Then he fought back with the letter of the law and accused the defense attorneys of dragging up all kinds of evidence that should not have been mentioned. If they wanted to claim the death penalty was used in a racist fashion, they should have done that back at the original trial; it was not correct procedure to raise it now. Bill Srack's experience was irrelevant because he was a juror in the first trial, whereas this hearing was concerned with the conviction that had arisen from the second trial. The loss of the exhibits was no longer a debatable issue since it had already been dealt with by the court in Austin, as had the allegation that there was a conspiracy to conceal their loss, although, he added, the word "conspiracy" might not have been used. The only evidence that Judge Martin and Jim Keeshan had held secret meetings was hearsay, he complained. The evidence that Brandley was innocent was unbelievable, and anyway, even if everything the defense said was true, it made no difference because according to the law, new facts were not relevant to the courts more than thirty days after a conviction.

At some point during Peter Speers's speech, Mike De Geurin's blood started to boil. He had seen DA's doing this before, trying to use the law to obstruct justice. He loathed it. As soon as the district attorney had finished, he jumped forward, glanced once at his padful of notes, shoved them under his left arm, and never consulted them again. How could all this be irrelevant? he asked. What about Janet Dial and her courage? What about Mary Johnson and her tears? At what personal cost had these people dared to tell the truth?

"Apparently, Mr. Speers has never done such a thing or he would know how difficult it is and what a terrible price a person pays for telling the truth in Montgomery County when it's embarrassing to the officials. Where is Mary Johnson tomorrow? Where is Janet Dial? What do they have to gain from testifying the way they did?

"William Srack. What has he had to endure because he did his duty and when he found that the evidence was insufficient, he so voted and didn't go along with the pack?

"Is it irrelevant to prove the 'project' atmosphere, the chilling effect, the judge that tells his court reporter 'Keep your mouth shut or you lose your job'?"

And what about the secret meetings between Judge Martin and the DA? Were they irrelevant? What about the secret meeting between an earlier judge, Judge Alworth, and the DA when they raised Brandley's bail bond without telling the defense?

"The only legal argument we learned about in that hearing is the Sheriff didn't want the little nigger on the street."

What about Don Brown and George Morris, "struggling along in Conroe, fighting for this man's liberty, going along with the Rules of Evidence and law, like they're supposed to?

"And then let's skip from there to after the trial, what can we prove beyond doubt . . ."

De Geurin suddenly abandoned the sentence and turned on Peter Speers. "And, by the way, Mr. Speers, you questioned whether or not I used the word 'conspiracy.' If I have not used it, I'll use it now. They conspired against Clarence Brandley. They conspired to trick Don Brown and they conspired to trick George Morris.

"Not only did they try to keep secret that all of the evidence was lost in the case, but much more, much worse than that. In addition to that, in keeping it secret, they made fake exhibits and entered fake exhibits into official records hoping that Don Brown wouldn't find out about it. And not only that, but they thought it was funny. . . .

"Now, that's not irrelevant. If it is, then I have missed the boat, Your Honor, all the way through."

He finally paused and turned back toward the defense table. Paul Nugent saw his eyes were brimming with tears.

Then his words rushed on again, over the missing exhibits, and the district clerk's birthday, and the blind focus of the investigation, and all the evidence that had now emerged about Brandley's innocence.

He turned to Judge Perry Pickett. "You put all that together, Judge. What you have is this county sucking the oxygen out of the courtroom until you suffocate, And I ask for a new trial for Clarence Brandley—breathe some fresh air back into the justice system."

From his bench Judge Pickett looked solemnly down on the attorneys gazing up, and at the reporters with their pens poised, and at Clarence Brandley still sitting solid as a rock at the defense table, and at all the rows of spectators with their hopes written across their faces, and he put down his pipe and began to speak.

"This is the two hundredth anniversary of our Constitution. One of the basic rights of this noble document is equal justice under the law and the inherent dignity of mankind.

"For the past ten days, I have presided over an evidentiary hearing, tried to determine if equal justice under the law has been self-evident from all the evidence adduced under oath.

"The litany of events so graphically described by the witnesses—some of it chilling and shocking—leads me to the conclusion that the pervasive shadow of darkness has obscured the light of fundamental decency and human rights. I can only sadly state that justice has been on trial here, but of more significance, injustice has been on trial.

"My statement of facts and conclusions of law to the Court of Criminal Appeals will be conclusive and unequivocal.

"I shall recommend a new trial for the defendant and, if granted, recommend the trial be removed from Montgomery County."

Chapter Ten

Judge Pickett had hardly finished speaking before pandemonium seized the courtroom. Don Brown was hugging Brandley. Reyna and McCloskey were swaying in each other's arms. Nugent and De Geurin were shaking hands and smiling their thanks all over the court. The reporters were shouting and shoving. Reverend Boney was leading a victory chant, and all the old ladies were standing up, clapping and cooing and praising the Lord.

As the jubilation flooded around Clarence Brandley, the mask of self-control that had concealed him through the hearing finally broke, and he began to weep.

Peter Speers swept up his papers and scuttled swiftly through the crowd toward a waiting car, pressing through the howling pack of newspaper and TV reporters with their babble of questions, pausing only briefly as he ducked into his car to mumble a hasty "no comment."

The people of Dugan bubbled out of the courthouse, past the scowling Montgomery County deputies and the sour-faced Texas Rangers, hugging and kissing the attorneys and the investigators, singing and chanting "Jus-tice! Jus-tice!"

For a while the defense camp were tempted to believe that all would be well. They had only to wait for justice to take its course: Judge Pickett would produce his detailed findings of fact; the Court of Criminal Appeals would agree that Brandley should have a new trial; Peter Speers would have to acknowledge that there could be no trial since all the evidence had been either thrown away or discredited. Brandley, the defense believed, would be free by Christmas.

On November 19, 1987, the wheels of justice began to turn. Judge Pickett produced his findings, forty-seven pages of unyielding analysis. The judge's opening words set the tone for what followed. "After ten days of trial," he wrote, "the court became convinced that Clarence Lee Brandley did not receive a fair trial, was denied the most basic fundamental rights of due process of law, and did not commit the crime for which he now resides on death row."

The judge went on to give the defense a clean sweep of the case. He found that the evidence showed not only that Clarence Brandley was innocent but that "Gary Acreman and James Dexter Robinson are prime suspects and probably were responsible for the death of Cheryl Dee Fergeson." Both Acreman and Robinson, he said, had lied at the Galveston hearing.

He moved through the Conroe courthouse like vengeance.

Judge John Martin, he said, was a liar. "The court finds that Judge Martin's testimony, perhaps tempered by a motive for self-preservation, was simply not credible." Judge Martin, he concluded, had held secret meetings with the DA during the trial as well as after the disappearance of the exhibits, and he had been hostile to Brandley and to any other black people who came into court.

The former district attorney, now the Honorable Judge James Keeshan, he found, was a liar. Specifically, Pickett ruled that despite his denials, Keeshan had held secret meetings with Judge Alworth at which Brandley's bail bond was hiked, that he had also held secret meetings with Judge Martin at which they had rehearsed key rulings in Brandley's second trial, that he had referred to Brandley as "this little nigger," that he had intended to cover up the disappearance of the exhibits and tried to deceive the defense with fakes, that he had deliberately and wrongly concealed other evidence from the defense, and that he had showed a "personal white versus black posture."

Peggy Stevens, he said, was a liar. She was "not a credible witness and her testimony was untruthful." In particular, he found that despite her denials, she had asked Judge Martin to arrange for Brandley to die on her birthday and that she had hidden with Jim Keeshan and laughed while Don Brown stood outside trying to find the missing exhibits. This was, he said, "a sordid instance where the 'project-like' mentality overbore any sense of justice and decency at the courthouse."

Wesley Styles was also a liar. The judge found that the ranger had threatened John Sessum, that he had roughed up Icky Peace and threatened to blow out his brains, that he had deliberately concealed the tape recording of his conversation with Peace and then lied about it in court, and that he had consistently kept a blind focus on Clarence Brandley. "Styles failed to conduct a proper investigation in that the Ranger operated with the state of mind that he had already gotten his man, and that he was not going to investigate any leads that might prove his preconception wrong."

Judge Pickett even jabbed at Peter Speers, whose behavior had never been formally examined by the court, and recorded his failure to tell the defense of evidence that tended to show Brandley's innocence, first when he buried Brenda Medina's statement and then when he failed to disclose that Ranger Styles had found his tape recording of Icky Peace ten days before the Galveston hearing began.

Judge Pickett left no doubt about why, in his view, the courthouse had conspired to put Clarence Brandley to death for Cheryl Fergeson's murder. "The court unequivocally concludes," he wrote, "that the color of Clarence Brandley's skin was a substantial factor which pervaded all aspects of the State's capital prosecution against him, and was an impermissible factor which significantly influenced the investigation, trial and post-trial proceedings. The tone of the courtroom, as fostered by the District Attorney's office, the judge and the District Clerk's office, was white against black."

Once the black janitor had been elected as the prime suspect, Judge Pickett wrote, the courthouse set out to convict him, regardless of the facts. "The authorities wholly ignored any evidence, or leads to evidence, which might prove inconsistent with their premature conclusion that Brandley had committed the crime. The conclusion is inescapable that the investigation was conducted not to solve the crime, but to convict Brandley."

By the time he reached the last page of his findings, Judge Pickett, this conservative veteran of the Texan bench, had made ruins of all the pillars that supported the reputation of Conroe and its courthouse. "In the thirty years this court has presided over matters in the judicial system, no case has presented a more shocking scenario of the effects of racial prejudice, perjured testimony, witness intimidation, an investigation the outcome of which was predetermined, and public officials who for whatever motives lost sight of what is right and just.

"The continued incarceration of Clarence Lee Brandley under these circumstances is an affront to the basic notions of fairness and justice."

All those who had been put on trial by the defense— Acreman, Robinson, Conroe and its courthouse—had been found guilty. And Clarence Lee Brandley had been declared innocent. The victory was total.

Soon after Judge Pickett published his findings, John Henry Faulk found himself once again by the riverside north of Conroe with his fishing rod and his old friend, and once again, just as they had on the day after Cheryl Fergeson's murder, they fell to talking about these sad events and about the judgment of Perry Pickett. After all these years Faulk had learned to live with his friend's opinions about black people. Underneath it all he knew his friend was intelligent and well informed in his way. So Faulk was pleased to hear him admit that it looked as if Clarence Brandley might be innocent.

The two men waited awhile, watching the water, and then his friend spoke again. "Yep." He sighed and scratched his chin. "Ah reckon it must a bin some other nigger done it."

Conroe is the kind of town where a stranger might never notice the truth. It seems clean and efficient, traffic lights blinking on and off, a smiling policewoman handing out parking tickets, ordinary people going about their business. No one stands in the courthouse square denouncing black people. There are no signs on the edge of town like those that used to stand in redneck towns warning NIGGER, DON'T LET THE SUN SET ON YOU HERE. It is part of the change that has taken place since the civil rights movement that the *Courier* now reports the Miss Black Conroe Pageant and gives space on its sports pages to black football players at the high school. In conversation white people in Conroe speak about black people with calm confidence.

When Perry Pickett effectively convicted the town of racism in the fall of 1987, many white people seemed shocked. Carl Barton, Jr., for example, who had been reelected mayor of

Conroe every two years since 1978, insisted he had never come across such a thing in all his years in the town. "We don't have racism here. We never have had. This is a real tight little community, black and white together. It's just never been a problem."

Barton was sitting in his office near the courthouse square, rolling a cigar as thick as a swan's neck between the fingers of his right hand. Although he had been a businessman for most of his working life, he still had the build of a workingman, like his father, who had been a pumper in the East Texas oil fields: a stocky frame, muscular hands, and forearms matted with thick black hair. Mayor Barton was unmoved by Judge Pickett's findings.

"I'll tell you the truth about that Brandley case," he said, lighting up his cigar at last. "The crime shocked a lot of people. People were upset about it all right, but the evidence was such that it seemed at the time that the right man had been got. And I'll tell you this: if there was any doubt at all, I certainly would be the first to say that he deserves a new trial. But I don't see where a judge can start deciding who all is guilty or innocent. That's for a jury and, you know, twenty-three jurors agreed that Brandley was guilty."

In the mayor's eyes Conroe was a happy town. Fueled by workers from the Northeast moving south in search of better living standards, Montgomery County had become the fastest-growing county in the USA. Mayor Barton had personally pioneered the floating of a public works bond that had raised $19 million and given Conroe new roads, huge reservoirs of water, new sewers, new garbage disposal—all the public facilities it needed for the foreseeable future. Now new industries were moving in. The town was booming. "This is a great little place," he said. "And the best thing about it is the people. They're the friendliest you'll ever meet."

A cynic might have listened to the words of Mayor Barton and dismissed him as a liar, but the truth about the white people of Conroe was more subtle than that. That fall almost all of them agreed with the mayor that their town was not racist, and in saying that, they showed every sign of sincerity. To an outsider, armed with the Brandley case and the history of their town, it might have been obvious that they were wrong, but they seemed genuinely not to realize that. They were happy to talk about their town and about the Brandley case, eager to discuss the role of black people in Conroe, to admit the problems of the past, and to explain the success of the present. Yet when they did so, they protested too much. It was like listening to an alcoholic who swears he has not been drinking and who launches into a lengthy account of his movements that might be persuasive if it were not for the smell of alcohol on his breath that becomes more obvious and more destructive of his story with every word he speaks. So it was in Conroe after the Galveston hearing. The more people sincerely denied their racism, the clearer it became.

At the Chamber of Commerce, Don Moore, the president, declared his satisfaction that black people had the same chance as white people to run big businesses in Conroe, and to prove his point he produced a glossy color fifty-five-page brochure about the town's business community in which every face was white.

Art Rohsner, a retired frozen-food salesman who had lived in Conroe for more than fifty years, insisted that all this talk about racism was a misunderstanding. "I was born in Pennsylvania, and I have no doubt that there is less discrimination in the South—and I mean true discrimination—than there is in the North. When I came down here, I was amazed at how kindly the colored people were treated. But the blacks don't try to mix in. You never see them at council meetings. They may be poor, but I can't see any reason why they should not have prospered. People have to work for a living. I only wish that some of these blacks would understand that."

Rohsner lives the life of a full-time citizen, constantly writing letters to the *Courier*, attending council meetings, and harrying local politicians. Just like his mayor, he was sure that Brandley was guilty. "Those janitors down there, their first testimony was true, and at this point their testimony is not worth a damn. They may have thrown out some old evidence, but that was years after the conviction and years after the appeal was refused—years after. How long are they supposed to keep it? Keeshan and Speers are just politicians like the rest of them, but I don't see how they've mishandled this case. That judge down in Galveston was strictly out of line. How in hell can a judge say Brandley is innocent when a jury says he is guilty? Under law he is guilty. Nobody has proved he is innocent. I am sure that if somebody came up and proved that he is innocent, then the people of Conroe would applaud and get him out of there, but nobody has proved it. No, sir. All they have is Brandley's word for it."

Faye Cryar was the same. An elderly white woman with pearl earrings and a grandmotherly smile, she said she had definitely heard that Brandley was guilty because he was the only one who could have got in that auditorium. She was sure of that, and, she continued in her gentle voice, she had lived in Conroe most of her life and she had never had anything against colored folk. To illustrate her point, she recalled the time of integration, which she said was never needed in Conroe.

At that time, in the 1960s, she belonged to a Home Demonstration Club that was a product originally of the land-grant college. Cryar and the other women in the club taught people how to sew, how to prepare food. But when integration came, the college sent a woman to say they had to integrate with the colored women, who had their own group. "Well, we didn't want to do that. Why should we? We didn't know the colored women and the colored women didn't know us." So she and her friends all resigned and formed their own club, nothing to do with the land-grant college. They called it the Lamplighters because it was shedding light. They had their own bylaws. You couldn't join unless you were invited and then you had to be voted in. Cryar said the colored women didn't mind. "They had their own club, and you know how colored people stick together. White people have their friends, and colored people have theirs. Colored people have different customs. They wouldn't want to be in a club for white people." Just the same as her church, which has three thousand members, and there are only two or three colored people that ever go to the church. "Colored people are different."

As a matter of fact, Cryar said, there was more opposition to integration from the blacks in Conroe than from the whites. "They wanted to keep things the way they were because they felt secure in their own group. They were afraid of being shunned." She and her friends helped them all the same because, as she said, she has never had anything against colored folk.

This was not the legendary racism of the Old South, red in tooth and claw. There was no venom, no scorn, and certainly no guilt. This was a deeper, subtler, more mysterious approach, which took heed of the new climate in which the brazen simplicities of the old days were no longer acceptable. This was racism with a smiling face—the easy assumptions of white people who had always lived with black underdogs. The mayor and people like Art Rohsner and Faye Cryar took it for granted that black people lived in shinny shacks while white people lived in brick houses with carports and central air conditioning. It was not an issue; it was simply a fact of life. And if black people were too poor to eat in the white restaurants and spent their time instead in their dirty juke joints, then that, too, was just the way things were. White children played in sandpits; black children played in the dirt. In their eyes black people not only naturally lived in these conditions but liked it. There was no hint that people in Dugan ever feared their white neighbors or resented their own poverty or mourned the dead-end prospects of their young. In the same way the white people took it for granted that black people were different—lazy or stupid, like the black people in the old jokes column the *Courier* used to run. There had always been "good niggers" and "bad niggers," and even though the Chamber of Commerce might now refer to them as "ethnics," the myths about black people had not changed. The myths made it easy to accept their living conditions and to explain their separateness.

In the months after Judge Pickett's ruling the most senior black law officer in the town, Sergeant Leonard Taylor, complained of racism in the sheriff's department. He said the department was run on "a good ol' boy system." One of the incidents he complained about was the posting of a notice that announced: OPEN SEASON ON PORCH MONKEYS, ALSO KNOWN AS NEGRO, NIGGER, BURRHEADS, HOUSE APES, JUNGLE BUNNIES AND SAUCERLIPS. THIS SEASON HAS NO RELATION TO THE PORCH MONKEY BREEDING SEASON WHICH IS YEAR ROUND. When he complained, he was fired. No one in the town came to his defense. Around the same time a group of fifty black parents formed a committee to protest racism in Conroe schools. They said an "unwritten code" worked against their children. They were allowed onto the sports teams, but they were excluded from cheerleading. They were not encouraged to lead or to do well in class. There was a shortage of black teachers and guest speakers. The school superintendent, Dr. Richard Griffin, said he had taught in towns where they had problems, but Conroe really never had suffered that way. "I just don't see it," he said.

Much of this new, gentle racism was passive—failing to notice that the town was still physically segregated, failing to be shocked by black inequality. The active, aggressive racism that Judge Pickett had seen in the Brandley case flowed directly from these blithe assumptions. In spite of all that had been revealed at Galveston, these people still truly believed that Brandley should die, and they had gathered twisted scraps of fact to prove it. There might have been those in the courthouse who knew the true facts well enough to know beyond doubt that Brandley was innocent; their racism consisted in their belief that they could sacrifice a worthless black life for their pride and their careers. But in the town they were still happy to believe that Brandley was guilty. It was easy. It required no bad conscience or any wrestling with the facts. Their racism was so natural it was almost benign. White townspeople simply took it for granted that a black man would commit a crime like that.

A sheriff's deputy confided that Brandley not only had killed that girl at the high school but had also raped his own mother. Lucy Proctor, one of the reporters who had covered the Brandley case for the *Courier*, declared: "There is no way Brandley is innocent. I wouldn't believe him if he told me there was oxygen in the air."

There were a very few whites who admitted that Brandley was innocent and that there was racism in Conroe, but even they seemed unable to see the racism in themselves. In his office by the courthouse square the veteran attorney W.B. Etheridge, who had a reputation as a decent man and had helped the Brandley defense, recalled the day when as a child he had seen Joe Winters burned to death in the square outside the window where he now sat. "It's mob violence," he said. "You get carried away with things like that, and then later on you wonder why in the world did you ever do a thing like that. But I think the blacks took the attitude that he got what was coming to him. At that time we had some of the best black folk that ever were in Conroe. They weren't unruly; they didn't give any problems at all. Fact of the matter is, blacks haven't had that much to complain about. They are just a different kind of creature. We have some blacks who are intelligent, but most of them . . ." Etheridge waved his hand in the air, as if to dismiss the thought of them. Then he continued. "Anytime the blacks move into a place, it goes downhill. One or two blacks go into a neighborhood, land values drop, all the trash everywhere, the don't-care attitude—'Why should we work?' Crime everywhere. There are always exceptions. Some blacks are intelligent, but most of them . . ." Etheridge went on to describe the day that Bob White was shot dead in a Conroe courtroom, referring to White throughout his story as "the nigger."

The town's bad ways were plain to see for Peggy Riggle, the Bette Midler look-alike who had lost her job in the *Courier*'s telemarketing department after testifying for Brandley at Galveston. "I'm not going to say there's no racism in Conroe," she said, "because there is. Tell the truth, Conroe is one bigoted little town. You just don't see blacks hanging out with whites. The more you go out into the country, the worse it gets, and out in east county, well, the mentality there—no one ever taught them about charity. Montgomery County is just one hypocritical county, if you want to know the truth."

But Peggy Riggle insisted that each generation got a little better. Six generations back, her family had owned slaves, but her own father wouldn't stand for any racism. There was one Sunday, she recalled, when he took the family to a restaurant in Hillsboro and two black couples who were very well dressed and nice came in, but the restaurant refused them service. Her father got the family up and made them leave. "If you won't serve them, you won't serve me," he said. Of course, Riggle added, her father and mother never would have let a black person visit their house, never would have dreamed of it. They didn't even know any black people. But each generation got better, she believed. "I've had black friends," she said. "Sure I have. Not boyfriends, you understand. I'd never do that because right, wrong, or indifferent, I can't help the way I feel. It just wouldn't be right. One of my kids now, they might go out with blacks, and they might say, 'I'm in love with this black girl and she is decent,' but of course my first question would be 'Well, how decent?' "

As Conroe came to terms with Judge Pickett's findings, Clarence Brandley waited for his freedom. His hope that he would be released by Christmas soon faded as the nine judges of the Court of Criminal Appeals relapsed into silence, some of them evidently distracted by the election primaries they had to fight the coming March, none of them willing to speak out on Brandley's behalf. Twice before, this court had failed him. Despite all the joy of the victory at Galveston, Brandley now began to wonder whether his life was safe, whether these nine white judges had the political courage to stand up for him.

He saw the backlash against Judge Pickett gather strength in Conroe. Peter Speers publicly denounced the judge, telling the press that he was illogical and irrational and "totally lacking in any attempt at objectivity." The *Courier* ran a front-page report detailing some of the conclusions of the attorney general's investigators. Soon after Christmas Judge John Martin fired his court reporter, Mary Johnson. Since the day she had tearfully put her fears behind her and testified at Galveston, Johnson had never been allowed back to her work. She had been suspended immediately after the hearing. No one from the courthouse would have anything to do with her. She had tried to work as a free-lance, hiring herself out as a court reporter, but all the judges and the attorneys shied away from her. Some of the defense attorneys told her they were sorry but they could not jeopardize their clients' chances by being seen with her. She no longer felt safe going into town and drove miles in the opposite direction to do her shopping. Someone called her up and warned her to get out of Montgomery County. Someone went to her little office in The Woodlands, south of Conroe, and painted an obscenity on her window. Now she had been formally fired, just as she had always said she would be if she dared to tell the truth.

In Houston, the Reverend Don Boney was arrested. The police said they had found a small amount of cocaine in his pocket. Boney, a Baptist minister, furiously denied the charge. He said that he was "completely against drug use" and that the police had searched him twice before claiming to find anything. He suggested that the law was being abused to punish him for his role in the campaign for Clarence Brandley.

Finally, in March 1988, after a delay of more than four months and after the election primaries were over, the judges in Austin announced that both sides in the Brandley case would have to submit written briefs before they could make a decision. In the meantime, despite Judge Pickett's declaration that it was an affront to the basic notions of fairness and justice, the incarceration of Clarence Brandley continued.

Jim McDougal sat at his kitchen table, his body hunched forward, pools of sweat filling the armpits of his shirt, his right hand shoved across the table, fingering his heavy black pistol. "I'll kill 'em," he said. "I'm not kidding. If they come for me, I'll kill 'em."

McDougal had never thought he would hear himself talk that way about anyone and certainly not about law enforcement officers. Now, after all that had happened, he admitted he had been pretty damned innocent in the past, but he had truly believed that law officers were basically honest, and that had had a lot to do with why he had become one. Now it was all over. After twelve years' service he had been fired by Joe Corley, the sheriff of Montgomery County, and his former colleagues were threatening his life. His offense had been simple.

Working on traffic duty, he had kept coming across cases in which drivers who were involved in one-car accidents were not having their blood tested for alcohol. He knew that was bullshit. How else were you going to know if the man had been drinking? Then there were cases of driving while intoxicated that he would bring in only later to be told to drop the charges. It did not take him too long to find out what was going on. These drivers were paying bribes to some of the senior deputies to have evidence destroyed or to get the paperwork fixed. McDougal started taking his own blood samples. Then he tape-recorded some conversations in the sheriff's department, and the next time he found a driver bribing his way out of trouble, he went and complained to his bosses and told them that law enforcement in Montgomery County was a joke. That was when they fired him.

Since then he had been fighting and looking over his shoulder. He had taken his evidence to the DA's office, and just in case the prosecutors got any ideas about covering it up, he had taken it to the press, too. Already three senior deputies had been forced to resign, and Jim McDougal was still gathering evidence—about illegal phone tapping, about the reason why no cocaine dealers had been busted in Montgomery County, and about the hit squad of deputies that settled scores with people who dared to cross the courthouse. That was what worried him. Just the other day his neighbor had seen a car going by really slow, stopping right by his driveway. The neighbor had taken the number, and McDougal had traced it. Sure enough, it belonged to a detective from the hit squad. "I went straight into the sheriff's department, and I told them to get their people away from me or there's gonna be trouble. And I told 'em I'm not kidding."

Jim McDougal's allegations were only part of an avalanche of complaints that tumbled down on Conroe as the Clarence

Brandley case came to a head. In a way it was like the summer when the Brandley case had started, back in August 1980, when the land had been poisoned by the sun and every living thing was withered and brown, and wildfires were breaking out every day in some different corner of the county, and the firemen were racing from one outbreak to another, trying to keep control. Only now it was not fire but some kind of rottenness in the town that kept breaking out, as if all the corruption and greed could no longer be contained. Peter Speers was in the middle of it all, rushing from one crisis to another.

There was a wrecker driver, Vernon Cowan, who said he had been pushed out of business by Sheriff Joe Corley because he refused to pay him money. Since then, Cowan said, he had been shot at, beaten and robbed by a deputy, had his house burned to the ground by deputies, had three cars and two trucks torched, seen police cars prowling around his house, and been the victim of a failed attempt to plant stolen goods in his truck. One of Cowan's sons, John, said he had been beaten by deputies until he had agreed to make a statement against his father. Another son, Jay, said deputies had brutalized him and threatened him with homosexual rape until he agreed to make a similar statement. A Houston journalist who started to investigate had his windows shot out, and Cowan's attorney, a former FBI agent named Phil Swisher, said that deputies had tried to plant cocaine in his car and that someone had fired shots into his home.

A federal jury found that Sheriff Corley had been routinely beating up prisoners in his custody. The jury ordered the county to pay forty thousand dollars in damages, but the sheriff lodged an appeal. A former chief deputy, Steve Graeter, told the federal jury how Sheriff Corley had strapped a prisoner into a barber's chair and punched him until he was exhausted and how he himself had been victimized for trying to expose the incident. A prisoner who complained that the sheriff broke his nose and jaw said he had been shot at, hit by a speeding car, and arrested by deputies who carried machine guns, ordered him to crawl through the dirt, and tried to force him to drop his complaint.

A group of ex-prisoners joined the wrecker driver's family in suing the Montgomery County Sheriff's Department under the RICO statute. As far as anyone knew, it was the first time the anti-Mafia law had ever been used against a law enforcement agency.

A scandal rocked the county's Republican party, which had ridden to power in Conroe on Ronald Reagan's coattails, ending decades of Democratic supremacy, and which now numbered numerous former Democrats, including Jim Keeshan and Peter Speers, among its members. One of the party's biggest wheels, County Commissioner Weldon Locke, was arrested and charged with swindling the county out of $220,000. A justice of the peace had been helping him in the swindle. A local couple, Kaye and Joe McCoy, who helped to unearth the evidence of his corruption, complained that the DA's office had tried to persuade them that Locke had committed no offense, and that a Conroe judge had issued an unlawful gagging order against them forbidding them to say anything that might embarrass Locke. On the day he was due to appear in the courthouse to be arraigned, Locke was run down by a cement truck on I-45. Some people in the town said he had been murdered to stop him from exposing corruption by other big wheels in the Republican party. But the Houston medical examiner, Dr. Joseph Jachimczyk, looked into it and said it was certainly suicide.

Another county commissioner, Bo Calfee, admitted accepting nine thousand dollars from a businessman. In separate incidents five different justices of the peace were caught embezzling public money. A seventy-six-year-old municipal judge admitted soliciting sexual favors from a twenty-one-year-old woman who was trying to pay a delinquent traffic ticket. An official in the county tax collector's office was charged with stealing nearly three thousand dollars from public funds. A county constable admitted forging records to conceal the disappearance of money from his office. Three jailers were fired for taking a prisoner on a two-day shopping spree. Eight Conroe officials admitted they had received illegal campaign contributions. The minister of the First Methodist Church was jailed for ten years after failing to pay eighty-nine thousand dollars in restitution to two elderly spinsters he had swindled in a crooked land deal. Two employees of the school district were investigated, one for embezzling twenty-five thousand dollars, the other for molesting young children. A deputy who had been fired from two previous law enforcement jobs for sexually assaulting young women was fired again after a seventeen-year-old Californian complained that she had been forced to have oral sex with him. A new hearing for a convicted murderer, Glenn Earl Martin, was delayed because key evidence was missing from the courthouse.

Yet just as the white people of Conroe overlooked the truth about black people in their town, so they appeared to accept the corruption of officials as if it were part of their way of life. There was no campaign in the *Courier* to clean up the courthouse. There was no outcry from the city council or the county commissioners. Corruption had become so common that it was no longer controversial. For generations the courthouse authorities had respected the law in the morning and ignored it in the afternoon. If the rules were in the way, they were simply set aside as an inconvenience. It had been that way in the old days, and it had not changed. Corruption had become a habit. And the people of Conroe continued to tolerate it, as if by denying that their leaders were corrupt, they could excuse themselves for having elected them.

In the fall of 1988 there were elections in Conroe. The townspeople had a chance to register their feelings about some of the people who had run the Brandley case and who had been hit by the avalanche of new complaints. Peter Speers and Judge John Martin were the only officials from the Brandley case who had to run that year. Both had been condemned by Judge Pickett, both had played key roles in pursuing a man who had now been declared innocent, but the people of Conroe voted both of them back into office for new four-year terms. Sheriff Joe Corley also had to run for reelection. A federal jury had condemned him for beating prisoners, and he, too, was given the support of his town.

By the fall of 1988 Clarence Brandley had seen twenty-seven men led to their death through the door at the end of death row in Huntsville. Every time it happened, it was tough. Inside that place you got close to people. You had to if you were going to survive. So when another man was taken away, everybody felt it. After Galveston it had been different. The other guys could hardly believe the things that were coming out of that hearing. Then he had won. And when he won, they all won. They all scored a point against the system, and more than that, if he finally ended up raising some big legal issue, there were guys in there whose lives might also be saved because of it. Then as the months passed and the judges in Austin still showed no sign of interest in Judge Pickett's urgent demand for justice, they relapsed into pessimism and hopelessness.

Brandley was more and more afraid that the judges were more interested in pleasing their white voters than in seeing justice done. They had waited for the primaries to be out of the way before they decided that they needed written briefs from the attorneys. They had had the briefs since June, yet they had said nothing.

In July of that year, 1988, in Princeton, in an elegant house where Woodrow Wilson once lived, a man with a white collar around his neck and a crucifix on the wall heard that the nine judges had gone off for their summer vacations without a word about Clarence Brandley. "Those sons of bitches," he said.

Brandley believed that the judges were now holding out for the November election. Sure enough, no sooner had the judges been reelected to their jobs than they announced that they would hold a hearing to consider Brandley's case. They made their announcement one year and eleven days after Judge Pickett had ruled that his incarceration was an affront to justice.

Brandley's brother O.T. told the press: "I guess this is progress, but it takes longer for a black person to get justice than it takes for a white person." The hearing was set for January 18, 1989.

The day before the hearing Mike De Geurin flew into Austin from Houston holding a legal notepad on which he had written four words. They were the heart of the message he was going to try to present to the nine judges the next day. He had written: "Bumblebee on a billboard."

It was something his father, who had been an attorney and then a judge, had once told him: that you must never get so close to the fragmented details and dry legalities of a case that the big picture is lost the way the message on a billboard is hidden from a bumblebee in the middle of it.

De Geurin was trying hard to feel confident, but it was not easy. If these judges had wanted to see the big picture—that Brandley was innocent and had to be released—then they would have opened the door of his cell months ago, back when the case was fresh after the hearing in Galveston. Instead, it seemed, they had crawled over the meat of the case like so many fat-bellied flies and dropped little seeds of doubt all over it, which were now hatching out into a squirming mass of tiny questions, eating into the case, completely obscuring its true shape.

In purely legal terms, Clarence Brandley's claim on freedom had come down to seven "grounds for relief," yet the court had now asked the attorneys to address them on only three of them. That suggested that the judges had already made up their minds on the other four. And surely, De Geurin believed, if they had made up their minds in favor of the defense on even one of those four points, they would have declared that there was a reason for Brandley to have a new trial. Their silence suggested that the defense had already lost four of the seven grounds.

Those four points covered all the evidence of secret meetings between Jim Keeshan and the Conroe judges; the whole story of the cover-up of the missing exhibits; the suppression of the ranger's recording of his conversation with Icky Peace; and, most important of all, the central contention that Clarence Brandley was an innocent man.

In De Geurin's mind, the only way that the appellate judges could possibly have rejected all that evidence, complete with Judge Pickett's conclusion that it was credible and true, was if they had allowed it to be eaten away by legal technicalities: that the evidence should not have been admitted at Galveston, or that the complaints had already been rejected at previous hearings, or that the issues should have been raised earlier, or—worst of all—that innocence was irrelevant if it could be proved only with facts that were introduced more than thirty days after the original conviction.

The big picture was being lost. Still, De Geurin believed there was great power in the three remaining points. The first was the blind focus of the investigation into Cheryl Fergeson's murder: the intimidation of witnesses and the suppression of any clue that led anywhere other than to the black janitor. The second, and linked, argument was about racism and the history of a black man accused of a crime in a white town. The third defense point was that Brandley had been denied due process by the loss of crucial evidence such as the semen swabs and the hairs from the dead girl's body.

Even though there was power in the remaining arguments, De Geurin was still troubled—by the judges themselves. Only two of them had been elected as liberals. Several of the others were notoriously conservative. There was a chance that the defense was dealing with a built-in majority that had already secured a fifteen-month delay and demolished four of its arguments and that would shy away from the political consequences of accepting that Conroe and its courthouse were corrupt. The defense had left Galveston with a total victory. Now it was fighting for survival again, with its chances of winning perhaps as low as two out of nine.

The possibility that Brandley could yet be cheated of his life was now more galling than ever. As the weeks dragged by, new evidence to confirm all the theories of the defense attorneys about the case kept dropping into their laps. Two of the members of the grand jury that had indicted Brandley in September 1980 separately approached Don Brown—nervously and secretly—to confide that Jim Keeshan had done something highly irregular at the end of the hearing. Despite Keeshan's ferocious questioning of the black janitor, fewer than the required nine members of the grand jury had wanted to indict him. Keeshan, according to both grand jurors, finally swung the vote only by telling the grand jury that he had more evidence against Brandley, evidence that would prove beyond any doubt that he was guilty but that he was unable to put before them at that moment. The DA's claim had swung the grand jury, according to Brown's informants, even though it now appeared that the claim had been dishonest.

Then there was a woman who approached the defense—again nervously and secretly—to say that at the time of Brandley's trials a janitor from the high school had been lodging in her house. She was not saying he was involved with the murder. It was a smaller, but revealing, point. This janitor had keys to doors all over the school. She had seen them in her house, so she knew that Brandley was telling the truth when he said he was not the only one with keys. She thought it was important, and back in 1980 she had called the district attorney's office to report it. According to the rules, the DA should have passed on her information to the defense. But he had not.

The most tantalizing new information surfaced in early January, as the attorneys prepared for their hearing in Austin. A woman called up Don Brown and said that Gary Acreman had confessed to her that he had killed Cheryl Fergeson.

Her story was that Acreman had been working for her as a security guard and had wanted to be licensed to carry a gun. Looking into his background, she had come across his connection with the Brandley case and started talking to him about it. Acreman had told her first that he had been a witness in the case, next that he had been present at the school on the day of the killing, then that he knew who had really committed the crime. Finally, he had told her: "I was one of them that done it, but the nigger's gonna swing for it."

That was not all. The woman said that she had immediately fired Acreman and had then contacted the Montgomery County Sheriff's Department to report what he had said. And the sheriff's people had told her not to say anything to anyone about it.

The difficulty was knowing how to use all this information. Reyna and McCloskey wanted to hold a press conference, so that the court in Austin would be forcefully reminded of the big picture. But the three attorneys were not so sure. They saw a risk of alienating the judges, who might complain that the defense was trying to put improper pressure on them. There was also the risk—closer to a certainty—that the people in the courthouse in Conroe would start twisting and turning the new information: investigators in big boots would go around and tell the woman she was a liar; Gary Acreman would say he had never said any such thing; Peter Speers would tell the *Courier* that this was all illogical and offensive; the whole issue would soon become mired in lies. The defense decided to hold on to its affidavit and trust the nine judges to do their job.

The hearing was due to start at half past one on Wednesday, January 18, 1989. All through the morning, knots of people gathered beneath the heavy stone memorials to Confederate heroes around the pink granite Capitol in the center of Austin. It was a cool gray day. Reverend Boney was there. Since Galveston, he had been organizing sporadic raids to keep the Brandley case alive: rallying outside the Huntsville Jail; burning the Confederate flag outside the State Capitol; filling a section of the Astrodome during a Houston Astros game with people wearing "Free Clarence Brandley" T-shirts; running a "Bike Ride for Brandley" and a rolling hunger strike in which supporters took turns day by day fasting for twenty-four hours in solidarity with Brandley. That morning Boney and thirty supporters had visited the state Commission on Judicial Conduct to file a formal complaint against Judges James Keeshan and John Martin, calling for their immediate removal from office because of their "heinous and reprehensible judicial misconduct."

As more supporters arrived by car and by bus from Dugan and from Houston, some after journeys that had started before sunrise, the lobby outside the Court of Criminal Appeals filled to capacity and then kept filling, first scores and then hundreds of people swarming and pushing around the door to the court, which was closed.

Brandley's mother and father were there, leaning on each other's arms, united despite their long divorce by fear for their son. Richard Reyna was there with Mike De Geurin's wife and elderly mother and Paul Nugent's wife. Jim Keeshan's father was there, holding the front of the line, with Peter Speers's wife and Carol Williams of the *Courier*. Gwynn Fergeson, sister-in-law of the dead girl, was there, too. Almost the whole cast of characters from the long saga of Clarence Brandley was there for this legal climax, not merely because it was a climax but because, despite all the certainties of Galveston, its outcome was now in doubt. The one figure who was conspicuously absent was the central character, who had not been allowed to come to court to be a spectator to his own fate.

Reverend Boney appealed for calm and reminded Brandley's supporters that they must neither cheer nor jeer. A second minister called for a moment's silent prayer. There were scuffles at the front of the line as reporters and supporters clashed. Then the doors were opened, and Clarence Brandley's supporters flooded in. Paul Nugent's wife Mary, a Texan with the looks of a Californian and the politics of a Massachusetts liberal, immediately spotted something that started her blood boiling. Peter Speers's wife had seized a seat in the front row and, despite the milling crowd, had reserved an empty seat next to her. Mary Nugent had learned to dislike Mrs. Speers at Galveston, and she could see no reason why she should be reserving seats while others were standing and waiting outside, so she went and sat right down in it. Mrs. Speers protested. Mary Nugent held her ground. The two women then sat, elbow to elbow, stealing hostile glances at each other.

Just after half past one, when the nine judges paraded onto their raised platform at the end of the room to take their places on the arc of high-backed green chairs, they looked down on rows of seats that normally stood empty but that were now filled from front to back with strangers and were surrounded on all sides, on every spare space on the carpet, with more spectators, many of them spilling back out of the doors and into the lobby, all of them gazing anxiously up at them. The judges looked nervous. A detective game began.

Everyone was looking for clues. The three defense attorneys—Brown, De Geurin, and Nugent—the two Conroe prosecutors—Peter Speers and Rick Stover—seated at their tables at the feet of the judges, the spectators and the supporters and the relatives and the friends were all looking for clues, all hanging on every hint of a movement from any of the judges that might betray the way they were thinking.

Mike De Geurin watched them as he stepped forward from his table to take the podium. "It's been a long journey to get here," he began, "and there's a lot to be said. So much to be said and so little time." It was a gentle dig at the judges, who had waited fifteen months to hear the case and who had now ordered each side to restrict its submission to a total of twenty minutes. To make room for Paul Nugent's submission and for any argument that might develop, De Geurin had to try to concentrate all his thoughts into exactly six minutes. The judges leaned into the high backs of their chairs, impassively ignoring the dig.

De Geurin struck for the heart of the matter. "There is one inescapable fact and that is that a truly innocent man has been condemned to death. How did this happen? What can be done about it? It's not realistic and probably impossible to point to any one minute fact that caused this tragic thing to happen. My fear and concern is that we might—at the urging of the prosecution—dissect this tragedy into such minute particles that we will lose sight of the big picture—much like a bumblebee on a billboard. Too close to read the message."

De Geurin scanned the faces on the platform. Not a flicker of a smile, not even a hint of irritation. He pushed the same point again, harder. "On behalf of Clarence Lee Brandley, on behalf of his family and on behalf of the people of Texas, I beg this court not to lose sight of the illness while it studies the germ."

Still no reaction. But if the judges were determined to remain unmoved, something was nevertheless stirring in the rest of the courtroom. There was no cheering or jeering, not even any whispering or sighing. It was nothing that was said, only an intense concentration, a silence so deliberate that it screamed, as one by one the faces in the seats settled into a mold of subdued resistance, a glowering resentment. The more De Geurin spoke, the more tangible it became. By the time he had finished his whirlwind legal argument, a kind of dignity had descended on the silent spectators, like mourners at a funeral whose pain is so deep that they choose not to share it.

Now Paul Nugent came to the podium and spoke directly to the heart of their pain, recalling the now-familiar incidents of racism in the case, trying to compel the judges to react. "As much as we would like to say it didn't happen, as much as we would like to say 'This is the 1980s and we are not in the 1930s or 40s,' as much as we would like to close our eyes to reality, the fact is that the color of Clarence Brandley's skin was a factor in this case."

The pain belonged not only to Clarence Brandley. The nigger who was "elected" to take the blame might just as easily have been any other black man in Conroe. The nigger who was not allowed to get bail might just as easily have been any other black man or woman trapped in a white courthouse. The black man who had been dispatched to death row by white prosecutors and a white jury serviced by white officials and supervised by a white judge could just as easily have been any one of these black spectators sitting here now—before nine white judges, five white attorneys, six white security men, and a scattering of white court officials. Black people came to court only as victims. Clarence Brandley's pain belonged to all those in the court and to all those beyond the court who shared the color of his skin, to all of them.

At the podium Nugent was remembering the white woman who sat in a crowded courtroom chanting "Kill the nigger," and the sheriff who said Brandley was a "little nigger," and the DA who said Brandley was a "little nigger" and who spoke for whites and not for blacks. "As much as we would like to say that this does not happen in 1980 or 1981, that that was part of our past, the record shows that it did happen. The jury would have to have been deaf, dumb and blind not to be influenced by what happened in that courtroom."

Nugent went back to his seat. Perhaps now the tide of emotion that had risen in the court was beginning to lap around the feet of the judges. As Peter Speers stepped up to the podium, the judges were still frozen in silence. But as he spoke, they began to break out. Finally, there were some clues to their thinking. Speers was trying to put technical arguments. This idea that the trial was infected by racism, he complained, had never been spelled out in the defense's original writ. "From a legal point of view," he said, "that issue is not even before the court." Speers agreed that a police officer had said that "the nigger is elected" and explained that the officer had said this only because he thought Peace as too small to have hauled the dead girl up into the props loft.

One of the judges leaned forward. "How does that diminish the racial overtone?" he asked.

"If he used a racial epithet," said Speers, "that's not to be tolerated or condoned, but it was not his race, it was his stature and build that he was making reference to."

The judge leaned back again and listened while Speers explained that although the sheriff had called Brandley a "nigger," that was just because old-time East Texan sheriffs spoke that way. Anyway, the defense had never mentioned that in any previous appeal or writ, so technically it was not an issue for this court. The judge stared at him grimly.

A moment later Speers launched into an attack on Judge Pickett, and another judge leaned forward. "If there is evidence to support a trial judge's findings of fact, then this court will defer to that finding," he said.

Speers protested. "You are free to reject them," he said.

Another judge joined in. "Has this court ever rejected findings of fact that were supported by the record?"

Speers stammered, and the judge repeated his question, which was beginning to sound more like a challenge.

"Right off the top of my head, I can't remember a case," said Speers, anxiously pinching one thumb with his fingers. "But if I find such a thing I will absolutely make the court aware of it."

As the judges started sniping at Peter Speers, Mary Nugent watched the DA's wife beside her starting to pick nervously at the polystyrene cup she was holding. By the time Speers had finished his submission, four different judges had thrown hostile questions at him and the polystyrene cup was in shreds.

Then the time was up. The nine judges stood up and paraded out of the court. The attorneys and the spectators turned and swarmed into the lobby, everybody adding up the clues and exchanging guesswork.

No one could be sure what those judges were thinking. It looked as if at least four of them were on Brandley's side. They included the known liberals and none of the hard-line conservatives. The defense attorneys would need five judges to win a new trial. They were still stuck on the politics of the court. Minnie Ola Brandley spoke for everyone who had come from Dugan and from Houston to support her son. "I don't know," she said, "but I feel better."

In his cell, nine feet by three feet, Clarence Brandley waited and waited and shaped his life around the court in Austin.

He had been told that the nine judges would announce their decision on a Wednesday. To begin with, after the Austin hearing, he waited all week until Wednesday morning came around and built up his anticipation to nine o'clock, which was the first moment he reckoned he could hear if the judges had left a decision about him on the table outside their court. Then he sat by his radio to listen for news.

But there was none, and he soon decided that he was cutting it too fine, so he started spending all Wednesday listening to the radio on the hour, every hour, in case the news came through later in the day. But there was none, and he thought that maybe he was still not covering all the options, so he developed a routine where every hour on the hour from Monday through Friday he turned on his radio to try to find out if the judges had decided to spare him. He took Saturday and Sunday off and then started again on Monday. He found it gave him something to look forward to.

Death row had changed him. He had grown, and he had been awakened to all kinds of things, a bit like the way someone who has lost his or her sight develops much sharper hearing to make up for the loss. He had lost his life out there in the world, so he had developed a life inside his mind to make up for the loss. He read black history and politics and good novels as well as the Bible. He talked; he thought; he wrote down his thoughts; he still meditated. People who had always known him could hardly believe the change. He had once been shy with people—unless he was out drinking—and he had been bad at putting his ideas into words. But now he seemed to have become more intelligent. He was more articulate and reasoned than he had ever been, and he believed he understood a whole pack of things he never had before.

He had no illusions anymore. It seemed crazy now, but for a long time he had thought he was the victim of nothing worse than bad luck, that he was just in the wrong place at the wrong time and that if only he had stayed in bed with Beverley, he would have been free. It was only now, after Galveston and after all his thinking, that he saw the truth. The truth hurt. What hurt the most was that he had never seen it. The truth, which was now as clear as the sun in the sky, was that he had been the victim of racism, not bad luck. If everything that day at the school had been the same, except that he was white, he would never have been arrested. Those dumb cops would have railroaded Icky Peace instead. His skin had shadowed him through every step in that courthouse. It was still shadowing him now. As he looked back, it was clear. Yet he had not seen it. He hadn't seen it all his life. Now he could see how the white people in Conroe had been conditioned, all going to the same schools and then to the same churches and the same social functions. They were all in this white man's union. And he saw how the black people had been living in fear. Ever since he was a child in Dugan, he had been conditioned to be frightened: his grandma warning him about going downtown, his daddy telling how Putt had died, the old people who remembered what happened to Joe Winters and Bob White and then Greg Steele. He had known Greg Steele, played basketball with him. Every day he had lived with that fear. It had become part of him, like skin. Now, at last, he could see it. He knew things had changed. Sure enough, just twenty or thirty years ago he would have been dead by now. If a mob hadn't gotten him, the old white courts would have finished the job by now. Things had changed just that much. But his skin had not, and he was still trapped in it.

It was not only the people in Dugan who knew about Joe Winters and Bob White and Greg Steele. The white people in town remembered, too, but they remembered them a different way. They wrapped up their deaths in the same bundle of discarded history as slavery and the Jim Crow laws. They were all in the past, part of a time when the whole South was like that, nothing to do with Conroe, nothing to do with today. Anyway, hadn't Winters and White been rapists? Greg Steele might not have died so long ago, but hadn't the officer who shot him been tried and acquitted in a court of law? Didn't that prove the killing was just?

But there was something else, something that had vanished entirely from the white people's history of their town. Even the old people in Dugan could hardly grasp it. Their memories were fogged with fear and confusion, but they knew there was more. It was the stuff of legend and rumor, hardly there as memory anymore, more like a stain at the back of their minds, something they knew only vaguely and something they knew that they did not really want to know.

Nevertheless, the truth that had been swept aside by the fear of the black people and the self-delusion of the whites did survive—not in living memory but in yellowed old bundles of newspapers in dusty archives. The truth survived there in all its grim detail, a hidden history of the seeds of violence that had produced the story of Clarence Brandley. For the truth was that in their short history the white people of Montgomery County had repeatedly indulged in the public murder of black people. Joe Winters and Bob White and Greg Steele were just three names from a much longer list. These people had killed at least eight other young black men in collective acts of racial hatred. Lynchings. Clarence Brandley was the latest in their roll call of victims.

Andrew McGehee was shot to death in his cell by a mob of white men in Willis, ten miles north of Conroe, on May 15, 1887. He had been accused of attacking a wealthy young white man and was being held for trial, but when the mob of white men arrived, Marshal Goss walked away and let them break in and empty their guns into McGehee as he lay curled up in chains on the floor.

Clem Scott was hanged on February 27, 1908, from the old elm tree outside the courthouse where the people of Conroe used to shelter themselves from the sun. A group of white men said he had been prowling outside a white woman's house, intending to attack her. Sheriff Maben Anderson and his men did nothing to save Clem Scott as the white men bound him tight, slipped a noose over his head, and slowly heaved him into the tree, squeezing the breath out of his neck as his feet danced wildly above them. The next day a justice of the peace, C.T. Darby, investigated the death and concluded that he had died "in the hands of unknown parties." Darby later became mayor of Conroe.

In one week in March 1980 three men were killed by Montgomery County mobs. On Monday, March 17, James Kinder and Alf Riley were shot to death by an angry crowd in Magnolia, fifteen miles southwest of Conroe, because, it was said, they had tried to assault a white girl. On Sunday, March 23, in Conroe, an unnamed black man was accused of prowling near a white woman's house and shot through the head.

Warren Lewis died on June 23, 1922, only a month after Joe Winters. Lewis was mentally retarded and made the mistake of walking up to a white woman's house in Dacus, fifteen miles northwest of Conroe, to ask for water. She screamed, and Lewis ran. A group of white men went to his house, where a crowd of three hundred watched as the tearful eighteen-year-old was pushed up onto the back of a horse, had a rope hooked under his chin, and was sent choking into the air. His death was reported on the front page of the *Courier* underneath an advertisement that welcomed the citizens of Conroe to the Conroe Methodist Episcopal Church.

Tom Payne was hauled out of a patrol car on North Frazier Street on February 2, 1927, and hanged. He had been arrested earlier that day for robbing and wounding a white lumber mill worker named Jack Rogers. The mob was led by Doc Medley, a friend of Rogers's and a famous Conroe figure who weighed some four hundred pounds, wore a bushy beard, and had a belly like a barrel. The officers in the patrol car, however, said they were unable to identify any of the men who stole and killed their prisoner.

All this could not be thrown away as unwanted history. No matter what the whites might say, this was part of Conroe today. The sheer number of killings in itself made Brandley's ordeal seem almost inevitable, like the recurrence of an unstoppable pattern. Despite all the years that separated these other victims from the time of Clarence Brandley, frail threads linked their ordeals to his. Like Brandley, each of them was black, and each of them had been accused of attacking a white person—almost always a white woman—and like him, they had been condemned by the whole community without hope of defending themselves, while law officers turned a blind eye. There was one victim in particular whose short life was full of potent symbolism for Brandley's supporters: Bennett Jackson, a young farm laborer who died a few days before Christmas 1885, aged only nineteen, the first of Montgomery County's victims.

Jackson was born the son of emancipated slaves in 1866, the first year of his parents' freedom, the child of a new generation growing up, like Brandley a hundred years later, with the promise of liberty. He lived in a lumber town called Mink Prairie, a mean, dusty little place that once stood about fifteen miles southwest of Conroe, near where Magnolia stands today.

No one knows too much about why he died. It is said he had attacked a white woman and her children. Maybe he had. Maybe not. Maybe he was insane. Maybe he committed cold-blooded murder. No one knows because he was never put on trial, except by "Judge Lynch," in whose court the regular rules of law meant nothing.

Bennett Jackson's life was as good as over the moment a Mink Prairie farmer named John Smith came home and found his wife and two children beaten and bloody on the floor of their house. John Smith was one of the most prominent white men in Mink Prairie, and as news of the crime spread, the whole town rose to find the attacker. Within the day the whites of the community had arrested Bennett Jackson. At first they were content to send him up to Montgomery, which was then the county seat, to be tried and dealt with by old Judge Masterson. Then came word that one of John Smith's children had died from injuries inflicted in the attack. Now the whole community rose again.

There was never any doubt about what was going to happen. In Houston the *Post* of Saturday, December 19, 1885, declared in its headline JUDGE LYNCH WILL PRESIDE IN MONTGOMERY TODAY. The *Post* explained that Judge Masterson had tried to send Jackson to Houston for safekeeping but that "the people in the majesty of their might would not permit it." The townspeople had planned to kill Jackson on Friday, but then, out of respect for Judge Masterson, who was still holding court in Montgomery, "the lynching picnic was postponed until Saturday."

The *Post* understood the way the town felt: "No man in this country feels that his wife and children are safe from outrage and murder as long as so fearful a demon lives. . . . A thrilling time is expected here. If he is lynched, however, it will be openly and boldly done without disguise or any attempt at secrecy. It will be an act of the people. . . . Every good citizen approves of the lynching as the negro outrages are too frequent in this section."

In the small hours of Saturday a crowd of white men took Bennett Jackson from his prison cell and led him into the woods. History does not record what they did to him there, but Jackson was still alive at noon, when he was dragged into the middle of Montgomery. The whole town had gathered in front of the courthouse to see the spectacle. Men, women, and children filled the square. According to the *Houston Post*, it was "the leading citizens of the county" who then bundled Bennett Jackson onto the back of a horse, ran a rope over the branch of a stout tree, looped the noose around the young man's neck, and jerked the horse away. Bennett Jackson was soon dead.

The story of Clarence Brandley rang with echoes from Bennett Jackson's ordeal: the rules of law that had been abandoned; the judge who had fallen in with the mob; the press that had relished his fate; the "leading citizens of the county" who had committed the crime; the bodyguard of new civil rights that had turned and deserted him; the whole town that had stood by and let it happen. And that was the loudest echo of all.

The whole town had been tangled in the death of Bennett Jackson. There were those who held the rope and those who held the man and those who hurled the rope over the limb of a stout tree and those who sent his body wriggling into the air, and then there were also all those who watched and even a few who looked away; but all of them—the ringleaders and the bystanders—were involved in Bennett Jackson's death.

That was how it was in Conroe as Clarence Brandley waited for his freedom. The whole town knew what its ringleaders in the courthouse had been doing. It knew what Judge Pickett had found and it knew about the cloud of corruption swirling around its courthouse, and yet it did nothing. The link to the past was more than mere symbolism. This history of public murder went to the heart of the treatment of Clarence Brandley.

It was part of the corruption that had become a way of life. The townspeople had always gotten away with taking the law into their own hands. After Joe Winters was burned to death, reporters from outside East Texas came to Conroe to find out what had happened. One of them asked Sheriff Hicks why he had not intervened to save the man. The sheriff shrugged him off, saying, "I just looked away for a moment and when I looked back, the negro was tied to a burning stake." The law in Conroe had always looked away. That was why Dude Cochran had been able to walk free after killing Bob White in front of a courtroom full of witnesses. Killing black men was easy.

Not only had the whites always got away with it, but they had also always been able to justify it. Killing one black man was a means of disciplining the whole of his

community. Just as a secret police force tries to quell the
courage of a whole people by arresting its figureheads, just
as terrorists try to frighten a whole society by throwing fear
into the lives of each of its members, so the white people of
Montgomery County had for years ruled black people with
fear by picking off their young men. Murder was disguised
as a necessary social task. If it was true, as the myths and
the jokes pretended, that all niggers were lazy and dishonest
rapists, then it was essential for whites to teach them a lesson,
to keep them in line. They were always open and sincere about
it. In March 1908, when the people of Montgomery County
murdered three young black men in one week, the *Houston
Post* reported an incident in Palestine, north of Conroe, outside
Montgomery County, in which a black hack driver had been
attacked for complaining about the way one of his friends
had been abused. The *Post* reported: "A band of determined
men took him in hand and when they finished their work, the
negro's hide would not hold shucks. There is an element of
lawless negroes in Palestine who become very insolent just
before an election. The people, however, because of several
recent trying situations, have become of one mind, and that
is to suppress this element, and the Saturday affair is but
an indicator of what will happen if this element persists in
lawlessness."

In Conroe, in 1989, the ringleaders of the attack on Clarence
Brandley were still getting away with everything they had
done, still proudly justifying themselves.

Behind his large wooden desk in the DA's office, Peter
Speers was full of boyish enthusiasm for the cause. Brandley
was a vicious killer who deserved to die, he said, and all
of Brandley's defenders were crooked. "I'm convinced that
a large part of what the defense has been doing is literally
for publicity—not because they think it is legally valid in any
way. De Geurin and those attorneys are not working for free.
Do you think McCloskey and Reyna are working for free?
The more sensational they can make this case in the news
media, the more money they can raise for themselves. That's
what this is all about." And Judge Pickett? He was crooked,
too. "All this crap about the Constitution. I categorically deny
that any injustice was done to Clarence Brandley. Pickett gives
off all this mumbo jumbo. It's outrageous. I have been told
that Judge Pickett is an old personal friend of Percy Foreman,
which might explain why he was so totally biased."

Jim Keeshan was just as confident. Reverend Boney might have reported him and John Martin to the state Commission on Judicial Conduct. A veteran judge might have ruled that he had lied on oath and perverted the course of justice, but he was unmoved. "I'm proud of my efforts in the Brandley case," he said. "I'm proud of how I carried out my duties the best way I know how. I don't have anything I should feel ashamed about regarding that prosecution."

If any doubt remained that the killing of unruly young black men was still an acceptable necessity in East Texas, it was soon dispelled when the roll call of victims gathered two more names.

Loyal Garner died in the county jail in Hemphill, about a hundred miles north of Conroe on December 27, 1987. He had never been in trouble in his life and was, in the words of a white friend, "the finest man I ever met in my life, white or black." He was stopped by a group of white policemen, who accused him of drunken driving and locked him up without allowing him to call his wife to tell her and his six children what had happened. According to two friends who were arrested with him, the police lost their tempers when Garner beat on his cell door, demanding to be released, and several officers took him away, beat him unconscious, and then left him lying unattended on his cell floor all night, breathing unsteadily through his bloody mouth. He died the next day without regaining consciousness. According to the police, they hit Garner only once after he attacked them in a drunken rage. They suggested he might have hurt himself by falling over a chair and they claimed he was a drug trafficker. A Hemphill jury cleared the police of all wrongdoing.

Hambone Simpson had been in trouble all his life. He was found dead in a cell in the Cleveland police station (where Icky Peace was questioned by Wes Styles) after being "subdued" by eleven officers on March 16, 1988. The man in the next cell said he had heard Simpson pleading for his life. An autopsy found that pressure had been applied to his neck, and a justice of the peace said his neck was bruised with fingermarks. The Texas Rangers were called in to investigate. The police explained that they had had to subdue him because they had found him smoking marijuana, which had not been detected by any search. One officer claimed that he had tape-recorded the whole incident and that the tape proved that Simpson was still alive when they left his cell. The assistant attorney general for Texas, David Hess (who supervised the inquiry into the Brandley case), announced that Simpson had probably died from "positional asphyxia"—a condition in which someone lying in an awkward position may block his windpipe with his own body weight. Hess conceded that this was a rare cause of death but added that it had been found to occur in police cells. The Texas Rangers concluded that no officer should be prosecuted for any offense, and a Cleveland grand jury agreed.

Hemphill. Cleveland. Conroe. They are all the kinds of towns that strangers never notice because they are all the same. They all have the railroad tracks that split the whites from the blacks, and they split the power and the wealth the same way. They are all peaceful and plump and content to remain obscure. The civil rights laws hit the racism in these towns like a knife stabbing the wind. The laws might have changed them more if the racism were part of a criminal conspiracy, but towns like Conroe do not work that way. Jim Keeshan and his judges might have put their heads together to plot Brandley's fall, but for the rest there was no need for conspiracy among the smiling racists. Keeshan did not have to go to the *Conroe Courier* and persuade it to prejudice Brandley's trial or, later, to misreport the Galveston hearing. No one had to bribe or bully twenty-three jurors into finding Brandley guilty. No one had to organize the phone calls that rained down on Bill Srack's head. Mayor Barton did not have to race around town telling his citizens to deny there had ever been racial problems in Conroe. No one had to persuade the white people of Conroe to insist on Brandley's guilt. There was no need for conspiracy because each of them in his or her own right agreed with what was happening. The bystanders not only stood by but welcomed events, just as they always had.

The project to convict Clarence Brandley was never a guilt-riddled conspiracy. It was a popular event, just like the public lynching of Bennett Jackson a hundred years earlier. It was exactly as the *Post* had recorded at the time: "If he is lynched, it will be openly and boldly done without disguise or any attempt at secrecy. . . . Every good citizen approves of the lynching as the negro outrages are too frequent in this section." It was truly, as the *Post* had said, "an act of the people."

On December 13, 1989, more than two years after Judge Pickett called for Clarence Brandley's immediate release, the nine judges in Austin finally published their decision. By six votes to three, they supported all of Perry Pickett's findings of fact, ruled that there had been a blind focus on Clarence Brandley, and overturned his conviction. His treatment, they said, had been blatantly unfair and "a subversion of justice."

On death row in Huntsville Clarence Brandley met reporters and cried with relief. His family and supporters prayed and celebrated and prepared for his release.

But the ringleaders in the courthouse still would not yield in their righteous mission to kill the black man. Jim Keeshan went on radio stations in Houston to denounce Brandley as a killer. Peter Speers attacked the Austin judges, demanded a second hearing, claimed he would go to the Supreme Court, and called press conferences to declare this was "the biggest miscarriage of justice I've ever seen." For a month they succeeded in stalling Brandley's release. Then, on January 22, the court in Austin spoke again and formally rejected Speers's request for another hearing. Conroe might still be anchored safely in its history, the good ol' boys might still be standing proud, but there was a new wave of courage sweeping past them. The truth was not their property anymore. Things had changed just that much. Peter Speers still insisted that he would go all the way to the Supreme Court in Washington, but Mike De Geurin flew to Austin and told the judges that it was over. Peter Speers could do whatever he liked, but it was time for the victim to be released. The judges agreed and gave him bail.

And so, on Tuesday January 23, 1990, just after noon— nine years, four months, and twenty-five days after he was first put in chains—Clarence Lee Brandley walked through the heavy gates of death row and out into the sunlight. There were photographers and film crews, a whole lot of cheering and crying and general confusion, but the final fact was clear as day. He was free at last.

Epilogue

Because this is a true story, it does not have the tidy, convenient ending that a piece of fiction might. Despite numerous investigations, there are still little mysteries lurking in the background. It is impossible, for example, to be sure what really happened to the exhibits that disappeared from the courthouse in Conroe in January 1982. The same is true of all the disappearing evidence: the swabs from the postmortem; the photographs that would have shown that Brandley was not wearing a belt on the day of the crime, the original statement made by Jo Ellen Parrish. In the context of all that is now known about the case, it is reasonable to guess that one or more malevolent figures in the courthouse were responsible for the disappearance of all this material. But it can only be a guess, and so I have held back from giving any definitive conclusion.

The story is unfinished, too, in the sense that justice is still catching up with its various characters. Some of the minor players have already been caught. The police officer who killed Greg Steele has been jailed for robbing a bank. Jo Ellen Parrish, the prostitute whose claim that she had been raped by Clarence Brandley helped Jim Keeshan have him sentenced to death, has been charged with possession of cocaine. Duke Bodisch has been sacked from the attorney general's office for exploiting his position there to try to write a book about the Brandley case.

At the other end of the moral scale, Jim McCloskey has now won the freedom of six innocent men who had been wrongly jailed, and Richard Reyna has become a regular partner in his investigations. Don Brown is still tussling with the courthouse in Conroe and has succeeded in running a campaign to have a woman Democrat elected mayor instead of Carl Barton. Percy Foreman died in the summer of 1988, but Mike De Geurin and Paul Nugent are still fighting the good fight in the courtrooms of East Texas and telling Percy Foreman stories. The Reverend Don Boney was cleared of possessing cocaine and has launched a new campaign in support of black workers in Houston. Clarence Brandley spent the first nine months of his freedom under a cloud, while Peter Speers petitioned the Supreme Court in Washington to send him back to death row. Finally, on October 1, 1990, the Court threw out Speers's application, and the district attorney conceded defeat. Brandley became a Baptist minister in Houston, trained to work as an electrician, and got married. He never set foot in Conroe again.

There are others for whom justice is still waiting in the wings. Two and a half years after Judge Perry Pickett found that they had perverted the course of justice and lied under oath, Jim Keeshan and John Martin still sit in judgment in the Conroe courthouse, and the Texas Commission on Judicial Conduct has still not seen fit to take action against them. The various law officers who conspired to send Brandley to death row have all kept their jobs or retired peacefully. Gary Acreman and James Dexter Robinson have never been arrested and questioned.

The ordeal Clarence Brandley suffered was an attempt at a legal lynching. It was the law, not an old rope, that was twisted into a deadly weapon, but the intention of those who attacked him was just as surely to kill him, as their predecessors had killed young black men in the past. His supporters were strong enough to rescue him and save his life. Their strength derived from their own inner resources and also from the past victories of others like them who had fought in the civil rights movement, but there was still a limit to what they could do. As a result, the lynch mob remains free and in that very important respect this story still has no ending.

About the Author

Nick Davies was born in London in 1953. He has been a regular contributor to the *Observer*, the *Guardian*, and the *Evening Standard*, among other publications, and spent two years in the United States as a columnist while researching and writing *White Lies*. In 1980 he was named Crime Reporter of the Year by the British Press Awards. He is currently producing documentaries and films for British television.